The International Dictionary

of

Food & Nutrition

Kenneth N. Anderson
and
Lois E. Anderson

John Wiley & Sons, Inc.
New York • Chichester • Brisbane • Toronto • Singapore

This text is printed on acid-free paper.

This publication is designed to provide accurate and authoritative information
in regard to the subject matter covered. It is sold with the understanding
that the publisher is not engaged in rendering legal, accounting, or other
professional service. If legal advice or other expert assistance is required,
the services of a competent professional person should be sought. FROM A
DECLARATION OF PRINCIPLES JOINTLY ADOPTED BY A COMMITTEE OF
THE AMERICAN BAR ASSOCIATION AND A COMMITTEE OF PUBLISHERS.

Library of Congress Cataloging-in-Publication Data

Anderson, Kenneth, 1921–
    The international dictionary of food and nutrition / by Kenneth N.
Anderson and Lois E. Anderson.
        p.   cm.
    ISBN 0-471-55957-1 (alk. paper)
    1. Food—Dictionaries.   2. Cookery—Dictionaries.   3. Nutrition—
dictionaries.   I. Anderson, Lois E.   II. Title.
TX349.A236   1993
641'.03—dc20   92-38971
                                                        CIP

Printed in the United States of America

10 9 8 7 6 5 4 3 2 1

Introduction

This may be the best of times to examine the language of eating. Never before in human history has there been such a proliferation of viands, or food items, ingredients, equipment, and recipes available to the general public. Among the several reasons for the increasing popularity of cookery interest are the explosive expansion of supermarket and gourmet shop inventories, new cooking methods and equipment such as microwave ovens and food processors, and the hurried life-styles of working adults. Our ancestors may have found time to prepare their breakfast sausage and eggs by butchering a hog, grinding the meat, checking the henhouse for fresh eggs, and stoking a fire in a wood-burning kitchen range, but the consumer of the 1990s gets the same food, microwave ready, in minutes from the neighborhood grocer. However, the modern customer may have to decide between white and brown eggs, large, medium, or small, regular or low cholesterol, or an egg substitute. The sausage may be in bulk, patties, or links, beef, turkey, or pork, with or without sage seasoning, and so on.

Also contributing to our expanding food language is the dynamic movement of populations across national boundaries, as expatriates and as vacation or business travelers. Even the armchair traveler is exposed to a flood of new food words—a newspaper travel article about Switzerland may contain details about Emmenthaler cheese processing while a magazine article about Caribbean travel is likely to extol the gustatory pleasures of shaddock and callaloo. And while North Americans learn to appreciate fajitas and flautas, pirogis and blinis, or miso and sembei, Russians and Japanese are testing Big Macs and Cokes.

Food, or the lack of it, has shaped the course of civilization since before humans began counting goats on clay tablets. The earliest bands of people constantly battled over food supplies. Nomadic tribes wandered the earth in search of a good meal and often ended their quest by plundering the food supplies of more fortunate tribes. For some primitive tribes, to save surplus food for another day would be an admission that their men were not capable of finding tomorrow's food. One historian has suggested that fighting for food was such a traditional way of life among early ancestors that the first words for food were probably synonymous with raiding. The primitive mind needed no ideological hypocrisy to justify attacking a neighbor, and "war" was simply a way of saying, "We want your sheep."

Although the earliest words for food items may never be known, archeologists have given us an idea of what may have been on a Neolithic menu. The clues range from Bronze Age and Iron Age fishhooks and pottery jugs for storing grain and wine to an axe blade made from an antler resting in the skull of a prehistoric whale. When Chinese began producing rice on flooded fields 5,000 years ago the Egyptians were already growing wheat on the flood plains of the Nile. A Babylonian carving of 3,500 years ago shows a farmer plowing a field. The early Babylonians also knew how to bake breads and cakes and how to collect honey. Grapes and olives were cultivated in Mesopotamia, Persians grew peaches, and cherries thrived along the shores of the Black Sea. The Chinese developed meals of millet, wheat, rice, vegetables, and fish, although milk was virtually unknown. Milk and milk products were common food items in the Middle East but pasta, a Chinese invention, was unknown. Both early cultures had developed a taste for alcohol: grape wine and beer were developed in the Middle East while the Chinese made rice wine.

Until about the sixth century B.C., most dinners were probably quite bland, composed of whatever edibles the population could scrounge from the land and water, including insects, minnows, and wild berries. Around that time, the Greeks began combining meats, cereals, and vegetables with herbs and wine. The first menus were therapeutic, not unlike the Oriental scheme of balancing ying and yang for health benefits. The Romans later adapted the Greek cuisine, improved it with herbs and spices imported from Asia and Africa, and later transplanted their own recipes throughout Europe and the Middle East. But a craving for strong flavors persisted and one of the favorite Roman condiments was a yellowish fluid called *liquamen*, made by fermenting fish with wine and salt. At one time, liquamen manufacture was a major industry and Romans argued about the relative virtues of different forms of the fluid, which reportedly has the aroma of overripe cheese.

Until the very recent past, food choices evolved slowly but did not progress much past the meals and cookery methods of the Middle Ages. Fresh foods were important because refrigeration was unknown. Cooked foods required fire. There were no "convenience foods," but plenty of "inconvenience" foods. A perusal of the 1796 cookbook, *American Cookery of Viands, Fish, Poultry, and Vegetables*, by Amelia Simmons, reveals much about the food language of that era. Readers were advised about the differences between "cow beef" and "ox beef," how to tell if a chicken was fresh by smelling it and checking for the presence of a "tight vent," and how to distinguish four kinds of cabbage, nine kinds of beans, and seven kinds of peas. One also needed to know how to dress wild ducks, snipes, woodcocks, partridges, hares, rabbits, geese, capons, turkeys, and turtles. Recipes led mainly to puddings, pies, cakes, dried fruits, boiled vegetables, and pickles.

Almost a century later, Isabella Beeton's 1861 _Book of Household Management_ provided more interesting recipes, but the cook was still expected to know about such things as "the art of taking and killing birds," and how to make stews, soups, and stew soups using rabbit, pheasant, teal, partridge, quail, lark, and hare. Recipes were becoming more imaginative and included "minced fowl a la bechamel" and "boudin a la reine," both made from cold roast fowl, and "poulet a la Marengo," honoring Napoleon Bonaparte's defeat of the Austrians in 1800. It was a step, albeit a short one, toward modern cuisine.

Today's cookbooks and restaurant menus are obviously more sophisticated and require a much wider knowledge of food ingredients, nutrition, cookery, and serving. To entertain at home or order in a restaurant, one needs to be aware of the meanings of such terms as _bain-marie_, _kombu_, _lotus root_, _polenta_, _focaccia_, _wasabi_, _vitello tonnato_, _timbale_, _tahini_, and _tamari_. Even school lunch menus for children today require some knowledge of foods and nutrition.

The need for such knowledge is likely to increase in the future as new food-processing techniques, jet transport, and telecommunications enable a person in almost any part of the world to order a meal from another region of the world. It is already possible to obtain by telephone overnight delivery of Dublin Bay prawns from Ireland, Norwegian salmon, Italian sardines, or Japanese sea urchin roe. Meanwhile, other airships pass in the night with Louisiana crayfish or New England lobster bound for overseas palates. Thus, dishes that were once beyond the reach of the world's most powerful monarchs are available today to the ordinary person.

The International Dictionary of Food and Nutrition presents a comprehensive cross section of the world's current literature on foods and cookery. The total international language of dining is nearly infinite and space is limited. Therefore, the authors have selected some 7,500 representative definitions of food ingredients, garnishes, sauces, entrées, and appetizers. The choices are based on food words that are interesting, useful, and most likely to appear on your menu or shopping list. Oshokuji o dōzo! (Good appetite!)

The following is a list of the abbreviations used to indicate the more than forty languages used in this book. In some cases, an abbreviation is modified in the definitions to further clarify. For example, (Gr–Swiss) means German spoken in Switzerland or (Af–Swahili) means the Swahili spoken in vast areas of Africa.

(Aa)	Australian	(Jp)	Japanese
(Af)	African	(Jw)	Jewish (includes American-
(Ar)	Arabic		Jewish terms and Israeli terms)

(Bl)	Belgian	(Kr)	Korean
(Bu)	Bulgarian	(Ml)	Malaysian
(Ca)	Canadian	(Mx)	Mexican
(Cb)	Caribbean	(Nw)	Norwegian
(Ch)	Chinese	(Pg)	Portuguese (includes Portugal and Brazil)
(Cz)	Czechoslovakian		
(Da)	Danish	(Ph)	Philippine
(Du)	Dutch	(Pl)	Polynesian (includes Hawaii)
(Fi)	Finnish	(Po)	Polish
(Fr)	French	(Ro)	Romanian
(GB)	British (includes England and Wales)	(Rs)	Russian
		(Sc)	Scottish
(Gk)	Greek	(SC)	Serbo-Croatian
(Gr)	German	(Sp)	Spanish
(Hu)	Hungarian	(Sw)	Swedish
(Ia)	Hindi (India)	(Th)	Thai
(In)	Indonesian	(Tr)	Turkish
(Ir)	Irish	(US)	American
(It)	Italian	(Vt)	Vietnamese

Note: Terms that appear in a definition as a cross reference are shown in boldface or italics to help guide the reader to further information. A word in boldface means that it can be found in the dictionary with its own definition. Italicized words are not defined elsewhere, but are heightened to bring them to the reader's attention. Because this book is about foods from many countries and the entries explain the terms used in some forty languages, one point to notice is that cross references in an entry will most likely be in languages other than English. For example, the entry on smelt explains that it is also called **éperlan.**

This does not mean that in the United States, smelt is familiarly known as éperlan. If the reader is interested and observes that the foreign term is in boldface type, he or she can find in the entry for éperlan that it is French. Thus, as you, the reader, explore *The International Dictionary of Food and Nutrition*, you will find many ways to bring together the languages of the world on the interesting subject of what people eat.

A

aab ghosht (Ia) Meat, often lamb, boiled in milk.

Aal (Gr, Du) Eel; served boiled, smoked, jellied, and in soups and stews.

Aalbutte (Gr) Eelpout, a bony fish resembling an eel. Also called **burbot.**

Aalgeräuchert (Gr) Smoked eel.

aalgestoofd (Du) Eel stewed with wine and herbs.

Aalgrün (Gr) Eels cooked in white wine with herbs, onions, and sour cream.

aal i gélé (Da) Jellied eel.

Aalmutter (Gr) Muttonfish.

aalsoep (Du) Eel soup.

Aalsuppe (Gr) Eel soup with vegetables and fruit; served with dumplings.

aam (Ia) Mango.

a'ama (Pl) A small black rock crab, a Hawaiian delicacy.

aam chatni (Ia) Mango chutney, made with unripened mangos.

aamiainen (Fi) Breakfast.

aamiaisherkku (Fi) Breakfast egg casserole.

aamiaispaistos (Fi) Breakfast sausage stuffed with minced onion and tomato sauce and baked.

aamiaissämpylät (Fi) Breakfast bun.

aardappel (Du) Potato.

aardappelsoep (Du) Potato soup.

aardbei-chipolata (Du) A mixture of crushed fruit with eggs and cream.

aardbeien (Du) Strawberries.

aardvark (Af) Large ant-eating mammal used for food in Africa.

aardwolf (Af) Hyenalike mammal eaten in Africa.

Aargauer Rüeblitorte (Gr) Swiss cake made with carrots and glazed almonds.

Aaron's rod (US) 1. Common name for mullein, a species of *Verbascum* used in herbal teas. 2. A common name for the almond tree, *Amygdalus communis*.

aassida (Af) A kind of dumpling made of flour and butter and boiled in water.

aata (Ia) Whole wheat flour; used in making unleavened bread such as chapati.

aawa (Pl) A black-spot wrasse, a bony saltwater fish found in the Pacific Ocean around the Hawaiian Islands.

abacate (Pg) Avocado.

abacate batida (Pg) Avocado whip or puree.

abacaxi (Pg–Brazil) Pineapple.

abadejo (Sp) Any of a variety of saltwater fish, including grouper, pollock, and codfish.

abaisse (Fr) A layer or sheet of pastry, sometimes used as an undercrust.

abalone (US) A flat mollusk, genus *Haliotis*, found in warm seas; the relatively tough muscular foot is edible. May be thinly sliced to be sautéed, fried, or stewed or minced for chowder and served in salads. Also called **awabi, mutton fish, sea ear.**

abats (Fr) Offal; giblets and animal head.

abats d'agneau (Fr) Variety meats or offal of lamb, including the heart, brains, kidneys, and testicles.

abats de boucherie (Fr) Offal; variety meats of an animal.

abattis (Fr) External and internal giblets of poultry.

abattis de volaille (Fr) Chicken giblets.

abattis en ragoût (Fr) Stewed giblets.

abba (Ia) Mustard made from black mustard seed, used in curries.

abbacchi arrosto (It) Roast baby lamb.

abbacchio (It) Young spring lamb; legs may be served whole; often seasoned with rosemary and garlic or braised in a sauce of egg, lemon, and white wine.

abbacchio al forno (It) Roast spring lamb flavored with garlic and rosemary.

abboccato (It) Semidry or semisweet wine.

abborr (Nw) Perch.

abbrustolire (It) To broil or toast.

abdug (Ar) A drink made with yogurt.

abelmosk (US) A mallow herb, *Hibiscus moschatus*, native to tropical Asia and the East Indies. Its musky seeds are used to flavor Middle Eastern coffee.

Abendessen (Gr) The evening meal.

Aberdeen Angus (Sc) Breed of beef cattle developed in Scotland and noted for its fine quality beef.

Aberdeen roll (Sc) A buttery scone made with yeast.

Abernethy biscuit (Sc) A hard biscuit with caraway seeds; originally promoted by a nineteenth century British doctor as an easily digested food.

Abertam (Cz) A hard sheep's milk cheese produced in the Carlsbad region.

abfetten (Gr) To skim off the fat.

abfüllen (Gr) To decant wine.

abijau (Ar) Beer.

abkochen (Gr) To boil down or extract by boiling.

abkochen Milch (Gr) To scald milk.

à blanc (Fr) Describes food, such as onions or meat, cooked or partially cooked without browning or coloring.

ablette (Fr) A small, silvery, freshwater fish, usually served fried. Also called **bleak.**

abóbora (Pg) Pumpkin, squash, vegetable marrow.

aboloo (Af) Steamed patties of fermented corn meal.

abon ayam (In) Shredded chicken, fried with spices.

aborinha (Pg) Zucchini.

aboukir (Ar) A Red Sea shrimp used in Middle Eastern seafood dishes.

a brasileira (Pg) Brazilian style.

abricot (Fr) Apricot.

abricot-péche (Fr) Nectarine.

abricots Condé (Fr) Poached apricots arranged around a ring of rice pudding, decorated with glacé cherries, angelica, and almond, and served with an apricot and Kirsch sauce.

abrikos (Rs) Apricot.

abrikosovi povidlo (Rs) Apricot jam.

abrikosovi sup (Rs) Cold apricot soup, served with rice and sour cream.

abrikossnitte (Da) Pastries shaped like bowties and filled with apricot preserves.

abuñolado (Sp) 1. Eggs turned or frittered. 2. Fried in batter.

abura (Jp) oil.

abura age (Jp) Thick slices of soybean

curd (tofu), fried in oil; may be filled with rice, meat, or vegetable mixtures.

aburakkokunai (Jp) Lean, without fat.

abura miso (Jp) Miso, or fermented soybean curd, sautéed in sesame oil and usually added to vegetable or rice mixtures.

abutilon (Pg) A leafy vegetable similar to spinach grown in South America and Asia. In Brazil, the flowers are cooked with meat dishes.

acacia (US) See **gum arabic.**

Acadian blueberry grunt (Ca) Stewed blueberries topped with scone batter and served with cream.

Acadian cheese bread (Ca) A dessert bread from the Maritime Provinces made with cranberries, orange juice, Cheddar cheese, and chopped walnuts.

açafrão (Pg) Saffron.

acajou (Fr) Cashew nut.

acajú (Pg) Cashew nut.

acara (Pg) Shrimp and bean fritters fried with onions and green peppers.

acaramelado (Pg) Caramel-flavored or caramel-like.

acar campur (In) Cooked and pickled vegetable salad.

acar ikan (In) Pickled fried fish.

acarne (Fr) Sea bream.

Ac'cent (US) Name for a commercial brand of monosodium glutamate.

acciughe (It) Anchovies.

acras de morue (Cb) Codfish fritters, a Creole dish made with salt cod, chives, and green and red peppers.

acecinado (Sp) Smoked, dried meat.

acedera (Sp) Sorrel.

aceite (Sp) Oil.

aceitunas (Sp) Olives.

aceitunas negras (Sp) Black olives.

acelga (Sp) Chard.

acelgas con crema (Sp) Creamed Swiss chard.

acerola (Cb) A small, red cherrylike fruit of a tropical plant, genus *Malpighia*; used in desserts and preserves; reported to contain more vitamin C per weight than any other known fruit. Also called **Barbados cherry.**

acesulfame-K (GB) An artificial, noncaloric sweetener reported to be about two hundred times sweeter than regular sugar. It was developed for use in dietetic beverages.

aceteria (Sp) Pickled vegetables.

acetic acid (US) An organic acid; the acid of vinegar and spoiled wine; used in pickling as a vinegar substitute and as a flavoring in commercial products such as yogurt and cheese.

acetini (It) Pickles, gherkins.

aceto (It) Vinegar.

aceto balsamico di Modena (It) See **balsamic vinegar.**

aceto-dolce (It) Sour-sweet, usually applied to a mixture of sour and sweet vegetables and fruit.

acétomel (Fr) A syrup of vinegar and honey.

acétoselle (Fr) Wood sorrel.

achar (Ia) Salad; raw or cooked vegetables steeped in a dressing of vinegar, salt, sugar, and ginger, to become mildly pickled; may be tinted with turmeric or saffron.

achara zuke (Jp) Sliced turnips in a vinegar and dried kelp dressing.

achari (Af–Swahili) Pickle.

achar tandal (Ia) Pickled cauliflower.

ache (Fr) Wild celery; smallage.

achicoria (Sp) Chicory.

achigan (Fr) Black bass.

achiote (Sp) See **annatto.**

acidophilus milk (US) A cultured milk prepared in a process similar to that used for buttermilk and yogurt.

acids (US) Active chemicals present in some foods. Naturally occurring acids give a sour flavor to foods; these include acetic acid, citric acid, and lactic acid. Pure acids, such as those used in cooking and sold as crystalline powders, include citric acid and tartaric acid.

acidulated water (US) Water made slightly acid by adding lemon juice or vinegar; used to prevent darkening of cut fruits and vegetables.

acini di pepe (It) Dried pasta shaped like tiny peppercorns used in soup.

ackee (Cb) A bright red tropical fruit, *Blighia sapida*, introduced to Jamaica from Africa; only the creamy aril is eaten, often cooked with salt cod. Also spelled **akee.**

açorda (Pg) Bread softened in olive oil with garlic and various other ingredients such as vegetables, chicken, fish, pork, or snails.

açorda alentejana (Pg) A thick, cold soup made with bread soaked in fish stock, olive oil, tomatoes, peppers, coriander, garlic, and cucumbers.

açorda de alho (Pg) A thick soup made with soaked bread, garlic, and herbs.

acorn (US) The nut of the oak tree, genus *Quercus*; all species are edible; used boiled, roasted like chestnuts or as a coffee substitute, and ground for flour.

acorn squash (US) Winter squash variety with a deep green ribbed shell streaked with yellow or orange; deep yellow to orange flesh; usually cut in half, seeds removed, and baked, cooked, or steamed.

acqua (It) Water.

acquacotta (It) Vegetable soup with sweet peppers and tomatoes.

acqua minerale (It) Mineral water.

acrid (US) Having a bitter, sour, or burning taste or smell.

acrolein (US) A bitter chemical produced by overheating fats, particularly by frying; causes poorly digested nutrients.

active dry yeast (US) See **yeasts.**

açúcar (Pg) Sugar.

adafina (Sp) A stew of chicken or beef, vegetables, and hard-boiled eggs.

additive (US) Any substance added directly or indirectly that becomes part of a food product. Substances added with no planned function may be acquired in processing, packaging, or storage. More than three thousand chemicals are used as food additives in more than thirty categories such as leavening agents or nutritive sweeteners. The safety of any such additive is regulated by the U.S. Food and Drug Administration.

ådelost (Sw) Dessert cheeses.

aderezo de comida (Sp) Condiment.

adobo (Ph) National Philippine dish with chicken, beef, or pork marinated in palm vinegar, garlic, and spices then simmered in a mixture of the marinade with soy sauce; many variations.

adobo criollo (Sp) Thick spicy Creole style sauce.

adobo de pescado (Sp) Fish casserole with tomatoes, ancho chilis, and spices.

adobong labong (Ph) Adobo with bamboo shoots, pork, and shrimp.

adobong pusit (Ph) Adobo with squid.

adobo sauce (Mx) Dark red sauce made with ancho chilis and tomatoes; used for meat, poultry, and vegetables.

adrak (Ia) Green gingerroot.

adrak chatni (Ia) Chutney made with fresh gingerroot and white raisins.

adrak murgh (Ia) Pepper chicken with gingered tomato sauce.

adriatico, dell' (It) Marinated in olive oil and lemon juice and then grilled over a wood or charcoal fire.

advocaat (Du) Eggnog with brandy.

adzhersandal (Rs) Eggplant baked with fried onions and tomatoes.

adzuki (Jp) See **azuki.**

æbleflæsk (Da) Bacon with fried apple rings and onion.

æblegrød (Da) Applesauce.

æblekage (Da) Pudding made with apples, toasted sugar, buttered breadcrumbs, and cream.

æbleskiver (Da) Deep-fried, sugared doughnut with an apple filling.

æg (Da) Egg.

æggekage (Da) Literally, "egg cake"; scrambled eggs with chopped onions, potatoes, and bacon.

æg og sild (Da) Egg with herring.

aemono (Jp) Salads of fish or shellfish and vegetables served raw or lightly cooked with a dressing based on tofu, miso paste, or crushed sesame seeds.

ærter (Da) Peas.

affettato (It) Sliced cold meats.

affogato (It) Poached or steamed.

affumicato (It) Smoked.

agachadiza (Sp) Snipe.

agar-agar (Ml) Odorless, colorless jelling agent obtained from red algae, *Rhodophyceae*, similar to gelatin; used in ice creams, custards, jellies, bakery products, and other foods. Also called **kanten.**

agedashi (Jp) Deep-fried soybean curd in a soy sauce with daikon, dried bonito, and gingerroot.

agemono (Jp) Deep-fried foods of two kinds: tempura, coated with batter; and kara age, lightly dusted with cornstarch.

ageta (Jp) Fried.

age, to (US) To tenderize and improve the flavor of freshly butchered meat by hanging it in a cold environment for a period of time; to mature and ripen cheese by storing; to bring wine to a peak of flavor by storing in a cool place.

ägg (Sw) Egg.

äggröra (Sw) Scrambled eggs.

aglio (It) Garlic.

aglio e olio (It) A dressing of hot olive oil and garlic for pasta.

agnautka (Rs) Flat, whole-grain bread of the Ukraine.

agneau (Fr) Lamb.

agneau de lait persillé (Fr) Grilled baby lamb served with parsley.

agneau grillé au thym (Fr) Grilled lamb seasoned with thyme.

5

agnello (It) Lamb.

agnello all' arrabbuata (It) Literally, "angry lamb"; lamb cooked over a high flame.

agneshko magdanoslija (Bu) Lamb with onions, parsley, and lemon slices.

agnolotti (It) Literally, "little lambs"; pasta packets filled with meat, cheese, and spinach, seasoned with nutmeg, often poached in chicken stock, and served with grated cheese.

agnolotti di grasso (It) Pasta packets filled with roast beef and veal, served with the roasting juices.

agoni (It) Freshwater shad; often served cold as an appetizer cooked with thyme.

agoni seccati in graticola (It) Freshwater shad grilled and marinated in vinegar with bay leaves.

agourelo (Gk) Young olive oil pressed from an early harvest.

agresto (It) Sour juice of unripe grapes used in some sauces and as a condiment.

agrião (Pg) Watercress.

agro (Sp) Acid, sour.

agrodolce (It) Sweet and sour, as with vinegar and sugar mixed.

agua (Sp) Water.

água (Pg) Water.

aguacate (Sp) Avocado.

aguacate encamaronados (Mx) Avocado with shrimp.

aguacate picante (Sp) Spiced avocado.

aguacates rellenos (Sp) Avocados stuffed with seafood or salad vegetables.

água com gelo (Pg) Water with ice.

água mineral (Pg) Mineral water.

agurk (Da) Cucumber.

agurkai su rukcscia grietine (Rs) Salad of cucumbers and sliced eggs in a dressing of mustard and sour cream.

agurker (Nw) Cucumbers.

agurkesalat (Da) Sliced cucumber salad in a dressing of vinegar, sugar, and dill.

ahds (Ar) Lentils.

ahds imqala (Ar) Lentil, potato, and onion soup.

ahds imsafa (Ar) Mashed lentils with rice and onion browned in olive oil.

ahds majroosh (Ar) Split dried red lentils.

ahds polo (Ar) Lentils with rice, lamb, raisins, and onions.

ahi (Pl) Hawaiian fish, yellowfin tuna, that has red flesh with a meaty texture and flavor; used grilled or sautéed.

ahjeen (Ar) Dough.

ahjeen il fatayer (Ar) Yeast dough used for turnovers or pies.

ahmeeghthalota (Gk) Almond cookies.

ahngooree (Gk) Cucumber.

ahsal (Ar) Honey.

ahududu (Tr) Raspberry.

ahven (Fi) Perch.

ai ferri (It) Cooked on the spit; grilled.

aiglefin (Fr) Haddock.

aïgo sau d'iou (Fr) A fish soup similar to bouillabaisse with potatoes added; a Provençal dish.

aigre-doux (Fr) Sweet-sour, tart.

aiguillette (Fr) A long, thin slice of fowl or meat.

aiguillette de canetons Montmorency (Fr) Strips of duckling breasts sautéed in butter and flambéed in cognac; served in a port and orange juice sauce.

ail (Fr) Garlic.

aile de poulet (Fr) Chicken wing.

aillade (Fr) A mayonnaise sauce flavored with garlic and walnuts, served with fish.

aïoli (Fr) A garlic-flavored sauce with the consistency of mayonnaise, made with egg yolks, vinegar or lemon juice, and olive oil; usually served with poached fish, but may be used with vegetables or meat.

aipo (Pg) Celery.

air (In) Water.

airelle (Fr) A variety of blueberry.

air jeruk manis (In) Sweet orange juice.

air tomat (In) Tomato juice.

aish (Ar) Bread.

aisu kōhi (Jp) Iced coffee.

aisu kurīmu (Jp) Ice cream.

aisu tī (Jp) Iced tea.

ajawn seeds (Ia) Seeds similar to caraway but smaller, used in curry and lentil dishes.

aji (Jp) Pompano.

aji (Sp) Capsicum peppers; chili sauce.

aji-no-moto (Jp) See **monosodium glutamate.**

ajmoda (Ia) Parsley.

ajo (Sp) Garlic; garlic sauce for meat.

ajo cebollino (Sp) Chive.

ajókamártas (Hu) Anchovy sauce.

ajonjoli (Sp) Sesame seeds; a term used in Africa for yellow to red sesame seeds roasted like peanuts and ground for flour.

ajo porro (Sp) Leek.

akadashi (Jp) Red-bean paste soup.

aka miso (Jp) Red miso.

akee (Cb) See **ackee.**

åkerbøne (Nw) Partridge.

akevitt (Nw) See **aquavit.**

akhinos (Gk) Sea urchin.

akhladhi (Gk) Pear.

akhrot (Ia) Walnuts.

akkra (Cb) Fritters made with beans.

akuri (Ia) Scrambled eggs with coriander and ginger.

akvavit (Da, Sw) See **aquavit.**

al (It) At the; to the; on the.

ål (Da, Nw, Sw) Eel; served boiled, smoked, and in aspic.

à la, à l' (Fr) With; in the style of.

a la (Sp) In the style of.

alabalik (Tr) Trout.

alabega (Sp) Sweet basil.

à la carte (Fr) According to the menu; describes a price list for menu items selected and charged individually.

alajú (Sp) 1. Almond paste with honey and walnuts. 2. Gingerbread.

à l'algérienne (Fr) Served with sweet potatoes either pureed for soup or sautéed or in croquettes, and with garlic-flavored chopped tomatoes.

à l'alsacienne (Fr) 1. With a garnish of ham or sausages and sauerkraut. 2. With a garnish of noodles, foie gras, and truffles. 3. With a Madeira sauce.

à l'amiral (Fr) Literally, "admiral's style"; served with a garnish of oysters, mussels, crayfish, mushrooms, and truffles; used for large fish.

à la mode (Fr) In the style; usually meaning "served with ice cream," as in the dish, pie à la mode; or meaning "braised with vegetables and served with a gravy," as in beef à la mode.

à la mode de (Fr) As prepared in, by, or for. See **tripes à la mode de Caen.**

à l'ancienne (Fr) With a garnish of small onions and mushrooms; used with dishes such as chicken fricassee or lamb stew.

à l'andalouse (Fr) With a garnish of rice-stuffed sweet peppers, eggplants au gratin, and a tomato sauce.

à l'anglaise (Fr) In the English style; vegetables, meat, and poultry cooked in either water or stock; meat and fish breaded or floured and fried.

al arancio (It) Orange-flavored; with an orange sauce.

à l'Argenteuil (Fr) Garnished with asparagus.

à l'arlésienne (Fr) With a garnish of stuffed tomatoes, eggplant, and rice sometimes colored with saffron.

alaskačorba (SC) A hearty "fisherman's soup" made with whitefish, egg, and lemon.

à l'autrichienne (Fr) In the Austrian style; with sour cream, paprika, and onions.

alb (Ar) Heart.

albacore (US) A species of tuna, *Thunnus alalunga*, sold as white meat tuna and used baked or grilled.

albaricoque (Sp) Apricot.

Albert, sauce (Fr) A white sauce with horseradish used on braised beef.

albicocca (It) Apricot.

albillo (Sp) White grape, or wine of a white grape.

albóndigas (Sp) Spicy meatballs or molded ground meat; sometimes a thick soup with ground beef and rice; in Mexico dish may be flavored with chilis, cumin, oregano, and contain chopped zucchini.

Albuféra, sauce (Fr) A béchamel sauce with sweet pepper butter.

albumin (US) A sulfur-rich form of protein found in many vegetable tissues such as peas, wheat, and soybeans and in nearly all animal tissues including blood plasma and milk. Egg whites are a common source. Albumins coagulate when heated and will partially coagulate when whipped, as with egg whites.

al burro (It) Dressed with butter.

alcachofas a la vinagreta (Sp) Artichokes in a vinaigrette dressing.

alcachofra (Pg) Artichoke.

alcaparras (Pg) Capers.

alcaravea (Sp) Caraway.

alcohol (US) A term that usually refers to ethyl alcohol although there are a large number of substances, from liquids to waxy solids, that can be called alcohol. Ethyl alcohol, found in wine, beer, and whiskey, is produced through the fermentation of sugar by yeast. The starch content of cereals, when used to produce alcohol, must first be converted to sugar by a malting process.

alcool (Fr, Sp) Alcohol.

al dente (It) Literally, "to the tooth"; refers to pasta that is cooked only to the point it loses the taste of flour and is chewy.

ale (US) An alcoholic beverage brewed from a cereal; may be used to flavor soups, stews, and casseroles.

ålesuppe (Da) Eel soup; served with dark bread.

alewife (US) A saltwater fish, genus *Alosa*, related to the herring with oily flesh; used fried, grilled, or baked.

alface (Pg) Lettuce.

alfajor (Sp) Cake made with nuts and honey.

alfalfa sprouts (US) The mild-flavored sprouted seeds of a legume, *Medicago sativa*, eaten as a salad food.

al forno (It) Baked, roasted.

älgstek (Sw) Elk steak; roast elk.

alho (Pg) Garlic.

alho-poró (Pg–Brazil) Leek.

al horno (Sp) Baked.

ali (It) Wings, such as chicken wings.

alice (It) Anchovy.

alici sott'olio (It) Anchovies preserved in olive oil.

alicot (Fr) A ragout of poultry giblets braised with garlic, carrots, and potatoes.

aliñado (Sp) Seasoned.

aliño (Sp) Seasoning.

ali-oli (Sp) Garlic-flavored mayonnaise.

alkali (US) Any of a number of chemical compounds that react with acids to form salts or with fats to form soaps. Bicarbonate of soda, commonly used in cooking, is an alkali.

alkanet (US) Plant of the borage family, native to the Mediterranean, with roots containing a red dye used to color margarine, sausage skins, and other products.

Alkohol (Gr) Alcohol.

alkupalat (Fi) Appetizers, hors d'oeuvres.

alla, alle, allo (It) In the style of; prepared with.

alla brace (It) Charcoal-broiled.

all'agliata (It) With a garlic, bread, and wine vinegar sauce.

all'amatriciana (It) In the style of Amatrice in central Italy; pasta with a sauce containing tomatoes, red peppers, and lean salt pork.

alle acciughe (It) Prepared with anchovies.

alle cozze (It) With mussels.

allemande, sauce (Fr) A velouté sauce bound with egg yolks.

alle vongole (It) Prepared with clams.

Allgäuer Emmenthaler (Gr) A cow's milk cheese with yellow to brown rind, a yellow interior with large holes, and a milder taste than Swiss cheese.

Allgewürz (Gr) Allspice.

alligator pear (US) See **avocado.**

all'olio ed aglio (It) Prepared with olive oil and garlic.

alloro (It) Bay leaves.

allo spiedo (It) Roasted on a spit.

allspice (Cb) Dried berry of a tropical tree, *Pimenta dioica*, grown in Jamaica; taste resembles a mixture of spices including cloves; used in pickling, for stews, soups, fish, and meats. Also called **Jamaica pepper.**

allumettes (Fr) Potatoes cut to the thickness of matchsticks; also, puff pastry strips.

all'uovo (It) With eggs.

Allspice

alma (Hu) Apple.

almamártás (Hu) Applesauce.

almás rétes (Hu) Apple strudel.

almejas (Sp) Clams, cockles, mussels.

almejas en salsa de ajo (Sp) Clams served in a sauce of olive oil, garlic, and parsley.

almendra (Sp) Almond.

almendra amarga (Sp) Bitter almond.

almendrado (Sp) Macaroon.

almendras confitadas (Sp) Candied almonds; pralines.

almendras de cacao (Sp) Cocoa beans.

almendras garapiñadas (Sp) Sugared almonds.

almendras tostados (Sp) Almonds toasted in butter.

almibar (Sp) Syrup.

almíbares (Sp) Preserved fruit.

almirón (Sp) Wild chicory.

almodón (Sp) Baking flour.

almodrote (Sp) Eggplant sauce.

almojábana (Sp) 1. Cruller. 2. Cheesecake. 3. Paste of butter, eggs, and sugar.

almond (US) The kernel of a fruit of the almond tree, *Prunus amygdalus*, native to the Mediterranean. The almond used as a food is the *sweet almond*, sold in many forms such as blanched, sliced, chopped, ground, and roasted. **Bitter almonds**, which form lethal prussic acid unless correctly processed, are not sold in the United States, but are used in amaretti and confections in other countries.

almôndegas (Pg) Meatballs or croquettes made with a mixture of pork and veal.

almori (Sp) Sweetmeat; cake.

almorzar (Sp) To breakfast or lunch.

ål og røræg (Da) Eel with scrambled eggs.

aloque (Sp) Describes a clear white wine, or a mixture of red and white wines.

alosa (Sp) Shad.

alose (Fr) Shad.

alouettes (Fr) Larks.

alouettes sans têtes (Fr) Veal birds; thin veal slices rolled around a filling of ground pork, bread crumbs, egg, and garlic and sautéed in olive oil.

aloyau (Fr) Beef sirloin.

alperche (Pg) Apricot.

alpistela (Sp) A cake with sesame seeds, flour, honey, and eggs.

Alpkäse (Gr–Swiss) Literally, "cheese made in the Alps"; soft to firm cow's or goat's milk cheese; has a sweet, mellow taste when made with cow's milk.

al ragù (It) With meat sauce.

al sangue (It) Served rare (meat).

Alse (Gr) Shad.

al sugo (It) With meat sauce.

alu (Ia) Potato.

alubia (Sp) French bean; haricot.

alu bukhara (Ia) Plum.

alu chat (Ia) A snack made with potatoes and peas flavored with chilis, tamarind, and coriander.

alu matar (Ia) Potato and green pea curry.

alu pakoras (Ia) Potato fritters.

amai (Jp) Sweet.

amande (Fr) Almond.

amande amère (Fr) Bitter almond.

amandel (Du) Almonds.

amandine (Fr) Prepared with almonds; often used to describe fish fillets.

amaranth (US) A plant of the family Amaranthaceae, with large seed heads; seeds are ground into flour for bread and popped like popcorn; greens are used stir-fried.

amarelle (US) A cultivated sour cherry, *Prunus cerasus*, with colorless juice. Also called **klarbär.**

amaretti (It) Small macaroons made with sweet and bitter almonds.

amaretto (It) A liqueur flavored with almonds and apricots; may be used in whipped cream and fruit salads.

amaro (It) Bitter.

amazake (Jp) Literally, "sweet cake"; a thick hot drink made with rice and water.

amazu (Jp) Sweetened vinegar sauce.

ambrosia (It) A dessert made with sliced oranges and bananas, sugar, and coconut.

Ambrosia (Sw) A pale yellow cow's milk cheese with a somewhat soft interior and a mild, slightly tart taste.

amchoor (Ia) Dried mango powder; used like a seasoning.

amêijoas (Pg) Clams; cockles.

amêijoas na cataplana (Pg) Steamed clams with sausages, ham, tomatoes, and spices.

ameixas (Pg) Plums; prunes.

amêndoas (Pg) Almonds.

amendoim (Pg) Peanuts.

américaine (Fr) See **homard à l'américaine.**

American cheese (US) Term applied to American Cheddar or Cheddar-style cheeses and also to processed, presliced sandwich cheese.

amino acid (US) An organic chemical compound that occurs naturally in animal tissues and is a building block for protein molecules. There are more than twenty different kinds of amino acids, most of which can be produced by the body. However, at least eight, called essential amino acids, must be obtained from food. See **essential amino acids.**

amirty (Ia) Deep-fried, crisp yellow spirals of urad dal; soaked in syrup.

amóras (Pg) Berries.

amrood (Ia) Guava.

anacard (Pg–Brazil) A vinegar made from cashew nuts.

anadama bread (US) Bread made with yeast dough, cornmeal, and molasses.

anago (Jp) Conger eel.

Anaheim chili (US) Bright, shiny green pepper, 5 to 8 inches long, about 2 inches wide, tapering to a point; flavor

11

ranges from mild to moderately hot. Also called **California green chili.**

ananas (Cz, Fi, Nw, Rs, Tr) Pineapple.

ananas au kirsch (Fr) Pineapple in Kirsch.

ananasový meloun (Cz) Cantaloupe.

ananasso (It) Pineapple.

ananász (Hu) Pineapple.

anar (Ia) Pomegranate.

anchellini (It) Ravioli stuffed with meat and fried.

ancho (Mx) A mild chili that resembles the green bell pepper; sold fresh when green or a ripe red; or dried and black; often used in Mexican cooking.

anchoas (Sp) Anchovies.

anchois (Fr) Anchovies.

anchoussi s yaitzami (Rs) Anchovies on eggs.

anchouwa (Ar) Anchovies.

anchova (Pg) Anchovy; bluefish.

anchovies (US) Small saltwater fish, *Engraulis encrasicholus*, found in Mediterranean waters or along the coasts of southern Europe; when salted and cured develop a red color; usually sold canned in oil or in a paste; used often in Italian, Spanish, and Portuguese cooking. Around the world other small fish are known locally as anchovies.

anchoyade (Fr) Puree of anchovies mixed with garlic and olive oil, served with raw vegetables or on bread.

ançuvez (Tr) Anchovies.

and (Da, Nw) Duck.

anda (Ia) Egg.

anda ki kari (Ia) Egg curry.

andalouse, sauce (Fr) Mayonnaise sauce with tomato puree, green peppers, and parsley.

andesteg (Da) Roast duck.

andijvie (Du) Escarole.

andouille (Fr) Thick sausage made with tripe and encased in a pig intestine; black from smoke and wrinkled.

andruty (Po) Wafers.

anellini (It) Pasta shaped like little rings; usually served in soup.

anequim (Pg) See **mackerel shark.**

aneth (Fr) Dill.

aneto (It) Dill.

angel food cake (US) A light sponge cake made with beaten egg whites and no shortening and baked in a tube pan; usually a white cake but may be flavored with chocolate, vanilla, or almond extract.

angel hair (US) Very thin, cylindrical pasta. Also called **capellini.**

angelica (US) A tall herb, *Angelica archangelica*, with thick, hollow stems and large, serrated leaves; used chopped as a garnish, prepared like celery or rhubarb, or candied.

angélique (Fr) Angelica.

anglerfish (US) Monkfish.

Anglesey eggs (GB) A Welsh dish of mashed potatoes topped with hard-boiled eggs and a cheese sauce and baked.

angoor (Ia) Grapes.

angrešt (Cz) Gooseberries.

angsa (In) Goose.

anguila (Sp) Eel.

anguilla marinata (It) Marinated eel.

anguille (Fr) Eel.

anguille alla veneziana (It) Eels cooked in tuna and lemon sauce.

anguilles au vert (Bl) Sautéed eels in a sauce of egg yolks, white wine, and herbs including sorrel and mint.

anguria (It) Watermelon.

anice (It) Anise.

anijs (Du) Anise.

animelle (It) Sweetbreads.

animelles à la crème (Fr) Sliced sweetbreads cooked in butter and a cream sauce; used as a garnish.

anise (US) An aromatic seed of an herb, *Pimpinella anisum*, with a slight licorice flavor; brown when dried; used to flavor cookies, rolls, stews, sauces, and dishes of the Mediterranean, India, and Southeast Asia. Also called *aniseed*.

anisetta (It) A liqueur made with the aromatic herb, anise.

anitra (It) Duck.

anitra arrosto (It) Roast duck.

anitra selvatica (It) Wild duck.

anjeer (Ia) Figs.

Anjou (Fr) A pear variety with a yellow-green, often russeted skin; sweet flavor; used for a dessert pear, poaching, baking, broiling, and canning.

anjova (Sp) Bluefish.

anjovis (Fi) Anchovies.

anka (Sw) Duck.

ankerias (Fi) Eel.

ankka (Fi) Duck.

Annabella (It) A soft, white, creamy cow's milk cheese, eaten fresh with fruit.

annatto (US) A salmon-red dye produced from the fruit of a South American tree, *Bixa orellana*; used to color confections, cheese, and rice. The seeds are ground and used as a spice.

anolini (It) Small ravioli stuffed with minced cooked beef and Parmesan cheese.

Anschovis (Gr) Anchovy.

ansjovis (Sw) Marinated sprats.

antioxidants (US) Substances that prevent or retard the tendency of foods, particularly fats or oils, from absorbing oxygen from the air and becoming rancid. They may be natural agents such as ascorbic acid used to prevent the discoloration of fruit or synthetic chemicals.

antipasto (It) Literally, "before the meal"; a first course; appetizers, hors d'oeuvres.

antipasto variato (It) Assorted hors d'oeuvres.

antojos (Mx) "Whims"; appetizers.

aoyagi (Jp) Round clams.

apams (Ia) Rice and coconut pancakes cooked with coconut milk.

apel (In) Apple.

apelsin (Sw) Orange.

apel'sin (Rs) Orange.

apenoten (Du) Peanuts.

apéritif (Fr) Any drink such as sherry or champagne usually taken before dinner as an appetite stimulant.

aperitivo (It) Apéritif.

Apfel (Gr) Apple.

Apfelkuchen (Gr) Apple custard tart.

Apfelmus (Gr) Applesauce.

Apfelpfannkuchen (Gr) Apple pancakes.

Apfelreis (Gr) Rice pudding made with apples.

Apfelrotkohl (Gr) Red cabbage and apples, cooked together and served with roast pork.

Apfelsinen (Gr) Oranges.

13

Apfelsinensaft (Gr) Orange juice.

Apfelstrudel (Gr) Apple strudel.

Apfelwein (Gr) Apple cider or wine.

aphelia (Gk) Pork fillets marinated in red wine with bay leaves and crushed coriander then sautéed in olive oil and wine.

aphrodisiac (US) A food or drink believed to arouse or intensify sexual drive.

api'i (Pl) A form of taro, gray in color.

apio (Sp) Celery.

apio-nabo (Sp) Celeriac.

à point (Fr) Medium done (meat).

appelbeignets (Du) Apple fritters.

äppelkaka med vaniljsås (Sw) Layers of fried bread crumbs and apples with vanilla custard.

appelmoes (Du) Applesauce.

appelsap (Du) Cider.

appelsiini (Fi) Orange.

appelsiinimehua (Fi) Orange juice.

appelsin (Nw) Orange.

appelsinsaft (Nw) Orange juice.

appeltaart (Du) Apple cake.

Appenzell (Gr–Swiss) A cow's milk cheese with a smooth brown rind, a pale gold interior with small scattered holes and a mild to fruity and spicy taste.

appetizer (US) Any food or drink served before a meal to stimulate the appetite, such as hors d'oeuvres or a dry sherry.

apple (US) The fruit of a temperate-zone tree, genus *Malus*, member of the rose family; some 7,000 varieties are known in the United States; may be roughly classified into wild crab apples, cultivated all-purpose apples, and cooking apples. Skin color ranges from green to pale yellow to dark red. Eaten raw or cooked in numerous ways. A few of the many common varieties include Granny Smith, Jonathan, Golden or Red Delicious, McIntosh, and Winesap.

äpple (Sw) Apple.

apple amber pudding (GB) A tart filled with sweet, flavored apple puree topped with meringue.

apple butter (US) See **fruit butters.**

apple charlotte (GB) A pudding of layered, buttered bread crumbs and stewed apples, sweetened and topped with more bread crumbs, and baked. Bread strips may be used in place of crumbs. Said to be named for Charlotte, wife of George III.

apple dumplings (GB) Peeled and cored apples, filled with a sweet mixture, wrapped in a pastry crust and baked; served with cream.

applejack (US) Apple brandy.

äppleknyten (Sw) Apple dumplings.

apple pandowdy (US) A New England and Pennsylvania Dutch cross between a pudding and a deep dish apple pie; a baked mixture of sliced apples, sugar, molasses, butter, cinnamon, and nutmeg covered with a pie crust.

apple pie (US) A traditional two-crust pie, the filling is an apple mixture spiced with cloves, cinnamon, and nutmeg; served with cheddar cheese or ice cream. Green apple pie is made with sour apples.

applesauce (US) Strained, cooked apple puree recooked with sugar and sometimes lemon juice; may be seasoned with cinnamon.

apple slump (US) Apple pandowdy topped with biscuit dough.

apple snow (US) A dessert made with beaten egg whites, lemon juice, cinnamon, nutmeg, and sometimes gelatin mixed with applesauce.

appum (Ia) Rice flour pancakes made with coconut milk.

apricot (US) The fruit of a tree, *Prunus armeniaca*, many varieties; skin color ranges from pale yellow to orange-red; white, yellow, or orange flesh; sweet, juicy; eaten fresh, dried, or canned; used cooked in many Middle Eastern dishes.

aprikoosi (Fi) Apricot.

aprikos (Nw, Sw) Apricot.

Aprikosen (Gr) Apricots.

aprósütemények (Hu) Cookies.

aquavit (US) Literally, "water of life";

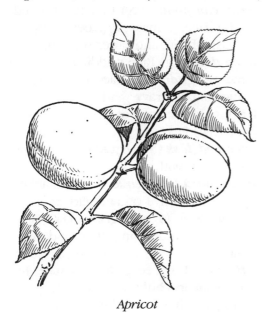

Apricot

Scandinavian spirits distilled from potatoes, rye, or barley and flavored with caraway seeds. Also spelled *akevitt, akvavit*.

arachide (Fr, It) Peanut.

arachis huile (Fr) Groundnut or peanut oil.

aragosta (It) Lobster.

arak (Ar) An anise-flavored spirit.

arancia (It) Orange.

aranciata (It) Orangeade.

arancini (It) Little rice balls mixed with liver, meat, mushrooms, onions, and spices, then breaded and fried in olive oil.

arándano (Sp) Bilberry; blueberry.

aranygaluska (Hu) Dumpling cake.

arare (Jp) Small rice crackers.

arbei (In) Strawberries.

arborio (It) An Italian short-grain rice used in risotto.

Arbroath smokies (Sc) Smoked haddock stuffed with butter and baked or grilled.

arbuz (Rs) Watermelon.

archiduc, à la (Fr) Prepared with a cream sauce containing white wine, onion, and paprika.

arenque (Pg) Herring.

arenque ahumado (Sp) Smoked herring.

arepas (Sp) Venezuelan corn cakes cooked on a griddle.

arhar dal (Ia) Pigeon pea.

aringa (It) Herring.

aringa affumicata (It) Kippered herring.

aringa marinata (It) Marinated herring.

arista (It) Pork loin roasted on the spit or in the oven.

15

armadillo (US) An armor-covered mammal, *Dasypus novemcinctus*, hunted in the southwestern United States and used in soups or chili con carne; various species are eaten in South America.

armagnac (Fr) A dry, pungent brandy from Gascony.

Arme Ritter (Gr) Bread dipped in beaten egg or batter, fried, sprinkled with sugar and cinnamon, and served with applesauce.

armoricaine (Fr) An old term for Brittany and sometimes confused with a lobster dish created by a French chef. See **homard à l'américaine.**

armut (Tr) Pear.

arnab (Ar) Rabbit.

arnabeet (Ar) Cauliflower.

arnavut ciğeri (Tr) Lamb's liver fried with onions, parsley, and paprika.

arni (Gk) Lamb.

arni exokhiko (Gk) "Country style" lamb in phyllo pastry with a mixture of peas, potatoes, cheese, and tomatoes; baked.

arni steen stamna (Gk) Lamb baked in a dough-sealed clay dish.

aromatic (US) Having an agreeable fragrance from food or drink; flavored with plants or herbs such as ginger, parsley, garlic, or thyme that give a pungent odor.

arraia (Pg) Skate, ray.

arrayán (Sp) Myrtle.

arreganato (It) Prepared with oregano.

arrôs (Pg–Brazil) Rice.

arroser (Fr) To baste.

arrostire sulla (It) Broiling.

arrosto (It) Roast, roast meat.

arrosto di agnello con patatine (It) Roast spring lamb with new potatoes.

arrowroot (US) A fine, white, edible starch made from the ground pith of the roots of several tropical plants, mainly *Maranta arundinacea*; used as a glaze and to thicken sauces, puddings, and other cooked foods.

arroz (Pg, Sp) Rice.

arroz abanda (Sp) Saffron rice steeped in seafood stock; served with fish and shellfish; many variations.

arroz blanco con mejillones (Sp) White rice with mussels.

arroz con azafrán (Sp) Saffron rice.

arroz con costra (Sp) A casserole of rice and rabbit with an egg crust.

arroz con frijoles (Sp) Rice with black beans.

arroz con leche (Sp) A pudding of rice cooked in milk with cinnamon and lemon. Also called **leché quemada.**

arroz con pollo (Mx) Chicken cooked with rice, tomatoes, green pepper, peas, saffron, and other seasonings.

arroz doce (Pg) Rice pudding.

arroz refogado (Pg) Rice in an onion and tomato gravy.

Art (Gr) In the style of.

ärter (Sw) Peas.

ärter med fläsk (Sw) A traditional yellow pea soup with pork.

artichauts à la grecque (Fr) Artichokes cooked in olive oil and garlic.

artichauts à la vinaigrette (Fr) Artichokes in a dressing of oil and vinegar.

artichoke (US) See **globe artichoke, Jerusalem artichoke.**

articsóka (Hu) Artichoke.

**Artischocken** (Gr) Artichokes.

**Artischockenherzen** (Gr) Artichoke hearts.

**artisjokk** (Nw) Artichoke.

**artisokka** (Fi) Artichoke.

**ärtsoppa** (Sw) Pea soup.

**artyčoky** (Cz) Artichokes.

**aru** (Ia) Peach.

**arugula** (It) A salad plant, _Eruca sativa_, member of the cabbage family, with pungent-flavored leaves. Also called **rocket cress.**

**arvi ki kari** (Ia) Yam curry.

**asadero** (Mx) Literally, "fit for roasting"; a white, cow's milk cheese sold in braids; melts smoothly, can be diced, or pulled into strands; similar to Monterey Jack.

**asado** (Sp) Cooked on a barbecue; roasted.

**asado de cerdo** (Sp) Roast pork.

**asadura** (Sp) Offal or variety meats; chitterlings.

**asafetida** (Ia) The dried resin of a fennellike plant, _Ferula asafoetida_, used in the cooking of India. When fried, the aroma and taste resemble that of onions.

**asafetida poori** (Ia) A spicy bread made with ground chick-peas and flavored with asafetida.

**asakusa nori** (Jp) A form of seaweed (nori) used in making norimaki sushi.

**asam** (In) Tamarind; sour.

**asar** (Sp) To broil, roast.

**asar a la lumbre** (Sp) To roast on an open fire.

**asar a la parrilla** (Sp) To grill.

**asatsuki** (Jp) Chives.

**ascalonia** (Sp) Shallot.

**asciutta** (It) A term for pasta used in a sauce or stuffed, as opposed to a pasta used in a broth (in brodo).

**ascorbic acid** (US) An alternative term for vitamin C. Synthetic ascorbic acid is used as an antioxidant in manufactured foods and sometimes in home cooking to prevent browning of cut fruits. Ascorbic acid does not increase the vitamin C content of manufactured foods because it is lost with cooking. See also **vitamin C.**

**aseer** (Ar) Juice; fruit juice.

**aseer burtuaan** (Ar) Orange juice.

**aseer il limoon** (Ar) Lemon juice.

**ash sak** (Ar) A hearty soup with yogurt, meat, spinach, and nuts.

**ashtarak tolma** (Rs) Apples or quinces stuffed with lamb.

**Asiago** (It) A Cheddar-like cow's milk cheese with a yellow interior and a pungent flavor. When young, used as a table cheese; when aged, used for grating.

**Asian pear** (US) Any of several varieties of a tree, _Pyrus pyrifolia_, native to Japan with edible fruit that resembles both apple and pear; skin color from yellow-green to brown; aromatic, crisp, juicy white flesh; usually eaten fresh but can be cooked, dried, or pressed into juice. Also called **Japanese pear, nashi, sand pear.**

**asopao** (Sp–Puerto Rico) A stew with rice, chicken, and seafood.

**asparagi** (It) Asparagus.

**asparagi alla fiorentina** (It) Asparagus mixed lightly in butter with Parmesan cheese and topped with fried eggs.

**asparagus** (US) A vegetable, _Asparagus_

17

officinalis, a member of the lily family with spearlike stems ending in tightly closed bud heads; color usually green but may be blanched white; delicate flavor; used steamed or gently boiled; often served with a sauce.

asparagus bean (US) See **yard-long bean.**

aspara-kopitas (Gk) A puff pastry stuffed with asparagus, feta cheese, garlic, and mushrooms.

asparges (Da) Asparagus.

asparges (Nw) Asparagus.

aspartame (US) An artificial sweetener almost two hundred times sweeter than table sugar; must be labeled because some persons are unable to metabolize an amino acid in it (phenylalanine).

asperges (Fr) Asparagus.

asperges à la crème (Fr) Creamed asparagus.

asperges en branches (Fr) Whole, boiled asparagus.

asperges mornay (Fr) Asparagus with a thick cheese sauce.

asperges mousseline (Fr) Asparagus with a sauce of egg yolks, lemon juice, and whipped cream.

aspergesoep (Du) Asparagus soup.

asperillo (Sp) Slightly tart or sour.

aspic (US) Cold, cooked food such as meat, fish, poultry, vegetables, or fruit set in a mold with aspic jelly.

aspic jelly (US) A clear, savory jelly made with reduced chicken or veal stocks, or clarified meat, fish, or poultry stocks with gelatin added. It solidifies when cooled; used for aspics, as a gar-

nish, and to glaze cold, cooked poultry, meat, or fish.

aspro (It) Sour, tart.

aspro krasi (Gk) White wine.

assado (Pg) Roasted; roast.

assaisonnement (Fr) Seasoning; salad dressing.

assaisonnement aromatique (Fr) An aromatic seasoning such as parsley or chervil.

Assam (Ia) A black, pungent tea from Assam in India.

ässät (Fi) S-shaped cookies.

assida bil bufriwa (Ar) Hazelnut pudding topped with nuts and a sweet sauce.

assiette anglaise (Fr) An assortment of cold, sliced meats.

assiette assortie (Fr) A mixture of cold hors d'oeuvres.

assiette de charcuterie (Fr) A plate of assorted sausages.

assortimento pazzo (It) A wild or extravagant assortment of meat, seafood, and vegetables.

assortito (It) Assorted.

astaco (It, Sp) Spiny lobster.

astakos mayioneza (Gk) Spiny lobster served with mayonnaise.

asuparagasu (Jp) Asparagus.

aşure (Tr) Pudding made with a mixture of navy beans, chick-peas, rice, dried fruit, and nuts.

ásványvizet (Hu) Mineral water.

atalvina (Sp) An almond meal porridge.

atayef (Ar) Folded pancakes stuffed with a sweet, flower-flavored mixture of walnuts.

atemoya (US) A hybrid fruit of the cherimoya and the sweetsop in the custard apple family, shaped like a large, scaly, green fir cone. Its custardlike flesh contains many seeds and is usually eaten raw.

atholl brose (Sc) A drink made by straining water from soaked raw oats (brose) and mixing with Scotch whiskey, honey, and sometimes cream. Reportedly named for a duke of Atholl.

atjar (In) Any of the sweet-and-sour relishes made from various pickled vegetables.

atjar rebung (In) Sweet-and-sour bamboo shoot relish.

atole (Sp) A sweet beverage or gruel made with milk, corn flour, and flavorings.

atpokat (In) Avocado.

attereau (Fr) An hors d'oeuvre of various ingredients coated in bread crumbs, laced on a skewer, and fried.

åttiksgurka (Sw) Pickled gherkins.

atum (Pg) Tuna.

atún (Sp) Tuna.

Aubergine (Gr) Eggplant.

aubergine (GB, Fr, It) Eggplant.

aubergines à la niçoise (Fr) Eggplant with garlic and tomatoes.

au beurre (Fr) With butter, browned or in a sauce.

au bleu (Fr) Describes the blue color that very fresh fish, usually trout, acquire when cooked by plunging immediately into boiling court bouillon.

Auflauf (Gr) Soufflé; pudding.

au four (Fr) Baked in the oven.

Aufschnitt (Gr) Plate of assorted sliced sausages.

au gratin (Fr) A baked or grilled dish sprinkled with grated cheese or bread crumbs or both.

augurken (Du) Pickles.

au jus (Fr) Served in its own juice or gravy; usually from beef.

au lait (Fr) With milk.

au lard (Fr) Cooked in salt pork.

au naturel (Fr) Served unseasoned, or without butter, sauce or garnishes.

aure (Nw) Trout.

aurore, sauce (Fr) A velouté sauce with tomato paste or puree, heavy cream, butter, and egg yolks; also, a béchamel sauce with paprika and cream.

au sang (Fr) With a sauce made from the blood of the meat used.

Austern (Gr) Oysters.

auszpik (Po) Aspic.

avakkai mangai (Ia) Mango chutney.

avêia (Pg) Oatmeal.

aveline (Fr) Filbert, hazelnut.

avellana (It, Sp) Filbert, hazelnut.

aves (Sp) Poultry; birds.

avgha (Gk) Eggs.

avgolemono (Gk) Lemon and egg sauce; often used to flavor and bind soups and other dishes.

avkokt torsk (Nw) Boiled cod.

avocado (US) The round or pear-shaped, smooth or rough-skinned, fruit of a tropical evergreen tree, *Persea americana*; skin colors ranging from green to almost black; creamy flesh with a buttery texture when ripe; used in salads, soups, ice cream and, best known, in guacamole. Also called **alligator pear.**

avocat (Fr) Avocado.

avocat farci de crevettes (Fr) Avocado stuffed with shrimp.

awabi (Jp) Abalone.

ayam (In) Chicken.

ayam panggang bumbu besengek (In) Roast, grilled chicken in coconut sauce.

ayam panike (In) Chicken cooked in an aromatic sauce.

ayam percik (Ml) Grilled marinated chicken with coconut sauce.

ayam tauco (In) Chicken cooked with fermented yellow beans.

ayran (Tr) A drink made with yogurt.

ayskrimu (Af–Swahili) Ice cream.

ayskrimu ya vanila (Af–Swahili) Vanilla ice cream.

ayu (Jp) Freshwater trout.

az (Tr) Rare or undercooked.

azafrán (Sp) Saffron.

azarole (US) A small, applelike fruit of a shrub, *Crataegus azarolus*; white to red skin; crisp flesh; eaten fresh or used in preserves. Also called **Naples medlar.**

azedinha (Pg) Sorrel.

azedo (Pg) Sour.

Azeitão (Pg) A cream cheese of ewes' milk with a yellow rind and mild taste.

azeite (Pg) Oil; olive oil. Also called **óleo.**

azeitonas (Pg) Olives.

azijn (Du) Vinegar.

azu (Rs) Beefsteak and vegetable stew.

azúcar (Sp) Sugar.

azuki (Jp) A legume, *Phaseolus angularis*, cultivated throughout Asia, Africa, and North and South America; sold as small, red-brown, dried beans; used boiled, mashed, sweetened, as a base for cakes, and in rice. Also spelled **adzuki.**

azukian (Jp) Sweet red bean paste.

azyme (Fr) Unleavened bread.

baars (Du) Bass.

bab (Hu) Beans.

baba (Fr) A sweet sponge cake molded in the shape of a turban and named for a fictional character, Ali Baba; many variations of flavorings.

baba au rhum (Fr) A turban-shaped sponge cake soaked in rum and dec orated with candied or glacéed fruits.

babaco (Sp) A yellow fruit, hybrid of the pawpaw, genus *Carica*, that appears star shaped when sliced. The pulpy flesh has a flavor of mixed fruits such as peach and strawberry; used in sweet and savory dishes.

baba ghannoug (Ar) Peeled eggplant, puréed and baked with sesame paste and served with lemon juice, garlic, and olive oil.

babassu (Pg) Several varieties of a palm, genus *Orbignija*, native to Brazil, with hard-shelled nuts from which a kind of coconut oil is made.

babat (In) Tripe.

bā bǎu dūng-gwā tāng (Ch) A winter melon ("eight treasure") soup made of stock, meat, and vegetables and served in the hollowed-out shell of the melon.

babeczki smietankowe (Po) Cream tarts with raisins, cherries, or walnuts.

babeurre (Fr) Buttermilk.

babgulyas (Hu) Bean goulash.

babi (In) Pork.

babi asam pedas (In) Pork in a spicy, sour sauce.

babka (Po) Literally, "grandmother"; a rounded pastry, a cross between a cake and a sweet bread, topped with sugar, cinnamon, and icing.

bableves (Hu) Bean soup.

bableves csipetkével (Hu) Bean soup made with smoked ham stock and sour cream.

bábovka (Cz) Crown-shaped yeast cake; Kugelhopf.

bacalao (Sp) Salted and dried cod; added to omelets and casseroles or boiled and served with potatoes.

bacalao al ajo arriero (Sp) Literally, "in the style of the muledriver"; salt cod with tomatoes, onions, and garlic.

bacalao al pil-pil (Sp) Salt cod simmered in olive oil and garlic with parsley and peppers.

bacalhau (Pg) The national dish of Portugal, salted and dried cod, often soaked, boiled, and served in melted butter and garlic and garnished with onions, black olives, and hard-boiled eggs.

baccalà (It) Salted and dried cod; when soaked to softness, often served sautéed with garlic.

back bacon (GB) A cut from the top of the pig, divided into rashers or chops; served fried, grilled, or boiled.

Backhendl (Gr–Austria) Breaded, fried chicken, garnished with lemon and parsley and served with boiled potatoes.

Backobst (Gr) Dried fruit.

Backpflaumen (Gr) Prunes.

Backwerk (Gr) Cakes, pastries.

bacon (US) Boned pork, usually the side or belly meat; may be smoked or unsmoked and cured with salt, sugar, and spices.

bacon (Nw) Bacon.

bacon (Fr) Lard; salt pork.

bacon med ägg (Sw) Bacon and egg.

bacon og æg (Da) Bacon and egg.

bacon rasher (GB) A slice of bacon.

bacon strip (US) A slice of bacon.

badakelu vinjal (Ia) A vindaloo or curry made with duck meat and apples.

badam (Ia) Almonds; used for sweets, pullao, and curries.

badam barfi (Ia) A fudgelike almond and chocolate sweet or dessert.

badami pasanda (Ia) A sweet stew of mutton with almonds and cashews.

badderlocks (US) A form of brown seaweed; used in cooking for its sugary, nutty flavor.

bær (Nw) Berries.

bagel (Jw) A hard, round yeast bun with a hole in the center. Two main types are the traditional water bagel, first simmered in water then baked, and a modern, rich egg bagel, both produced with variations. Often served with cream cheese and lox.

bagel chip (US) Snack food made of thin, seasoned pieces of bagels and baked in butter or oil.

baghari jhinga (Ia) A curried shrimp dish with garlic and mustard seed.

bagna cauda (It) Literally, "hot bath"; a sauce of garlic, olive oil, anchovies, and sometimes truffles used as a hot dip for raw vegetables.

bagnare (It) To wet, moisten, dip, steep.

Bagnes (Fr–Swiss) A cow's milk cheese that has a rough crust, a firm interior, and a fruity taste; often used to make raclettes.

bagoong (Ph) A pungent sauce or paste made from tiny fermented shrimp or fish in brine.

bagt kartoffel (Da) Baked potato.

baguette (Fr) Long loaf of crusty bread.

bái-cài (Ch) A Chinese vegetable, *Brassica rapa* var. *Chinensis*, in the mustard family that has white stalks, dark-green leaves, and a sweet flavor; used in soup or stir-fried. Also called **bok choy.**

baicoli (It) Slices of pastry.

baidakov kulebiaka (Rs) A twelve-layer rectangular pie with a different meat or fish filling for each layer.

baies (Fr) Berries.

bái-gwo (Ch) Lime.

bái-lwó-bwō (Ch) Turnips.

baingan (Ia) Eggplant. Also called **brinjal.**

baingan bharta (Ia) An appetizer made with broiled eggplant mashed with onions, tomatoes, ginger, and chilis.

baingan pakora (Ia) Deep-fried eggplant.

bain-marie (Fr) A pan of water, kept uniformly hot, in which other pans containing various foods such as sauces or stews may stand to maintain warmth without further cooking.

baiser (Fr) A sweet or petit four called a kiss; two meringues sandwiched with a cream filling.

bái-shǔ (Ch) Sweet potatoes.

bái-tsài (Ch) See **Chinese cabbage.**

bái-tsài bai yú-ywán (Ch) Braised Chinese cabbage served over fish croquettes.

bái-yú tāng (Ch) "White jade" soup; chicken broth with bean sprouts, soybean curd, bamboo shoots, and mushrooms.

bajia (Af–Swahili) Cakes made of bean or lentil flour.

bajra (Ia) Millet.

bakalar (SC) Cod.

bakaliaros (Gk) Salt cod.

bakarkhani (Ia) Fat, round bread loaves made by throwing balls of dough into a fire.

bake, to (US) To cook foods in an oven enclosed with circulated heat and a constant temperature.

bakeapple (Ca) See **cloudberry.**

bake blind, to (GB) To bake an unfilled pie crust or pastry shell.

baked Alaska (US) A block of hard-frozen ice cream on a base of sponge cake that is completely covered with meringue and baked at high heat until the meringue is browned but the ice cream remains frozen.

bakelse tart (Sw) Pastry.

baker's cheese (US) A dry cheese used commercially by bakers for cheesecake and similar foods; made from skim milk powder or skim cow's milk and high in rennet.

baking powder (US) A leavening agent, a mixture of baking soda combined with an acid substance, such as cream of tartar, and a base of flour, cornstarch and salt; used to cause dough to rise.

baking soda (US) Sodium bicarbonate, which by itself does not have a leavening effect; an acid such as sour milk or lemon juice must be added.

baklava (Ar, Gk, Tr) A sweet strudellike pastry of phyllo dough layered with nuts, honey, and spices; covered with honey or lemon-flavored syrup.

baklazhan (Rs) Eggplant.

baklazhan s ovoshami (Rs) Chopped eggplant fried with onions, carrots, tomatoes, and squash; served cold.

bak mie (In) Vegetables such as green beans, cabbage, and leeks with noodles; similar to chow mein.

bak pao (In) Steamed, meat-filled rice cake.

bakré ka gosht (Ia) Mutton; goat meat.

balachan (Ml) See **trassi.**

balachong (Ia) A kind of pickled relish made with shrimp, tomatoes, onions, hot chilis, turmeric, and vinegar.

balah (Ar) Dates.

balik izgara (Tr) Broiled fish.

balik tavasi (Tr) Fried fish.

ballon (Fr) A ball of meat, usually lamb, formed from a boned joint.

ballottine (Fr) A stuffed roll of boned meat, fish, poultry, or game birds coated in aspic jelly; served sliced.

baloney (US) Bologna.

balsamella (It) White sauce made with milk, flour, and butter; béchamel sauce.

balsamic vinegar (US) A mild, dark red, fragrant vinegar with a sweet-sour taste; made from the juice of a white grape; aged in wood barrels. Also called **aceto balsamico di Modena.**

Balsamkraut (Gr) Costmary.

balsam pear (US) See **bitter melon.**

Baltic herring (US) A subspecies of herring, smaller than Atlantic herring and with a lower fat content.

balungi (Af–Swahili) Grapefruit.

balushahi (Ia) Deep-fried sweet pastry dipped in sugar syrup.

balyk i siomga (Rs) A combination of smoked sturgeon and salmon.

bamboo shoots (US) The young, ivory-colored shoots of a huge grass, genus *Bambuseae*, with many species; the edible variety must be cooked before use if sold raw; available canned; used in many Chinese or Japanese dishes.

bamia (Af–Swahili) Okra.

bamja (SC) Okra.

bamya (Ar) Okra.

ban (Ia) Rolls.

banaani (Fi) Banana.

banan (Nw, Rs, Sw) Banana.

banán (Cz, Hu) Banana.

banana (US) The fruit of a large tropical plant, *Musa sapientum*, that grows in clusters. The most common commercial variety has an elongated, curved shape with an easily removed yellow skin and pulpy flesh. Can be eaten raw, baked, fried, or combined with other ingredients. A sweet variety with red skin is also available. See also **plantain.**

banana pepper (US) A mild, sweet, yellow chili pepper.

bananas Foster (US) A New Orleans dessert of fresh bananas, banana liqueur, butter, brown sugar, cinnamon, and rum served flambéed over vanilla ice cream. Named for a 1950s New Orleans businessman.

banana split (US) A whole banana split lengthwise and topped with vanilla ice cream, whipped cream, and chopped nuts.

banane (It, Gr) Banana.

banane (Fr) Banana.

bananes à crème chantilly (Fr) Bananas with whipped cream.

bananes flambées (Fr) Bananas doused with rum and ignited.

Banbury cake (GB) A flat, glazed cake of puff pastry with a sweet filling of dried fruit and spices.

bancha (Jp) Coarse green tea.

band gobbi (Ia) Cabbage.

banger (GB) Fried sausage.

bangers and mash (GB) Fried sausages and mashed potatoes.

banh cuon (Vt) Shredded pork with mushrooms, onion, and spices wrapped in rice paper; served with chicken marinated in five-spice powder.

banh xeo (Vt) A mixture of pork and shrimp cooked in a batter of mung beans, coconut milk, and flour.

banitsa (Bu) A goat cheese pastry made with phyllo dough.

bankebiff (Nw) Browned and stewed beef.

bankekød (Da) Stewed beef, similar to Swiss steak.

bàn ming-há (Ch) Shrimp poached in an egg-and-mustard sauce.

bannock (Sc) A flat round cake that resembles shortbread; made of oatmeal, wheat meal, or barley meal; may contain almonds and orange peel; baked on a griddle.

Banon (Fr) A cheese usually made with goat's milk that is cured in green leaves and has a natural rind, a creamy interior, and lactic to savory taste.

bàn-shù de jī-dàn (Ch) Soft-boiled eggs.

bap (Sc) A traditional breakfast roll of Scotland that is flat and oval shaped with a central dent and heavily dusted with flour.

bar (Fr) Sea bass.

bär (Sw) Berry.

barackleves (Hu) Apricot soup.

barackpálinkát (Hu) Apricot brandy.

baranii bok s kashei (Rs) Breast of mutton cooked with a kasha filling.

baranina (Po) Lamb.

bárány (Hu) Lamb.

báránypörkölt (Hu) Lamb stew with paprika.

barashek (Rs) Lamb.

barbabietole (It) Beets.

barbacoa (Mx) Barbecue.

Barbados cherry (Cb) See **acerola.**

Barbados sugar (Cb) Dark brown sugar.

barbecue (US) Term usually applied to outdoor cooking on a charcoal grill. However, barbecuing of foods is also done on indoor grills and oven rotisseries.

barbecue sauce (US) A spicy sauce often containing vinegar, Worcestershire sauce, Tabasco sauce, onion, spices, herbs, and sometimes wine; used as a marinade and to brush on foods that are being barbecued.

barbel (US) A European freshwater fish, *Barbus barbus*, related to the carp family; used poached, grilled, or baked. Also called **parma.**

barberry (US) The small, usually red fruit of a bush, genus *Berberis* that has an acid taste and is used in preserves and pies.

barbes-de-capuchin (Fr) Literally, "beard of a Capuchin"; a slightly bitter winter salad made with bleached wild chicory roots.

barbue (Fr) Brill.

barbunia (Gk) Red mullet.

bardana (It) See **burdock.**

bardé (Fr) Covered with strips of bacon or other fat that are placed on the surface of meat, fish, or poultry before cooking to add moisture and flavor to the meat.

barfi (Ia) A thick, cooked, fudgelike dessert flavored with coconut, rose water, nuts, or cocoa; served cut in squares; may be decorated with silver leaf.

bar grillé (Fr) Broiled bass.

barigoule (Fr) A preparation of braised, stuffed artichokes, with ham and mushrooms of the same name.

barkoukess (Ar) A kind of couscous made with semolina and served with a tomato and fava bean sauce.

bar-le-Düc (Fr) Red or white currant preserves in a syrup; other fruits may be used.

barley (US) A grain, *Hordeum vulgare*, with less gluten than wheat used to make malt; when husked and polished (**pearl barley**), it is used in cereals, stews, soups, casseroles, and puddings.

barley flour (US) Ground barley; unless

combined with wheat flour, does not make good bread.

barley sugar (GB) A brittle candy originally made with barley.

barmbrack (Ir) A yeast fruitcake made with currants, raisins, and candied fruit peel.

Bärme (Gr) Yeast.

barnacle (US) A crustacean with a long stalk, the part eaten. Considered a delicacy in Spain and Portugal.

barna kenyér (Hu) Brown bread.

baron (US) A term meaning a large cut of meat. In the United States, the hindquarters, both legs and both loins of meat, usually lamb; in France, the saddle and two legs of mutton or lamb; in England, both sirloins, left uncut, of beef.

baroo (Ar) Plums.

bar pochè á l'oiseille (Fr) Poached bass with sorrel.

barquette (Fr) Boat-shaped pastry shell containing either a sweet or savory filling.

barquettes ostendaise (Fr) Pastry shells filled with oysters in a cream sauce.

barracuda (US) Term used for a group of long, slim, aggressive fish, genus *Sphyraena* resembling freshwater pike; meat flavor and texture similar to the dark meat of tuna; used as steaks for barbecuing or in chunks for casseroles.

bar raye (Fr) Striped bass.

Barsch (Gr) Bass.

barszez (Po) A soup of meat, fish, or vegetable stock with boletus mushrooms, beets, sour beet juice, garlic salt, and sugar.

basal (Ar) Onion.

basar (Jw) Meat.

basar bakar (Jw–Israel) Beef.

basar egel (Jw–Israel) Veal.

basar keves (Jw–Israel) Lamb.

basil (US) An herb, genus *Ocimum*, related to the mint family; a number of varieties include sweet basil, lemon basil, and holy basil; the leaves are used for tomato sauce, soups, egg dishes, steaks, and salads.

basilic (Fr) Basil.

basilico (It) Basil.

Basilienkraut (Gr) Basil.

basmati rice (Ia) An aromatic, long-grain beige colored rice, native to India; traditionally served with curries; used in savory or sweet dishes.

basquaise (Fr) With a garnish of mushrooms, ham, and potatoes.

bass (US) A term applied to many unrelated saltwater and freshwater fish in different parts of the world. See **sea bass.**

baste, to (US) To moisten the surface of food with melted fat, water, or meat drippings to prevent drying and to add flavor.

batā (Jp) Butter.

bata (Af–Swahili) Duck.

bâtarde, sauce (Fr) A hot, butter sauce made with flour, butter, egg, water, and lemon juice and served with fish and vegetables.

batata (Ar) Sweet potato.

batatas (Pg) Potatoes.

batatas (Sp) Sweet potatoes.

batatas doces (Pg) Sweet potatoes.

batatis (Ar) Potatoes.

batatis maleeya (Ar) Fried potatoes.

bata wa bukini (Af–Swahili) Goose.

batér (Ia) Quail.

Bath bun (GB) A sweet yeast bun made with currants and topped with nuts and candied fruit.

batido (Sp) Beaten eggs; biscuit batter.

bàtonnets (Fr) Small, thin sticks of pastries, almond paste, or cut vegetables.

battak (Ia) Duck.

batteekh (Ar) Melon; round watermelon.

batter (US) A mixture of flour, milk, eggs, and often a leavening agent, the consistency of which is liquid enough to pour.

batter bread (US) Bread made with batter that can be poured into the baking pan; does not require kneading.

battre (Fr) To whip or beat (eggs).

baudroie (Fr) Monkfish.

bāu-dz (Ch) Steamed dumplings.

Bauernart (Gr) Farmer or country style.

Bauernbrot (Gr) Farm or rustic bread.

Bauernsuppe (Gr) Hearty cabbage and sausage soup.

bauletto (It) Rolled veal.

Baumtorte (Gr) Multilayered log-shaped cake.

Baumwollöl (Gr) Cottonseed oil.

bāu-yú (Ch) Dried abalone.

Bavarian cream (US) Dessert made with vanilla-flavored egg custard, gelatin, whipped cream, and sometimes fruit puree chilled in a mold.

bavarois (Fr) Bavarian cream. The term may also refer to a similar dish using cream cheese.

bawang (In) Onions.

bawang putih (In) Garlic.

bawd (Sc) Hare.

bayam (In) Leafy vegetable similar to spinach.

bayd (Ar) Eggs.

bayd masloo (Ar) Boiled eggs.

bay leaf (US) An aromatic leaf of the sweet bay (laurel) tree, *Laurus nobilis*, with a pungent taste. Used dried in soups, gravies, puddings, and to flavor meats and fish. Native to the Middle East. In ancient times, kings and heroes wore crowns of bay leaves.

bayonnaise, à la (Fr) In the style of Bayonne; with ham produced in the Basque region included in the dish.

bay scallop (US) A small, white-to-black, bivalve shellfish, *Chlamys irradians*, whose lean muscle meat may be poached, baked, fried, or grilled.

bažant (Cz) Pheasant.

bean (US) Any of many plants in the legume family with edible pods and seeds, dried or fresh. Among the most important are the soybean, the haricot bean, and the broad bean. Beans are high in protein and are good meat substitutes.

bean curd (US) See **soybean curd.**

bean sprouts (US) The sprouted seeds of a variety of beans, including azuke, mung, and soybeans; grown from mung beans, the fresh sprouts are white and crisp with tiny caps; used in stir-fried dishes and salads.

bean thread noodles (US) See **cellophane noodles.**

beard (US) The gills of an oyster and the fibrous extrusion of a mussel. The beard may or may not be removed before serving.

béarnaise, sauce (Fr) Thick sauce made with shallots, tarragon, thyme, bay leaf, vinegar, white wine, and egg yolks; often served with grilled or sautéed meat or fish.

beat, to (US) To mix or stir vigorously with a spoon or a machine with a paddle.

Beaumont (Fr) Yellow, smooth, full-flavored cow's milk cheese.

becada (Sp) Woodcock.

bécasse (Fr) Woodcock; served roasted.

bécassine (Fr) Snipe.

beccaccia (It) Woodcock.

beccaccino (It) Snipe.

beccaccino allo spiedo (It) Snipe roasted on a spit; served on toast.

béchamel, sauce (Fr) Milk blended with a mix of butter and flour (roux). Also called **white milk sauce.**

bêche de mer (Fr) Also called **sea cucumber.**

beckasin (Sw) Snipe.

bécsi szelet (Hu) Breaded veal cutlet.

beebeek (Ia) Custard cake.

beechnut (US) The edible, small triangular nut of several species of beech trees. Beechnuts are rich in oil that has been used for a salad oil, mainly in France.

beef (US) The flesh of a slaughtered adult cow, bull, or steer. Most commercial beef comes from steers. Baby beef refers to meat intermediate between veal and beef.

beef à la mode (US) Braised beef, sliced thin, served in a gravy made with the red wine braising stock; garnished with carrots and glazed onions. Also called **boeuf à la mode.**

beef Stroganoff (US) Of Russian origin, this dish features thin strips of beef sautéed with mushrooms and onions and served with sour cream and rice. Said to be named for a Count Stroganoff whose chef when in Siberia found that the beef was frozen and could only be shredded.

beef tartar (US) See **tartar steak.**

beef tea (US) A drink made from simmering beef in water.

beef Wellington (US) A fillet of beef roasted and cooled, spread with a mixture of mushrooms and liver pâté, encased in a glazed puff pastry crust, and baked; served sliced.

beer (US) Alcoholic drink made by the fermenting of malted cereal. Also used in cooking.

beer cheese (US) Variation of brick cheese.

beet (US) Any of several varieties of plants, *Beta vulgarus*, with a fleshy root and long leaf stalks. The common red beet or beetroot may be spherical, cylindrical, or top-shaped; juicy, sweet taste; prepared boiled, steamed, or baked, eaten hot or cold and served in salads, savory dishes, and in soups. The leaves may also be cooked and eaten as greens.

beetroot (GB) Edible root of the red beet.

beet sugar (US) Sugar processed from the white root of the sugar beet.

befsztyk (Po) Steak.

befsztyk tartarski (Po) Chopped raw beef. See **tartar steak.**

beignets (Fr) Fritters made from a choux pastry batter.

Beet

beignets de pommes (Fr) Apple fritters.

beignets niçoise (Fr) Tuna fritters.

Béi-jīng fén (Ch) Literally, "Peking dust"; sweetened chestnut puree topped with whipped cream and preserved fruit.

Béi-jīng jyău-dz (Ch) Peking-style dumplings with a sauce made with soybeans, garlic, and chili.

beinasu iradashi (Jp) Deep-fried eggplant.

Bekassine (Gr) Snipe.

bēkon to tamago (Jp) Bacon and eggs.

belegde broodjes (Du) Small appetizers on rolls.

belegtes Brot (Gr) Open-face sandwich.

Belgian endive (US) A small, cylindrical variety of chicory, *Cicorium endiva*, with many tightly wrapped leaves forced and blanched to white or pale yellow; a slightly bitter, astringent flavor; eaten raw or cooked.

beli luk (SC) Garlic.

belimbing (In) See **carambola.**

belle-dijonnaise, à la (Fr) Served with black currants, a specialty of Dijon.

bellevue (Fr) Describes a beautiful presentation of food on a dish.

bell pepper (US) See **sweet pepper.**

belon (Fr) Variety of pink oyster named after the Belon River.

belo vino (SC) White wine.

Bel Paese (It) A semisoft cow's milk cheese with a pale interior and a mild, creamy, fruity taste; melts easily for casserole or pizza toppings.

beluga caviar (US) The large roe of beluga sturgeon, *Huso huso*, a highly valued and expensive caviar.

ben cotto (It) Well done (meat).

benishoga (Jp) Pickled red gingerroot.

benløse fugle (Da) Meat loaf molded like a game bird.

benne seeds (US) See **sesame seeds.**

berberé (Af) A fiery red pepper seasoning mixed into a paste with water.

Bercy, à la (Fr) Prepared with wine and shallots, or served with shallot butter.

berenjena (Sp) Eggplant.

bergamot (US) A variety of orange with fruits used like the citron, preserved

29

and candied. Used mainly in perfumery.

bergère (Fr) A dish prepared with sweet butter, heavy cream, and mushrooms.

Bergkäse (Gr) Literally, "mountain cheese"; made in the Bavarian alps with raw milk and containing up to 60 percent butterfat.

beringela (Pg–Brazil) Eggplant.

Berliner Pfannkuchen (Gr) Pancake with jelly filling.

Bermuda onion (US) Large onion with yellow skin and mild taste.

Berner Sauce (Gr) Béarnaise sauce with wine, vinegar, spices, butter, and egg yolks.

berro (Sp) Cress.

berry (US) 1. Small fruit with seeds in a juicy pulp. 2. Groat.

berry sugar (US) Finely granulated sugar; castor sugar.

berza rizada (Sp) Savoy cabbage.

besan (Ia) Chick-pea flour; high in protein. Also called **gram.**

beschuit (Du) Hard rusk.

beschuittaart (Du) Rusk cake.

besciamella (It) Béchamel sauce.

besengek daging sapi (In) Boiled beef in a spicy sauce.

bessenvila (Du) Currant pudding.

besugo al horno (Sp) Baked sea bream.

beta-carotene (US) One of the most important of the carotenes, the yellow pigment in some foods. It is converted to vitamin A in the body and is more active than other carotenes in lowering the risk of cancer.

betelloh (Ar) Veal.

betteraves (Fr) Beetroots, beets.

betteraves à l'orange (Fr) Beets with orange sauce.

beurre (Fr) Butter.

beurre à la maitre d'hôtel (Fr) Butter melted with parsley, salt, pepper, and lemon juice and served with meat, fish, or vegetables.

beurre blanc (Fr) A classic sauce made from a mixture of white vinegar, white wine, shallots, and butter; served with vegetables and fish dishes. Also called **white butter sauce.**

beurre d'ail (Fr) Garlic butter.

beurre d'anchois (Fr) Anchovy butter.

beurre d'échalote (Fr) Butter and shallots; used on meat or fish.

beurre de citron (Fr) Lemon butter.

beurre de crevettes (Fr) Shrimp butter, used as a sandwich spread or filling for eggs.

beurre fondu (Fr) Melted butter served with poached fish or boiled vegetables.

beurre manié (Fr) Butter kneaded with flour, used to thicken stews and sauces.

beurre noir (Fr) Clarified butter heated slowly until deep brown, then flavored with vinegar; served with eggs, fish, or vegetables and often used in the preparation of brains.

beurre vert (Fr) Butter mixed with pureed spinach.

beyaz peynir (Tr) A Turkish white cheese.

beyin (Tr) Brains.

bezelye (Tr) Peas.

bharta (Ia) Curried eggplant.

bhéja (Ia) Brains.

bhelpuri (Ia) Savory snacks served on fried bread (puri).

bhindi (Ia) Okra.

bhujiya (Ia) Sliced vegetables coated in a batter of besan (chick-pea) flour and deep-fried.

bhuna chaval (Ia) Brown rice.

bhuna hua (Ia) Grilled.

bialy (Po) Onion roll made with yeast, with a depression in the center and topped with finely chopped browned onions.

bianchette di vitello (It) Veal stew with gravy.

bianchetti (It) Small fish; whitebait.

bianco (It) White.

bianco de Spagna (It) Large white beans; cannellini.

bianco d'uovo (It) Egg white.

Bibb lettuce (US) Small, tender-leafed variety of head lettuce.

biber (SC, Tr) Pepper.

biber dolmasi (Tr) Stuffed green pepper.

bibimpap (Kr) Traditional Korean dish of rice and sautéed vegetables flavored with kochu jang, a hot red pepper sauce.

bibita (It) Soft drink.

bicarbonate of soda (US) Sodium bicarbonate; baking soda.

bidingehn (Ar) Eggplant.

bief (Du) Beef.

biefstuk (Du) Beefsteak.

bien asado (Sp) Well-done (meat).

bien cuit (Fr) Well-done (meat).

Bienenstich (Gr) Honey and almond cake.

bier (Du) Beer.

Bier (Gr) Beer.

bière (Fr) Beer.

Bierkaltschale (Gr) Cold beer soup.

Bierkäse (Gr) "Beer cheese"; a type of Limburger, but firmer, with a bacon-like taste.

Bierwurst (Gr) A coarse-textured sausage; may be spiced with juniper berries, cardamom, and sometimes garlic.

bieten met appelen (Du) Beets with apples.

bietola da coste (It) Chard.

bife (Pg) Beef; beefsteak.

biff (Nw) Beefsteak.

biff à la Lindström (Sw) A Swedish ground beef dish made with cream, beets, potatoes, and eggs.

biffstek (Sw) Beefsteak.

bifsztek (Hu) Beefsteak.

biftec (Sp) Beefsteak.

biftec de ternera (Sp) Veal steak.

bifteck (Fr) Beefsteak.

bifteck entrecôte (Fr) Usually means a good cut of beef.

bifteck pavé au poivre (Fr) A thick steak served with pepper.

biftek (Cz, Tr) Beefsteak.

bifuteki (Jp) Beefsteak.

bigarade, sauce (Fr) A brown sauce made from the pan drippings of duck or veal, orange and lemon juice, grated orange peel, vinegar, and curacao; served on duckling.

bigaro (Sp) See **winkle.**

bignè (It) Cream puff.

bignè al formaggio (It) Cheese puffs.

bigorneau (Fr) See **winkle.**

bigos (Po) A casserole with sauerkraut,

apples, sausages, bacon, venison or other meat, dried mushrooms, and sometimes white cabbage.

bihon (Ph) Rice noodles.

biksemad (Da) Diced leftover meat mixed with onions; often served with candied potatoes.

bilberry (GB) A variety of blueberry.

bílé víno (Cz) White wine.

billi-bi (Fr) A cream soup made with mussels and white wine. Also spelled **billy-by.**

biltong (Af) Strips of meat cured by rubbing with salt and brown sugar, then air-drying; served raw or grilled.

binatang buruan (In) Game.

binder (US) Any ingredient or combination of ingredients, such as flour, eggs, breadcrumbs, and cheese, that thicken and hold a mixture together when added.

bing (Ch) Chinese baked bread, round and flat.

Bing cherry (US) A large, dark red, very sweet cherry.

bing-gān (Ch) Cookies.

bīng-gwo-dz-lù (Ch) Sherbet.

bīng-jī-líng (Ch) Ice cream.

biotin (US) A member of the vitamin B-complex active in the metabolism of fatty acids and amino acids; a recommended daily allowance (RDA) has not been established but 100–200 micrograms (mcg) per day is considered to meet normal adult requirements; good dietary sources include liver, soy flour, cereals, and yeast.

bira (Bu) Beer.

bird pepper (US) A very small, extremely hot, red pepper, species *Capsicum frutescens*, native to warm countries. Also called **cabe rawit.**

bird's nest (US) A Chinese delicacy; translucent, cuplike structures made with the gelatinous saliva of birds, genus *Collocalia*, similar to swifts; used for soup, stuffings, and sweets. Also called **yān wō.**

bird's nest soup (US) A Chinese delicacy made of chicken stock, chicken, and mushrooms simmered with cleaned, dried bird's nest. Also called **jī ěr yān wō tāng.**

biringani (Af–Swahili) Eggplant.

Birne (Gr) Pear.

birra (It) Beer.

biryani (Ia) Rich pilaf made with spiced saffron rice and lamb, chicken, beef, or shrimp.

biscoitos (Pg) Cookies.

biscotte (Fr) Rusk; biscuit.

biscotti (It) Cookies; crackers; biscuits.

biscotti all' anice (It) Anise-flavored cookies.

biscottini di mandorle (It) Almond macaroons.

biscotto tortoni (It) A frozen dessert made with egg whites, macaroons, and whipped cream; topped with chopped almonds.

biscuit (US) Small, unsweetened, flaky bread raised with baking powder or soda.

biscuit (GB) Thin, crisp unsweetened crackers or sweet cookies.

biscuit (Fr) Dry flat cake; cookie; cracker.

bisilla (Ar) Peas.

biskopskake (Nw) "Bishop's cake"; made with raisins and almonds.

Biskuit (Gr) Rusk; biscuit.

biskuti (Af–Swahili) Cookies.

Bismarck herring (Gr) Boned herring marinated in white wine, vinegar, and spices. Named for the founder of the German empire, Prince Otto von Bismarck-Schoonhausen.

bisque (Fr) A thick cream soup, usually made with pureed shellfish, although can be made of pureed vegetables or game birds.

bisque d'ecrevisse (Fr) A crayfish bisque.

bistecca (It) Beefsteak.

bistecca alla Fiorentina (It) Charcoal-broiled beefsteak served with lemon wedges.

bistik (In) Beefsteak.

bisuketto (Jp) Cookies.

bitamin (Jp) Vitamin.

bitok (Rs) Small beef patties flavored with minced beets and gherkins, fried and then simmered in sour cream.

bitter almond (US) See **almond.**

bitterballen (Du) Deep-fried balls of a mixture with chicken and ham in bread crumbs; served as a snack.

bitter chocolate (US) The pure hardened chocolate liquid without added sugar; used in cooking. See also **chocolate.**

bitterkoekjes (Du) Macaroons.

bitterkoekjesvla (Du) Macaroon pudding.

Bittermandel (Gr) Bitter almond.

bitter melon (US) An oblong, warty vegetable, *Momordica charantia*, used in the cooking of China (soup or stir-frys) and India (curries). Also called **balsam pear, kŭ-gwā, karela.**

bitter orange (US) See **Seville orange.**

bitters (GB) A bitter tasting liquor made from herbs, bark, roots, or fruits.

biwa (Jp) See **loquat.**

bixin (US) See **annatto.**

bizcochada (Sp) Biscuit and milk soup.

bizcocho (Sp) Biscuit, hardtack, sponge cake.

bizcocho genovesa (Sp) Ladyfinger.

björnbär (Sw) Blackberry.

bjørnebær (Nw) Blackberry.

blåbær (Nw) Blueberry.

blåbærpannekake (Nw) Blueberry pancakes.

blåbærsuppe (Da) Blueberry soup.

blåbär (Sw) Blueberry.

black bean (US) A legume, *Phaseolus vulgaris*, native to South America, with kidney-shaped beans in pods. The bean, dried for use in soup and casseroles, has black skin and white flesh. Also called **frijoles negros.**

blackberry (US) The black fruit of a shrub in the rose family; eaten raw and cooked. Also called **bramble.**

black-bottom pie (US) A chocolate custard pie topped with rum custard and whipped cream.

blackened (US) Describes the appearance of fish and meat cooked Cajun-style in a hot skillet.

black-eyed peas (US) The edible seeds of the cowpea, *Vigna unguiculata*; small, kidney-shaped, cream-colored with a black "eye" on the side; used in many dishes worldwide.

black pepper (US) A seasoning and con-

Blackberry

diment made from the ground, dried, unripe berries of a plant, *Piper nigrum*. The dark hulls and light inner kernels are mixed together in the grinding.

black pudding (GB) A smooth-textured, cooked blood sausage made with the blood of sheep, pig, or ox, and cereal, onions, pieces of fat, salt and spices; served fried or warmed in water.

black salsify (US) See **scorzonera.**

black sea bass (US) A gray to blue-black Atlantic fish, *Centropristis striatus*, with firm, white, mild-flavored flesh; used fried, baked, or poached.

blackstrap molasses (US) The concentrated liquid residue in sugar making that comes from the third boiling; rich, pungent flavor; high in iron.

black treacle (GB) Molasses.

black walnut (US) The nut of the black walnut tree, *Juglans nigran*, with a hard-to-crack shell; strong flavor of the nut meats is retained in cooking; used in cakes, candy, and ice cream.

bladselleri (Da) Celery.

blaeberry (Sc) Bilberry; whortleberry.

blanc de cuisson (Fr) A seasoned white liquor made of flour, water, lemon juice, and white vinegar used to aid whitening of foods.

blanch (US) To partially cook food a very short time in boiling liquid, steam, or hot fat; done to remove skins, to prevent nutritional loss before freezing and to prepare for further cooking.

blancmange (Fr) Any of various puddings or custards usually made with cornstarch and milk flavored with vanilla; may be topped with fruit or a sweet sauce. The traditional version uses pulverized almonds without cornstarch.

blandad (Sw) Mixed.

blanquette (Fr) A white stew of veal, chicken, or lamb in a cream sauce, garnished with small onions and mushrooms.

blanquette d'agneau à l'ancienne (Fr) Lamb stew with cream, onions, and potatoes.

blanquette de veau (Fr) Veal stewed in a cream sauce.

bláthach (Ir) Buttermilk.

Blaubeere (Gr) Bilberry; whortleberry; blueberry.

blaze (US) To ignite liqueur on foods; flambé.

blé (Fr) Wheat; corn.

bleak (US) See **ablette.**

blend (US) To mix and combine two or more ingredients until smooth.

blé noir (Fr) Buckwheat.

bleu (Fr) Describes meat that is served almost raw, just heated. See also *au bleu.*

blewah (In) Canteloupe.

blinde vinken (Du) Stuffed veal steaks.

blind Huhn (Gr) Chicken casserole with beans, bacon, vegetables, and apples.

blini (Rs) Thin buckwheat pancakes served with red or black caviar and sour cream.

blintze (Jw) A type of pancake made with matzo meal and eggs, filled with sweetened cottage cheese, rolled into an envelope shape, fried or baked, and served with sour cream. May have other fillings such as jam, fish, or fruits.

bloater (GB) Herring or mackerel, whole and gutted, prepared in brine then wood smoked; used for tea sandwiches when made into a paste.

blodbudding (Da) Literally, "blood pudding"; a dish of animal blood, barley, sugar, and seasonings baked as a pudding or as a sausage filling.

blodfersk (Nw) Blood fresh; describes freshness of fish.

blødkogte æg (Da) Soft-boiled eggs.

blodkorv (Sw) Blood pudding; black pudding.

blodpølse (Da) Fried pork blood sausage; served with butter, sugar, and cinnamon.

bloedworst (Du) Blood sausage made with oatbran and raisins.

bloemkool (Du) Cauliflower.

blomkaal (Da) Cauliflower.

blomkål (Da, Nw, Sw) Cauliflower.

blommer (Da) Plum.

blond de veau (Fr) White veal stock.

blond de volaille (Fr) Clear chicken stock.

blondir (Fr) To cook lightly in fat.

blood (US) Fresh blood of animals or chickens used as a sauce thickener. Baked blood is used in fried dishes in some European countries.

blood orange (US) Any of several varieties of sweet orange with red-orange pulp and rind.

blood sausage (US) See **black pudding.**

bløtkake (Nw) A sponge cake layered with cream and topped with marzipan.

bløtkokt (Nw) Soft-boiled (egg).

blueberry (US) The fruit of a bush, genus *Vaccinium*, related to cranberries; many species including bilberry and whortleberry; blue to blue-black skin; sweet, juicy flesh; eaten raw or cooked; used in ice cream, pies, muffins, soup, jam, and many other dishes.

blue cheese (US) A soft cheese, usually made from cow's milk, marbled with veins of edible blue-green mold; generally gives cheese an intense, piquant flavor. Examples are Stilton and Roquefort.

blue cheese dressing (US) A vinaigrette or French dressing flavored with crumbled blue cheese and served with various salads.

blue crab (US) A species of crab, *Calli-*

nectes sapidus, with blue claws, found along the U.S. Atlantic coast from Maryland to Florida and the Gulf of Mexico; mild, sweet meat; served boiled, steamed, or fried.

bluefish (US) A silvery fish in the family Pomatomidae with a delicate, rich flavor; often served baked or broiled with acid fruits or vegetables. Also called **anchova, anjova, tassergal.**

Blumenkohl (Gr) Cauliflower.

Blutwurst (Gr) Blood sausage made with pig's blood and bacon and flavored with marjoram and allspice.

bobi (Rs) Broad beans.

bobotee (US) Puddinglike dish of bread crumbs, almonds, onions, and hot sauce.

bobotie (Af) South African dish similar to moussaka; chopped lamb or beef and beaten eggs flavored with curry powder, onions, garlic, pepper, and almonds.

böbrek (Tr) Kidney.

bobwhite (US) See **quail.**

bocadillo (Sp) Sandwich of thin-sliced veal on a hard-crusted roll.

bocconcini (It) See **olivette.**

Bock (Gr) A dark Bavarian beer.

böckling (Sw) Smoked Baltic herring.

Bocksbart (Gr) Salsify.

Bockwurst (Gr) Spicy, plump sausage that resembles and is cooked like the frankfurter.

bodega (Sp) Wine cellar.

boerenkool (Du) Kale.

boerenkool met worst (Du) Casserole of kale and potatoes with sausage.

boeuf (Fr) Beef.

boeuf à la mode (Fr) See **beef à la mode.**

boeuf bouilli (Fr) Boiled beef.

boeuf bourguignon (Fr) Braised beef prepared in the style of Burgundy; with small glazed onions, mushrooms, and red wine.

boeuf en gelée (Fr) Sliced beef in a jellied sauce.

boeuf miroton (Fr) Beef stewed with an onion-based sauce.

boeuf rôti (Fr) Roast beef.

boeuf salé (Fr) Corned beef.

bøf med løg (Da) Fried ground beef with onions and brown sauce.

bøf tartar (Da) Raw scraped beef mixed with raw egg yolk and capers.

Bohnen (Gr) Beans.

boil (US) Submerge food in boiling liquid to thoroughly cook.

boiler (US) Stewing chicken, more than a year old.

bok choy (Ch) See **bái-cài.**

bokking (Du) A kind of herring.

bola (Mx) Ball-shaped, such as a meatball.

bolacha (Pg) Crackers.

bolets (Fr) Boletus mushrooms.

boletus (US) A genus of wild mushroom characterized by having tubes rather than gills under the cap, and usually a thick stalk; widely used because of its flavor; not all members are edible. Also known as **cèpe, funghi porcini, tatti.**

bolillo (Mx) A bread roll.

bolinchos de bacalhau (Pg) Codfish balls with parsley, coriander, and mint; topped with poached eggs.

bolle (Da, Nw) Bun, muffin, or soft roll.

boller (Da) Balls of meat or fish.

bollito (It) Boiled.

bollito misto (It) Mixed boiled meat,

such as veal, tongue, sausage, calf's head, and beef brisket; served with a tomato or pepper sauce or various condiments.

bollo (Sp) Bun, roll or small loaf.

bolltee (Ar) Large porgy.

bôlo (Pg) Cake.

bologna (It) Precooked and highly seasoned sausage made of beef, veal, and pork; eaten hot or cold.

Bolognese, alla (It) Served with a classic meat sauce from Bologna; made with beef, pork, chicken livers, tomatoes, and red wine.

bombas de camarones (Sp) Deep-fried potato cakes with shrimp.

Bombay duck (Ia) Dried, salted fish similar in size to herring caught off the coast of India near Bombay; fried and served with curry dishes and as a snack. Also called **bommaloe.**

bombe glacée (Fr) A frozen dessert molded in a round or cylindrical shape, made with a layer of ice cream surrounding a central core of an ice-cream-like mixture containing various ingredients such as nuts, glacé fruits, and liqueurs.

bombons (Pg) Candy.

bommaloe (Ia) See **Bombay duck.**

böna (Sw) Bean.

bonbon (Fr) Candy, confections.

bondas (Ia) Deep-fried snack made with besan (chick-pea) flour mixed with spices.

bondpige med slør (Da) Literally, "peasant girl in a veil"; a dessert made with pumpernickel bread crumbs, chocolate, and jam and topped with whipped cream.

bone, roll, and tie (US) To tie raw meat or fowl in a compact roll after removing bones.

bonen (Du) Beans.

bonensla (Du) String bean salad.

boniatos (Sp) Sweet potatoes.

boniatos confitadas (Sp) Candied sweet potatoes.

boning (US) To remove bones, usually from raw meat, fish, or poultry.

bonite à dos rayé (Fr) Bonito.

bonito (US) Tunalike member of the mackerel family with firm, oily, and savory flesh, found in the Atlantic and Pacific oceans; used baked, fried, steamed, poached, and barbecued. Meat from the belly is regarded as a delicacy and is baked with herbs. Much of the Pacific catch is canned. Used fresh or dried in Japanese cooking, such as in sushi.

bonne-dame (Fr) See **orache.**

bonne femme, à la (Fr) Cooked with bacon, onions, potatoes, and a thick brown gravy.

bønner (Da, Nw) Beans.

bönor (Sw) Beans.

boonchi (Cb) Yard-long beans.

boquerónes (Sp) White anchovies; usually pickled in salt and vinegar.

borage (US) An herb, *Borago officinalis*, with cucumber-flavored leaves used in salads, beverages, boiled for a ravioli stuffing, and fried with a batter-coating. The blue flowers can be candied.

boranija (SC) Green beans.

Borç (Tr) Borsch.

bordelaise, à la (Fr) In the style of Bordeaux; served with a sauce made with wine, bone marrow, and other ingredients varying according to the dish, such as eggs, fish, or steak.

börek (Tr) Layers of thin pastry filled with cheese or meat.

borjúhús (Hu) Veal.

borjúpörkölt (Hu) Veal stew with paprika.

borjúvelö (Hu) Calf's brains.

borleves (Hu) Soup made with white wine, egg yolks, sugar, and lemon and spiced with cloves.

borrego (Pg) Lamb. Also called **cordeiro.**

bors (Hu) Pepper.

borsch (Rs) Many soups are known as borsch and vary from region to region. Most are deep red from beet juice and generally contain beef, beets, carrots, potatoes, and other vegetables.

borscht (Po) Borsch.

borsó (Hu) Peas.

borsóleves (Hu) Pea soup.

borstplaat (Du) Hard fondant.

borststuk (Du) Brisket.

borůvky (Cz) Blueberries.

bosbessen (Du) Blueberries.

Boscaiola, alla (It) Seafood sauce with tuna, anchovies, tomatoes, and mushrooms.

Boston baked beans (US) A dish of white beans slow-cooked with molasses, mustard, salt pork or bacon, and sometimes onion; served with brown bread.

Boston brown bread (US) A steamed, rye-flour bread made with molasses.

Boston lettuce (US) Small head lettuce with glossy, dark-green leaves on the outside and inner yellow leaves; mild, sweet flavor.

boszorkánybab (Hu) "Witches' froth"; a chilled dessert made with mashed apples, whipped egg whites, and apricot brandy; topped with whipped cream.

bot (Du) Flounder.

botargo (It) Salted, pressed roe of the mullet or tuna.

boter (Du) Butter.

boterhamkoek (Du) A sweet cake flavored with anise.

botifarra amb mongetes (Sp) Blood sausage and white beans cooked in port wine.

boti kabab (Ia) Pieces of lamb marinated in yogurt and spices, then skewered and charcoal grilled.

botvinya (Rs) A cold soup made with spinach, stock, and kvass; also used as a fish sauce; Polish origin.

botwina (Po) A summer soup of whole young beets, veal stock, vegetables, cream, lemon, and sour beet juice; served with hard-boiled eggs, dill, and parsley.

boubliki (Rs) Yeast dough rings similar to doughnuts served with butter.

bouchée (Fr) A "mouthful"; very thin, small patties or cakes.

bouchée à la reine (Fr) Pastry filled with sweetbreads in a cream sauce.

bouchère, sauce (Fr) Literally, "as the butcher's wife makes it"; a meat sauce with tomatoes and onions.

boudin (Fr) A form of sausage; served fried.

boudin blanc (Fr) A sausage made with

white meat, bread, cream, eggs, and seasonings. A Creole mixture uses rice instead of bread.

boudin noir (Fr) Blood sausage made with pig's blood; many variations with additions such as chestnuts, apples, or spinach.

bouillabaisse (Fr) A well-known dish from Provence made with fish and shellfish cooked either in water or wine with garlic, parsley, pepper, oil, and tomatoes; ingredients vary. In France sturgeon and perch are often used; the Creoles use redfish and red snapper.

bouilli (Fr) Boiled.

bouillon (Fr) A clear soup, stronger than broth but not as strong as consommé.

bouillon de boeuf (Fr) Stock made with a beef base.

boulangère, à la (Fr) "In the style of the baker's wife"; meat or poultry oven-baked with onions and potatoes in stock.

boule-de-neige (Fr) A small, ball-shaped cake covered in whipped cream.

boulette (Fr) Meat, fish, or other foods, mashed and formed in small balls, sometimes coated with crumbs, and usually fried.

bouquet (Fr) The aroma produced from volatile oils in plants; also, in wine.

bouquet garni (Fr) A small bunch of herbs, usually bay leaves, thyme, marjoram, and parsley, tied together or enclosed in a muslin bag; used to flavor stocks, stews, soups, casseroles, and braised dishes.

bouquetière, à la (Fr) Meat or poultry served with a garnish of vegetables.

bourgeoise, à la (Fr) Family style; often braised meat prepared with carrots and onions.

bourguignon, à la (Fr) In the style of Burgundy; eggs, meat, fish, or chicken poached in red wine with small onions, mushrooms, and bacon.

bourride (Fr) A fish stew made with monkfish and aïoli.

boysenberry (US) The red, oval fruit of a shrub similar to blackberries and raspberries; a sweet, tangy flavor; used fresh or canned.

Brachsenmakrele (Gr) A species of bream.

braciola (It) A chop or cutlet; rib steak.

braciola di maiale (It) Pork chop.

braciola di manzo (It) Beef cutlet.

braciolette d'abbacchio (It) Grilled lamb chops or cutlets.

bräckkorv (Sw) Smoked pork sausage.

bradán (Ir) Salmon.

braga (Rs) Mead, a drink made with honey.

brain (US) An organ meat, generally from calf; has a soft, creamy texture when cooked first in a vinegared court bouillion, then browned in butter or deep-fried with a batter coating; often scrambled with eggs.

braise, to (US) To brown meat or vegetable pieces first in fat; then slowly cook in a small amount of liquid or sauce in a covered pan.

braisé (Fr) Braised.

braisé de boeuf (Fr) Beef stew in wine.

bramble (US) See **blackberry.**

brambor (Cz) Potato.

bramborák (Cz) Potato pancake.

Braise

bramborová kaše (Cz) Mashed potatoes.

bramborová polévka (Po) Potato soup.

bramborový knedlík (Cz) Potato dumpling.

bramborový salát (Cz) Potato salad.

bran (US) The coarse outer layer of a whole grain kernel such as wheat or rye; provides dietary fiber, B vitamins, and minerals including iron, zinc, and magnesium.

brancin (SC) Bass.

brandade (Fr) A puree of salt cod, olive oil, and milk; other ingredients may be added. A sauce called brandade is served with cod.

brandewijn (Du) Literally, "burned wine"; brandy.

brandy (US) Distilled, aged wine, usually from grapes. When made with other fruits, brandy must be so labeled, such as peach brandy.

branzino (It) Sea bass.

brasato (It) Braised beef.

braskartofler (Da) Fried potatoes.

brasserie (Fr) An informal restaurant.

Braten (Gr) Braised or roasted meat.

Bratfisch (Gr) Fried fish.

Brathänchen (Gr) Roast chicken.

Bratheringe (Gr) Fried, boned herring marinated in vinegar with onions and spices.

Bratkartoffeln (Gr) Fried potatoes.

Bratwurst (Gr) Literally, "frying sausage"; a fresh, pale-colored, finely ground pork or veal link sausage; mildly seasoned; served fried, braised, broiled or grilled. Some smoked varieties.

braune Tunke (Gr) Brown sauce.

Braunschweiger (Gr) A sausage made with seasoned, smoked, minced liver; served cold as a spread on bread or crackers.

brawn (GB) See **headcheese.**

Brazil nut (US) The hard-shelled seeds of a large, South American tree, *Bertholettia excelsa*; high fat content, rich taste; used in bread, cake, and other desserts.

brazo mercedes (Ph) A log cake of meringue with a filling made of egg yolk and condensed milk.

breac geal (Ir) Sea trout.

bread (US) Any of various baked or griddle-cooked food made with flour or meal, salt, a moistening agent and that may or may not have a leavening agent such as yeast, baking powder, or soda. Leavened bread is kneaded, allowed to rise, shaped, and baked. Many kinds of bread are unleavened including tortillas and chapatis.

bread, to (US) To coat a food with bread or cracker crumbs before cooking;

the food may also be dipped in egg and milk before breading.

bread and butter pickles (US) Sweet pickles made with sliced, unpeeled, young cucumbers, onions, and pepper slices.

breadfruit (US) A fruit of a tropical tree, *Artocarpus communis*, related to the jackfruit; many varieties with round to elongated shapes and smooth to bumpy green skin; a staple, starchy food of Southeast Asia and the Pacific. Also called **mei.**

bread pudding (US) A pudding made of crumbled bread, milk, egg yolks, sugar, flavorings such as vanilla or chocolate, raisins, and nuts; served cold or hot with a sweet sauce.

bread sauce (GB) A thick sauce for poultry made with bread crumbs, milk, and onion.

bread sticks (US) Long, thin sticks of crisp bread; served with soup like crackers.

bream (US) Term given to various unrelated species of fish worldwide. In the United States the name is loosely applied to the freshwater bluegill, sunfish, and the saltwater porgy. Freshwater bream found throughout most of Europe is carplike and used mainly in stew or matelotes. The French daurade is the best known sea bream.

brécol (Sp) Broccoli.

bredflab (Da, Nw) Monkfish.

bree (Sc) Pot liquor; stock; soup.

Brei (Gr) Cooked cereal.

brème de mer (Fr) A species of bream.

brennesnut (Nw) Barley and frankfurter soup.

breskva (SC) Peach.

bretonne, à la (Fr) Served with beans.

brew (US) To prepare a beverage such as tea by steeping and boiling; also, to make beer or ale by steeping, boiling, and fermenting malt and hops.

brewat (Ar) A mixture for sweets made with almond paste, rice, and honey.

brewer's yeast (US) A yeast used in brewing beer and also as a dietary supplement high in protein and B-complex vitamins.

Brezel (Gr) Pretzel.

brick cheese (US) A yellow, brick-shape, cow's milk cheese with a semisoft interior and mild to pungent flavor; served with dark breads or on grilled sandwiches.

brick tea (US) A Chinese tea product made of tea leaves and tea dust compressed into bricks; expands when covered with boiling water in the cup or pot.

Brie (Fr) A white cow's milk cheese with a light edible crust and a soft interior; creamy taste intensifies as it ripens;

Breadfruit

served at room temperature as a dessert or appetizer.

brigidini (It) Aniseed wafers.

brik (Ar) Paper-thin sheets of pastry dough. Also called **filo, phyllo.**

brik bil lahm (Ar) Ground lamb and egg wrapped in thin pastry and fried in oil.

brill (US) A flatfish, *Scophthalmus rhombus*, similar to turbot, with firm, sweet flesh; used poached, baked, steamed, fried, or grilled. Also called **barbue.**

brine (US) Salt dissolved in water; used for processing or pickling vegetables and fruit and for curing meat and fish.

bringa (Sw) Brisket.

bringebær (Nw) Raspberry.

brinjal (Ia) Eggplant. Also called **baingan.**

brioche (Fr) A cakelike bread with light texture made of rich yeast dough; many variations with added ingredients and flavorings; usually baked in fluted tins and topped with a small dough ball.

brioche de fois gras (Fr) Brioche dough stuffed with goose liver pâté.

brioška (Cz) Brioche.

brisket (US) A fatty cut of beef from the underside of the animal, the breastbone and the five lower ribs, often braised or slow roasted.

brisler (Da) Veal sweetbreads.

brisling (Da, Nw) Sprat.

broa (Pg) Corn bread or muffin.

broad bean (US) The oval, flat seeds in long pods of a plant, *Vicia faba.* Green, young beans in the pod are used as a boiled vegetable. Seeds are light brown when dried. Also called **fava bean.**

broccoletti di Brusselle (It) Brussels sprouts.

broccoli (US) A vegetable, *Brassica oleracea* var. *italica*, related to cauliflower; long green stalks with branching shoots end in clusters of immature, green flowers; the flower heads, peeled stems, and leaves may be eaten; used in salads and cooked dishes.

broccoli (It) Broccoli.

broccoli al formaggio (It) Broccoli with melted cheese sauce.

broccoli all' agro (It) Broccoli served with olive oil and lemon juice.

brochan (Sc) Porridge, gruel.

broche, à la (Fr) Cooked on a spit or skewer.

brochet (Fr) Freshwater pike.

brochette (Fr) A skewer; anything cooked on a skewer may be called a brochette.

brochette de mouton (Fr) Mutton on a skewer, broiled; shish kebab.

bröd (Sw) Bread.

brød (Da, Nw) Bread.

brodetto (It) Served in rich, thick gravy.

brodetto di pesce alla veneziana (It) Fish stew with thick gravy and saffron.

brodo (It) Broth; consommé; vegetable stock.

brodo di manzo (It) Clear beef broth, often with tiny pasta.

brodo di pollo (It) Chicken soup.

brødsuppe (Da) Bread soup made with fruit juice and raisins and garnished with whipped cream.

broil (US) To cook by direct heat, either

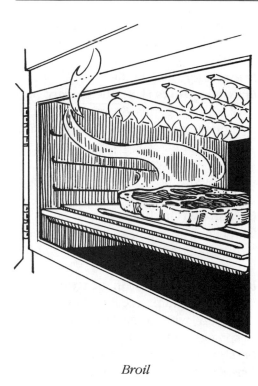

Broil

over or under the heat source. Also called **grill.**

broiler (US) A young chicken weighing about 2½ pounds (1.25 kilograms).

brood (Du) Bread.

broodjes (Du) Rolls, buns; sandwich.

broodpap (Du) Bread pudding.

broqueta (Sp) Skewer; brochette.

Bröschen (Gr) Calf's sweetbreads.

brose (Sc) A thin porridge eaten with butter, cream, or milk; made by pouring boiling water or stock over oatmeal.

broskev (Cz) Peach.

Brot (Gr) Bread.

Brotaufstrich (Gr) Any spread for bread such as jam or meat paste.

Brötchen (Gr) Rolls.

broth (US) The liquid in which any meat or vegetable has been boiled; thin soup made from vegetable, meat, or poultry stock; rice or pearl barley may be added.

Brotkoch (Gr) Molded bread pudding.

brouillés (Fr) Scrambled (eggs).

broulaï (Cb) Fish stew made with cassava roots or potatoes, tomato purée, onion, and chili pepper.

brown (US) Describes foods that are unrefined, unpolished, or untreated, such as brown rice and brown sugar.

brown, to (US) To turn the surface of food a light brown by using a small amount of fat in a pan or by using intense or direct heat.

brown betty (US) A pudding made with bread crumbs, spices, sugar, and cooked fruit, often apples but may be other fruit such as peaches.

brownie (US) A rich, thick bar cookie containing nuts and usually chocolate.

brown rice (US) Unprocessed rice with a brown-red skin and an intact bran layer; only the husk has been removed; has a stronger flavor and is more nutritious than white rice. Also called **unpolished rice.**

brown sauce (US) One of the classic basic sauces; traditionally made of meat stock with a roux (usually flour and butter browned together), braised or browned vegetables, various seasonings, and red wine.

brown stock (US) Seasoned water simmered with roasted meat.

brown sugar (US) Unrefined or partly

refined sugar; may be light or dark brown, and coarse or fine.

brugnon (Fr) Nectarine.

Brühe (Gr) Gravy, sauce, broth.

bruin bonen (Du) Kidney or brown beans.

bruin brood (Du) Whole wheat bread.

brûlé (Fr) Literally, "burned"; a term used in various ways, such as made or served with a caramelized sugar or sauce.

brûlot (Fr) Alcohol that is doused on a food and ignited at the time of serving. See also **flambé.**

bruna bönor (Sw) Brown beans cooked with vinegar and brown sugar and served with fried pork.

brunch (US) A late breakfast combined with lunch, serving some of the foods of both.

brunede kartofler (Da) New potatoes browned in butter and sugar.

brunekager (Da) Brown spice cakes or cookies.

brun fisksuppe (Nw) Fish soup made with flour browned in butter.

brunkaalsuppe (Da) Brown cabbage soup.

Brunnenkresse (Gr) Watercress.

brunoise (Fr) A garnish of diced vegetables; also, any food cut or diced into small pieces.

Brunswick stew (US) A stew with many variations; usually contains chicken, tomatoes, corn, beans, garlic, and seasonings; originated in the South where the meat used was squirrel.

brus (Nw) Soft drink.

bruschetto (It) Tart, sour.

brush, to (US) To use a pastry brush to coat foods with beaten egg, milk, oil or fat, syrup, or some other glaze or icing.

Brussels lof (Du) Endive.

Brussels sprouts (US) The axillary buds of a plant, genus *Brassica*, related to cabbage and broccoli, first cultivated in Belgium. The sprouts resemble small cabbages. Used boiled or steamed, and in savory dishes with meat or poultry.

Bruststück (Gr) Brisket.

brut (Fr) Unrefined, as applied to sugar; unadulterated or very dry, as applied to wine.

bruxelloise, à la (Fr) In the style of Brussels, Belgium; meat or egg dishes served with a garnish of Brussels sprouts and chicory.

brylépudding (Sw) Caramel cream.

bryndza (Po) Ewe's milk cheese.

brynt potatis (Sw) Browned potato wedges.

brynza (Cz) A white cheese made from sheep's milk, similar to Feta.

brysselkål (Sw) Brussels sprouts.

brzlík (Cz) Sweetbreads.

brzoskwinia (Po) Peach.

buah anggur (In) Grapes.

buah ara (In) Figs.

buah ceri (In) Cherries.

buah zaitun (In) Olives.

bubble and squeak (GB) A dish of pan-fried, leftover mashed potatoes with chopped cabbage; pieces of roast meat may be added. Named for the sound made while frying.

bubbly jock (Sc) Turkey.

bubrezi (SC) Kidneys.

bucatini (It) Long noodles.

buccellato (It) A cake made with pastry flour, sugar, vanilla, aniseed, and currants and shaped in rings or rolls.

buccin (Fr) Whelk.

bûche (Fr) Swiss roll; sponge cake rolled around a jelly or cream filling.

bûche de Noël (Fr) A Christmas cake made from a Swiss roll and decorated with chocolate butter cream or whipped cream to look like a yule log.

buchta (Cz) Cake.

Buchweizen (Gr) Buckwheat.

Bückling (Gr) Smoked herring; eaten with brown bread.

buckwheat (US) The small, triangular seeds of a plant, *Fagopyrum esculentum*, in the sorrel family. Not a true cereal or grain, it is cooked like rice and used whole in Russian kasha or in stuffing for fish or meat. Also called **Saracen corn.**

buckwheat flour (US) A brown flour made from ground buckwheat, used in bread, pancakes, and blinis.

budding (Da) Pudding.

budin (Sp) Pudding.

bù-ding (Ch) Pudding.

budino (It) Pudding.

budino di pasta (It) Noodle pudding.

budino di ricotta (It) Custard or pudding made with ricotta or cream cheese, walnuts, candied orange peel, and grated lemon rind.

budō (Jp) Grapes.

budyń (Po) Custard.

bue (It) Beef.

buey (Sp) Beef.

Buffalo chicken wings (US) Spicy, barbecued chicken wings named for the city where the snack originated.

buffet (Fr) A refreshment bar; a variety of foods on a table.

buggyantott tojás (Hu) Poached eggs.

buisson (Fr) An arrangement of food, particularly asparagus or crayfish, in a pyramid.

bulgar saláta (Hu) A vegetable salad named for Bulgaria.

bulgur (Ar) See **burghul.**

buljong (Sw) Bouillon.

hully heef (GB) Corned beef.

buluchki (Rs) Rolls.

bul'yon (Rs) Broth.

bun (GB) Small yeast loaves, usually sweet and with dried fruit.

bun (US) A roll.

buncis (In) Green beans.

Bundnerfleisch (Gr–Swiss) Salted, air-dried beef; served in thin slices with dark bread.

buntil (In) Taro leaves stuffed with spiced coconut.

buñuelo (Sp) Fritter; pancake; bun; waffle.

buñuelos de bacalla (Sp) Cod fritters.

buraki (Po) Cooked apples with grated beets in a sauce; served hot.

buras (In) Steamed rice dish.

burbot (GB) See **Aalbutte.**

burdock (US) Any of several plants, genus *Arctium* with large, slightly wooly, rough leaves that are used, when young, as salad greens or boiled. Burdock is also used as a root vegetable. In Japan, it is cultivated as a vegetable. Also called **bardana, gobo.**

burekakia (Gk) Little stuffed pies made with phyllo pastry.

burghul (Ar) Whole wheat that has been cooked, dried, partially debranned, and cracked into coarse fragments; the cracking occurs from boiling the grain. The coarse product may be used in dishes such as pilaf and as a substitute for rice and potatoes. When ground into a flour, burghul is used in dishes such as kibbeh and tabbouleh. Also called **bulgur.**

burgonya (Hu) Potatoes. Also called **krumpli.**

burgonyagombóc (Hu) Potato dumplings.

burgonyaleves (Hu) Potato soup.

burgoo (US) A hot, spicy stew associated with Kentucky; made with various meats and vegetables including pork, beef, veal, chicken, potatoes, onions, carrots, peppers, beans, okra, and seasonings.

Burgos (Sp) A mild flavored ewe's milk curd cheese, eaten as a dessert cheese.

Burgundy (Fr) The full-bodied red and dry white wines produced in the Burgundy region of France.

burnet (US) See **salad burnet.**

burnt cream (GB) British version of crème brûlée.

burritos (Sp) Wheat flour tortillas rolled around a variety of fillings such as chili con carne; served with grated cheese.

burro (It) Butter.

burro di acciuga (It) Anchovy butter.

burro fuso (It) Melted butter.

burro maggiordomo (It) Butter melted with parsley and lemon juice.

burské ořísky (Cz) Peanuts.

buřtíky (Cz) Knockwurst.

burtuaan (Ar) Oranges.

busecca (It) Highly spiced veal tripe with beans and onions.

buta (Jp) Pork.

butaniku (Jp) Pork dishes.

buta no kakuni (Jp) Stewed, cubed pork.

butifarra (Sp) A highly seasoned sausage, usually white, made with pork and spiced with nutmeg.

butifarrón sabroso (Cb) Meat loaf with minced beef, pork, ham, hot chili peppers, onion, coriander, and oregano; fried.

Butt (Gr) Flounder.

butta (Ar) Duck.

butter (US) A food made from churned cream; the agitated fat forms a compact mass. Unless qualified, the term butter usually means salted butter. *Sweet butter* is made from sweet cream and usually means without salt. *Whipped butter* means it has been beaten to incorporate air. This process increases its volume and softens the texture, so it is useful as a spread but not in cooking.

Butter (Gr) Butter.

butter bean (US) A vegetable, genus *Phaseolus*, used fresh or dried; kidney shaped with a pale yellow-green color; a traditional ingredient in succotash. Also called **lima bean.**

buttercream (US) A sweet, rich cream made with butter and icing or castor sugar, often flavored and colored, and used to fill and cover cakes. Variations may use margarine and milk.

buttercup squash (US) A turban shaped winter squash with a taste similar to a sweet potato.

butterfat (US) The fat found in milk and used to make butter.

butterfish (US) A small, bony, marine flatfish with oily, tender white flesh; used baked or fried.

butterfly cut (US) Slit partly open and spread out, such as done with thick steaks or chops.

Butterkäse (Gr) A cow's milk cheese with a light brown rind, a butter-colored interior, and a butter taste; some times with caraway seeds.

Buttermilchquark (Gr) Quark, a cheese similar to cottage cheese, made from a mixture of buttermilk and skim milk.

buttermilk (US) A liquid drained from butter as it is churned. Commercial or "cultured" buttermilk is made from skim milk with the addition of lactic acid bacteria to cause the milk to thicken.

butternut (US) A member of the walnut family, *Juglans cinerea*, native to the United States, with an eliptical shape and a tough shell. Its sweet, oily kernels are used in breads, cakes, and cookies. Also called **white walnut.**

butternut squash (US) A cylindrical winter squash, *Cucurbita maxima*, with a hard, light brown shell and sweet flavor; often grilled with chicken or spareribs.

butterscotch (US) 1. A cooked, brown sugar and butter flavoring. 2. A hard candy.

Butterteig (Gr) Short pastry; puff pastry.

button mushroom (US) The common mushroom, *Agaricus bisporus*, at its youngest stage, before the cap has opened.

butyric acid (US) Fatty acid that gives butter its characteristic flavor.

buz (Tr) Ice.

buzhenina (Rs) Ham baked in beer.

bwó káu-bing (Ch) Pancakes.

bwō-lwó (Ch) Pineapple.

bwō-tsài (Ch) Spinach.

bygg (Nw) Barley.

C

caballa (Sp) Mackerel.

cabbage (US) A vegetable, genus *Brassica*; overlapping smooth or curly leaves form a loose or dense head; many varieties; colors vary from white to red; used many ways including raw in cole slaw, boiled, baked, deep-fried, sautéed, stuffed, pickled, and made into sauerkraut.

cabbage palm (US) See **hearts of palm.**

cabe (In) Hot chili peppers.

Cabécou (Fr) A goat's milk cheese shaped in small cones or logs; blue crust with soft, white interior; zesty, nutty flavor; sometimes wrapped in leaves, soaked in vinegar, and eaten when the color turns pink.

cabellos de ángel (Sp) Literally, "angel's hair"; a jam made with spaghetti squash.

cabe rawit (In) See **bird pepper.**

cabillaud (Fr) Fresh cod.

cabinet pudding (GB) A steamed pudding made from sponge cake or ladyfingers layered with chopped, crystallized fruits and sometimes soaked with brandy.

Caboc (Sc) A cow's milk cheese in a cylinder covered with oatmeal; nutlike, slightly sour taste.

cabra (Sp, Pg) Goat.

Cabrales (Sp) A sheep's and goat's milk cheese in a cylinder; crusty rind, blue-veined interior; crumbly texture; sharp, piquant taste; considered a delicacy.

cabrito (Sp, Pg) Kid; young goat.

cabrito al horno (Sp) Roast kid.

caça (Pg) Game.

cacao (Du, Fr, It, Sp) Cocoa.

cacao (US) The raw or semiraw product of the cacao tree, *Theobroma cacao*, such as the beans, pod, and butter.

cacau (Pg) Cocoa.

cacciagione (It) Game.

cacciatora, alla (It) Prepared in the style of a hunter; usually with mushrooms, herbs, shallots, tomatoes, and wine.

cacciucco (It) Fish stew, Tuscan-style; with red wine and lobster or shrimp as well as fish, usually mullet, and highly seasoned.

cacerola (Sp) Casserole baking dish.

cacerola de pollo y elote (Mx) Casserole of chicken and corn.

cachaca (Pg) An alcoholic beverage made from sugarcane.

cachorro (Pg) Frankfurter; hot dog.

Cabbage

cachumbar (Ia) A mélange of cucumber, tomato, onion, fresh coriander, and green chilis.

cacik (Tr) Sliced cucumbers in yogurt with garlic, mint, and olive oil.

cacio (It) Cheese.

Caciocavallo (It) A pear or gourd-shaped cow's milk cheese with yellow rind, white interior, a Cheddar-like texture, and a mild, smoky taste.

cacio grattato (It) Grated cheese.

cactus pear (US) See **prickly pear.**

Caerphilly (GB) A cow's milk cheese in cylinders or blocks; white interior; moderately firm, crumbly texture; mild, slightly acidic taste; used like Greek Feta in salads or as a dessert cheese.

Caesar salad (US) A salad of greens, cheese, anchovies, and garlic-flavored croutons tossed with raw or coddled egg; dressed with olive oil and lemon juice; originated in Mexico and named for its creator, Caesar Cardini.

Caesar's mushroom (US) A common name for *Amanita caesarea*, a large, orange, delicate Amanita mushroom. Historically, it was a taste treat reserved for Roman emperors.

café (Fr, Sp, Pg) Coffee.

café au lait (Fr) Coffee with milk.

café brûlot (Fr) Spiced coffee with orange and lemon peel; flamed with brandy.

café com crème e açúcar (Pg) Coffee with cream and sugar.

café com leite (Pg) Coffee with milk.

café complet (Fr) The continental breakfast of coffee, milk, rolls, and butter.

café con leche (Sp) Coffee with milk.

café cortado (Sp) Cappuccino.

café corto (Sp) Espresso.

cafedaki (Gk) Heavily sweetened coffee.

café express (Fr) Espresso.

café filtre (Fr) Filtered coffee; served black in demitasse cups.

café gelado (Pg) Iced coffee.

café glacé (Fr) Ice cream with coffee flavoring.

café noir (Fr) Black coffee.

cafézinho (Pg) A syrupy-sweet dark espresso coffee; popular in Brazil.

caffè cappuccino (It) Coffee with whipped cream topping and cinnamon flavor.

caffè espresso (It) See **espresso.**

caffeine (US) An organic chemical that occurs naturally in a wide variety of plant products including coffee, tea, cola, and cocoa. It is a central nervous system stimulant.

caffè latte (It) Coffee with milk.

caffè nero (It) Black coffee.

cahn tom chua cai (Vt) A spiced hot and sour prawn soup.

caille (Fr) Quail.

caillebotte (Fr) Curds.

caille-lait (Fr) Rennet.

cailles en sarcophage (Fr) Literally, "quails in nests"; boned, stuffed, and poached quails served in baskets formed with deep-fried matchstick potatoes.

čaj (Cz, SC) Tea.

cajeta (Sp) A caramel candy.

čaj s ledem (Cz) Iced tea.

cajú (Pg) Cashew nuts.

Cajun (US) A French-Southern style of cooking developed by French settlers in Louisiana based on the use of rendered pork fat as a cooking oil.

cake (US) A baked dessert made with sweet dough, often with a filling between layers, and topped with a frosting. There are two basic types: those that contain fat, usually butter; and those without fat but with air beaten into egg whites as a leavener.

cake (Du) Cake.

calabash (US) See **kaddu.**

calabaza (Sp) A pumpkin, squash, or other gourd.

calamares en su tinta (Sp) Squid served in a sauce made with the ink of the squid.

calamaretti (It) Small or baby squid.

calamari (It) Squid, cuttlefish.

calamari affogati (It) Steamed squid.

calamari imbottita (It) Squid stuffed with chopped fish, raisins, nuts, basil, and egg.

calamondin (US) A small, tart citrus fruit, *Citrus mitus*; used candied and for acidic flavorings.

calcium (US) The most abundant mineral in the human body; essential in maintaining bone mass, nerve conduction, muscle contraction, and clotting of the blood; the recommended daily allowance (RDA) is 800 milligrams for adults; good dietary sources include milk and other dairy products, sardines, broccoli, kale, and calcium-fortified foods.

calda de papa (Sp) Potato soup with tomatoes, onions, jalapeño chilis, and other spices. Raw egg whites and yolks are drizzled into the hot mixture, making strands.

caldeirada (Pg) Fish chowder with onions, garlic, tomato, green pepper, and coriander; similar to bouillabaisse.

caldo (It) Warm, hot.

caldo (Pg, Sp) Broth; consommé.

caldo de patas (Sp) A broth made with cow's feet, white corn, and peanut butter.

caldo de pescado (Sp) Fish soup.

caldo de pimentón (Sp) Fish and potato soup with green peppers.

caldo gallego (It) A soup of white beans and mustard greens in meat stock with bits of meat or chicken.

caldo gallina (It) Chicken soup.

caldo verde (Pg) A soup or stew of shredded kale, chorizo or other sausage meat, potatoes, and olive oil.

caléndula (Sp) See **marigold.**

calico scallops (US) Large, flavorful scallops with mottled shells found in the Gulf of Mexico.

cálido (Sp) Hot; piquant; heating, as with seasonings.

çali fasulye (Tr) String beans.

California green chili (US) See **Anaheim chili.**

Calimyrna fig (US) Amber-colored succulent Smyrnan-type fig that originated in Turkey.

callaloo (Cb) The bitter-tasting heart-shaped leaves of the taro plant; cooked like spinach; often used in Creole-West Indian dishes with okra, onions, peppers, pork or ham, and shellfish.

callaloo soup (Cb) A soup made with

callaloo leaves, fresh coconut milk, okra, yam, and sweet green peppers.

callos (Pg, Sp) Tripe.

callos a la madrileña (Sp) Tripe cooked with calf's foot, sausage, onion, garlic, chili and sweet peppers, white wine, and seasonings.

callos de porco com amèijoas (Pg) Marinated pork tripe with clams, tomatoes, and coriander.

calmar (Fr) Squid.

calorie (US) A unit of energy-producing value in foods. The calorie referred to is the kilo calorie. The numbers of calories per type of food are rounded-off averages. The caloric value of a food does not refer to its nutritive value but to the heat released in the metabolism of food. The higher the calorie content, the higher the rate of burn needed to prevent excess storage of fat in the body.

calorie-free (US) A term meaning that a product contains less than 5 calories per serving; proposed by the U.S. Food and Drug Administration for food labels.

calvados (Fr) Apple brandy.

calzone (It) A pastry of pizza dough filled with ham, cheese, anchovies, and olives; deep-fried.

camarão (Pg) Shrimp marinated in lemon juice.

camarones (Sp) Prawns, shrimp.

Camembert (Fr) A cow's milk cheese with white orange-flecked rind in small discs; pale, oozy interior; creamy, rich taste; a dessert cheese eaten at room temperature.

camote (Sp) Sweet potato.

campagnola, alla (It) In the country style; usually with mushrooms, onions, tomatoes, and herbs.

Canadian bacon (Ca) Meaty, less fatty bacon made from the lean muscle of the loin of a pig.

canalons (Sp) Pasta sheets rolled around meat, fish, or vegetable filling.

canapé (Fr) Literally, "couch"; a small, toasted slice of bread or biscuit topped with a variety of spreads; used as an appetizer.

canard (Fr) Duck.

canard à l'orange (Fr) A classic dish of roast duck garnished with orange slices and watercress; served in a rich sauce containing orange juice, red currant jelly, and red wine.

canard aux cerises (Fr) Duck with cherries.

canard rôti (Fr) Roast duck.

canard sauvage (Fr) Wild duck.

candát (Cz) Pike perch.

candito (It) Candied.

candy (US) A sweet confection including fondant, fudge, caramels, butterscotch, and many others.

candy, to (US) To cook a food such as fruit pieces in sugar syrup until coated or until the syrup is reduced and thick.

canela (Sp) Cinnamon.

cane syrup (US) The concentrated sap of sugarcane.

caneton (Fr) Duckling.

cangrejo (Sp) Crab.

cangrejo de rio (Sp) Crayfish.

canja (Pg) Chicken and rice soup.

canneberge (Fr) Cranberry.

cannella (It) Cinnamon.

cannelle (Fr) Cinnamon.

cannellini (It) Oval or kidney-shaped white beans, *Phaseolus vulgaris*, with a firm texture; used in soups and cold salads.

cannelloni (It) Large hollow tubes of egg pasta; boiled and usually stuffed with minced meat, chicken, or fish mixtures, then baked, and served with grated cheese or a sauce.

canning (US) A method of preserving food in which it is sterilized usually by heat from boiling water or steam and then kept in sterilized containers.

cannoli (It) A dessert of hollow rolls of pastry, fried crisp and filled with ricotta; candied fruits or chocolate may be added to the cheese; a Sicilian specialty.

canola oil (US) A free-flowing oil obtained from a special form of rape-seed, an oilseed for salad and cooking oils.

Cantal (Fr) A cow's milk cheese similar to Cheddar; firm, yellow interior and mellow, nutty flavor.

cantaloupe (US) A melon in the muskmelon family; common varieties have heavily netted skin, broad ribs, and orange flesh with a fruity scent; used as an appetizer with prosciutto, in fruit salads, and cold soup.

cantarello (It) Chanterelle mushrooms.

canterellen (Du) Chanterelle mushrooms.

cap cay (In) Chop suey.

capellini (It) Literally, "fine hair"; very fine cylindrical pasta.

capercaillie (Sc) A large wood grouse favored as game; cooked like turkey.

capers (US) Small flower buds of the caper plant, genus *Capparis*; pickled and used as a condiment, to garnish salads, and to flavor sauces for meats and fish.

capirotada (Mx) Bread pudding with nuts and raisins.

capitone (It) Large eels.

capocollo (It) Spiced, smoked pork.

capon (US) A male chicken, castrated when young; tender flesh; used roasted or braised.

caponatina (It) Eggplant, capers, celery, and anchovies in a vinegared sauce with pureed tomatoes.

cappelletti (It) Literally, "little hats"; round, cap-shaped pasta with a filling of chicken or veal and ricotta cooked in broth.

Caper plant

cappelli d'angelo (It) Literally, "angel hair"; very thin, cylindrical pasta.

capperi (It) Capers.

cappesante (It) Bay scallops.

cappone (It) Capon.

cappuccino (It) Coffee espresso with hot, foaming milk added; sugar, nutmeg, or cinnamon may also be added.

câpres, sauce aux (Fr) Caper sauce; often used on lamb.

capretto (It) Kid, young goat.

capsicum (US) Any of various plants, genus *Capsicum*, in the nightshade family; round, conical or elongated fruits; green when immature and yellow to red when ripe; the two important species are the chili pepper (also sold as red or cayenne pepper) and the sweet pepper (also sold as paprika and pimento); eaten as a vegetable, used in relishes, or ground into powders.

capuchino (Sp) 1. Nasturtium. 2. A confection made with the yolk of an egg.

caracóis (Pg) Snails.

caracoles en salsa (Sp) Snails cooked with a sauce of tomato, onion, garlic, and parsley.

carambola (US) An oval, ribbed, orange-yellow fruit of a tree, *Averrhoa carambola*, with a slightly sweet, acidic taste; when sliced in cross-section produces a star shape; used as a garnish, in fruit salads, jellies, and preserves. Also called **belimbing, kamrakh, star fruit.**

caramel (US) 1. Describes any dish flavored or coated with browned sugar syrup, such as crème caramel. 2. A firm, chewy candy.

caramelize, to (US) To heat sugar until it melts into a brown syrup; used for flavoring and to add color to dishes including stews, gravies, custards, and flans. Also, to coat food with sugar and brown under a broiler or in an oven.

caramelle (It) Hard candy; taffy.

caranguejo (Pg) Crab.

caraway seeds (US) Hard, brown, tapered seeds of an herb, *Carum carvi*, in the parsley family; pungent flavor similar to anise; used in breads, cakes, cheeses, sauerkraut, potato salad, and noodles.

carbohydrate (US) A general term for a large group of sugars, starches, and celluloses. Carbohydrates are often divided into two groups identified as simple sugars and compound sugars. Glucose is the basic simple sugar used by the body as a source of energy. A compound sugar is composed of two or more molecules of simple sugars. Most compound sugars are tasteless, are sometimes difficult to digest, and may not dissolve in water.

carbonara, alla (It) With a sauce of lightly-cooked eggs, bacon, and garlic.

carbonated water (US) Describes water that has been made fizzing or bubbling by forcing a gas, carbon dioxide, into the water under pressure. Various beverages are made from carbonated water by adding flavorings such as syrups and spices. Soda water, no longer made with bicarbonate of soda, is a carbonated water.

carbonnade à la flamande (Fr) Beef cooked with beer.

carbonnades de boeuf (Fr) Sautéed and braised sliced beef.

carcakes (Sc) Pancakes; derived from a word meaning "to toss."

carciofi (It) Artichokes.

carciofini all'olio (It) Artichoke hearts cooked in white wine; preserved in olive oil.

cardamom (US) The brown to black seeds of a plant, *Elettaria cardamomum*, related to ginger; sold ground or whole within their seed capsules; used to flavor soups, curries, punch, pastries, and other sweets; important in the cooking of India.

carde (Fr) Chard.

cardon (Fr) Cardoon.

cardoon (US) A vegetable, *Cynara cardunculus*, of the thistle family, related to the globe artichoke. The clustered prickly leaf stalks, like large sticks of celery, are used cooked or raw in French and Italian dishes.

cari (Fr) Curry; curry powder.

carne (It, Pg, Sp) Meat.

carne al sange (It) Meat cooked rare.

carne asada (Sp) Thinly sliced beef, broiled.

carne ben cotta (It) Meat cooked well done.

carne de membrillo (Sp) "Quince meat"; a confection of sweet, pureed quince; served with cheese.

carne de res (Mx) Beef.

carne de venado (Sp) Venison.

carne de vinho e albos (Pg) Pork braised in white wine with herbs.

carneiro (Pg) Mutton.

carne non troppo cotto (It) Meat cooked medium.

carnitas (Mx) Literally, "little meats"; oven-browned pork, first cooked in stock with cumin, coriander, and oregano, then shredded for tacos or served in chunks.

carob (US) The dark brown, flat pods of a tree, *Ceratonia siliqua*; with a sweet taste, sometimes eaten as a candy; used as a substitute for chocolate. A legend calls it "St. John's Bread" as it is thought to be the locusts eaten by John the Baptist in the desert.

carote (It) Carrots.

carotene (US) A yellow pigment in various foods such as carrots, pumpkins, egg yolks, and peas. The body converts it to vitamin A. It is also used commercially to color foods.

carottes (Fr) Carrots.

carp (US) A freshwater fish, *Cyprinus carpio*; medium oily flesh; served usually with a sauce, baked, poached, or fried and traditionally used for gefilte fish; important in many Chinese and central European dishes.

carpe (Fr) Carp.

carpio (It) Carp.

carrageenin (US) A food additive used as a suspending agent in food, to control ice crystal growth in frozen foods and as a clarifying agent in beverages; made from a red algae, carrageen (Irish moss) found on the coasts of Europe and North America.

carré d'agneau aux herbes (Fr) Roast loin of lamb with a variety of herbs.

carré de porc provençal (Fr) Roast of rib loin with spices.

carrelet (Fr) Plaice; flounder.

carrot (US) A root vegetable, *Daucus carota*; shape varies from long and conical to short and round; commonly an orange color; good source of vitamin A; eaten raw or cooked.

carrot cake (US) A cake made with grated raw carrots, raisins, chopped walnuts, and spices (cinnamon, nutmeg, cloves), usually with a cream cheese frosting. Fruit such as crushed pineapple may be included.

casaba (US) A large globe-shaped melon in the muskmelon family; yellow to pale green rind with deep grooves; sweet, juicy, white to yellow flesh.

casalinga (It) Homemade.

cascabel (US) A small, plum-shaped chili pepper used in salsa.

casein (US) A substance composed of a number of different proteins in milk; it contains all of the essential amino acids.

cashew (US) A pale beige, kidney-shaped dry fruit or nut of a plant, *Anacardium occidentale*, native to Brazil; used whole or ground, as a snack, in salads, curries, and casseroles.

cassareep (Cb) A syrup made from a variety of cassava and used as a condiment, primarily in highly spiced dishes such as Caribbean pepperpot.

cassata (It) Cheesecake flavored with liqueurs.

cassava (US) A large starchy tuber of the cassava plant, genus *Manihol*. Sweet varieties are eaten as a vegetable; bitter varieties contain a poison when raw and are used to make cassava bread, starch, and as the source of tapioca. Also called **manioc.**

casserole (US) An oven-proof cooking pot with lid; also, the food cooked in it, consisting of more than one ingredient usually in sauce; considered a one-dish meal.

cassia (US) The bark of a tree, *Cinnamomum cassia*, related to cinnamon with a similar, more pungent flavor; may be used instead of cinnamon.

cassis (Fr) Black currant.

cassoulet (Fr) A savory stew made with white beans, onions, garlic, herbs, and meats, such as pork, lamb, goose, or duck; many variations. Traditionally, baked in an earthenware pot.

cassoulet toulousain (Fr) Navy bean stew with lamb, pork sausage, or poultry.

castagna (It) Chestnut.

castagnaccio (It) Thick fritters made with chestnut flour, pine nuts, almonds, candied fruit, and currants.

castañas con jaraba (Sp) Chestnuts in syrup.

castanha (Pg) Chestnut.

castanha-do-pará (Pg) Brazil nut.

caster sugar (GB) Very fine granulated sugar that dissolves rapidly in water; used in cakes and as a sweetener. Also spelled *castor*.

catfish (US) A marine and freshwater fish with long barbels by its mouth like cat's whiskers; many species; firm, white flesh; used fried, grilled, baked, and in stews.

cat's tongue (US) See **ladyfingers.**

catsup (US) See **ketchup.**

caul (US) The fatty, nearly transparent membrane that covers and holds the abdominal organs of animals; sometimes used to protect meat while roasting or as a skin for sausages.

cauliflower (US) A vegetable, genus *Brassica*, member of the cabbage family; with compact, edible flower heads called curd, usually white; also green and purple varieties; good source of vitamin A and C; served raw or cooked.

cavatelli (It) Short, ripple-surfaced pasta shells made with noodle strips.

caviale (It) Caviar.

caviar (US) The prepared, ripe eggs (roe) of various species of sturgeon including **beluga, osëtra** and **sevruga**; colors range from black to white and from golden to orange-brown. The roe of fish such as lumpfish and salmon is also treated as caviar; colors range from black to pink. Traditionally served in small dishes with a silver spoon accompanied by chopped onion, sour cream, and toast squares.

cavolfiore (It) Cauliflower.

cavoli (It) Cabbage.

cavoli imbottiti (It) Stuffed cabbage leaves.

cavolino di Brusselle (It) Brussels sprouts.

cavolo riccio (It) Kale.

cavolo rosso (It) Red cabbage.

cavolrapa (It) Kohlrabi.

çay (Tr) Tea.

cayenne pepper (US) A fiery, red powder ground from the seeds and pods of various chilis; used for a condiment.

cazabe (Sp) Cassava; cassava bread.

cebolas (Pg) Onions.

cebollas (Sp) Onions.

cebula (Po) Onion.

ceci (It) Chick-peas.

cecina (Sp) Dark, lightly salted, air-cured beef from Burgos.

cefalo (It) Mullet.

céklasaláta (Hu) Beet salad.

celer (SC, Cz) Celery.

céleri (Fr) Celery.

celeriac (US) A variety of celery grown for its large turnip-shaped root;

Celeriac

brown skin; used raw or cooked. Also called **turnip-root celery.**

céleri-rave rémoulade (Fr) Celeriac in sauce.

celery (US) A vegetable, _Apium graveolens_, with a cluster of stalks usually blanched to light green while growing; crisp, juicy and slightly sweet; used raw or cooked; leaves are also used, often as a garnish.

celery salt (US) A combination of salt and ground celery seeds.

celery seeds (US) Seeds of a variety of celery commonly called smallage; a somewhat bitter taste; used to season fish, meats, and stews.

cellophane noodles (US) Fine, transparent noodles made from mung bean flour; used stir-fried or deep-fried and in soups. Also called **bean thread noodles.**

cendawan (In) Mushrooms.

cenouras (Pg) Carrots.

centeno (Sp) Rye.

cèpe (Fr) See **boletus.**

cèpes farcis (Fr) Stuffed mushrooms.

ceppatella (It) Mushroom.

cereale cotto (It) Cooked cereal.

céréales (Fr) Cereals.

cerejas (Pg) Cherries.

cereza (Sp) Cherry.

çerezler (Tr) Appetizers; hors d'oeuvres.

cerfeuil (Fr) Chervil.

cerfoglio (It) Chervil.

cerise (Fr) Cherry.

çerkez tavuğu (Tr) Shredded chicken with walnut sauce containing garlic and paprika.

čerstvé (Cz) Fresh.

cerveja (Pg) Beer.

cervelles (Fr) Brains.

cervelles au beurre noir (Fr) Brains prepared in brown butter.

cervelli fritti (It) Calf brains, sliced, breaded and fried.

červená řepa (Cz) Beets.

červené vino (Cz) Red wine.

cerveza (Sp) Beer.

česnek (Cz) Garlic.

cetriolo (It) Cucumber; gherkin.

ćevapčići (SC) Grilled meat rolls.

ceviche (Sp) A classic appetizer of raw fish marinated in lemon or lime juice and chili peppers; served with sliced onions and tomatoes. Also spelled **seviche.**

chá (Ch) Tea.

chá (Pg) Tea.

Chablis (Fr) A dry white Burgundy wine.

chá com limão (Pg) Tea with lemon.

chá gelado (Pg) Iced tea.

cha gio (Vt) A Vietnamese specialty; spring rolls with minced pork and shrimp, wrapped in rice paper and deep-fried until crisp; served with rice noodles and fresh mint or coriander.

chai (Af–Swahili) Tea.

chai (Rs) Tea.

chakchouka (Ar) A spicy stew of potatoes, onions, tomatoes, and eggs seasoned with chili peppers.

chakleti (Af–Swahili) Chocolate.

chakula (Af–Swahili) Food.

chalky (US) 1. A term used to describe very white cheese, not a reference to taste. 2. A fine-grained texture in cheese, usually Chèvres.

challah (Jw) A traditional egg-rich,

braided or rectangular Sabbath bread loaf.

chamomile tea (US) A drink made from the dried flowers and leaves of either of two herbs, *Anthemis nobilis* or *Matricaria chamomilla*; with a pleasant aroma and slightly bitter, fruity taste.

champ (Ir) Creamed potatoes with scallions.

champagne (Fr) A sparkling wine, usually white, some pink; traditionally, from the Champagne district in France but now produced in many countries.

champagne, au (Fr) Prepared with a champagne sauce; often used with fish.

champanhe (Pg) Champagne.

champignons (Fr) 1. Cultivated mushrooms. 2. Mushroom-shaped foods such as small rounded breads.

champignons (Du) Mushrooms.

champignons à blanc (Fr) Stewed mushrooms.

champignons à la grecque (Fr) Marinated mushrooms.

champignons, aux (Fr) Garnished with mushrooms or topped with a mushroom sauce.

champignons farcis (Fr) Stuffed mushrooms.

champiñones (Sp) Mushrooms.

champurrado (Sp) A chocolate drink made with sweetened corn flour.

channa (Ia) A fresh cheese similar to cottage cheese.

chanoki (Rs) Braised lamb with potatoes, tomatoes, beans, and eggplant.

chanterelle (Fr) A wild, funnel-shaped mushroom, *Cantharellus cibarius*;

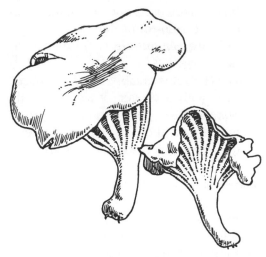

Chanterelles

yellow with an apricot aroma; favored in French cooking. Also called **girolle.**

Chantilly (Fr) See **crème Chantilly.**

chapati (Ia) Flat, unleavened, whole wheat bread; shaped in rounds and fried on a griddle or in a pan without oil.

chapon (Fr) Capon.

chapon de Gascogne (Fr) A bread crust rubbed with garlic and added to salad.

char (US) A freshwater and saltwater fish, genus *Salvelinus*, with flesh similar to salmon or trout, usually ranging in color from white to pink; delicate flavor; prepared by baking, broiling, poaching, and grilling.

charcuterie (Fr) Pork products such as ham and sausages.

chard (US) A vegetable, *Beta vulgaris cicla*, a member of the beet family; grown for its edible, thick white stalks and green leaves used like spinach. A red variety is known as rhubarb chard. Also called **spinach beet, Swiss chard.**

charlotte (Fr) A baked dessert of fruit puree flavored with lemon and cinnamon and made in a deep mold lined with bread. Said to be named for Queen Charlotte of England, wife of George III.

charlotte russe (Fr) Bavarian cream or chocolate mousse in a mold lined with ladyfingers; sometimes topped with whipped cream.

chartreuse (Fr) A dish made with braised cabbage and meat or game such as partridges, and sometimes eggs.

chǎ shǎu (Ch) Barbecued pork.

chashmé ka paani (Ia) Mineral water.

cha soba (Jp) Noodles made of buckwheat and green tea.

chàtaigne (Fr) Chestnuts; with chestnuts.

chateaubriand (Fr, Nw) Thick slice of tenderloin from the middle of filet mignon; classically grilled and served with a béarnaise sauce and a garnish of potatoes cut in strips.

chatini (Af–Swahili) Chutney.

chǎu bái-tsài (Ch) Sautéed cabbage served with meat, fish, or soybean curd and a sauce.

chaud-froid (Fr) Describes a dish prepared hot but served cold; cooked salmon, chicken, or game coated with a cream sauce and glazed with aspic jelly.

chǎu dòu-fú (Ch) Sautéed soybean curd.

chǎu-fán (Ch) Fried rice.

chǎu ji-dàn (Ch) Scrambled eggs.

chǎu-myàn (Ch) Fried noodles.

chausson (Fr) Turnover.

chǎu syā-rén (Ch) Sautéed large shrimp.

chaval (Ia) Rice.

chawan mushi (Jp) Savory egg custard with chicken, shrimp, ginko nuts, and vegetables steamed in individual cups.

chayote (US) A vegetable, *Sechium edule*, in the squash family; shaped like a spiny, ridged pear; green to white skin and light green flesh; a crisp, light taste, similar to a cucumber; eaten raw, stir-fried, steamed, or baked. Also called **mirliton, vegetable pear.**

chaza (Af–Swahili) Oysters.

chebureki (Rs) Spicy lamb dumpling made with dough similar to strudel.

Cheddar (US) A cow's milk cheese; many varieties; firm, noncrumbly texture; yellow to orange color; mild to sharp taste; named for a village in England where it originated. Used as a dessert and a cooking cheese.

cheese (US) A food made from milk curdled by the action of heat or rennet and with the curd separated from the liquid whey. The curd or the whey may be used to make the cheese.

cheesecake (US) A dessert with a basis of a soft cheese such as cream cheese, ricotta, or cottage cheese.

chelo (Ar) Cooked rice served with butter and raw egg yolk.

chenza (Af–Swahili) A large tangerine.

cherimoya (Sp) A tropical fruit of a tree, *Anona cherimolia*, in the custard apple family; shaped like a green fir cone; white flesh; sweet taste between pineapple and strawberry; used in dessert dishes.

cherry (US) The small fruit of a tree,

genus *Prunus*, member of the rose family; many varieties in three main groups: sweet, sour, and hybrids; with round to heart shapes and colors from yellow to red to black-red. Depending on the variety, cherries are eaten fresh, used for cooked dishes, liqueurs, and brandies.

cherrystone clam (US) See **quahog.**

chervil (US) An herb, *Anthriscus cerefolium*, relative of parsley; lacy leaves; slight anise taste; used in salads, *fines herbes*, egg, and seafood dishes.

chess pie (US) A deep, flaky pastry shell filled with custard and pecans; other variations include sour cream, dates, and raisins.

chestnut (US) The edible fruit of a tree, genus *Castanea*; sweet, starchy flesh within a hard, brown husk; used in many ways including roasted, in stuffings, mixed with vegetables and sweetened for desserts. Also called **marron.**

cheval, à (Fr) Topped with a fried egg.

chèvre (Fr) Goat.

Chèvre (Fr) A goat's milk cheese similar to Greek feta.

chewa (Af–Swahili) Cod.

chianti (It) Dry red wine from Tuscany; served with meats and pastas.

Chiboust (Fr) A pastry cream mixed with beaten egg whites and flavored with vanilla; traditionally used to fill Saint-Honoré cakes.

chichinda (Ia) A long, thin gourd native to India; used in vegetarian dishes.

chicken (US) The common domesticated fowl, *Gallus gallus.*

chicken à la king (US) A dish of cooked chicken pieces served in a cream sauce with mushrooms, green peppers, and pimentos. The origin of the dish and its name has been claimed by restaurants from New York to London.

chicken-fried steak (US) Thin, pounded steak coated with seasoned flour and crisp-fried like chicken; served with gravy made by adding milk to brown particles left in the skillet.

chicken Kiev (US) A classic Russian style of cooking boned chicken breasts. They are pounded flat, folded around butter, coated in egg and bread crumbs, and deep-fried. When cut open, the butter pours out as a rich sauce.

chicken tetrazzini (US) Cooked chicken pieces in a cream sauce; served over spaghetti and topped with bread crumbs and Parmesan cheese; then oven-browned. Turkey may be substituted. Said to be named for an Italian opera singer, Luisa Tetrazzini.

chick-pea (US) The seed of a legume, *Cicer arietinum*; color varies from cream to black; sometimes eaten green but usually dried; important in Arab and Spanish cooking; used in soup, stews, pureed, and ground into flour. Also called **ceci, garbanzo.**

chicorée (Fr) Chicory.

chicory (US) A green leafy plant, *Cicorium intybus*; slightly bitter-tasting; used for salad greens; the root may be used like parsnips and is sometimes roasted for a coffee extender. See also **Belgian endive, endive.**

Chicory

chikuwa (Jp) Broiled fish cake.

chile (Mx, Sp) The chili pepper, the most used flavoring in Mexican cooking.

chiles en nogada (Sp) Chilis in walnut sauce.

chiles rellenos (Sp) Fried poblano chili peppers coated in batter and stuffed with ground pork or cheese.

chili con carne (US) A dish that originated in Texas; well-seasoned, browned beef cooked with chili peppers; beef sizes range from ground to large chunks; many variations but beans, pasta, or other starchy fillers are not included in the basic recipe.

chili con queso (US) An appetizer dip made with chili peppers and cheese, usually Monterey Jack.

chili paste (US) A paste of chilis, garlic, black beans, and salt.

chili pepper (US) A vegetable in the capsicum family, with many varieties; an oil in the seeds and membranes causes a spicy hot taste; the smallest and most fiery are in the species, *Capsicum frutescens*; used often in Mexican and Indian cooking. See individual kinds.

chili powder (US) A mixture of pulverized chilis, dried garlic, cumin, oregano, cloves, coriander, and dried onion.

chimichangas (Mx) Fried wheat flour tortillas rolled around a variety of fillings.

Chinese anise (US) See **Star anise.**

Chinese artichoke (US) A tapered, segmented tuber from a plant, *Stachys sieboldii*, with a flavor similar to globe and Jerusalem artichokes; used fried or boiled and served in butter with parsley or a sauce. Also called **chorogi, crosnes.**

Chinese black vinegar (US) A dark vinegar made from fermented rice.

Chinese cabbage (US) A vegetable of the cabbage family, *Brassica pekinensis*; tightly packed, wide, white stalks and yellow-green wrinkled leaves; used for soup, stir-fried dishes, and as a wrapper for fillings when steamed. Also called **bái-tsài, napa cabbage.**

Chinese gooseberry (US) See **kiwifruit.**

Chinese parsley (US) See **coriander.**

Chinese sausage (US) Highly spiced dried sausages made with chopped lean and fat pork.

61

chīng-jyāu (Ch) Green peppers.

ching tāng (Ch) Broth.

chīng-yú (Ch) Mackerel or herring.

chín-jyāu (Ch) Red pepper.

chinook salmon (US) A species of salmon, one of the most important food fishes of the North Pacific with meat that ranges in color from white to orange; used in a variety of dishes including quenelles, mousseline, and teriyaki. Also called **king salmon, quinnat.**

chín-tsài (Ch) Celery.

chiòdo di garofano (It) Clove.

chipolata (Fr) Small, fresh, spicy sausages; fried or grilled and used as a garnish, an appetizer, and in stew.

chipotle chile (Mx) Dark red to brown, fiery, medium-sized peppers; sold pickled in cans.

chipped beef (US) Thinly sliced beef, smoked and dried; prepared like corned beef.

chirashizushi (Jp) Vinegared rice mixed with eggs, mushrooms, and chopped vegetables.

chiri mushi (Jp) Steamed salmon casserole.

chirinabe (Jp) Fish and vegetables cooked at the table.

chispe (Pg) Pig's trotters.

chitterlings (US) Pig's intestines first cooked in a vinegared stock, then coated with batter and fried. Also called **chitlins.**

chitlins (US) See **chitterlings.**

chive (US) An herb, *Allium schoenoprasum*, member of the onion family; with thin, tubular, grasslike leaves; used as a garnish or flavoring for soups, omelets, salads, and sauces.

Chivry (Fr) 1. A sauce made with fish stock, served with fish; or a velouté sauce served with chicken or eggs. 2. A flavored butter for hors d'oeuvres.

chi-yú (Ch) Swordfish.

chléb (Cz) Bread.

chlodnik z ryby (Po) A summer soup with beets, fish, cucumbers, onions, carrots, dill, parsley, and sour cream; served cold.

chocola (Du) Hot chocolate.

chocolate (US) The ground and refined beans from the pods of the cacao tree, *Theobroma cacao*; a liquid produced is turned into a solid block. From this comes all the many forms in which chocolate is used, such as sweet chocolate, milk chocolate, and baking chocolate (bitter or unsweetened).

chocolate quente (Pg) Hot chocolate.

choix (Fr) Choice.

chokladglass (Sw) Chocolate ice cream.

cholent (Jw) Beef brisket simmered with beans, barley, and potato; a traditional Sabbath dish.

cholesterol (US) A pearly, waxlike substance found in animal fats. Although cholesterol is needed for cell membranes, certain hormones, and the formation of vitamin D, authorities advise against an excess taken in through foods.

cholesterol-free (US) A term for a food product that contains less than 2 milligrams of cholesterol per serving and no more than 2 grams of saturated fat per serving; proposed by the U.S. Food and Drug Administration for food labels.

chop, to (US) To cut into small pieces.

chop suey (US) A version of a Chinese dish made of shredded meat or chicken, bean sprouts, mushrooms, bamboo shoots, and water chestnuts; served with soy sauce and rice.

chorizo (Mx) Highly seasoned smoked sausage made of garlic-spiced, chopped pork, hot paprika, and sweet red peppers; served as an hors d'oeuvre and used as an ingredient in dishes such as paella, omelets, and with tortillas.

chorogi (Ch) See **Chinese artichoke.**

chou (Fr) Cabbage.

chou-broccoli (Fr) Broccoli.

choucroute (Fr) Sauerkraut.

choucroute garnie (Fr) Sauerkraut baked with ham, bacon, and sausages.

chou de Milan (Fr) Savoy cabbage.

chou-fleur (Fr) Cauliflower.

chou frisé (Fr) Kale.

chou-rave (Fr) Kohlrabi.

chouriço (Pg) Sausage.

chou rouge (Fr) Red cabbage.

chou vert (Fr) Green cabbage.

choux (Fr) Small filled or garnished buns.

choux à la crème (Fr) Cream puffs.

choux de Bruxelles (Fr) Brussels sprouts.

choux de Bruxelles à la grandmère (Fr) Brussels sprouts sautéed with onions and bacon.

choux pastry (Fr) See **cream puff pastry.**

chow chow (US) A relish of chopped mixed vegetables in a mustard and pickle sauce.

chowder (US) A thick soup usually made from seafood and milk.

chowder clam (US) See **quahog.**

chow mein (US) A version of a Chinese dish served with fried noodles; similar to chop suey, adding celery, and green pepper.

chřest (Cz) Asparagus.

chromium (US) A trace element required for normal glucose metabolism; a recommended daily allowance (RDA) has not been established but 80–100 micrograms (mcg) is considered an average adult intake per day; good dietary sources include meat, dairy products, and whole grain cereals.

chrysanthemum (US) A common flowering plant with leaves that in general are used for decoration of foods; when called for in Japanese cooking, they are of a particular species. See **shungiku.**

chrzan (Po) Horseradish.

chub (US) Any of various fishes including a North American freshwater whitefish, genus *Coregonus*, and a Eurasian freshwater species related to the carps. There are also marine fish known as chubs. The whitefish identified as chub is often sold smoked.

chuletas de cordero (Sp) Lamb chops.

chuletas de res (Sp) Prime ribs.

chuletas de ternera (Sp) Veal chops.

chumvi (Af–Swahili) Salt.

chungurro (Sp) Crabmeat with sherry and brandy.

chungwa (Af–Swahili) Orange (fruit).

churrasco (Pg, Sp) Barbecue; charcoal-grilled beef or sausage.

churros (Sp) Strips of deep-fried pastry resembling doughnuts in flavor and texture.

chutney (Ia) A relish made of fresh and dried fruit, often mango, raisins, spices, and vinegar; served with curry dishes and meat. There are many variations and a selection may be served with a meal.

chwūn-jywǎn (Ch) Spring roll.

chyáu-mài (Ch) Buckwheat.

chyé-dz (Ch) Eggplant.

chyōu-kwèi (Ch) Okra.

chywán-shú de jī-dàn (Ch) Hard-boiled eggs.

chywè-mài (Ch) Oats.

cialda (It) Wafer; waffle.

ciambelle (It) Ring-shaped buns; doughnuts.

ciasteczka (Po) Cookies.

ciastka drozdzowe (Po) A light yeast cake.

ciastka miodowe (Po) Cookies made with honey.

ciasto (Po) Cake.

ciboulette (Fr) Chives.

cibréo (It) Stewed eggs and giblets.

cibule (Cz) Onions.

cicoria (It) Chicory.

cider (US) A beverage; sweet apple cider is pure apple juice; hard cider is fermented apple juice; applejack is a distilled spirit made from hard cider.

cielęcina (Po) Veal.

cigala (Sp) A variety of crayfish.

cigány gulyás (Hu) Gypsy-style goulash, with a variety of meats.

ciğer (Tr) Liver.

çikolata (Tr) Chocolate.

cilantrillo (Sp–Puerto Rico) Fresh coriander.

cilantro (Sp) Coriander; also, a similar herb used in Mexico and Central America.

çilek (Tr) Strawberry.

çilek-kaymali (Tr) Strawberries in egg white beaten with sugar, cream, and orange-flower water.

ciliege (It) Cherries.

cima di vitello (It) Jellied veal.

cimino (It) Cumin.

cinnamon (US) A spice made from the dried, rolled bark of the cinnamon tree, *Cinnamomium zeylanicum*, native to Ceylon; sold in sticks but usually ground; used in sweet dishes and savory meat dishes. The bark of cassia is also used like cinnamon. See **cassia.**

cioccolata calda (It) Hot chocolate beverage.

cioppino (US) A fish stew reported to have originated at Fisherman's Wharf in San Francisco; said to come from "chip in" with whatever spare fish was available.

ciorba (Ro) Vegetable soup made with fish or beef.

cipolle (It) Onions.

cipolline (It) A name applied to several members of the onion family including tiny onions, chives, scallions, and shallots.

cipolline in agrodolce (It) Spring onions in a sweet-and-sour tomato sauce with vinegar and sugar.

ciruela (Sp) Plum.

citric acid (US) A water-soluble acid found in citrus fruits and other plants.

citroen (Du) Lemons.

citron (Fr) Lemon; citron.

citron (US) The fruit of an evergreen tree, *Citrus medica*, from the Middle East and Mediterranean regions; an appearance like a large lemon; the thick skin is used commercially as candied peel.

citrouille (Fr) Pumpkin, gourd.

citrus (US) Fruits from shrubs or trees of the genus *Citrus*; sweet species include the sweet orange, tangerine, and mandarin orange; less sweet, sour, or acid are the Seville orange, grapefruit, lemon, and lime. Kumquats, in another genus, are also included as citrus.

civet (Fr) A wild game stew made with red wine, onions, salt pork, and mushrooms. Traditionally, fresh blood of the animal is used to thicken the sauce. Civet may also be applied to some seafood or fish dishes.

civet de lièvre (Fr) Jugged hare.

clabber (US) A thick, white liquid, not separated into curds and whey, that forms at the bottom when milk is allowed to stand. It is sour and similar to yogurt but different in flavor and texture. When churned, it becomes buttermilk.

clafouti (Fr) A fruit pastry or thick pancake, usually made with black cherries; served warm sprinkled with sugar or with cream or a vanilla sauce.

clam (US) A bivalve mollusk eaten cooked or raw; many species, sizes, and names, including soft-shell clams: steamers and long clams; hard-shell clams; quahogs, littlenecks, cherrystones, and chowder clams.

Clamart (Fr) Describes various dishes that include green peas, whole or pureed, such as a garnish of artichoke hearts stuffed with green peas.

clambake (US) Traditionally, a meal cooked on a beach with clams and corn on the cob steamed in a driftwood fire.

clam chowder (US) A chowder made with quahog clams, bacon, onions, and potatoes. Manhattan style cooks the basic ingredients in water adding tomatoes, carrots, and celery. New England style cooks the basic ingredients in milk or cream.

clarified butter (US) Butterfat separated from the solids and liquids of butter after slow heating. Clarified butter allows food to be heated at higher temperatures without scorching of protein in butter.

clarify (US) To clear by filtering or straining soups, stocks, and jellies or by cooling fats until solid and removing them.

clavo (Sp) Clove.

clotted cream (GB) A thick, slightly grainy, yellow cream formed in a process of slowly heating then cooling milk; eaten as a spread with scones or as a topping for fruit.

cloudberry (Ca) The yellow fruit of a plant, *Rubus chamaemorus*, related to the blackberry, that grows in Canada and northern Europe; tastes like slightly green but sweet apricots;

eaten in any dish using blackberries. Also called **bakeapple, hjortron.**

cloud ear (US) A fungus used for its interesting texture and colors. Also called **tree ear, wood ear, yùn er.**

clou de girofle (Fr) Clove.

cloves (US) The dried, dark brown flower bud of an evergreen tree, *Eugenia aromatica*; aromatic with a strong, sweet flavor; used whole or ground in a variety of dishes.

coat, to (US) To cover food with egg, bread crumbs, batter, flour or other similar ingredients in preparation for frying, broiling, or roasting.

cobbler (US) A deep-dish pie with a thick crust of biscuit dough and fruit filling; served with a sweet sauce or ice cream.

cochifrito (Sp) Fricassee of lamb with lemon and garlic.

cochinillo asado (Sp) Roast suckling pig.

cochon (Fr) Pig.

cochon au lait (Fr) Roast suckling pig.

cocido (Sp) Cooked, boiled; a stew with

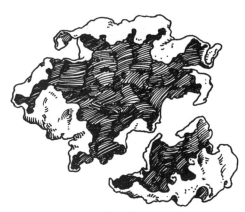

Cloud ear

meat, chicken, bacon, chick-peas, and vegetables; many variations.

cocido al vapor (Sp) Steamed.

cocido de riñones (Sp) Kidney stew.

čočka (Cz) Lentil.

cock-a-leekie (Sc) A traditional soup of chicken and leeks, sometimes with oatmeal or prunes.

čočková polévka (Cz) Lentil soup.

coco (Sp) Coconut.

cocoa (US) A beverage made from cocoa powder, sugar, and milk.

cocoa bean (US) See **chocolate.**

cocomero (It) Watermelon.

coconut (US) The fruit of a tropical palm, genus *Cocos*, with a fibrous, hard husk and sweet, white flesh; eaten fresh or dried and grated for many uses; often used in the cooking of Southeast Asia and India.

coconut milk (US) The liquid expressed from grated coconut meat after it has steeped in water.

coco quemado (Sp) Toasted coconut dessert.

cocotte, en (Fr) Cooked in an earthenware utensil.

coctel de mariscos (Sp) Seafood cocktail.

cod (US) A large, cold-water fish, family Gandidae, found in the Atlantic and Pacific oceans; lean, white, large-flaked flesh with a neutral flavor adaptable to almost any cooking method. Sold many ways including fresh, salted, pickled, filleted, and shredded.

coddle, to (US) To soft-cook eggs by placing them in a pan of boiling water removed from the heat and covered.

codorniz (Sp) Quail.

coêlho (Pg) Rabbit.

coeur à la crème (Fr) A rich dessert molded in a heart shape; made with cottage or cream cheese and topped with fresh cream and strawberries.

coeur d'artichauts (Fr) Artichoke hearts.

coeur de laitue (Fr) Hearts of lettuce.

coeur de palmier (Fr) Hearts of palm.

coffee (US) A beverage made from the roasted and ground beans of the berrylike fruit of an evergreen tree, genus *Coffea*, native to Africa and cultivated in tropical regions. Of the many different species, the most important is *C. arabica*; next is *C. canephora* which produces the coffee known as "robusta" used for blending. To produce a coffee that is balanced in flavor, acidity, and strength, a blend of two or more kinds of beans is usual. Roasting, which may be light, medium, or dark, gives coffee beans their characteristic taste.

cognac (Fr) A highly regarded brandy produced near the town of Cognac.

cogumelos (Pg) Mushrooms.

coing (Fr) Quince.

Çok (Tr) Well-done or over-cooked.

col (Sp) Cabbage.

Colby (US) A cow's milk cheese; a soft Cheddar with a yellow-orange color; mellow flavor; popular for snacks or sandwiches.

colcannon (Ir) A dish of chopped cabbage, mashed potatoes, and leeks mixed with butter and milk; similar to British bubble and squeak.

cold cuts (US) A selection of sliced cold meats, such as roast beef, salami, and ham.

col de Bruselas (Sp) Brussels sprouts.

cold pack (US) Describes cheeses mixed together into a spreadable paste without cooking. Also, a method in canning fruit or vegetables by packing into jars uncooked, then covering with boiling liquid.

coleslaw (US) A salad of shredded raw cabbage, grated carrots, onions or other crisp vegetables, sometimes chopped apples and nuts, combined with a dressing such as mayonnaise, sour cream, or yogurt.

coliflor (Sp) Cauliflower.

coliflor al ajo arriero (Sp) Deep-fried cauliflower, "muledriver style," with garlic and vinegar sauce.

colin (Fr) Hake.

collards (US) A form of kale with coarse leaves eaten as greens.

col lombada (Sp) Red cabbage.

collop (GB) A small thin slice of meat; escalope; scallop.

col rizada (Sp) Kale.

Collards

combine (US) To mix two or more ingredients together.

comida (Pg) Dinner, served midafternoon.

comino (Mx) Cumin, often used in Mexican cooking.

common edible crab (GB) A large, smooth-shelled crab, *Cancer pagurus*, most often eaten in Britain; pink-brown color; lean meat; boiled whole.

complete protein (US) A protein that contains all the essential amino acids. An example of a food source of complete protein is a chicken egg. Very few foods provide all of the essential amino acids. See also **essential amino acids.**

compota de manzana (Sp) Applesauce.

compote de fruits (Fr) Fruits, fresh or dried, stewed with syrup and served cold.

compound butter (US) A butter combined with other ingredients to alter flavor, aroma, or color, such as anchovy butter or fennel butter.

compressed yeast (US) See **yeasts.**

con (It) With.

concassé (Fr) Pounded or crushed, such as basil concassé.

conch (US) A large spiral-shelled mollusk with edible, somewhat tough flesh; used in chowders, fried, or marinated for salads.

conchiglie (It) Shell-shaped pasta.

concombres (Fr) Cucumbers.

condensed milk (US) A thick, creamy, canned milk that has been sweetened with sugar to hinder bacterial growth; used in cooking; a traditional base for Key lime pies.

condimentos (Pg) Condiments.

conejo (Sp) Rabbit.

confectioners' custard (US) See **pastry cream.**

confectioners' sugar (US) Fine, very white powdered sugar; used in whipped cream, uncooked sweets, and meringues. Also called **icing sugar, powdered sugar.**

confit (Fr) A form of preserving meat, such as capon, duck, goose, and pork, by salting and brining, then cooking and storing it in its own fat.

confit d'oie (Fr) Goose preserved in its own fat.

confiture (Fr) Jam; preserves.

congee (Ch) A thick gruel or porridge made from cooked rice; used with a variety of flavorings, meats, and seafoods; similar to kedgeree in India. Also called **zhou fàn.**

congee (Ia) The water in which rice has been boiled; used for an invalid's diet.

congelato (It) Congealed; frozen.

congelé (Fr) Frozen.

coniglio (It) Rabbit.

conserva (Sp) Jam; preserves.

conserve (US) A preserved fruit product that contains distinct pieces of fruit and with additions such as raisins and nuts.

conserve au vinaigre (Fr) Pickle.

consommé (Fr) A clear meat stock that has been enriched and concentrated to an almost jellylike stage, then clarified.

consommé à l'alsacienne (Fr) Broth with sauerkraut and sausages.

consommé à la bourgeoise (Fr) Broth with carrots, turnips, and potatoes.

consommé à la madrilène (Fr) Clear chicken soup with tomato pulp; served cold.

consommé à la reine (Fr) Chicken broth served with sliced chicken.

consommé aux perles (Fr) Barley soup.

consommé doré (Fr–Creole) A golden yellow consommé.

consommé froid (Fr) Cold consommé.

consommé julienne (Fr) Clear soup served with sliced vegetables.

consommé printanier (Fr) Broth with a variety of spring vegetables added.

consommé queue de boeuf (Fr) Soup made with oxtails, turnips and carrots.

Conti (Fr) Dressings for meat or potato dishes made with puréed lentils; the purée may be used in soup.

contorno (It) Side dish vegetables.

contre-filet (Fr) Tenderloin.

cookie (US) Small, sweet cakes with many shapes and flavors.

cookie (Sc) A kind of bun.

Coon Cheddar (US) A crumbly-textured, sharp American Cheddar.

coppa (It) Pork sausage; type of salami.

copper (US) A trace element essential for the formation of collagen and important in the development of red blood cells; a recommended daily allowance (RDA) has not been established but an intake of about 2 mg per day for adults is considered safe and adequate; good dietary sources include liver, shellfish, and whole-grain cereals.

coq au vin (Fr) Chicken lightly browned with diced pork and butter with mushrooms, garlic and small onions; served in a wine sauce and flambéed.

coque, à la (Fr) Soft-boiled (eggs).

coquillages (Fr) Shellfish.

coquilles St. Jacques (Fr) Scallops.

coquilles St. Jacques à la parisienne (Fr) Scallops and mushrooms in white wine sauce.

çorba (Tr) Soup.

čorba od povrća (SC) Vegetable soup.

corbina y mariscos al vapor (Sp) White conger or sea bass steamed with mussels.

cordeiro (Pg) Lamb. Also called **borrego.**

cordon bleu (Fr) "Blue ribbon"; once an honor given to knights in France, the term became applied to food prepared with excellence and to outstanding female chefs.

core, to (US) To remove the seed section from top to bottom of a fruit.

coriander (US) An herb of the parsley family, *Coriandrum sativum*, grown for its aromatic seeds, green leaves, and roots; important worldwide as flavoring for pickles, roast meat, curries, and many other dishes. Also called **Chinese parsley, cilantro.**

corn (US) Any of a variety of a cultivated cereal plant, *Zea mays*, with a white or yellow sweet kernel; eaten fresh, cooked, made into oil. Also called **maize.**

corn bread (US) A bread made of corn meal, flour, salt, and water or milk, sometimes buttermilk; baked in a covered skillet.

corn dog (US) A hot dog wrapped in a corn meal-batter crust and skewered on a stick; eaten plain, with mustard or catsup, or another sauce.

corned beef (US) Beef brisket cured in

69

brine flavored with seasonings such as garlic, cloves, peppercorns, and thyme; used cooked in seasoned water until tender. The term refers to a word, *corn*, for something small as a salt grain, not the cereal grain.

cornet (Fr) A cone made with a wafer, such as an ice cream cone, or a horn-shaped pastry made with a strip of puff pastry wound on a conical metal mold and baked; may also be a ham or salmon slice rolled into a cone and then filled. See also **cream horn.**

cornflour (GB) Cornstarch.

cornichon (Fr) A small variety of cucumber with a horn shape; usually pickled.

Cornish pasty (GB) See **pasty.**

corn meal (US) Meal ground from yellow or white corn; used for corn bread, puddings, mush, and other dishes.

corn oil (US) A refined oil obtained from the dried, crushed corn germ. An unsaturated oil without cholesterol, it is a major component in most margarines.

corn salad (US) See **mâche.**

cornstarch (US) A starch obtained from processed, ground corn; contains no gluten; used as a thickener.

corn syrup (US) A nutritive sweetener composed of a blend of sugars derived from corn and containing enough water to be fluid; used to sweeten and thicken foods.

còscia (It) Thigh; leg.

còscia di agnello arrosto (It) Roast leg of lamb.

cos lettuce (GB) See **romaine.**

costelêta (Pg) Cutlet, chop.

costelêta de porco (Pg) Pork chop.

costillas de cerdo (Sp) Spareribs.

costmary (GB) An herb of the daisy family similar to tansy; used to season soups, salads, poultry, and veal.

costole (It) Ribs; spareribs.

costolette (It) Chop; cutlet.

costolette alla milanese (It) Veal cutlets flattened, dipped in egg batter, and sautéed in butter.

costolette alla Modenese (It) Breaded veal cutlets baked in wine and tomato sauce.

costolette di agnello piccante (It) Lamb chops fried with herbs; dressed with lemon juice.

costolette di maiale (It) Pork chops.

cotechino (It) Spiced pork sausage made with pork rind.

côte de boeuf grillé (Fr) Grilled beef rib steaks.

côtelette d'agneau (Fr) Lamb chop or cutlet.

côtelette de porc (Fr) Pork chop or cutlet.

côtelette de veau (Fr) Veal chop or cutlet.

cotignac (Fr) A confection made with quince puree and sugar.

cotognata (It) Quince jam or paste.

cotolette (It) Slice of veal, turkey, or beef or some vegetables like eggplant.

cotolette alla milanese (It) Veal cutlets, Milanese style; fried, breaded cutlets pounded thin; served with lemon juice.

cottage cheese (US) A moist, loose-textured, white cheese made from skimmed cow's milk; sold in various forms such as creamed, small-curd, and large-curd.

cottage pudding (US) Plain cake topped with a sweet sauce.

cotto (It) Cooked.

cotto a vapore (It) Steamed.

cotton candy (US) A confection made from sugar syrup cooked and spun into threads, then rolled around a stick.

cottonseed oil (US) Refined oil from the crushed seed of the cotton plant.

coulibiac de saumon de croûte (Fr) Salmon, rice, and mushrooms, sometimes hard-boiled eggs baked in a rectangular pastry shell. Based on a Russian dish.

coulis (Fr) Strained juice from meat.

coupe aux marrons (Fr) Chestnut dessert.

coupe de fruits frais (Fr) Fruit cup made with fresh fruits.

courgette (Fr) Zucchini squash.

court bouillon (Fr) A prepared liquid in which a food, usually fish or shellfish, is to be poached or boiled; may contain a variety of spices.

court bouillon à la Creole (Fr) A fish stew, usually made with redfish.

couve (Pg) Kale.

couveflor (Pg) Cauliflower.

cozida à portuguesa (Pg) A dish of boiled beef, chicken, and vegetables.

cozido (Pg) Boiled.

cozido no forno (Pg) Baked.

cozze (It) Mussels.

crab (US) A crustacean related to lobsters, crayfish, and shrimp with a large flattened body, small tail, and delicate flesh; many different species ranging in size from tiny to gigantic. Crabs are grouped as to certain qualities of their shells, such as hard-shell or soft-shell, and the stage of shedding. One with a shell that is loose but not yet shed ("buster") is considered the finest. Sold fresh, frozen, or canned and used in a variety of dishes.

crabe (Fr) Crab.

crab Louis (US) A salad of crabmeat topped with a Louis sauce, mayonnaise flavored with chili sauce, whipped cream, chopped green pepper, onions, and lemon juice; served on a bed of lettuce.

cracker (US) A thin, crisp wafer, usually unsweetened.

crackling bread (US) A Southern specialty of corn bread with cracklings mixed in the batter before baking.

cracklings (US) Crisp brown pieces of fat or skin that remain after pork is rendered; eaten as a snack.

cracknel (GB) A hard, brittle biscuit.

cranberry (US) The bright red fruit of an evergreen shrub, member of the heather family, *Vaccinium* species; sharp, acid flavor when raw; used cooked in sweet or savory dishes.

cranberry sauce (US) A red, sweet-sour sauce made with cranberries, water, and sugar; served with fowl and game.

crapaudine, à la (Fr) Describes a pigeon or chicken cut open and broiled; named for a resemblance to toadstools.

crappin (Sc) Stuffing.

crappit heids (Sc) Stuffed heads of fish such as haddock.

crawdad (US) A local term for crayfish.

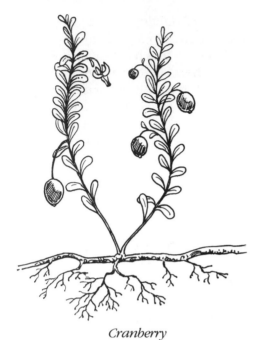

Cranberry

crawfish (US) See **crayfish.**

crayfish (US) A freshwater crustacean resembling a lobster without claws. Only the tail is used; braised, fried, steamed, served in sauce, in chowders and bisques. Also called **crawfish, crawdad.**

cream (US) The concentration of fat globules that collects on top when unhomogenized milk stands. Terms such as *half-and-half, light cream, light whipping cream*, and *heavy cream* are used to specify the amount of liquid milk allowed to dilute the milkfat.

cream, to (US) To beat fat and sugar or fat alone until fluffy and creamy.

cream cheese (US) An uncooked, unripened cow's milk cheese with 35 percent fat; sold in white bricks or whipped; soft with a tangy taste.

cream horn (US) A cornet or cone-shaped puff pastry filled with whipped cream, pastry cream, or jam.

cream of tartar (US) A white crystalline substance, acid potassium tartrate, with a slightly sour taste. It occurs naturally in wine, forming a crust. Decanting wine helps to avoid mixing the particles into the liquid. It is used in baking powder as a leavening agent and may be mixed with bicarbonate of soda as a substitute for the commercial product.

cream puff (US) A crisp, puffy-surfaced pastry that becomes hollow inside when baked. A variety of creamy or savory mixtures may then be inserted into the cavity.

cream puff pastry (US) A smooth, yellow paste made by combining a cooked mixture of flour, water, salt, sugar, and butter with eggs; then piped or spooned out on trays and baked. The many uses made for puff paste include éclairs, profiteroles, and gougères. Also called **choux pastry.**

Crécy, à la (Fr) Prepared with carrots, a specialty of Crécy, in northern France.

crema (It) Cream; custard.

crema catalana (Sp) Similar to crème brûlée.

Crema Dania (Da) A cow's milk cheese; white rind with creamy interior; mild, rich taste similar to Camembert.

crema pastelera al ron (Sp) Sponge cake rolled around a filling of rum cream.

crema pasticcera (It) Pastry cream.

crème (Pg) Cream.

crème (Fr) 1. Cream. 2. Custard. 3. Sweet liqueur.

crème anglaise (Fr) A thin custard used as a sauce, a pastry filling, and a base for chilled desserts. Also called **stirred custard.**

crème brûlée (Fr) A rich dessert pudding made with vanilla and cream; dusted with sugar and broiled; served cold.

crème caramel (Fr) Custard with a burnt sugar flavor.

crème Chantilly (Fr) Whipped cream with castor sugar and vanilla.

crème d'asperges (Fr) Cream of asparagus soup.

crème de tomates (Fr) Cream of tomato soup.

crème de volaille (Fr) Cream of chicken soup.

crème fouettée (Fr) Whipped cream.

crème fraîche (Fr) Very heavy cream with 35 percent butterfat; similar to sour cream but not as acid.

crème glacée (Fr) Ice cream.

Creole (US) Describes a style of cooking native to Louisiana and the Gulf States including French and Spanish cultures; generally depends on butter as a basic fat; typical dishes are the gumbos, jambalayas, and bouillabaisse.

créole, à la (Fr) Prepared with rice.

crêpe (Fr) A thin, delicate pancake made with flour and eggs; other ingredients may be included; often served folded or rolled and filled with sweet or savory mixtures.

crêpes alsaciennes (Fr) Thin pancakes rolled around a filling of jelly and topped with a sugar glaze.

crêpes de homard (Fr) Pancakes stuffed with lobster chunks.

crêpes Suzette (Fr) Thin pancakes made with a batter flavored with curacao and juice of mandarin oranges; usually served flaming.

crêpinette (Fr) Any mixture of minced meat, usually pork, with fat, herbs, spices, and seasonings; wrapped in bacon or a caul; fried, grilled, or roasted.

Crescenza (It) A cow's milk cheese; fresh, uncooked, soft-textured; creamy, mildly tart taste.

crescione (It) Watercress.

crespelle alla fiorentina (It) Thin pancakes rolled around a filling of spinach.

cress (US) Any of a number of plants with pungent or peppery leaves; included are watercress, garden cress, and rocket.

cresson de ruisseau (Fr) Cress.

crevette (Fr) Shrimp.

crevette rose (Fr) Prawn.

crimp, to (US) 1. To seal or decorate the edge of uncooked pastry by pressing with a fork or other tool. 2. To gash the sides of raw fish to allow penetration of a marinade.

crisp (US) Describes food with a crunchy texture.

crisp (GB) Deep-fried potato chips.

crisp, to (US) To warm food in an oven or to place food in chilled liquid or air until crisp.

crni bleb (SC) Dark or black bread.

crni luk (SC) Onions.

crno vino (SC) Red wine.

croccanti (It) Almond cookies or almond brittle; peanut brittle.

crocchetta (It) Croquette.

croissant (Fr) Crescent-shaped roll made with a puff pastry or yeast dough; most often served at breakfast.

croque madame (Fr) Grilled chicken and cheese sandwich.

croquembouche (Fr) An elaborate pyramid of small glazed or caramelized cream puffs.

croque monsieur (Fr) Grilled ham and cheese sandwich.

croquette (Fr) A small, cone-or sausage-shaped cake of minced food held together with a thick sauce; deep-fried so that the surface is crisp and the inside, soft. Meat is often the main ingredient but fish, eggs, vegetables, and fruit are also used.

crosnes (Fr) See **Chinese artichoke.**

crostacei (It) Shellfish.

crostata (It) Sweet pastry tart usually filled with cherry or plum jam.

crostini (It) Appetizers of toasted bread topped with cheese, anchovies, sausage, or chicken livers.

crostini en brodo (It) Croutons in broth.

croustade (Fr) A shell or case of pastry, rice, potato, or toasted bread; used to hold creamed foods including meats, seafood, and vegetables.

croûte, en (Fr) Cooked in a crust.

croûtons (Fr) Small pieces, usually cubes, of cut bread, fried or toasted; used as a garnish or base for soups, salads, stuffings, bread puddings, and other dishes.

crowdie (Sc) A dish made by pouring a cold liquid such as water, milk, or ale over oatmeal.

Crowdie (Sc) A cow's milk cheese; fresh curd combined with butter; white mold rind, white-yellow interior; buttery taste. Served at breakfast with oatcakes.

cru (Fr) Raw.

crudités (Fr) Raw vegetables served as appetizers.

crudo (It, Sp) Raw.

cruller (US) A round cake, similar to a doughnut, made with twisted strips of dough, deep-fried, and topped with sugar or icing.

crumb, to (US) To rub or grind a solid, dry or soft food such as bread to reduce it to small pieces; to coat a food with crumbs.

crumble (GB) A fruit dessert topped with a crumbled mixture of flour, fat, and sugar.

crumpet (GB) A round, somewhat flat, tea cake, with a pitted top surface; baked on a griddle, then toasted; served with butter and jam.

crust (US) 1. A layer of pastry used to top or encase a food. 2. A hardened top formed on cooked food.

csalamádé (Hu) Salad of pickled vegetables.

cseresznye (Hu) Sweet cherries.

csiga (Hu) Snails.

csipetke (Hu) Little pinched dumplings of egg noodle dough; cooked and served with gulyás and paprikás.

csirke (Hu) Chicken.

csirkeleves (Hu) Chicken soup.

csuka (Hu) Pike.

cube, to (US) To cut into cube shape.

cucumber (US) The fruit of a trailing vine, *Cucumis sativus*; many varieties worldwide including thick, stubby, long, prickly, warty and smooth; and rind color from brown to dark green to yellow; used many ways such as pickled, dressed with yogurt or sour cream, stuffed, and cooked with meat.

ćufte (SC) Meatballs.

cuicere alla graticola (It) Grilling.

cuisine (Fr) 1. Kitchen. 2. A style of cooking.

cuisine minceur (Fr) A type of diet or

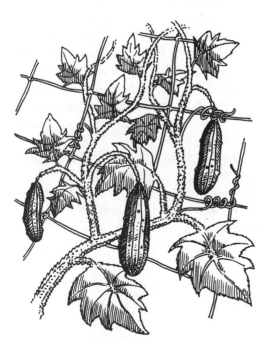

Cucumber

slimmer's cooking devised by French chef Michel Guérard.

cuisses de grenouilles (Fr) Frogs' legs.

cuissot de porc (Fr) Roast of fresh ham.

cuissot de marcassin (Fr) Roast leg of wild pig.

cuit (Fr) Cooked through; well-done (meat).

cuit au four (Fr) Baked.

cukier (Po) Sugar.

cukor (Hu) Sugar.

cukr (Cz) Sugar.

cukrovi (Cz) Cookies.

ćulbastija (SC) Grilled meat.

cullen skink (Sc) A creamy soup of flaked Finnan haddock, onions, mashed potatoes, milk, butter, and seasonings.

cumin (US) The tiny, aromatic seed of a plant, *Cuminum cyminum*, member of the parsley family; a slightly bitter, strong taste; used whole or ground for curry powders and spice mixes; used often in the cooking of Mexico, India, and Southeast Asia.

cuore (It) Heart.

cupcake (US) A small cake baked in a cup-shaped mold.

curd (US) The solid part (casein and fat) of milk coagulated by acids, rennet, or other souring agents; the liquid or whey is drained away. Curd also describes the white part of cauliflower.

cure, to (US) To preserve food, usually in salt or by drying.

currant (US) A berry of the genus *Ribes*, member of the gooseberry family; red and black currants are used in jams and jellies; white currants are used in salads and fruit cups. Currant also describes tiny, dried seedless grapes used in cakes and cookies.

curry (US) Spiced sauces and meat, poultry, or vegetable stew dishes containing characteristic spice blends; native to India; usually served on rice accompanied by a variety of side dishes such as chutney, nuts, and salads.

curry leaves (US) Small, green leaves of a plant, *Murraya koenigii*, used fresh in India and Indonesia in curry dishes; sold dried or powdered in Western countries.

curry powder (US) A blend of ground spices including turmeric, fenugreek, cuminseed, coriander, and red or cayenne pepper. Various other spices such as allspice, ginger, cardamom, fennel, and mace may be used depending on the dish being made.

curry sauce (GB) A sauce made of flour or cornstarch, tomato puree, cooked vegetables, curry powder, spices, and herbs; served with meat, fish, poultry, or eggs.

cuscinetti di vitello (It) Veal roast.

custard (US) A cooked or baked dessert made with eggs, milk, sugar, and flavorings.

custard apple (US) Any of several tropical fruits of the family *Annonaceae*, including the soursop, sweetsop, cherimoya, and pawpaw (not to be confused with papaya also called pawpaw); with scaly skin and soft white to yellow flesh varying in taste from acid to sweet; eaten fresh or used to make ices and drinks.

cut in (US) To work or combine solid fat with dry ingredients using two knives or a wire blender.

cutlet (US) Thin piece of meat, usually veal or lamb, cut from the leg or ribs; used for frying or broiling. Also, a flat croquette of boned, minced meat, poultry or fish.

cuttlefish (US) A member, *Sepia officinalis*, of the cephalopod group of mollusks including squid; an oval body with an internal shell or bone; two tentacles and eight arms attached to the head; lean flesh; used poached, steamed, baked, or fried.

cwikla (Po) A relish of grated cooked beets, horseradish, lemon, and sugar; served with cold meats or sandwiches.

cyanocobalamin (US) See **vitamin B-12.**

cymling (US) See **pattypan.**

cytryna (Po) Lemon.

czekolada (Po) Chocolate.

czosnek (Po) Garlic.

dab (US) A flatfish of the genus *Limanda* found on both sides of the Atlantic Ocean that has white, lean flesh; served baked, fried, and grilled.

dà-bi-mù-yú (Ch) Halibut.

dacca (Ia) A smoked cheese made from cow's and buffalo's milk.

dacquoise (Fr) Layers of baked meringue with ground almonds and hazelnuts; between each layer is a filling of whipped cream or butter cream, flavored with coffee, chocolate, or fruit; topped with confectioners' sugar or more cream.

dadar (In) Omelet.

dadar kepiting (In) Omelet with crab meat.

dadlar (Sw) Dates.

dadler (Nw) Dates.

dagaa (Af–Swahili) Sardines.

daging (In) Meat.

daging masak djahe (In) Braised beef with ginger.

daging redang (In) Meat cooked in coconut milk.

daging rusa (In) Venison.

daging sapi (In) Beef.

daging sapi cincang (In) Ground beef.

daging sapi gulung (In) Stuffed beef rolls.

daging sapi panggang (In) Roast or grilled beef.

dag kavush (Jw) Pickled carp fillets.

dagnje (SC) Mussels.

dahi (Ia) Yogurt.

dahi alu puri (Ia) Crisp little wafers mixed with potato cubes and chickpeas in a yogurt sauce flavored with chilis and tamarind.

dahi bara (Ia) Fried cakes of lentils coated with yogurt sauce; served cold.

dahi bath (Ia) Rice with yogurt.

dà-hwáng (Ch) Rhubarb.

daikon (Jp) A giant, tapering variety of radish, *Raphanus sativus*, with thin skin; crisp, white flesh; sweet taste; widely used in Oriental cooking, Japanese sauces, salads, grated, braised, and pickled. Also called **Japanese white radish.**

daizu (Jp) Soybeans.

dajaj mahshi (Ar) Roast chicken with rice and pine nut stuffing.

dal (Ia) 1. All members of the legume or pulse family, including beans, peas, and lentils. 2. A puree of lentils, which may be thick or smooth and liquid, according to regional preferences.

dalchini (Ia) Cinnamon.

dalia (Ro) A cows' milk cheese.

dal papri (Ia) Lentil crisps served with potatoes, yogurt, onions, and tamarind sauce.

dà-mài (Ch) Barley.

damascos (Pg) Apricots.

Dampfnudeln (Gr) 1. A dessert made of baked rounds of dough served with fruit compote or vanilla ice cream. 2. Steamed noodles usually served with a salad.

damper (Aa) Unleavened bread made from flour and water; often baked barbecue-style.

Damson (US) A species of plum, the fruit

of a tree, *Prunus damascena*; oval shape with a central stone; tough, blue-black skin and yellow-green, sharp-flavored flesh; used in cooked dishes and in preserves.

Damwildkeule (Gr) Roast leg of venison.

dana (Tr) Veal.

Danbo (Da) A cow's milk, Swiss-style cheese; semifirm texture with holes; creamy color and mild, buttery taste; sometimes contains caraway seeds.

dàn-bù-dīng (Ch) Custard.

dandelion (US) Any plant of the genus *Taraxacum* that grows wild in many regions of the world. The roots are dried, roasted, and used as a coffee substitute; the leaves are eaten cooked or in salads.

dandelion greens (US) Leaves of dandelions, often grown in a hothouse for culinary use with a larger, smoother leaf than wild variety and a milder flavor similar to escarole; used as other leafy greens.

dango (Jp) Dumplings.

dàn hwā tāng (Ch) Egg drop soup.

Danish Blue (Da) A cows' milk cheese, white streaked with blue veins, a crumbly texture, and a piquant flavor.

Danish pastry (US) A specialty of Denmark known worldwide; a yeasted puff pastry baked in a variety of shapes including pinwheels, crescents, snails, stars, and cockscombs.

Danska weinerbrød (Da) Literally, "Danish Vienna bread"; the term for Danish pastry.

Dansk leverpostej (Da) A liver pâté made with calfs' liver; served with potatoes or sliced when cold and used as topping for open-face sandwiches.

daragaluska (Hu) Small semolina and egg dumplings.

darált marbahús (Hu) Ground beef.

dariole (Fr) 1. A small, bucket-shaped mold used for making caramel creams and madeleines. 2. The name of the tart or other food item prepared in the mold.

Darjeeling (Ia) A fine, black tea grown in India.

darne (Fr) A fish steak, cut crosswise, with a bone; sautéed, braised, or grilled.

darne de saumon (Fr) Thick slice of salmon.

dartois (Fr) A savory or sweet filling between strips of puff pastry.

dasheen (US) A tropical tuber of the genus *Colocasia* with brown skin and bland-flavored, white flesh; taro root. Flavor combines with chestnut and potato. Said to have been named from the French phrase "de Chine" or "from China."

dashi (Jp) A light broth prepared by steeping dried kelp and bonito flakes in hot water; used as soup, cooking stock, or as a sauce base.

dà-syār (Ch) Prawns.

date (US) A small elongated fruit of a palm, genus *Phoenix*, with a thin central stone; intensely sweet flesh; sticky when dried and usually brown when sold packaged; eaten as a sweet or may be added to desserts and sweet or savory dishes.

datle (Cz) Dates.

datte (Fr) Date.

Datteln (Gr) Dates.

dattero (It) Date.

dattero di mare (It) Mussels.

daube (Fr) A rich casserole of slow-cooked meat, usually beef, in red wine with vegetables, herbs, and stock.

daube de moreton (Fr) Mutton stewed with herbs and vegetables.

daubiére (Fr) An earthenware, lidded casserole traditionally sealed shut with a flour paste to retain the juices of daube.

daumont, à la (Fr) Describes a garnish for fish that includes mushrooms, roes, crayfish tails, and sometimes quenelles of fish.

daun selada (In) Lettuce.

daun sup (In) Parsley.

dauphine, à la (Fr) Pureed vegetables, such as potatoes, eggplant, or celery root, shaped into balls and deep-fried; served with meat and used as a garnish; named for the Dauphiné region of France.

daurade (Fr) See **sea bream.**

debreceni rántotta (Hu) Omelet with smoked sausage and green peppers.

deep-fry (US) To submerge food in hot fat to cook until crisp.

deglaze (US) To add stock, wine, or water to the particles left in a pan after browning or cooking foods and reduce to make a brown sauce.

del giorno (It) Of the day.

délices (Fr) "Giving delight"; a term applied to various desserts, pastries, and sweetmeats.

Delmonico (US) Usually a rib steak or a top loin cut of beef.

demerara sugar (GB) Brown crystal-ized sugar from the West Indies; used to sweeten some desserts, breakfast cereals, and tea or coffee.

demi-deuil (Fr) Literally, "half-mourning"; describes dishes containing black and white ingredients, such as chicken stuffed with truffles.

demi-glace (Fr) Literally, "half-glaze"; a thick, brown sauce made by roasting veal bones with vegetables and spices; used in some French sauces.

demi-tasse (Fr) A small cup, usually of strong, black coffee.

demoiselles de Maine (Fr) Maine lobsters.

dendê (Pg) A thick orange oil of palm nut, used mainly in Brazil.

dendeng pedas (In) Crisp beef strips in a spicy sauce.

dendeng ragi (In) Crisp beef with grated coconut.

dengaku (Jp) Eggplant coated with tofu and coated with sesame seeds skewered on bamboo slats and broiled.

dent-de-lion (Fr) Dandelion.

dentelle (Fr) Literally, "lacework"; thin cookies rolled into a cup or other shape.

Derby (GB) A cow's milk, Cheddar-style cheese with an orange interior, a flaky texture and mild taste. Sage Derby has a flavor and color of the herb.

derma (US) A beef casing or sausage casing into which various ingredients are stuffed.

désossé (Fr) Boneless.

deviled (US) A food marinated in or combined with a spicy, hot mixture, such as mustard, Worcestershire sauce, and vinegar.

deviled ham (US) A variation of English potted ham; a homemade version uses minced or ground country ham cooked with cream, butter, flour, red pepper, and dry mustard then chilled.

dextrose (US) A white, free-flowing sweetener made from cornstarch with fewer calories than sugar; used in beer and as a binder in sausages.

dhania (Ia) Coriander.

dhansak (Ia) A casserole of breast of lamb and tripe, lentils, and vegetables such as pumpkin, tomatoes, and eggplant cooked to a puree with a spice mix (masala).

dhoka (Ia) A steamed or fried lentil cake.

dhuli urad (Ia) Yellow lentils.

diable, à la (Fr) Deviled; bread crumbed, grilled meat, usually chicken, served with a diable sauce.

diable, sauce à la (Fr) Spicy sauce of white wine, vinegar, shallots, cayenne pepper, and sometimes mustard.

diabloki (Po) Cheese croutons.

diablotins de fromage (Fr) Grilled, small bread rounds spread with cheese.

dia rau song (Vt) Vegetable platter.

diavolo, alla (It) Deviled; seasoned with red or black pepper, usually grilled meat.

dibakar (In) Baked or roasted.

dibs (Ar) A term for various syrups including a thick syrup of dates; molasses; and pomegranate syrup; used in layered bread dishes and in a bread salad.

dice (US) To cut shreds or strips of food smaller. If the pieces are about ¼ inch in size, they may be called dice. Larger pieces are identified as cubes.

Dicke Bohnen (Gr) Broad beans.

diente de ajo (Sp) Garlic clove.

dieppoise, à la (Fr) Describes a method of cooking fish in white wine and serving with a mussel garnish and a white wine sauce.

dietary fiber (US) Edible material, the most important from whole grains, which passes through the digestive tract and is indigestible.

digestif (Fr) An after-dinner liqueur.

digestive biscuit (GB) Lightly sweetened, whole wheat cookie; often served with butter and cheese and used crushed as a base for cheesecake.

digestivi (It) Liqueurs, brandies.

dijonnaise, sauce (Fr) Egg yolks, Dijon mustard, salt, and pepper beaten with oil and lemon juice to the consistency of mayonnaise.

dil (Tr) Tongue.

dil baliği (Tr) Sole.

dill (US) An annual herb, *Anethum graveolens*, used in pickling and with fish dishes and cucumber salads.

dillkött (Sw) Boiled veal with dill sauce.

dilly beans (US) Green beans pickled in salt, white vinegar, dill seed, mustard seed, and pepper.

di mare (It) Seafood with lemon juice dressing.

dim sum (Ch) Literally, "little heart"; the Chinese snack food, tiny sweet or savory dumplings, variously filled with chicken, crab, pork, and many other morsels; steamed, deep-fried, or baked.

dinde (Fr) Turkey hen.

dinde rôtie (Fr) Roast turkey.

dindonneau (Fr) Young turkey.

ding syang (Ch) Cloves.

dinja (SC) Canteloupe.

dinnye (Hu) Melon.

diós kifli (Hu) Pastry crescents filled with walnut paste.

diós metélt (Hu) Walnut noodles.

diples (Gk) Fried dough shaped like wide ribbons and covered with almonds and walnuts.

diplomat (Fr) A pudding of Bavarian cream and apricot preserves; or a sauce normande made with white wine, lobster and lobster butter, truffles, and Cognac.

dirty rice (US) A Cajun-Creole dish in which cooked long-grain rice is darkened with sautéed ground beef and pork, chicken livers, onions, celery, parsley, and garlic.

disznóbús (Hu) Pork.

disznókocsonya (Hu) Aspic of pig knuckles, hooves, and ears; requires a day to cook and a night to jell.

ditali (It) "Thimbles"; macaroni cut in lengths shorter than elbow macaroni; served with meat sauce.

divinity (US) A candy made with egg whites, sugar, corn syrup, nuts, candied fruit, and vanilla.

divljač (SC) Game; venison.

djuveč (SC) A rich casserole of rice, many vegetables, and cubed meat.

dobin mushi (Jp) Mushrooms and chicken steamed in an earthenware pot.

dobostorta (Hu) A seven-layer sponge cake with chocolate cream between each layer and covering the whole; topped with a glaze of caramel.

dobrada (Pg) Tripe with beans and sausage.

doce (Pg) Candy; confection, sweet.

dodine de canard (Fr) Boned duck with the skin intact, stuffed with chopped pork, veal, slices of the duck breast, mushrooms, and seasonings and braised in white wine.

doen jang (Kr) Red pepper and leek miso.

dogfish (US) A strongly flavored saltwater fish, genus _Scyliohinus_, with a texture like codfish and fat, sweet flaky flesh; served in soups or stews to which cereals or pastas have been added; also used in English fish and chips.

dojrzale oliwki (Po) Ripe olives.

dolce (It) Sweet.

dolce antico (It) A cake with fruits, nuts, and honey spiraled between leaves of serrated pastry.

dolce e agro (It) Sweet and sour.

dolce Maria (It) A round chocolate cake served in an espresso sauce.

dolci (It) Pastry and desserts, sweetmeats, cakes.

dolma (Gk, Tr) A vine leaf or other leaf, such as cabbage or fig, stuffed with cooked rice and minced lamb and braised.

dolmadakia (Gk) Rolled grape leaves filled with ground meat and rice.

dolmades (Gk) Stuffed vine leaves.

domashniaia lapsha (Rs) Homemade noodles.

domates (Tr) Tomatoes.

domatesli fasulye (Tr) Stewed white

beans covered with thick tomato sauce.

domates yemistes me rizi (Gk) Baked tomatoes stuffed with mint and garlic-flavored rice.

domatorizo pilafi (Gk) A pilaf containing puréed tomatoes.

domba (In) Lamb.

domburi (Jp) A bowl with an individual serving of soup or other food.

dôme blanche (Fr) A dessert of white and dark chocolate mousse and chocolate genoise constructed with a cupola-shaped top.

dom ke kai (Th) A soup of shredded chicken, coconut milk, lemon grass, and lemon juice.

domuz (Tr) Pork.

domyoji ko (Jp) Rice flour nuggets.

dondurma (Tr) A kind of Turkish sherbet of frozen fruit juice or frozen milk.

doner (Gk) Gyro made with lamb.

döner kebabi (Tr) Slices of lamb marinated in oil, herbs and spices, and layers of ground lamb broiled on a vertical spit. As the outside layer cooks, it is cut off and served.

doopiaza (Ia) Literally, "two onion"; a dish with many onions prepared in two ways, minced and sliced.

doree (Fr) Any food that has been given a golden tint in cooking.

doreshingu (Jp) Salad dressing.

doriani (Af–Swahili) Durian.

Dorsch (Gr) Codfish.

dort (Cz) Torte.

dosas (Ia) Pancakes made with ground rice and lentils; dough ferments overnight before cooking in oil. The pancakes are stuffed with curried vegetables and served with chutney.

dot, to (US) To scatter bits of butter or other seasonings over the surface of food to be cooked.

dòu (Ch) Beans.

double consommé (US) Consommé that has been cooked down twice to increase flavor.

double cream (GB) A rich cream with a butterfat content of 55 percent; whipping cream.

double cream cheese (US) A fresh cheese, such as cottage cheese, that has been enriched with more cream, also increasing the butterfat content by more than 60 percent. Gervais is an example.

dòu-fú (Ch) Soybean curd.

dòu-fú chīng-tsài tāng (Ch) Soybean curd and vegetable soup.

dough (US) A pliable, combined mixture of dry ingredients including flour or meal, sometimes sugar or salt or both and usually a leavening agent, with liquids, such as water, milk, and eggs. May be worked with the hands.

doughboy (US) A pan-fried or deep-fried dumpling.

doughnut (US) A deep-fried cake of sweetened, leavened dough, usually ring-shaped but may be other shapes. May be filled with jelly or custard and topped with frosting.

doughnut hole (US) A small fried doughnut without a hole.

dòu-shā bāu (Ch) Steamed buns filled with black bean jam.

doux (Fr) Sweet; fragrant.

dòu-yá-tsài (Ch) Bean sprouts.

Dover sole (GB) Considered finest flatfish of the sole family; must be caught off coast of England; white, lean flesh.

dragées (Fr) Almonds or chocolate drops with a hard coating of sugar; small sugar balls coated with silver.

draw, to (US) 1. To remove the entrails of poultry or game birds. 2. To extract the essence of an item, as in steeping tea.

drawn butter (US) 1. Clarified butter to which chopped herbs, lemon juice, or seasonings may be added. 2. Melted butter to which flour and stock or hot water has been added to make a sauce.

dredge, to (US) To coat with flour or crumbs prior to frying.

dress, to (US) 1. To clean and ready fowl, game, or fish for cooking, such as pluck, scale, truss, or trim. 2. To add dressing to a salad. 3. To garnish a dish.

dressing (US) 1. Any sauce for a salad, such as oil and vinegar or mayonnaise. 2. Stuffing for poultry, fish, or meat.

dried meat (US) Strips of cured, salted, usually air-dried meat, such as beef or game. Also called **biltong, jerky.**

drizzle (US) To pour melted fat or other liquids in a thin stream.

drop biscuit (US) Biscuits made by dropping tablespoons of dough onto a greased baking sheet.

drozhzhevoe testo (Rs) Yeast dough.

dršťková polévka (Cz) Tripe soup; pepper pot.

druer (Nw) Grapes.

druiven (Du) Grapes.

drum (US) Any of many species of saltwater fish related to croakers that make a drumming sound. Drums vary considerably in size and are sold whole, as fillets, and steaks. Fried steaks may be served with a spicy Chinese pepper sauce.

drupe fruit (US) A term for soft, fleshy fruit, such as the peach, plum, or cherry, with thin skins and hard-shelled stones or seeds.

dry curries (Ia) Curries prepared by allowing moisture to evaporate after the food is cooked tender; a coating of spices remains on the ingredients; usually served with unleavened bread.

dry milk (US) Powder or granules made from homogenized whole or skim milk with the moisture removed by heat. It is reconstituted with water or may fortify liquid milk. Used as a beverage or in cooking. Dried skim milk is high in protein and low in fat.

du Barry, à la (Fr) Garnished with florets of cauliflower; named for the mistress of King Louis XV.

Dublin coddle (Ir) A stew of onions, potatoes, sausage, and bacon; served with soda bread.

duchesse (Fr) Pastry shells filled with sweet or savory mixtures and served as appetizers.

duchesse potatoes (US) Puréed potatoes, egg yolks, and butter piped into various shapes and baked; served with meat and used as a garnish.

duck (US) Edible swimming birds, family Anatidae, with webbed feet, a broad flat beak, and dark, mild-flavored meat. Often stuffed and roasted. Among the more important breeds are the Long Island duck of Chinese ancestry, the English Aylesbury, the Nantes duck of France, the Muscovy duck from South America, and the mallard, wild or domesticated.

duck ham (US) Salt-cured duck breast.

duck sauce (US) See **plum sauce.**

due (Nw) Pigeon.

duff (GB) Pudding made with flour, eggs, seasonings, and often fruit; steamed or boiled in a cloth bag.

dugléré, à la (Fr) With a cream sauce made with wine and tomatoes; served with sole and other white-fleshed fish.

dulce (Sp) Sweetmeat; confection; candied fruit.

dulce de elote (Sp) A stew of green corn with milk and sugar.

dulce de higos (Sp) Green figs stewed with molasses or brown sugar and flavored with cinnamon.

dulse (US) An edible seaweed, *Rhodymenia palmata*, found on both Atlantic and Pacific coasts; with thin fronds ranging in color from yellow-green to brown; remains soft when dry and has a briny, spinachlike flavor; used in salads, soups, seafood dishes, and as a condiment.

dum (Ia) A form of steam cooking in which the pot is placed on hot charcoal with more charcoal on the pot lid.

dum alu (Ia) "Perfumed potatoes"; steamed potatoes with onion, yogurt, coconut, ginger, almonds, cumin, coriander, cardamom, nutmeg, ground chili pepper, garlic, and turmeric.

dumplings (US) Balls of dough often made with seasoned flour, water, and fat; cooked in stock, soup, water, or stews.

Dundee cake (Sc) A fruit cake flavored with orange juice and containing citrus peel; topped with rings of almonds.

Dungeness crab (US) The favored crab, *Cancer magister*, with large legs and claws containing lean, slightly pink meat; boiled whole, the shell becomes red; caught off the Pacific coast.

dūng-gǔ (Ch) Mushrooms.

dūng-gwā (Ch) Winter melon.

Dunlop (Sc) A cow's milk, Cheddar-type cheese; mellow, buttery taste; good with oatcakes.

durazno (Sp) Peach.

durazno en crema (Sp) Peaches in cream.

durian (In) An oval, yellow, spiky-skinned fruit similar to jackfruit, with a delicious taste but famous for its putrid aroma; used in sweet and savory dishes. The large, edible seeds are prepared like chestnuts.

durum wheat (US) A variety of hard wheat used in the production of semolina flour; high in protein and gluten.

duru-ten (Jp) Potato patties fried tempura-style.

duruwakashii (Jp) An Okinawan dish of mashed potatoes mixed with pork, fish cake, and shiitake mushrooms.

Duse, à la (Fr) Large joints of meat served with a garnish of tomatoes,

French beans, and potatoes; named in honor of Eleonora Duse, the great Italian actress.

dušené (Cz) Sautéed.

dust, to (US) To cover food lightly with flour, sugar, or other similar ingredient.

duva (Sw) Pigeon.

duxelles (Fr) Chopped mushrooms browned in butter and oil; mixed with onions, shallots, wine, and parsley; used as a sauce or stuffing.

dyăn-syīn (Ch) Pastry.

dyàu-wèi-pin (Ch) Condiments.

dybbavsreje (Da) A deep-water prawn.

dynia (Po) Pumpkin.

dyrestek (Nw) Roast venison; reindeer or elk meat.

dzău-dz (Ch) Dates.

džem (SC, Cz) Jam.

dzieczyzna (Po) Game.

džigerica (SC) Liver.

dzsem (Hu) Jam.

é (Ch) Goose.

e (It) And.

ears (US) The grain clusters of a cereal, such as corn, wheat, or rye, including both the kernels and their supporting structures; also, the ears of animals, usually pigs or calves, used in cooking.

earshell (US) See **abalone.**

eau (Fr) Water.

eau-de-vie (Fr) Literally, "water of life"; any of a variety of fragrant fruit liqueurs or dry fruit brandies made by distillers in the Alsace region; usually 80 to 90 proof.

eau-de-vie de poire (Fr) Ripe pears in brandy.

ebi (In) Dried shrimp.

ebi (Jp) Shrimp; prawn.

ebi furai (Jp) Fried shrimp.

ebi-sembei (Jp) Rice cake with shrimp.

ebi suimono (Jp) Clear soup with shrimp.

écarlate, à l' (Fr) Literally, "in the scarlet"; describes food that has been prepared in a way that colors it red, such as a butter mixed with crayfish; or a dish served with a tomato sauce; or with a process for pickled pork or beef, often beef tongue.

Ecclefechan tart (Sc) A pastry made with cream, eggs, currants, raisins, apples, and syrup.

Eccles cake (GB) A glazed, crunchy cake made with currants, chopped peel, butter, brown sugar, and spice; similar to Banbury cakes, but larger; originated in Eccles, Lancashire.

ecet (Hu) Vinegar.

échalote (Fr) Shallot.

echaude (Fr) Small crisp biscuit, leavened or unleavened.

éclade (Fr) A dish made with mussels.

éclair (Fr) Small, log-shaped puff pastry filled with cream or custard; topped with icing.

écossaise, à l' (Fr) In the style of Scotland; usually Scotch broth or an egg dish with salmon.

écrevisse (Fr) Freshwater crayfish; crawfish.

écrevisses à la nage (Fr) "Swimming crayfish"; freshwater crayfish served in the shells.

Edam (US) A Dutch cow's milk cheese made in Edam; ball-shaped, firm, yellow with a red wax coating; smooth, mellow taste that sharpens with age.

edamame (Jp) A type of green soybean; cooked in the pod or as a combination of shelled beans and rice.

Edammer kaas (Du) Edam cheese.

eddik (Nw) Vinegar.

eddike (Da) Vinegar.

Edelkastanie (Gr) Chestnut.

édeskömény (Hu) Caraway seeds.

édesnemes (Hu) "Noble sweet"; paprika.

édességet (Hu) Dessert.

Edinburgh fog (Sc) A dessert made with macaroons, chopped almonds, and sweetened whipped cream flavored with vanilla.

EDTA (US) Ethylenediaminetetraacetate; an additive used in mayonnaise and other processed foods for preventing trace metals from causing rancidity.

eel (US) A sweet-flavored fish, genus _Anguilla_, with a long, snakelike shape. Fresh eels are grilled, baked, pickled, and smoked. Also called **aal, anguille.**

eend (Du) Duck; fowl.

efterrätt (Sw) Dessert, sweet.

egg (US) A shelled ovum of a bird; when used for food, usually from a domesticated fowl, although eggs of wild birds such as quail may also be eaten. Eggs are sized by weight, averaged by the dozen, and are graded by their physical condition. The yellow yolk makes up about a third of the weight and is the most nutritious part. Egg white, over half the weight, consists of about 9 percent protein.

egg bløtkokt (Nw) Soft-boiled egg.

egg bread (US) An unleavened corn bread.

egg butter (US) A Finnish spread of butter, salt, ground ginger, and chopped hard-cooked eggs.

egg cream (US) A confection made from chocolate syrup, milk, and seltzer; the

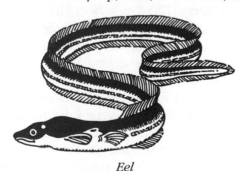

Eel

foam on top resembles beaten egg white; a popular New York City soda fountain drink.

eggerøre (Nw) Scrambled egg.

egg flip (GB) A hot drink with eggs, beer, and spirits, similar to eggnog.

egg foo yung (US) An American version of a Chinese dish (fú-rŭng dàn); omelet with chopped meat or seafood and Chinese vegetables; flavored with soy sauce.

egg forlorne (Nw) Poached egg.

egg hårdkokt (Nw) Hard-boiled egg.

eggnog (US) A beverage made with eggs and spirits traditionally served at Christmas.

egg og bacon (Nw) Egg and bacon.

egg pie (GB) An egg custard with bacon in a crust; similar to quiche.

eggplant (US) The egg-shaped fruit of a plant in the nightshade family, _Solanum melongena_, native to India; with purple-black skin and white, spongy flesh; served boiled, sautéed, or baked. Also called **aubergine.**

eggplant caviar (US) See **ikra iz baklazhanov.**

egg roll (US) Small, thin, egg-noodle wrappers rolled around fillings of chopped vegetables, meat, poultry, or seafood, and deep-fried. Also called **spring roll (chwūn-jywăn).**

eggs Benedict (US) English muffins topped with a slice of ham, poached eggs, and hollandaise sauce. The name is reported to have come from the creation of the dish for a customer of Delmonico's Restaurant in New York City.

eggs Sardou (US) A dish of poached eggs, chopped ham, artichoke hearts, anchovies, truffle, and hollandaise sauce. The dish was created and named for the nineteenth century French playwright Victorien Sardou at Antoine's restaurant in New Orleans.

egg wash (US) A mixture of water, sometimes milk or cream, beaten with egg yolk or egg white; used as a glaze on bread or pastry, and as a glue between pieces of pastry or as a base for seeds or sugar. Also called **wash.**

églefin (Fr) Haddock.

egres (Hu) Gooseberries.

ebu (Pl) Pink snapper.

Eier (Gr) Eggs.

eieren (Du) Eggs.

eieren met ham (Du) Ham and eggs.

eieren met spek (Du) Bacon and eggs.

eierenpannekoeken (Du) Pancakes.

Eierfrüchte (Gr) Eggplant.

eiergebak (Du) Eggs mixed with ground meat.

Eierkrem (Gr) Custard.

Eierkuchen (Gr) Pancakes; sweet omelets.

Eier mit Speck (Gr) Eggs and bacon.

Eiersalat (Gr) Egg salad.

Eierschaum (Gr) Whipped custard of egg yolks and sugar, flavored with wine; similar to **zabaglione.**

Eierspeisen (Gr) Egg dishes.

Einbrenn (Gr) Flour cooked in fat until mixture is golden; used to give color, flavor, and thickening in soups and stews.

Eingemachte (Gr) Jam; preserves; pickles.

eiró (Pg) Small eel.

Eis (Gr) Ice; ice cream. Also called **Eiskrem.**

Eisen (Gr) Iron.

Eisenbein (Gr) Ham hocks; often pickled and served with sauerkraut and mashed potatoes.

Eiskrem (Gr) Ice cream. Also called **Eis.**

Eistee (Gr) Iced tea.

Eistorte (Gr) Ice cream cake.

Eiswein (Gr) Ice wine; made from grapes picked and pressed while frozen.

ejotes (Mx) String beans; green beans.

ejotes con limon (Mx) String beans with lemon juice.

ekmek (Tr) Bread.

ekmek kataifi (Gk) Honeyed, two-layer pastry with shredded wheat, custard, and whipped cream.

ekşi (Tr) Sour.

elaichi (Ia) Cardamom.

elaichi murgh (Ia) Braised chicken with cardamom.

Elbo (Da) A yellow cow's milk cheese; Swiss-like; mild, buttery taste.

elbow pastas (US) Semicircles of any hollow tubular pasta; may be small or large, smooth or ridged. Elbow macaroni is most common.

elderberry (US) A member of the honeysuckle family, *Sambucus canadensis*, with edible flowers and fruit. The flowers may be deep-fried in batter; the fruit is used in chutney, soup, pies, jelly, and in making elderberry wine.

election cake (US) A raised fruitcake. The name comes from a New England tradition of serving cake on election day. Also called **Hartford election cake.**

Elefantenlaus (Gr) Cashew nuts.

eleoladho (Gk) Olive oil.

elft (Du) Shad.

elies (Gk) Olives.

ellinikous mezedhes (Gk) Hors d'oeuvres.

elma (Tr) Apple.

elote asado (Mx) Grilled, young corn ears.

elvers (US) The young of eels; considered a delicacy; boiled and pressed into eel cakes.

embe (Af–Swahili) Mango.

émincés (Fr) Leftover meat sliced thin and reheated in the oven with a cream and white wine sauce.

Emmentaler (Gr–Switzerland) A cow's milk cheese; brown-yellow rind; pale yellow interior with many large holes; mild, nutty taste.

empada (Pg) Meat pie.

empada de galinha (Pg) Chicken pie.

empal (In) Fried meat.

empalpedas (In) Fried beef with spices.

empanada (Sp) A filled pastry turnover; the dough is cut in a circle, filled with a sweet or savory mixture, folded over and fried or sometimes baked.

empanada de pulpo (Sp) A pie or turnover filled with cooked octopus.

empanada de verde (Sp) Green turnovers; made with plantains.

empanaditas (Sp) Small turnovers or meat pies.

empanaditas de queso (Sp) Deep-fried cheese turnovers.

empanado (Sp) Breaded.

emulsifier (US) A substance added to food to keep oils and water together. Lecithin, present in egg yolk, is a natural emulsifier, thus the use of egg yolk to keep sauces from separating. Paprika and dry mustard are also used.

emulsion (US) A mixture of two unlike liquids that would normally repel each other held together by the use of an emulsifier. Mayonnaise is an emulsion.

en bianco (It) Sautéed in white wine, onion, and mushrooms.

en bordure (Fr) Served with a border, commonly of duchesse potatoes.

enchilada (Sp) A Mexican-American dish of a tortilla stuffed with a mixture of meats, chorizo sausage, cheese, and chili pepper sauce; often served with refried beans.

en cocotte (Fr) Simmered or slow-cooked in an oven-proof, two-handled, round pan with a well-fitting lid.

en croûte (Fr) Baked in a pastry crust.

encurtidos (Sp) Pickles.

endive (US) A salad herb, *Cicorium endiva*, with several forms, including escarole and Belgian endive. It belongs to the same genus as chicory. See **Belgian endive, chicory, escarole.**

endive à la normande (Fr) Endives simmered in cream.

endive belge (Fr) Belgian endive.

endōmame (Jp) Peas.

eneldo (Sp) Dill.

enginar (Tr) Artichoke.

Englischer Kuchen (Gr) Pound cake.

English muffin (US) A round, flat muffin made with flour, malted barley, farina, yeast, and vinegar. Despite its name, it is only English through its originator, Samuel Bath Thomas, who is reported to have used his English mother's recipe in making muffins at his New York bakery in 1880.

English walnut (US) See **walnut.**

enguia (Pg) Large eel.

en meurette (Fr) In a red-wine-based sauce.

enoki (Jp) Cream-colored mushrooms with long stems and tiny caps; native to Japan where they are grown on the enoki tree; exported fresh, they have a mild flavor and crisp texture.

enriched products (US) Describes products such as flour, bread, rice, pasta, and milk to which vitamins, calcium, or iron have been added within the limits specified by the U.S. Food and Drug Administration.

enrollados (Mx) A batter-dipped, deep-fried taco.

ensalada (Sp) Salad.

ensalada variada (Sp) Mixed green salad.

Ente (Gr) Duck.

entrecosto de porco (Pg) Spareribs.

entrecôte (Fr) Literally, "between the ribs"; the steak cut from between two ribs of beef; usually grilled or fried.

entrecôte à la Bordelaise (Fr) Beef rib steak in red wine sauce.

entrecôte aux cèpes (Fr) Grilled beef rib steak served with mushrooms.

entrecôte marchand de vin (Fr) Beef rib steak cooked with red wine and shallots.

entrée (Fr) A dish served essentially as the third course, after the hors d'oeuvres and the fish course; in England, it is a prepared dish served before the roast; in the United States, it is the principal dish of a meal, the main course.

entremets (Fr) Literally, "between foods"; the dessert course served after cheese.

épaule (Fr) Shoulder.

épaule d'agneau (Fr) Lamb shoulder.

épaule de veau (Fr) Shoulder of veal.

epazote (Mx) A tall pungent herb, with serrated leaves, popular in Mexico for seasoning black beans, soups, and tortilla fillings. Also called **Mexican tea, wormseed.**

éperlan (Fr) See **smelt.**

épice (Fr) Spice.

épigramme (Fr) Two cuts of lamb, a chop and a breast slice, dipped in egg and bread crumbs and fried.

épinard (Fr) Spinach.

épinards au beurre noisette (Fr) Spinach in browned butter.

eple (Nw) Apple.

eplekake (Nw) Apple pie.

equatorial cuisine (US) Foods and cooking techniques of the Caribbean and other warm climates; spicy foods and grilled foods are common.

érable (Fr) Maple.

eramaahiekhaa (Fi) Literally, "wilderness sands"; browned butter cookies.

erbe (It) Herbs.

Erbsen (Gr) Peas.

Erbsensuppe mit saurer Sahne (Gr) Green pea soup with sour cream.

Erdäpfel (Gr–Austria) Potatoes.

Erdartischocke (Gr) Jerusalem artichoke.

Erdbeeren (Gr) Strawberries.

erik (Tr) Plum.

eros (Hu) Hot paprika.

ersatz food (US) Food products created to resemble natural foods, such as textured vegetable protein molded and colored to look like bacon strips.

erter (Nw) Peas.

ervilhas (Pg) Peas.

erwtensoep (Du) A thick, green pea soup made with diced salt pork, sometimes spareribs, pig's feet, sausage, potatoes, and leeks.

erwtjes (Du) Peas.

Esau (Fr) Any dish containing pureed lentils; often a thick soup. Named for a biblical figure who sold his birthright for potage.

Esbare Muscheln (Gr) Clams.

escabeche (Sp) Fish, poultry, and game that have been marinated in vinegar with herbs and spices, often with slices of lemon, lime, onion, and garlic; fried fish preserved in vinegar.

escalibada (Sp) A dish of braised, slivered eggplant with onions, red bell peppers, and zucchini.

escalopes (Fr) Scallops; boneless slices of meat or fish, slightly flattened and fried in butter or any fat.

escalopes de bar à l'oseille (Fr) Scaloppine of bass with sorrel.

escalopes de sanglier (Fr) Cutlets of wild boar.

escalopes de saumon à l'oseille (Fr) Slices of salmon with sorrel.

escalopes de ternera (Sp) Veal cutlets.

escalopes de veau (Fr) Veal cutlets.

escalopes de veau cordon bleu (Fr) Thin slices of boneless veal with ham and cheese.

escalopes de veau sautées à l'estragon (Fr) Veal scallops with tarragon.

escargots (Fr) Snails; usually removed from the shells, cooked in wine, stuffed back in shells filled with a butter sauce, and then baked.

escargots à la bourguignonne (Fr) Snails baked in their shells; served with garlic butter.

escargots de Bourgogne (Fr) Snails of Burgundy; famous for their succulence.

escarola alla monachina (It) Escarole "nun's style"; a dish of steamed greens baked under a mixture of bread crumbs, raisins, pine nuts, capers, oregano, parsley, and anchovies.

escarole (US) A form of endive (chicory); curly, crisp green leaves around a central heart of white to yellow leaves; used raw in salads or cooked like spinach.

espadarte (Pg) Swordfish.

espadilha (Pg) Sprat.

espadin (Sp) Sprat.

espadon (Fr) Swordfish.

espagnole, à l' (Fr) In the Spanish style; dishes containing or garnished with tomatoes, sweet peppers, onions, and garlic; often fried in olive oil.

espagnole, sauce (Fr) A basic brown sauce made from meat or poultry stock, a brown roux, and mixed vegetables with tomato puree, and seasonings; strained after simmering for several hours and used as a basis for many other brown sauces.

espargos (Pg) Asparagus.

espárragos (Sp) Asparagus.

espárragos con tomatillos (Mx) A salad of cooked asparagus spears topped with diced raw tomatillos, tomatoes, and grated cheese.

especialidade da casa (Pg) Specialty of the house.

espinaca (Sp) Spinach.

espinacas a la Catalana (Sp) Catalonia-style spinach with pine nuts and raisins.

espinafre (Pg) Spinach.

espresso (It) Literally, "pressed out"; a concentrated, dark, bitter Italian coffee made in a special espresso machine by forcing steam through freshly ground beans.

esprot (Fr) Sprat.

essence (US) The concentrated juice, flavor, or essential oil of a substance obtained by some method of extraction such as distillation. Certain flavored waters such as orange-flower water and rose water are essences. See also **extracts.**

essential amino acids (US) Amino acids contained in protein foods that must be included in the diet to maintain optimum health. They are: isoleucine, leucine, lysine, methionine, phenylalanine, threonine, tryptophan, valine, and arginine. See also **complete protein.**

essential fatty acids (US) See **fatty acids.**

essential nutrient (US) Any substance necessary for normal development and health maintenance that must be supplied in the diet. Examples include the essential amino acids, essential fatty acids, and certain vitamins and minerals.

essential oils (US) Strong-flavored, oily substances extracted from the various parts of certain plants; examples include citrus oil, almond oil, and peppermint oil; used for flavoring.

Essig (Gr) Vinegar.

Essigsäure (Gr) Acetic acid.

Esterhazy Rostbraten (Gr) Roast beef named for an aristocratic family of the Austro-Hungarian Empire, sixteenth to nineteenth century nobles and intellectuals.

estofado (Sp) Meat stew; braised meat or poultry coated in flour; usually served in a sauce of tomatoes, onions, and garlic.

estofado almendrado de pollo (Sp) Braised chicken in a sweet chili and almond sauce.

estofado de carnero (Sp) Lamb stew.

estouffade (Fr) A dish that is slowly stewed; a brown stock used to dilute brown sauces and moisten braised dishes.

estouffade de boeuf (Fr) Stew with braised beef in wine.

estragon (Fr) Tarragon.

esturgeon (Fr) Sturgeon.

esturión (Sp) Sturgeon.

esturjão (Pg) Sturgeon.

et (Tr) Meat.

etikka (Fi) Vinegar.

étoile de beurre (Fr) Literally, "star of butter"; a star-shaped pastry sprinkled with sugar and syrup.

étouffée (Fr) Literally, "smothered"; applied to dishes cooked on low heat in a tightly closed utensil with little or no liquid.

et suyu (Tr) Meat broth.

étuvé (Fr) 1. Applied to Dutch cheeses, such as Edam and Gouda, that are matured for up to 9 months in a special humidified cellar. 2. Stewed with a small amount of water.

étuver (Fr) To stew.

evaporated milk (US) Unsweetened whole milk that has been evaporated to half its original volume. It is heated in the can to sterilize the milk.

ewe (US) A female sheep.

exohiko (Gk) Of the countryside; a method of baking in parchment paper or phyllo pastry in a conventional oven.

extracts (US) Concentrated flavorings obtained from foods such as herbs, roots, flowers, fruit, and meat by various methods such as boiling down stock or distillation. Essences are extracts, as are meat concentrates.

extra grouse (Aa) Australian slang for delicious food.

extra-sec (Fr) Pertaining to wine, a term indicating semisweetness.

F

fabada (Sp) A white bean soup with salt pork, bacon, ham hocks, beef, onions, tomatoes, green peppers, potatoes, cloves, and morcillas, a Spanish sausage.

fadge (Ir) Fried potato cakes.

faggot (GB) Literally, "bundle"; various herbs tied in a bunch; bouquet garni.

faggots (GB) Country sausages of minced pork offal mixed with fat, bread crumbs, onion, egg, and seasonings wrapped in pig's caul and baked; served cold or hot with gravy; similar to Scottish haggis.

fagiano (It) Pheasant.

fagioli (It) White haricot beans.

fagioli al fiasco (It) "Beans in a flask"; beans with ham fat or olive oil, celery, and carrot simmered in an empty Chianti bottle placed in a kettle of water.

fagioli assoluti (It) White beans fried in olive oil with garlic.

fagioli con le cotiche (It) White beans simmered with pork rind and tomato sauce.

fagioli di lima (It) Lima beans.

fagiolini (It) Green string beans.

fagiolini in padella (It) String beans sautéed with onions and tomatoes.

fagioli toscani col tonno (It) White beans sautéed with tuna fish chunks; seasoned with olive oil, lemon, and black pepper.

fagottini (It) Pancakes; cannelloni.

fagottini di melanzane (It) Rolls of sliced eggplant with a spicy tomato sauce.

fagyasztott (Hu) Frozen.

faisan (Fr) Pheasant.

faisán (Sp) Pheasant.

faizan s gribami v smetane (Rs) Pheasant in a mushroom and sour cream sauce.

fajita (Sp) Soft tortilla rolled with grilled meats, chopped lettuce, tomatoes, green onion, and grated cheese; topped with sour cream.

fakba (Ar) Fruit.

faki (Gk) Lentil soup with garlic, onion, bay leaves, olive oil, and vinegar.

falafel (Ar) Fried balls of ground broad beans or chick-peas, cracked wheat, onions, garlic, cumin, and other seasonings; may be served with tahini in pita bread.

falsa (Ia) Blackberry juice.

falukorv (Sw) Smoked pork sausage; fried and served sliced.

fàn (Ch) Any food prepared from grains, such as rice or wheat.

fanchonette (Fr) Small pastry shell filled with custard or jelly.

fān-chyé (Ch) Tomatoes.

fān-chyé shā-là (Ch) Tomato salad.

fān-chyé tāng (Ch) Tomato soup.

farala (Ar) Strawberries.

faraona (It) Guinea hen.

faraona al cartoccio (It) Guinea hen stuffed with juniper berries, thyme, and garlic; covered in sage and bacon;

wrapped in parchment paper and oven roasted.

farce de poisson (Fr) Fish stuffing.

farcement (Fr) A cake of grated potato, eggs, and flour with the addition of prunes, pears, and sultana grapes; cooked in a mold greased with smoked bacon.

farces (Fr) Stuffing.

farci (Fr) Stuffed or filled; often with forcemeat.

farcito (It) Stuffed.

fårekjøtt (Nw) Mutton.

fårekotelett (Nw) Mutton chop.

fårerull (Nw) Spiced, pressed mutton roll.

farfale (It) Butterfly-or bowknot-shaped pasta; used in soup.

farfel (Jw) Dried pellets of egg dough used in soup or casseroles.

får i kål (Nw) Seasoned stew of mutton and cabbage or kale.

farin (Nw) Granulated sugar.

farina (US) A granular meal made from ground cereal grains, potatoes, or nuts.

farina dolce (It) Chestnut flour.

farina gialla (It) Maize or corn meal.

farine (Fr) Flour; meal.

farine de maïs (Fr) Cornstarch.

farinha (Pg) Flour; meal; manioc flour.

farinha de aveia (Pg) Oatmeal.

farkha (Ar–Egypt) Chicken.

fårkött (Sw) Mutton.

farl (Sc) A griddle bread such as an oat bannock cut in triangular wedges.

farmer's cheese (US) A dairy product similar to cottage cheese but firmer in texture and higher in fat content; shaped into bricks.

farofa (Pg–Brazil) Manioc flour browned in butter with egg, onions, and seasonings until it forms a dry, crumbly mass; used for stuffing meats and vegetables.

farófias (Pg) Meringue cooked in milk with sugar and lemon, chilled and sprinkled with cinnamon and served with egg custard.

farro (Sp) A soup of ham stock with vegetables and vermicelli.

farshirovanniye kambala (Rs) Flounder stuffed with bread crumbs, parsley, shrimp, butter, beaten egg, and nutmeg.

farshirovanniye luk (Rs) Stuffed onions.

fårsk oxbringa (Sw) Boiled beef.

färskt (Sw) Fresh.

fasan (Da, Nw) Pheasant.

Fasan (Gr) Pheasant.

fasaner (Da) Roast pheasant.

Fasan mit Weinkraut (Gr) Pheasant with sauerkraut in wine.

Fasan mit weissen Bohnen (Gr) Pheasant stewed with white beans.

Faschierter Braten (Gr) Minced meat loaf made from a mixture of pork, veal, and beef; eaten hot or cold.

faséole (Fr) Kidney bean.

faširane šnicle (SC) Fried meat patties.

fasirozott (Hu) Meat loaf.

fasola (Po) Beans.

fasolia (Gk) Beans.

fasoulakia (Gk) Lamb and potato stew.

fast food (US) A term for food, such as hamburgers, hot dogs, and pizza, dispensed quickly at inexpensive restaurants.

Fastnachtkrapfen (Gr) Doughnuts.

95

fasul (Bu) A mixture of white beans, carrots, onions, and parsley dressed with sugar, lemon juice, and olive oil; served cold.

fasulye (Tr) Beans.

fasulyeli paça (Tr) Calf's feet stewed with navy beans.

fasulye pilâkisi (Tr) Stewed navy beans with onions; served cold.

fatányéros (Hu) A dish of mixed grilled meats including pork chops, bacon, beef, and veal with fried potatoes.

fatayer (Ar) Savory pastries filled with a mixture of chopped spinach, onions, and olive oil.

fatback (US) A layer of pork fat that runs along the back over the midspine; may or may not be salt cured; sometimes used in cooking to line, insulate, and moisten a terrine.

fat-free (US) A term for a food product that contains less than 0.5 grams of fat per serving and no added fat or oil; proposed by the U.S. Food and Drug Administration for food labels.

fatia (Pg) Slice.

fatias frias (Pg) Sliced meats; cold cuts.

fatir (Ar) Large baked pancakes served with jam or honey.

fats and oils (US) Energy-giving food composed essentially of triglycerides, a term that means a typical fat molecule consists of three units of fatty acids and one of glycerol (glycerine). In general, liquid products are called oils and solid products are called fats. Sources are animal foods (meat, poultry, milk, cheese, eggs, and certain fish) and about a dozen vegetable fats and oils. Fat contains about two and one-quarter times the calories found in an equal dry weight of protein and carbohydrates. See also **fatty acids.**

fatta (Ar) Mutton, calf, or lamb feet stewed in broth with rice or bread; served with toasted bread, chick-peas, and yogurt.

fattiga riddare (Sw) Literally, "poor knights"; bread fritters, similar to French toast.

fatto in casa (It) Homemade.

fattoush (Ar) A salad of toasted bread, cucumbers, tomatoes, parsley, and mint.

fatty acids (US) A group of substances found in plant and animal fats. They are generally classified as saturated if they have a full complement of hydrogen atoms, or unsaturated if they can accommodate additional hydrogen atoms in their molecules. Humans use only about seven or eight fatty acids, which come from foods such as butterfat, coconut, peanut, and palm oils. Only three fatty acids are considered essential (normally required by humans) and must be supplied in the diet.

faux mousseron (Fr) A small mushroom common in meadows; dried caps can be crushed and used as a condiment.

faux-nuts (US) Doughnuts that are baked rather than fried for low-fat content.

fava bean (It) See **broad bean.**

fava frescas em salada (Pg) Salad of cooked, seasoned fava beans dressed with olive oil, parsley, and garlic.

Fayyoum duck (Ar) Roast duck from the oasis of Fayyoum, site of Egyptian duck farms west of the Nile.

fazan po-Gruzinski (Rs) Pheasant, Georgian-style; with green walnuts, orange juice, fresh grape juice, green tea, and Madeira wine.

fazant (Du) Pheasant.

fazole (Cz) Beans.

fazolky (Cz) Green beans.

fazolový salát (Cz) Bean salad.

fegatini di pollo alla salvia (It) Chicken livers fried in butter with fresh sage, ham strips, and Marsala wine; served with fried bread.

fegato (It) Liver.

fegato alla veneziana (It) Calf's liver thinly sliced and sautéed with onions in butter and olive oil, then finished with white wine and vinegar.

fegato di pollo alla salvia (It) Chicken livers cooked with sage.

fegato di vitello (It) Calf's liver.

fehérbort (Hu) White wine.

fehér kenyér (Hu) White bread.

Feigen (Gr) Figs.

feijão (Pg) Beans.

feijão guisado (Pg) Stewed kidney beans and bacon with tomato sauce.

feijão de vagens (Pg) Green beans.

feijoada (Pg) The national dish of Brazil; a thick stew of black beans and a mixture of fresh meats and cured meats including beef tongue, chorizo sausage, and pig's ears and feet; sprinkled with farofa (a coarse meal of manioc flour); served with rice, shredded kale, and orange slices.

Feingebäck (Gr) Pastry.

fejessaláta (Hu) Lettuce salad.

femöring med ägg (Sw) Small steak topped with fried eggs and onions.

fenalår (Nw) Cured, smoked leg of mutton.

Fenchel (Gr) Fennel.

fenesi (Af–Swahili) See **jackfruit.**

feng wei hsia (Ch) Large shrimp with the tails on, coated in batter and fried.

fen kuo (Ch) Crab dumpling; a dim sum snack.

fennel seeds (US) The small, dark yellow seeds of the dried fruit of an herb, *Foeniculum vulgare*, belonging to the parsley family; a flavor and aroma like mild aniseed; used in baking, with beef, pork, and some fish dishes.

fenouil (Fr) Fennel.

fenouil, au (Fr) Cooked over fennel stalks.

fenugreek (US) The oval, short, dark yellow seeds of a plant, *Trigonella foe-*

Fenugreek

num graecum, belonging to the pea family; a flavor like burnt sugar; used in chutney, curries, pickles, and meat dishes.

fer (Fr) Iron.

féra (Fr) Whitefish.

ferique (Ar) Spiced whole wheat kernels cooked with meat or squab.

fermière, à la (Fr) In the style of the farmer's wife; a method of preparing meat, pot-roasted with carrots, celery, turnips, and onions.

ferri, ai (It) Grilled on an iron rack over an open fire.

fersken (Da, Nw) Peach.

fesa di vitello (It) Leg of veal.

fesanjan (Ar) Braised chicken or duck in pomegranate sauce with walnuts.

feta (Gk) A white, soft, and fatty sheep's or goat's milk cheese; stored in brine or milk; with a rich, tangy, salty taste. Eaten as a snack cheese, in salads, and in dishes such as stifado.

fette (It) Slices.

fettine di manzo alla pizzaiola (It) Sliced beef topped with a thick tomato and oregano sauce.

fettucine (It) "Ribbons"; the Roman term for thin, flat egg noodles. Also called **tagliatelle.**

fettucine al burro (It) Egg noodles with melted butter.

fettucine alla panna (US) Fettucine noodles mixed with butter, Parmesan cheese, and heavy cream. A similar dish is known as *fettucine Alfredo.*

fettucine alla papalina (It) Thin egg noodles with ham and butter.

fettucine alla romano (It) Thin egg noodles served with beef stew.

fettucine all'uova (It) Thin egg noodles with meat sauce.

feuilles de betterave (Fr) Beet leaves.

Feuilles de Dreux (Fr) A cow's milk cheese wrapped in brown chestnut leaves; soft, creamy, yellow interior; fruity taste.

feuilles de vigne (Fr) Vine leaves stuffed with rice.

feuilleté (Fr) Slice of flaky pastry, pastry shell, or puff pastry filled or garnished with cheese, ham, or seafood.

feuilleté au fromage (Fr) Pastry shell with cheese.

feuilleté de fruits de mer (Fr) Pastry shell filled with a variety of seafood.

feuilleté de homard (Fr) Puff pastry with a lobster filling.

feuilleté de ris de veau (Fr) Puff pastry with a sweetbread filling.

fèves (Fr) Broad beans; fava beans.

fèves au lard (Fr–Canada) Pork and beans.

fèves de marais (Fr) Broad beans.

fiambre (Pg) Cooked ham.

fiambres (Sp) Cold cooked meat.

fiber (US) A substance in vegetable matter, including cellulose, pectin, and lignin, that absorbs water in the alimentary canal and gives bulk to enable stools to pass through the body. The quantity and quality of fiber needed varies with the type of food, such as wheat bran or fruit pectin. Also called **dietary fiber.**

ficat de pui cu ceapă (Ro) Chicken livers simmered in white wine with onions and parsley.

fichi (It) Figs.

fiddleheads (US) The young, unfurling

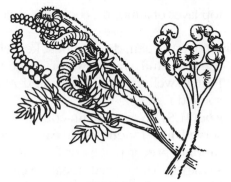

Fiddleheads

fronds of some ferns; eaten boiled in salt water and served in butter or in a salad.

fideos gordos (Sp) Large fat noodles.

fidget pie (GB) Apples, onion, and bacon layered in a pie.

fig (US) A sweet multiseeded fruit of a tree or shrub, *Ficus carica*; usually eaten dried; used as a filling in cookies.

figado (Pg) Liver.

figili (Af–Swahili) Radish leaves.

figl (Ar) Radishes.

figos (Pg) Figs.

figues (Fr) Figs.

fiken (Nw) Fig.

fikon (Sw) Fig.

fiky (Cz) Figs.

filbert (US) A species of hazelnut, *Corylus maxima*, from southern Europe and Mediterranean regions.

filé (US) A condiment of powdered, dried leaves of the sassafras tree, *Sassafras albidum*, used in Creole dishes to flavor and thicken foods such as gumbo; added when cooking is finished.

filet (US) See **fillet.**

filet, to (US) To cut into thin, tender, boneless slices. Also spelled **fillet.**

filet de boeuf (Fr) Tenderloin of beef.

filet de boeuf en croûte (Fr) Fillet of beef in a pastry crust.

filet de sole amandine (Fr) Fillet of sole cooked with butter and almonds.

filete de cerdo (Sp) Fillets of pork tenderloin.

filet mignon (Fr) A small, choice cut of beef prepared by grilling or sautéing.

filets d'anchois (Fr) Fillets of anchovies.

filets de hareng de la baltique crème (Fr) Herring in sour cream.

filetto di bue (It) Fillet of beef.

filetto di manzo (It) Thin beef steak.

filetto di pesce oreganato (It) Fillet of fish baked with oregano.

filetto di sogliole (It) Fillet of sole.

filetto di tacchino alla crema (It) Breast of turkey in a cream sauce.

filfil ahkdar (Ar) Green peppers.

filfil mahchi (Ar) Fried sweet peppers stuffed with meat, egg, and onions; served with a tomato and hot red pepper sauce.

filhó (Pg) Fritter; pancake.

fillet (US) A thin, tender, boneless piece of meat or other food; a boneless, skinless side of a small fish. Also spelled **filet.**

fillet, to (US) See **filet, to.**

filmjölk (Sw) Thick sour milk, similar to yogurt.

filo (Gk) See **phyllo.**

filosoof (Du) "Philosopher's dish"; a baked casserole of mashed potatoes, ground meat, and onion.

financière, à la (Fr) In the style of the captain of finance; made with a garnish

99

or sauce of sweetbreads, cockscombs and kidneys, truffles, mushrooms, and olives.

finanziera di pollo (It) Chicken giblets stewed with sweetbreads, mushrooms, and truffles in a sauce.

finbrød (Nw) Rye bread.

findik (Tr) Nuts.

fines herbes (Fr) Finely chopped fresh herbs including parsley, tarragon, chervil, and chives; often used in omelets or tossed green salad.

finger pies (US) See **hand pies.**

finnan haddie (Sc) Smoked finnan haddock grilled in butter or poached in milk; named for the fishing village of Findon.

finocchi (It) Fennel.

finocchio al forno (It) Fennel first boiled, then oven-baked with butter and grated cheese.

finsiktat mjol (Sw) Corn flour.

finta (Rs) Shad.

fiorentina, alla (It) In the style of Florence; applied to dishes such as roast saddle of pork with rosemary and garlic, or charcoal broiled steak with olive oil and lemon; not to be confused with the meaning of the French term, à la florentine.

fiori di zucchini (It) Zucchini blossoms.

fiori fritti (It) Fried blossoms, usually deep-fried zucchini blossoms in batter; sometimes stuffed with anchovies and cheese.

fi qa'atah (Ar) Literally, "at the bottom"; a layered dish with rose water and almond-flavored rice on the bottom, a middle layer of spiced meat and a top layer of almonds; cooked top-side down.

fireek (Ar) Green, dried, wheat kernels; used to stuff waterfowl or pigeons. Fireek swells from basting liquid. Also spelled **ferique.**

fire pot (US) An Asian main-course soup served like fondue with each diner dipping precut pieces of food into a stockpot. The sliced meats, vegetables, and seafood arranged on platters around the pot vary with the region. Included may be steamed pancake rolls or bread rolls, noodles and a sesame-seed flavored sauce. The enriched stock is served in bowls.

firinda (Tr) Roast.

firnee (Ia) A pudding made with ground rice flavored with cardamom or nutmeg and sometimes with nuts.

Fisch (Gr) Fish.

Fischbrühe (Gr) Fish broth.

fischietti (It) Literally, "small whistle"; smallest of the tubular pasta.

Fischmayonnaise (Gr) Cold fish salad.

Fischrouladen (Gr) Flatfish fillets rolled with a filling of bacon, onion, and mushroom; baked in butter and wine.

Fischschüssel (Gr) Fish and bacon pie.

fish slice (GB) A slatted spatula.

fish sticks (US) A fish fillet sliced into sticks about 1 inch wide, rolled in batter or bread crumbs, and baked or fried.

fish tartar (Jw) Minced fish mixed with salt, lemon juice, mayonnaise, chives, and grated white horseradish; a Passover alternative for gefilte fish.

fisk (Da, Nw) Fish.

fiskeboller (Nw) Fish balls made with flaked fish, bread crumbs, cream, and seasoning.

fiskegratin (Nw) Fish soufflé.

fiskekaker (Nw) Fish cakes.

fiskepudding (Nw) Fish pudding; made with the same ingredients as fiskeboller but made in a mold.

fisksoppa (Sw) Fish soup.

Fisolen (Gr–Austria) Green beans.

five-spice powder (US) A Chinese aromatic spice mixture of star anise, cinnamon, clove, fennel, and red pepper; uses include the seasoning of pork and chicken.

fjærfe (Nw) Poultry.

fläderbär (Sw) Elderberries.

Flädle (Gr) Pancake.

Flädlesuppe (Gr) A clear soup with strips of pancake.

flæskesteg (Da) Roast pork; usually served with spiced red cabbage and browned potatoes.

flæskeæggekage (Da) A thick omelet made with pork and eggs.

flæsk i kål (Da) Cabbage with meat, usually pork.

flageolet (Fr) A variety of haricot bean that is pale green and kidney-shaped with tender skin; used dried or fresh.

flake, to (US) To separate food particles into thin loose pieces. In fish cookery, to flake easily means the flesh separates in firm layers and is cooked.

flaki po polsku (Po) Tripe slices and vegetables simmered in stock; topped with cheese and bread crumbs.

flamande, à la (Fr) Braised with cabbage, carrots, potatoes, turnips, bacon, and sausage.

flambé (Fr) Describes a dish that has been doused with liqueur and ignited usually when served; the flaming may be done before cooking to brown and impart flavor to food.

flamiche (Fr) A tart shell filled with a mixture of eggs and chopped leeks stewed in butter; similar to quiche.

flan (Sp) A classic Spanish dessert of molded egg custard usually caramel-flavored; served with a caramel sauce.

flan (Fr) An open tart filled with fruit or a sweet or savory custard.

flan au lait (Fr) A pastry shell filled with custard.

flanchet (Fr) A cut of meat from the flank.

flan de manzanas (Sp) Apple tart or pie.

flank steak (US) A cut of beef between ribs and hips.

flannel cake (US) A large, thick pancake.

flapjack (US) A griddle cake; pancake.

fläsk (Sw) Pork.

fläsk korv (Sw) Large pork sausage.

flatbrød (Nw) Thin, crisp, unleavened flat bread.

flatfish (US) Best known are flounder, halibut, turbot, and sole.

flauta (Mx) Literally, "flute"; a tortilla tightly rolled with various fillings including meat, poultry, cheese, and sometimes fruit, and deep-fried.

Flecke (Gr) Tripe.

Fleischbrühe (Gr) Meat or beef broth; served with noodles, dumplings, pancake strips, or egg custard cubes.

Fleischklöschen (Gr) Meatballs.

flensjes (Du) A cake made of stacked pancakes layered with applesauce, jam, or other fruit purees; served in wedges.

flesk (Nw) Pork.

flet (Fr) Flounder.

flétan (Fr) Halibut.

fleurons (Fr) Small pieces of pastry.

fleurs de courgettes (Fr) Zucchini blossoms, stuffed with mashed zucchini, coated with batter, and deep-fried.

flingor (Sw) Dry cereal.

flitch (GB) A side of bacon.

floating island (US) A term used for several French desserts, **île flottante** and **oeufs à la neige.**

flocos de cereal (Pg) Dry cereal.

fløde (Da) Cream.

fløderand (Da) A blancmange molded in a ring; filled with stewed fruit.

fløde skum (Da) Whipped cream; served with many sweet pastries and dishes.

florentine, à la (Fr) In the style of Florence; prepared with spinach; with foods, usually eggs or fish, put on spinach, covered with mornay sauce, and sprinkled with cheese.

flory (Sc) A two-crust pie.

fløte (Nw) Cream.

fløtevaffle (Nw) Waffles made with a sour cream batter flavored with ginger or cardamom.

flounder (US) A generic term for nearly two hundred different kinds of flatfishes found in the Atlantic and Pacific oceans. The thin body results in fillets of even thickness; white, firm and delicately flavored; used stuffed and baked, poached in wine, sautéed, fried, and grilled.

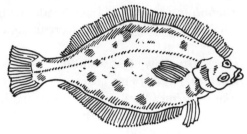

Flounder

flour (US) Finely ground meal made from grain. The main types of flour include hard wheat, soft wheat, all-purpose, whole wheat, semolina, farina, and stone-ground.

fluke (US) A flatfish belonging to the flounder family.

flummery (US) A dessert of simmered berries sweetened and thickened with cornstarch; served cold with cream.

flummery (GB) A molded dessert made with egg yolk, sugar, wine, lemon juice, and brandy and set with gelatine.

Flunder (Gr) Flounder.

flundra (Sw) Flounder.

fluoride (US) A compound of the element fluorine; not classified as essential but considered beneficial for the development of hard bone tissue and the prevention of tooth decay; a daily requirement for adults is around 1.5 milligrams; the best source is fluoride-treated drinking water.

Fluskrebs (Gr) Crayfish.

flying fish (Cb) A tropical fish, family Exocoetidae, with moist flesh, highly valued as food; usually fried; flying fish pie is a famous Caribbean dish served on Barbados.

flyndre (Nw) Flounder.

focaccia (It) Sweet or savory tarts, buns, or cakes; sometimes a flat bread similar in texture and flavor to pizza crust.

focaccia alla salvia (It) Savory buns seasoned with sage.

focaccia di vitello (It) Veal patties.

fogas (Hu) Large pike perch.

foie (Fr) Liver.

foie de canard (Fr) Duck's liver.

foie de poulet (Fr) Chicken liver.

foie de veau (Fr) Calf's liver.

foie de veau auvergnate (Fr) Calf's liver with bacon.

foie de volaille en brochete (Fr) Chicken livers, mushrooms, and bacon grilled on a skewer.

foie gras (Fr) The livers of especially fattened geese and ducks; served ground fine to a smooth paste. Highly prized are the fois gras of Toulouse and Strasbourg.

foie gras de canard en gelée (Ca) A paste of duck livers in aspic.

foie gras en croûte (Fr) Finely ground livers encased in pastry.

foie gras truffé (Fr) Goose liver with truffles.

foiolo (It) Tripe.

fokhagyma (Hu) Garlic.

folate (US) See **folic acid.**

fold, to (US) 1. To mix food by gently moving ingredients from the bottom up over onto the top. 2. To enclose a filling in a pastry or dough.

folic acid (US) A member of the vitamin B complex, working together with vitamin B_{12}, and essential for the formation of red blood cells; the recommended daily allowance (RDA) is 200–400 micrograms mcg for adults; good dietary sources include leafy, green vegetables, liver, and mushrooms. Also called **folate.**

folyami rák (Hu) Crayfish.

fond (Fr) A concentrated stock of meat, poultry, and game, used in sauces or to flavor other dishes. See also **fumet.**

fondant (Fr) Finely ground poultry mixture; usually served in a pear shape.

fondant (US) A soft, white cooked or uncooked candy used as a base for bonbons and icings; color and flavorings are often added.

fondas de alcachofas (Sp) Artichoke hearts.

fond blanc (Fr) White stock.

fond de volaille (Fr) Poultry stock or broth.

fonds d'artichauts (Fr) Artichoke hearts.

fondue (Fr) Melted; a dish, said to have originated in Switzerland, in which pieces of food are dipped into melted cheese mixed with white wine. There are also dessert fondues, such as made with chocolate.

fondue bourguignonne (Fr) Cubed beef cooked at the table in boiling oil; served with a variety of sauces.

fonduta (It) A cheese dish made with melted fontina cheese, egg yolks, milk, and truffles.

Fontainbleau (Fr) 1. A soft cow's milk cheese made with curds and whipped cream; wrapped in cheesecloth and drained; served with sugar, strawberries, and sometimes fresh cream. 2. A garnish of oven-browned potato boats filled with finely minced vegetables cooked in butter.

fontina Val d'Aosta (It) A cow's milk

cheese with a dark gold crusty rind and pale gold interior; a firm, dense texture and a rich, nutlike taste. The original fontina.

foo foo (Cb) Mashed plantain cakes or dumplings; poached or fried.

fool (GB) A dessert of chilled fruit or berries, sweetened and pureed, with whipped cream or custard.

forcemeat (US) Mixtures of finely chopped meats, poultry, or fish with herbs and spices, blended to a smooth paste. Fruit, vegetables, or other foods may also be used.

forel (Du) Trout.

forell (Sw) Trout.

Forelle (Gr) Trout.

Forelle blau (Gr) Trout poached in vinegar and water; served with melted butter.

Forellen in Gurkensosse (Gr) Trout in cucumber pickle sauce.

forel v vino (Rs) Trout cooked in white wine.

forestière, à la (Fr) In the style of the forester; meat or poultry served with woodland mushrooms, bacon, and diced potatoes.

forfar bridies (Sc) Short strips of beef sprinkled with suet, wrapped in pastry, and baked.

forloren (Da) Describes a mock dish made with ingredients flavored to imitate another dish, such as mock turtle stew or mock hare.

formaggio (It) Cheese.

formaggio di crema (It) Cream cheese.

formato (It) Loaf.

formato di carne (It) Meat loaf.

forno, al (It) Baked in an oven.

forno, no (Pg) Baked in an oven.

forretter (Nw) Hors d'oeuvre.

forró csokoládé (Hu) Hot chocolate.

forshchmak (Rs) Ground beef, herring, potatoes, and onion mixed with eggs, topped with bread crumbs and cheese, and baked.

Förstertopf mit Pilzen (Gr) Casserole of venison with mushrooms.

fortune cookie (US) A crisp, griddle-baked wafer folded around a bit of paper printed with a fortune forecast. The cookie, a Chinese-American invention, must be opened to find and read the fortune.

fött krumpli (Hu) Boiled potatoes.

four, au (Fr) Oven-baked.

fourrage à la crème d'orange (Fr) Orange and butter cream filling for cake.

fourrer (Fr) To insert a raw or cooked filling into a sweet or savory pastry, bread roll, cake, or other item.

fowl (US) Any edible wild or domestic bird.

Fra Diavolo (It) Literally, "Brother Devil," a monk who left the monastery to lead a life of crime; applied to lobster or other shellfish sautéed in olive oil and served with a spicy tomato sauce.

fragole (It) Strawberries.

fragoline (It) Wild or small strawberries.

fragoline di mare (It) Literally, "sea strawberries"; tiny squid.

frais (Fr) Fresh; cold.

fraises (Fr) Strawberries.

fraises aux liqueurs (Fr) Strawberries, sugared and sprinkled with a variety of liqueurs.

fraises chantilly (Fr) Strawberries with whipped cream.

fraises des bois (Fr) Tiny, intensely sweet, wild strawberries; a strawberry-flavored eau-de-vie.

fraises Romanof (Fr) Strawberries in a mixture of orange juice and curacao and topped with whipped cream.

framboesas (Pg) Raspberries.

framboises (Fr) Raspberries; a raspberry-flavored eau-de-vie.

frambozen (Du) Raspberries.

frambuesas (Sp) Raspberries.

francala (Tr) Rolls.

Franconia potatoes (US) Boiled potatoes baked with butter.

frangipane (US) 1. A pastry made with flour, egg yolks, butter, and milk, similar to cream puff or choux pastry; then baked and filled with forcemeat or another mixture. 2. A rich pastry cream flavored with ground almonds and used as a filling or topping for various cakes and pastries.

frango (Pg) Chicken. Also called **galinha.**

frango no espota à moda de Minho (Pg) Spit-roasted chicken brushed with olive oil and chili sauce.

frankfurters (US) Smoked, seasoned, precooked sausages made from beef, pork, veal, chicken, and turkey. They range in length from tiny to foot-long and may or may not have casings. Also called **hot dogs**, *weiners.*

Frankfurter Würstchen (Gr) Small sausages made with finely minced lean beef and pork, mildly seasoned, and lightly smoked; pink color comes from saltpeter; boiled and served with bread and mustard; origin of the hot dog.

Frankfurterplatte (Gr) A plate of sausage and sauerkraut.

frappé (Fr) A dessert, fruit juices, or drink that has been partially frozen, then stirred or beaten; a liqueur may also have been poured over ice chips.

freddo (It) Cold.

free-range (US) Describes poultry or animals allowed to roam and feed without confinement.

freestone (US) Describes fruit with a pit to which the flesh does not cling, such as a freestone peach.

freezer burn (US) A dry, discolored surface on frozen food that has been improperly preserved by freezing, such as with broken wrapping. Freezing removes moisture much as heating does, thus causing a burn.

French bean (US) A term applied to any young, tender, green string bean. Also, a variety of French haricot bean, the **flageolet.**

French cream (US) A blend of sour cream, heavy cream, cream cheese, gelatin, vanilla, and sugar; usually served with fresh berries.

French cuisine (US) The basic flavor principle of most French recipes involves wine vinegar and oil with herbs, mainly basil, thyme, tarragon, parsley, onion, garlic, shallots, and leeks. Many classic French sauces are based on combinations of wine and stock or butter and cream. Mediterranean French cooking is heavily dependent on olive oil and tomato combinations.

French dressing (US) A commercial American dressing that is red-orange, creamy, and slightly tart. See also **vinaigrette.**

French fries (US) Deep-fried potatoes that have been cut into thin to thick strips.

French pastry (US) Puff pastry filled with custard, whipped cream, or jam.

French toast (US) White bread soaked in a mixture of egg and milk, fried; Served with syrup or honey. Also called **pain perdu**, *lost bread.*

fresas (Sp) Strawberries.

fresca (It) Fresh.

fresh (US) A food-label term that applies only to raw foods that have not been processed, frozen, or preserved; proposed by the U.S. Food and Drug Administration for food labels.

Fresno chili (US) A hot, conical-shaped chili pepper about 2 inches long and bright red when mature.

friandises (Fr) Petits fours served with ice cream.

fricadelles (Fr) Croquettes of ground beef mixtures.

fricandeau (Fr) Sliced braised veal in a sauce.

fricandel (Du) Croquette of seasoned ground meat with onions.

fricando (Sp) Veal stew with wild mushrooms, onion, garlic, and jamon serrano.

fricassee (US) To braise food with a thick sauce, milk, or cream.

fricassée (Fr) A stew of braised meat, usually veal or poultry, flavored with onion, cloves, mace, or nutmeg and thickened with a roux; often contains mushrooms; served with a cream and lemon juice sauce; garnished with lemon wedges or bacon.

fried green tomatoes (US) Unripened green tomatoes, usually those right before the first frost, sliced and dredged in flour, beaten egg, and corn meal, then fried in hot oil.

fried rice (US) A Chinese side dish; cooked rice stir-fried in oil with spring onions and egg.

fries (GB) Calves' and lambs' testicles; fried, stewed, or braised.

frigărui (Ro) Mixed grill of meats with onions, mushrooms, and tomatoes.

frijolada (Sp) Bean stew with meats and vegetables.

frijoles (Sp) Beans, commonly applied to black, pinto, or red kidney beans.

frijoles negros (Sp) See **black bean.**

frijoles refritos (Mx) A term that means well-fried beans (not twice-fried); boiled, dried red beans prepared by mashing and frying to a thick paste with onions, chili peppers, garlic, and sometimes tomatoes. Used as a dip, an ingredient in tortilla dishes, or as a side dish with shredded cheese.

Frikadellen (Gr) Fried meatballs.

frikadeller (Da, Sw) Large oval meatballs made with mixtures of finely ground veal, beef, or pork, bread crumbs, onion, egg, milk, and seasonings; fried in butter; served hot or cold with pickled beets or cucumbers.

Frikase (Gr) Sautéed lamb with scallions, lettuce, and dill in an egg and lemon sauce.

frikassé (Nw) Stew.

Frikassee vom Huhn (Gr) Braised chicken.

frio (Sp) Cold.

frisch (Gr) Fresh.

friss (Hu) Fresh.

frit (Fr) Fried.

frites (Fr) Fried potatoes.

frito (Pg, Sp) Fried.

fritots (Fr) Fritters.

frittata (It) A thick pancakelike omelet made with vegetables; cooked in olive oil until browned; served hot or cold as a main dish or cut in pieces as appetizers.

frittata con funghi (It) Mushroom omelet.

frittata primavera (It) Omelet with peas or asparagus, parsley, and chives.

fritte de ciliegielle (It) Cherry fritters.

frittelle (It) Fritters; deep-fried rings of dough, sprinkled with sugar; served hot.

frittelle di polenta (It) Corn meal fritters.

fritter (US) Deep-fried chopped meat, fish, vegetables, or fruit mixed with or coated with a batter, creating a crisp texture. The batter may be made from wheat, rice, or other types of flour.

fritto (It) Fried.

fritto misto (It) Mixed fry of organ meats, steak, and other meats served with a variety of batter-coated, deep-fried vegetables.

fritto misto di mare (It) Mixed fry of seafoods, such as shrimp and squid, first boiled, then deep-fried; served with lemon.

fritura de pechugas de pollo (Sp) Fried chicken breasts.

fritura mixta (Sp) Assorted meats, chicken, vegetables, or fish; dipped in batter and deep-fried.

friture (Fr) Fried fish, mixed.

frizzle (US) To cook food quickly until edges curl, usually on a griddle.

frog's legs (US) The hind legs of frogs, sautéed, broiled, deep-fried, or cooked with a sauce.

froid (Fr) Cold.

fromage (Fr) Cheese.

fromage à la crème (Fr) Fromage blanc that has been refined with cream and sweetened with sugar.

fromage blanc (Fr) White cheese; cow's milk allowed to sour, then drained like cottage cheese.

fromage de tète (Fr) Headcheese.

fromage du pays (Fr) Local cheese.

fromage rapé (Fr) Grated cheese.

Froschschenkel (Gr) Frogs' legs.

frost, to (US) To coat with a frosting.

frosted (US) A half-frozen citrus juice drink, thick and icy.

frosting (US) Sweet spread or covering for cakes and cookies made cooked with egg white or uncooked with confectioners' sugar. See also **icing.**

Fruchtbrot (Gr) Fruit bread.

Fruchtkaltschale (Gr) Cold fruit soup made with cherries, strawberries, pears, plums, or apricots.

Fruchtpasteten (Gr) Fruit pies.

Fruchtsalat (Gr) Fruit salad.

fructose (US) A water-soluble sugar, sweeter than sucrose, occurring in invert sugar, many fruits, and honey.

frugt (Da) Fruit.

frugtsaft (Da) Fruit juice.

frugttærte (Da) Fruit tart.

Frühlingskäse (Gr–Austria) Open-face sandwiches of black bread spread with a mixture of cream cheese, caraway seeds, and paprika; garnished with pickles.

fruit (Du) Fruit.

fruit butters (US) Preserves made with fruit pulp such as apple, plum, cherry, rhubarb, and figs; cooked with sugar until thick.

fruitcake (US) A cake with dried, candied, or crystalized fruit and nuts held together with a small amount of batter; it may be dark from molasses or brown sugar and spices; or light with granulated sugar and no spices.

fruit cocktail (US) A mixture of diced fruits in syrup; served as an appetizer.

fruit cup (GB) A nonalcoholic fruit drink, similar to punch.

fruit givré (Fr) Sorbet or ice cream in shells of hollowed fruit.

fruit salad (US) A variety of prepared fresh fruits served on lettuce leaves and dressed with mayonnaise or with lime juice and honey.

fruits cuits (Fr) Stewed fruit.

fruits de mer (Fr) Literally, "fruits of the sea"; seafood or shellfish.

fruit sec (Fr) Dried fruit.

fruits frais (Fr) Fresh fruit.

frukt (Nw) Fruit.

fruktkompott (Nw) Stewed and mixed fruit.

fruktsaft (Nw) Fruit juice.

frullato (It) Whipped; milkshake.

frumenta (It) Grain, wheat or corn.

frumenty (GB) Pudding or porridge made with wheat cereal, milk, eggs, raisins, sugar, and spices.

fruset (Sw) Frozen.

fruta (Pg) Fruit.

fruta azucarada (Sp) Candied fruits.

frutta cotta (It) Stewed fruit.

frutta della stagione (It) Fruit in season.

frutta fresca (It) Fresh fruit.

frutta secca (It) Dried fruit.

frutti di mare (It) "Fruit of the sea"; seafood.

frutti misti (It) Mixed fruits.

fry (US) The young of fish; the fried organs of an animal.

fry, to (US) To cook pieces of food in a small amount of fat, some or all of which may come from the food itself, such as bacon.

fryer (US) Chicken usually 14 to 20 weeks old, about 2 to 3 pounds, tender enough for frying.

fu (Jp) Wheat gluten; mixed with flour made from glutinous rice and shaped into rolls and boiled; flavorings and coloring may be added; used in soup or other dishes.

fudge (US) A semisoft candy made of chocolate or cocoa, sugar, butter, milk, and vanilla or other flavorings.

fugath (Ia) Vegetables fried with onions, coconut, and masala.

füge (Hu) Figs.

fugl (Nw) Fowl.

fugu (Jp) A blowfish sometimes used in sashimi that may cause severe poisoning and death if not skillfully cleaned and prepared. Also called **makimaki.**

fugusashi (Jp) Sliced blowfish.

fuki (Jp) A Japanese spring vegetable

with a stem resembling celery; used in soups.

fukujinzuke (Jp) Sliced vegetables in soy sauce.

ful (Ar) Brown beans; broad beans.

Füllung (Gr) Stuffing.

ful medamis (Ar) A national dish of Egypt; broad beans and lentils slow-cooked until tender, mashed with olive oil and lemon, and garnished with chopped egg.

fumé (Fr) Smoked.

fumet (Fr) A concentrated stock of fish or mushrooms; used in sauces or to flavor other dishes. See also **fond.**

fundido (Sp) Melted.

funghetto, al (It) Sautéed in very hot oil.

funghi (It) Mushrooms.

funghi acciugati al forno (It) Baked mushrooms with anchovies.

funghi porcini (It) See **boletus.**

funghi ripieni (It) Stuffed mushrooms.

funghi sott'olio ed aceto (It) Pickled mushrooms.

funghi trifolati (It) Sliced mushrooms fried in olive oil and garlic; served with chopped anchovies, parsley, butter, and lemon.

fun gwor (Ch) Vegetable and shrimp dumpling; a dim sum snack.

funnel cake (US) A deep-fried pastry made from batter dripped through a funnel and swirled in spirals; a Pennsylvania Dutch specialty.

furaimono (Jp) Fried foods.

fursadi (Af–Swahili) Raspberries.

fursecuri (Ro) Small biscuits made with chocolate and walnuts.

fú-rŭng dàn (Ch) Deep-fried omelet with chopped meat, often pork, or seafood, or vegetables, such as scallions, mushrooms, and bean sprouts; egg foo yung.

fusilli (It) Thin, spiral-shaped noodles.

füszeres (Hu) Spicy.

füszeres hozzávaló (Hu) Condiments.

fyldt hvidkålshoved (Da) Cabbage stuffed with ground meat.

fylt kålhode (Nw) Stuffed cabbage.

Fynbo (Da) A Samsoe cheese originating on the island of Fyn; natural rind; firm texture with a sprinkling of holes; mild Swiss-like taste.

G

gaai ka gosht (Ia) Beef.

gâche (Fr) A small yeast cake or brioche; sometimes filled with sliced apples.

gädda (Sw) Pike.

gado-gado (In) A cold vegetable platter, often with as many as ten vegetables, usually steamed, and soybean curd cakes; served with a garlic and lemon-flavored peanut sauce.

gadon tahu (In) Steamed bean curd with coconut and chili peppers.

gaffelbitar (Sw) Herring tidbits.

Gaiskäsle (Gr) A goat's milk cheese made in the Allgäu region; white or red rind; pungent taste; strong aroma.

gajar (Ia) Carrots.

gajar ka halva (Ia) Sweet carrot pudding.

galabart (Fr) A large blood sausage, eaten cold, sliced.

galamb (Hu) Pigeon.

galangal (US) Either of two plants, genus *Alpinia*, with small, knobby, brown or reddish roots; a gingerlike, peppery flavor; grows in Southeast Asian and Mediterranean regions; used dry, raw, or roasted like chestnuts. Also called **galingale, leuqkuas.**

galantine (Fr) Boned turkey, duck, game birds, or chicken stuffed into a sausage shape then cooked in wine and bouillon and chilled; usually served in aspic.

galatoboureko (Gk) Cakes made with layers of phyllo and filled with orange custard.

galette (Fr) 1. A round flat cake with many variations; may be sweet or savory, of yeasted or puff pastry and made with walnuts or chestnuts, candied fruits, and curd cheese. 2. A term used for a small cookie.

galettes aux fruits de mer (Fr) Thin pancakes rolled around a filling of shrimp.

galingale (US) See **galangal.**

galinha (Pg) Chicken. Also called **frango.**

galinha assada (Pg) Roast chicken.

gallimaufry (GB) A term originally applied to a feast dish; then descended to mean hodgepodge, a combination of many things; used for a stew or ragout.

gallina a la pimienta (Sp) Chicken cooked in a black pepper and garlic sauce.

gallo pinto (Sp) A Costa Rican breakfast of rice and beans.

galushki (Rs) Buckwheat flour dumplings.

galuska (Hu) Small chewy dumplings.

galuşte (Ro) Dumplings.

gamba (It) Leg.

gambari (Ar) Shrimp.

gambas (Pg, Sp) Shrimp; prawns.

gambas a la plancha (Sp) Buttered shrimp cooked on the grill and served with lemon.

gamberello (It) Prawn.

gamberetti di laguna (It) "Sea crickets"; small shrimp.

gamberetto grigio (It) Shrimp.

gamberi di fiume (It) Crayfish.

game (US) Any edible undomesticated animals that are hunted, such as bear, bison, fox, squirrel, deer, rabbit, wild sheep, and goats; also includes "big game," such as elephant or lion. Usually well-flavored but can be tough; marinating is often recommended and less tender cuts are used in stews, pot roasts, or casseroles.

game birds (US) Any edible undomesticated birds that are hunted, including wild ducks and geese, quail, partridge, and thrush. Young birds are often roasted; older birds marinated or cooked with liquids.

game fish (US) Any food fish caught for sport such as trout, pike, bass, and tuna.

Gammelost (Nw) A cow's milk cheese made from sour milk; brown rind with yellow-brown interior with blue mold; a strong, aromatic, sharp flavor.

gammon (GB) A side of cured bacon, smoked or unsmoked, with the hind leg and thigh. The knuckle end may be braised, stewed, or boiled.

gamous (Ar) Water buffalo; meat used like beef as in steaks or kababs.

ganache (Fr) A chocolate cream with the texture of a mousse used to decorate or fill a variety of pastries and desserts; made with chocolate, heavy cream, and a vanilla bean.

gandofli (Ar) Oysters.

ganmodoki (Jp) Fried soybean curd and vegetables.

gans (Du) Goose.

Gans (Gr) Goose.

Gänseleberwurst (Gr) A liver sausage of goose liver and truffles.

ganso (Pg) Goose.

ganso relleno de castañas (Sp) Roast goose stuffed with chestnuts.

ga nuong ngu vi (Vt) Grilled chicken seasoned with soy sauce, five-spice powder, honey, and garlic.

garam (In) Salt.

garam masala (Ia) A basic blend of dried ground spices; usually includes cardamom, cinnamon, cloves, coriander, cumin, and black pepper; used alone or with other seasonings in a wide variety of dishes.

garang asam ikan (In) Spiced fish steaks.

garbanzo (Sp) See **chick-pea.**

garbanzos salteados (Sp) Stewed chick-peas (highwayman-style).

garbure (Fr) A thick stew made of potatoes, cabbage, beans, and other vegetables with preserved goose or other pickled meats. Served with fried bread.

garfish (US) A saltwater fish in the family *Belonidae*, with green bones; popular in Denmark, fried or used in soups. Also called **hornfisk.**

garlic (US) An herb, *Allium sativum*, with a papery skin around a bulb, which separates into divisions or "cloves"; strong taste; used for flavoring meats, dressings, salads, soups, and sauces; essential for dishes such as aïoli, bagna cauda, and skordalia.

garlic bread (US) Oven-browned sliced bread, usually Italian or French, spread with garlic butter and other seasonings, often paprika.

garlic butter (US) Seasoned butter mixed with crushed garlic.

Garlic

garlic salt (US) Ground dried garlic with salt.

garnalen (Du) Shrimp.

Garnele (Gr) Shrimp.

garni (Fr) Garnished or decorated.

garnish, to (US) To decorate food with colorful, tasty, cut pieces of other foods; may be placed around food or served separately.

garniture (Fr) Garnish, trimmings.

garretto (It) Knuckle; veal or pork shank.

garulla (Sp) A bread roll in Colombia.

garvie (Sc) Sprat.

gås (Nw, Sw) Goose.

găscă prăjită (Ro) Roast goose.

gåsesteg (Da) Roast goose.

gåsesteg med æbler og svedsker (Da) Roast goose stuffed with apples and prunes; a traditional Christmas dish.

gastrique (Fr) A sweet-and-sour preparation added to overly rich or fatty foods, such as duck; made with a reduced, caramelized mixture of sugar and vinegar.

gâteau (Fr) A term for pastries and cakes; usually identifies layered, filled sponge cakes with the egg yolks and whites beaten separately and often used to make a rolled cake.

gâteau à la brioche (Fr) A cone-shaped cake flavored with rum or orange-flower water; baked on a rotating spit.

gâteau de crêpes à la florentine (Fr) Layered crêpes filled with spinach and topped with a cheese sauce.

gâteau de crêpes à la Normande (Fr) Layered crêpes with apple slices and macaroons.

gatto (It) A pastry made with a sponge cake base soaked in rum, layered with custard and chocolate creams and topped with whipped cream.

gaudes (Fr) A corn meal porridge; served with milk or cream; may be browned and served with sugar.

gauffres (Bl) Waffles; served warm with butter and syrup or with whipped cream or fruits.

gaufrette (Fr) A small, thin wafer; may be fan-shaped or rolled up and filled.

gauloise, à la (Fr) With cockscombs and kidneys; as a garnish, in soups, on eggs.

gayette (Fr) A small flat sausage made of pig's liver, pork fat, garlic, and parsley; soaked in olive oil and served hot or cold.

gazar (Ar) Carrots.

gazpacho (Sp) A cold soup made with chopped fresh tomatoes, sweet peppers, and cucumbers mixed with garlic, olive oil, vinegar or lemon juice, and spices; may be served with croutons. Also, there are white gazpachos that do not include tomatoes or are made with almonds and grapes.

Gebäck (Gr) Pastry.

gebacken (Gr) Baked.

gebakken (Du) Fried.

gebakken paling (Du) Fried fillets of eel breaded with crushed rusks and served with lemon slices.

gebakken zeetong (Du) Fried sole.

gebraden (Du) Roast.

gebraden kip (Du) Fried chicken.

gebraten (Gr) Fried or roasted.

gedämft (Gr) Steamed.

Geflügelsalat (Gr) Chicken salad.

gefilte fish (Jw) A Jewish specialty; balls of minced fish, often carp, onion, matzo meal, egg, and flavorings; usually simmered in fish stock; served hot or cold.

gefüllt (Gr) Stuffed.

gefüllte Kartoffeln (Gr) Stuffed potatoes.

gegrillt (Gr) Grilled.

gehackt (Gr) Ground or chopped.

gehacktes Rindfleisch (Gr) Ground beef.

gehaktballetjes (Du) Small meatballs.

Gehirne (Gr) Brains.

gehoon (Ia) Wheat.

gekocht (Gr) Boiled.

gekookt (Du) Boiled.

gelado (Pg) Ice cream.

gelatin (US) A highly refined substance extracted from animal bones and cartilage boiled in water. The resulting clear, tasteless processed powder, granules, or sheets are soluble in wa-

ter and will set, or stiffen, sweet or savory mixtures when blended with them. Gelatin has little nutritive value as it is not a complete protein, lacking in tryptophan, an essential amino acid. Also spelled *gelatine.*

gelato (It) A rich ice cream that is folded rather than churned; an ice, sherbet.

gelato alle fragole (It) Strawberry ice.

gelato di crema (It) Vanilla ice cream.

gelbe Rüben (Gr) Carrots.

geléa (Pg–Brazil) Jelly.

gelée (Fr) Jelly.

gelée, à la (Fr) In aspic; or with a jelly.

gelée de groseille (Fr) Red currant jelly.

geléia (Pg) Jelly; citrus marmalade.

gèlo (Pg) Ice.

gemischter Salat (Gr) Mixed salad.

Gemüsesuppe (Gr) Vegetable soup.

genomstekt (Sw) Well done (meat).

genevoise, sauce (Fr) A sauce for fish made with a brown sauce from fish stock, red wine, and minced vegetables.

génoise (Fr) A light sponge cake filled with apricot preserves, chocolate cream, or mocha cream; origin in Genoa, Italy.

Genovese, alla (It) In the style of Genoa; with an aromatic sauce of basil, garlic, and pine nuts (pesto sauce).

geoduck (US) A large edible soft-shell clam, *Panope generosa,* of the Pacific coast of North America; lean flesh; usually fried.

geraniums (US) Garden blossoms shredded in salads, used as a garnish, and added to preserves.

germ (US) The heart or embryo of a grain kernel, such as wheat or oats;

113

provides B vitamins, vitamin E, minerals, and fat.

German potato salad (US) A potato salad dressed with vinegar, oil, or bacon fat, and bits of bacon; served hot or cold.

gerookt (Du) Smoked.

gerookte paling (Du) Smoked eel; garnished with lemon and gherkin; also eaten as an hors d'oeuvre.

gerookte zalm (Du) Smoked salmon.

geroosterd (Du) Grilled.

geroosterd brood en jam (Du) Toast and jam.

Geröstel (Gr) Hash-brown potatoes.

Gerste (Gr) Barley.

Gerstensuppe (Gr) Barley soup.

Gervais (Fr) A fresh double cream cheese with a slightly sharp taste; white rind.

geś (Po) Goose.

geschmort (Gr) Braised.

gestoofde bieten (Du) Stewed beets.

gestoofde pruimen (Du) Stewed prunes.

gesztenye szív (Hu) Chestnut-shaped cakes filled with chestnut cream and covered with chocolate.

getost (Sw) Goat cheese.

Getreide (Gr) Cereals.

gevuld (Du) Stuffed.

gevulde ui (Du) Stuffed onion.

Gewürze (Gr) Spices, seasoning.

Gewürzkuchen (Gr) Spice cakes.

ghai ka gosht (Ia) Beef.

ghala (Gk) Milk.

ghalopula (Gk) Turkey.

gharidhes (Gk) Shrimp.

ghee (Ia) Pure butterfat (usli ghee) from which all the milk solids have been removed; clarified butter. Also, various vegetable shortening oils are called ghee.

gherkin (US) A pickle made either with the small prickly fruit of a variety of cucumber or the immature fruit of garden cucumbers.

ghiacciata (It) Iced drink; icing for cake.

ghiaccio (It) Ice.

ghianda (It) Acorn.

ghiveci călugăresc (Ro) A stew of garden vegetables including fried onions, potatoes, celery, eggplant, zucchini, and green beans cooked with olive oil, garlic, and salt. Meat or fish may be added. Romania's national dish. Also called *Monk's Hotchpotch*.

ghleeko (Gk) Sweet.

ghurunopulo tu ghalaktos (Gk) Suckling pig.

giardiniera (It) A mixture of marinated vegetables.

gibanica (SC) Egg and cheese custard pie; may also be a fruit soufflé.

gibelotte (Fr) Fricassee of rabbit.

gibier (Fr) Wild game.

giblets (US) Poultry offal.

gibnah (Ar) Cheese.

gigot d'agneau (Fr) Leg of lamb.

gigue de chevreuil (Fr) Roast leg of venison.

gingembre (Fr) Ginger.

ginger (US) A brown, gnarled root of a plant, *Zingiber officinale*; about 3 inches long; pungent flavor; used fresh, grated or sliced, in Indian dishes and all the cusines of Asia. Dried, ground ginger is used in baked goods, sauces, cooked fruits, and savory meat or vegetable dishes. Also sold crystalized, pickled, and preserved.

gingerbread (US) A dark brown cake flavored with ginger and molasses; traditionally used to make decorated miniature houses and gingerbread figures.

gingersnaps (US) Crisp cookies flavored with ginger and molasses.

gingili (Ia) Sesame oil.

gingko nuts (US) The small oval nuts from the fruit of an ornamental tree, *Ginko biloba*, with light brown shells, ivory meats; widely used in Chinese and Japanese cooking.

ginjal (In) Kidneys.

ginnan (Jp) Gingko nuts.

ginseng (Ch) An aromatic, gnarled root of a plant, *Panax schinseng*, used in Chinese cooking and as a tonic.

gioulbassi (Gk) Salad of romaine, scallions, tomatoes, and rocket cress dressed with olive oil, dill, and lemon juice.

giovetsi (Gk) Orzo pasta with lamb.

girolle (Fr) See **chanterelle.**

gjedde (Nw) Pike.

Gjetost (Nw) A goat's and cow's milk cheese; brown paste; texture resembles peanut butter; sweet, caramellike flavor.

glace (Fr) Ice; ice cream.

glacé (US) Iced, glazed; candied.

glace aux noix (Fr) Walnut ice cream.

glace de viande (Fr) Meat glaze.

glaces tous parfums (Fr) Ice cream in all flavors.

gladzica (Po) Plaice.

glasmästarsill (Sw) Literally, "glass-blower's herring"; herring marinated in vinegar with carrots, onions, and horseradish.

glasswort (GB) A plant found in salt marshes; young shoots cooked, pickled, or eaten raw.

Glattbutt (Gr) Brill.

Glattroche (Gr) Skate.

glaze (US) A reduced stock added to some sauces.

glaze, to (US) To coat surface of food with syrup, egg white, or icing sugar until it glistens.

glazirovannye gretskie orekhi (Rs) Glazed walnuts.

gljive (SC) Mushrooms.

globe artichoke (US) A thistlelike, green, cone-shaped vegetable, *Cynara scolymus*, with partly edible flower bud scales and an edible heart or base; usually boiled and eaten as an hors d'oeuvre, in salads, or in cooked dishes.

glögg (Sw) A hot, spiced red wine with brandy, vodka, or aquavit; flavored with raisins, orange rind, and almonds.

Glücksschweinchen (Gr) Pig-shaped cookie, a holiday symbol of good luck.

glucose (US) A simple sugar that is the basic carbohydrate in many foods such as fruits, honey, and some vegetables. It is the chief source of energy for most body functions. All digestible carbohydrates in the diet are eventually converted to glucose in the body. When not immediately required, it is further converted to glycogen or body starch and stored. Too much glucose in the blood is a sign of diabetes; too little glucose is known as hypoglycemia or low blood sugar.

Glühwein (Gr) Literally, "glow wine"; mulled wine with cinnamon, allspice, nutmeg, and cloves.

gluten (US) An elastic protein substance present in some cereal grains, chiefly wheat and corn. It stretches and absorbs water, giving support and lightness to dough. Spring or hard wheat is high in gluten, making it a good flour for bread. Gluten flour (wheat flour with the starch removed) is used to make high-protein dishes, particularly in vegetarian diets.

gluten-free (US) A term applied to any food that contains no gluten; used by people who are allergic to the substance.

glutinous rice flour (US) A waxy type of flour made from glutinous or sticky rice. Also called **sweet rice flour.**

glycerine (US) The commercial term used for gycerol, an alcohol formed by the decomposition of fats. It is used as a moistening agent and as a solvent in some foods.

glykadakia (Gk) Sautéed sweetbreads in lemon sauce.

gnocchi (It) Small dumplings made of semolina or potato flour; served like pasta with sauce and Parmesan cheese.

gnocchi di patate al sugo di pomodor (It) Potato dumplings with tomato sauce.

gô (Jp) A puree of soaked soybeans.

gobo (Jp) See **burdock.**

godiveau (Fr) A forcemeat made from veal; used to make quenelles.

gogol'-gogol' (Rs) An eggnog dessert made with egg yolks, Cognac, orange liqueur, and lemon juice.

gohan (Jp) Long grain rice rubbed to remove surface starch then soaked in water, boiled, and dried; cooked rice.

gohanmono (Jp) Rice dishes.

goi (Vt) Salad.

goi cuon (Vt) An appetizer of minced pork and shrimp wrapped in rice paper; served cold with a chili-spiced bean sauce.

goi gia (Vt) A bean sprout salad; shrimp or crab may be added.

gôjiru (Jp) A thick soup prepared with gô (pureed soybeans), vegetables, mushrooms, daikon, taro, and deep-fried tofu.

golabki (Po) Stuffed cabbage rolls including ground beef, pork, rice, tomatoes, onion, lemon juice, nutmeg, and sour cream.

golden needles (US) Tiger lily buds, *Hemerocallis*; used fresh or dried in Japanese savory pork dishes, in salads, and floated on soups.

golden syrup (GB) A thick, sweet by-product of sugar making; resembles corn syrup in color and texture; used in baking, with stewed fruit, and as a spread.

golub (SC) Pigeon.

golubtsy (Rs) Stuffed cabbage rolls including ground beef, rice, egg, onion, and tomato; covered with tomato sauce; browned in butter and baked.

goma (Jp) Sesame seed.

goma abura (Jp) Sesame oil.

goma-sembei (Jp) A rice cake with sesame seeds.

gomba (Hu) Mushrooms.

gombaleves (Hu) Mushroom soup.

gombamártás (Hu) Mushroom sauce.

gombás hús (Hu) Beef rolls filled with mushrooms.

gombás palacsinták (Hu) Mushroom crepes.

gombóc (Hu) Dumplings.

gomoku gohan (Jp) A five-ingredient rice dish with green beans, carrots, peas, egg, chicken, or seafood in chicken broth.

goober (US) Peanut.

goose (US) A large web-footed bird, genus _Anser_, member of the duck family; usually roasted with a tart stuffing.

gooseberry (US) A fruit of a bush, _Ribes grossularia_, related to currants; oval shape, smooth or hairy skin; green to red color; used in preserves and desserts.

goosefish (US) See **monkfish.**

gorditas (Mx) A sausage-shaped dough of corn meal and potato with cheese, fried and served with ground pork and guacamole.

gorduroso (Pg) Fatty.

goreng (In) Fried.

goreng babat asam pedas (In) Fried tripe in a spicy and sour sauce.

goreng cumi-cumi (In) Fried squid.

Gorgonzola (It) A cow's milk cheese; soft, moist texture; white to straw color interior with blue-green mold; pungent aroma; rich, piquant flavor.

Gooseberry

goriachii shokolad (Rs) Hot chocolate beverage.

goriachii vinegret iz teliachikh mozgov (Rs) A hot salad with calf's brains.

gorp (US) A mixture of high-energy foods such as nuts or raisins. Also known as _trail mix._

gosht badaam pasanda (Ia) Fillets of lamb pounded thin and simmered in a sauce made with crushed almonds.

gosht do pyaza (Ia) Meat cooked with onions.

goshtaba (Ia) Lamb pounded to a paste seasoned with cardamom, cumin, and cloves; mixed with curds; formed into large balls and fried in ghee.

gosht quorma (Ia) Spiced lamb curry.

Götterspeise (Gr) A steamed pudding of pumpernickel crumbs, grated chocolate, beaten eggs, and almonds; served with whipped cream.

117

Gouda (Du) A rich, full-cream cow's milk cheese; cartwheel-shaped; yellow or red rind; yellow interior; mild, buttery taste.

gougère (Fr) Savory puff pastry containing cheese; may include other ingredients such as shrimp; an hors d'oeuvre.

goujon (Fr) Deep-fried, breaded strips of sole; served as appetizers.

goulash (US) A Hungarian meat and vegetable stew flavored with paprika, usually served on noodles.

gourd (US) Any of the trailing plants, genus *Cucurbita*, including the edible varieties such as squash, pumpkin, and vegetable marrow.

gourre (Fr) A potato cake.

goûter (Fr) An afternoon snack, similar to British four o'clock tea.

govedina (SC) Beef.

govedje pečenje (SC) Roast beef.

govedska juha (SC) Beef soup with noodles, parsnips, onions, and tomatoes.

goviadina (Rs) Beef.

goviadina po-Gusarski (Rs) Beef, Hussar-style; baked with Swiss-style cheese, egg yolks, and bread crumbs.

goviadina po-Stroganovski (Rs) See **beef Stroganoff.**

goviazhii kotlety (Rs) Ground beef patties.

grädde (Sw) Cream.

gräddost (Sw) A mild cheese.

grah (SC) Beans.

graham cracker (US) A sweetened, thin, flat biscuit made from graham flour.

graham flour (US) Unsifted, finely ground whole wheat flour; named for Sylvester Graham, early nineteenth century physician, who promoted the flour for breadmaking.

grahamkorputs (Fi) Graham crackers or rusks; baked rolls split in half and slowly dried in a cool oven.

grain (US) Seeds or fruit of plants such as grasses.

grain café (Fr) Coffee bean.

grain de poivre (Fr) Peppercorn.

gram (Ia) Chick-pea flour. Also called **besan.**

grana (It) A term used to mean cheeses suitable for grating; many varieties including Parmesan and Romano.

granada (Sp) Pomegranate.

granadillas (Sp) Pale green passion fruit.

Granatapfel (Gr) Pomegranate.

granchio (It) Crabs.

grand-duc, au (Fr) In the style of the Grand Duke; with a garnish of asparagus, truffles, and crayfish tails; used for chicken and served with a Marnier sauce.

grandmère (US) A Cajun term used for foods cooked with tender, loving care.

grandmère, à la (Fr) In the style of a grandmother; various dishes including scrambled eggs mixed with croutons and vegetable soup with pasta.

grand venure (Fr) A pepper sauce served with ground game or venison; made with red currant jelly and cream and sometimes with the blood of the animal.

grani di carvi (It) Caraway seeds.

granita (It) An iced dessert similar to sorbet but with a grainier texture; usually made with fruit juice.

granita al limone (It) Lemon ice.

granité (Fr) Grainy-textured ice usually made with fruit syrup and water.

granité au champagne (Fr) A flavored ice with syrup, sparkling wine, and Kirsch.

Granny Smith (US) An apple variety; green skin with green-white flesh and sweet, tart flavor; used in salads and cooked dishes. Originated in Australia.

grano (It) Grain; corn; wheat.

granola (US) A breakfast food made with oats, bran, shredded coconut, walnut pieces, sunflower seeds, raisins, honey, cinnamon, and butter or margarine; oven-toasted; served cold.

grano saraceno (It) Buckwheat.

granulated sugar (US) Refined, grainy, white sugar.

grãos (Pg) Chick-peas.

grãos com espinafres (Pg) Chick-peas cooked with onion and spinach.

grapefruit(US) The large, round fruit of an evergreen tree, *Citrus paradisi*; thick rind and segmented flesh; two main varieties: one with yellow skin and flesh and one with pink-yellow skin and pink to red flesh; usually eaten fresh.

grapefrukt (Nw) Grapefruit.

grape must bread (US) A Portuguese bread in which the must of crushed grapes is the leavening agent.

grapes (US) The round or oval, thin-skinned fruit of a climbing vine, *Vitis vinifera*; many varieties, which are divided into two classes, black and white; skin color varies from pale green to red to dark purple; pulpy,

Grapefruit

sweet flesh with or without seeds; eaten fresh or dried (as currants, raisins, and sultanas) in fruit salads, desserts, and used for jelly. Many grape varieties are grown for wine making.

grape sugar (US) Dextrose.

grappa (It) A brandy made from the fermented skins, seeds, and pulp of pressed grapes from the wine-making process; fiery, clear white to amber liquid.

grašak (SC) Peas.

gras-double (Fr) Tripe.

gräslök (Sw) Chives.

grătar amestecat (Ro) A hearty mixed grill of beef sausages, pork, liver, kidneys, and other meats.

grate, to (US) To scrape and shred the surface of food into small pieces.

gratin, au (Fr) Prepared with a topping of bread crumbs, melted butter, and

119

usually grated cheese, then oven-toasted or broiled.

gratin dauphinois (Fr) Potatoes, garlic, cheese, milk, and seasonings baked until golden brown.

gratin de poires (Fr) Pear gratin.

gratinée (Fr) Onion soup topped with bread crumbs and grated cheese and browned in an oven.

grauwe poon (Du) See **gurnard.**

gravlax (Sw) Marinated, spiced, sugar-cured fillets of raw salmon with dill; served with a mustard, dill, and sour cream sauce.

gravlaxsås (Sw) A mustard and dill sauce.

gravmakrell (Nw) Marinated mackerel.

gravy (US) 1. The juices and fats from cooked meat. 2. A sauce made with meat or poultry juices, a thickener of flour or cornstarch, stock or water, and seasoning.

grechnevaia kasha (Rs) Buckwheat.

grecque, à la (Fr) In the style of Greece; usually means a dish including olive oil and lemon such as vegetables in a marinade of olive oil and lemon; may also be fish in a wine sauce with fennel.

green cauliflower (US) A Dutch hybrid, a cross between broccoli and cauli-flower.

greengage plum (US) A *Reine-Claude* variety of plum, genus *Prunus,* with a green-yellow skin and yellow flesh; sweet, tart taste; used in fruit salads, cooked dishes, and as a dessert fruit; introduced to England from France in the eighteenth century by Sir William Gage and renamed.

green onions (US) Scallions.

green pepper (US) The unripe fruit of the sweet pepper or the hot pepper. See **capsicum.**

greens (US) The edible leaves and some-times stems of some plants such as spinach, beet tops, mustard, and kale; used cooked and in salads.

green sauce (US) A sauce made with vin-egar or lemon juice or both, oil and chopped green herbs; sometimes bread and hard-cooked eggs. See also **salsa verde.**

green tea (US) Tea leaves processed by withering, which retains the color.

greipin (Fi) Grapefruit.

greippimehu (Fi) Grapefruit juice.

grejpfrut (Po) Grapefruit.

grelhado (Pg) Grilled.

grelos (Pg) Turnip tops.

grenade (Fr) Pomegranate.

grenadine (US) A nonalcoholic fruit syrup made with pomegranate juice and sugar.

grenoblois (Fr) Sautéed with capers, brown butter, and lemon.

grenouille (Fr) Frog.

grenouilles à la provençale (Fr) Frogs' legs in garlic and butter.

grepfrut sok (SC) Grapefruit juice.

gresskar (Nw) Pumpkin.

gribi v smetane (Rs) Mushrooms in sour cream.

gribnaia ikra (Rs) Mushroom "caviar"; mushrooms marinated with minced onions, scallions, and garlic.

gribnye kotlety (Rs) Mushroom patties.

griddle (US) A flat, often rimless and heavy iron pan or stove surface used to cook pancakes, scones, and other similar foods.

griddle cake (US) Pancake.

Griessmehl (Gr) Semolina.

griglia, alla (It) Grilled; broiled.

grigliata di verdure (It) Grilled vegetables.

grillade panée (Fr) A Creole-American dish of veal marinated in egg, onion, and hot peppers, coated in corn meal, and deep-fried.

grillat (Sw) Grilled.

grillattu (Fi) Grilled.

grill (US) A gridiron or similar utensil used for broiling over hot coals or in modern stoves; also, the food prepared on a grill, as in mixed grill.

grillé (Fr) Broiled; grilled.

grind, to (US) To chop fine in a machine (grinder).

grinder (US) 1. A machine used to chop food. 2. A sandwich. See **hero.**

gris kob (SC) Farina pudding with apples, raisins, and whipped cream.

grissini (It) Pencil-thin bread sticks or long thin bread rolls.

grits (US) A form of hominy; a traditional Southern specialty made with dried, hulled, finely ground corn kernels, boiled and used as a breakfast food, a side dish, pudding, or soufflé.

groat (US) A grain kernel with the hull removed. Also called **berry.**

groenten (Du) Vegetables.

groentensoep (Du) Meat broth with vegetables and small meatballs.

gröna bönor (Sw) Green beans.

grønlangkål (Da) Kale; often served in a cream sauce.

grønnsaker (Nw) Vegetables.

grønnsaksuppe (Nw) Vegetable soup.

grøntsager (Da) Vegetables.

grönsakssoppa (Sw) Vegetable soup.

grönsallad (Sw) Green salad.

groseille à maquereau (Fr) Gooseberry.

groseille blanche (Fr) White currant.

groseille rouge (Fr) Red currant.

grosse Bohne (Gr) Broad bean.

groszek zielony (Po) Peas.

grøt (Nw) Cooked cereal.

gröt (Sw) Cooked cereal.

ground cherry (US) A round, tart, orange or red berry of several species of tropical plants, genus *Physalis*, used in preserves and in chili sauce.

groundnut (US) See **peanut.**

grouper (US) Any of the related warm saltwater fish, genus *Epinephelus*, members of the sea bass family; firm, lean, white flesh; may be grilled, poached, broiled, or baked; frying not recommended.

grouse (US) An important game bird, family Tetraonidae; plump body, delicate flavor; used broiled, stuffed, roasted, and cooked on a spit. The principal species are: in the United States, the ruffed grouse, prairie chicken, and the ptarmigan; in Europe, the capercaillie, the black and red grouse.

grovbrød (Nw) Pumpernickel bread.

grožđje (SC) Grapes.

gruel (GB) Thin porridge made with various cereals including oats, barley, and wheat.

grüne Bohnen (Gr) Green beans.

grüne Paprikaschoten (Gr) Green peppers.

121

grüner Salat (Gr) Green salad.

Grunkern (Gr) A type of unripe wheat roasted for use in a soup.

grunt (US) A steamed dessert made with berries and a dough cover; a dumpling topped with stewed fruit.

grunt (US) A tropical saltwater fish in the family Haemulidae, found in waters off Florida, that makes a grunting sound when alarmed; smaller fish are pan-fried.

Gruyère (Fr–Swiss) A cow's milk cheese; brown rind, pale yellow interior; smooth, firm texture; creamy, mild, piquant taste; used in fondues, cheese sauces, casseroles, and as a dessert.

grystek (Sw) A pot roast of beef or reindeer with a cream sauce; served with red currant jelly.

grzanka (Po) Toast.

grzyby (Po) Mushrooms.

guacamole (Mx) A side dish or dip made with mashed avocadoes with lemon or lime juice, green chilies, coriander or parsley, and seasonings; may also contain tomatoes and onions.

guajalote (Mx) Turkey.

guanabana (Cb) Custard apple; soursop.

guarapo de caña (Sp–Puerto Rico) A drink made with the juice of ground sugarcane served over ice.

guasacaca (Sp) A sauce from Venezuela similar to guacamole; a blended mixture of chopped avocado, tomato, hot chili pepper, green pepper, parsley, coriander, and hard-cooked egg in olive oil and vinegar; onion, garlic or mustard may be added; served with barbecued meats.

guava (US) The fruit of a tropical tree, *Psidium guajava*, related to myrtle; pear- or plum-shaped; pale yellow skin when ripe; white to pink flesh with many small, hard seeds; strawberry-like taste; eaten raw. Also sold canned.

guava duff (Cb) Steamed pudding with guavas.

guay tiaw (Th) Thin rice noodles; may be stir-fried and served with shrimp.

guazzetto (It) Stew; hash; ragout.

gubana (It) A snail-shaped pastry filled with fruits, nuts, and chocolate soaked in grappa.

gudeg (In) Chicken with jackfruit.

gudgeon (GB) A small freshwater fish in the carp family; deep-fried in bread crumbs or batter.

Gugelhupf (Gr) See **Kugelhopf.**

guinea hen (US) A domesticated bird, *Numidida meleagris*, related to the chicken, partridge, and turkey; with meat darker and gamier than chicken; may be prepared like a game bird.

guisado (Pg) Stew; stewed.

guisantes a la bilbaina (Sp) Stew cooked in the style of the seaport of Bilbao; with peas, potatoes, and onions.

guiso (Sp) Cooked dish; stew.

guiso de atun (Sp) A stew of fresh tuna and vegetables.

guiso de quimbombo (Cb) A stew made with okra, root vegetables, bacon, and plantain dumplings in beef stock flavored with sherry.

gula (In, Ml) Sugar.

gulab jamun (Ia) A dessert of small, deep-fried dumplings soaked in syrup containing rose water and cardamom.

gulai (In, Ml) Dish; curry.

gulai bagar (In) Curried braised beef.

gulai daging lembu (Ml) Beef curry simmered in coconut milk and tamarind water.

gulai ikan padang (In) Fish curry with chili peppers, tamarind, lemongrass, galangal, and coconut milk.

gulai otak (In) Brains in a spicy coconut sauce.

gul ärtsoppa (Sw) Yellow pea soup.

guláš (Cz) Goulash.

gulášová polévka (Cz) Spicy meat soup.

gule ærter (Da) A winter soup made with yellow split peas, vegetables, bacon, and sausage.

guleng (Ml) Milk.

gulerødder (Da) Carrots.

gullflyndre (Nw) Plaice.

gulrøtter (Nw) Carrots.

gulyás (Hu) Goulash; a thick dish of beef or veal braised in lard with tomatoes, potatoes, and onions seasoned with paprika.

gulyásleves (Hu) Goulash soup made with gulyás and water.

gum arabic (US) A gum from the bark of the acacia tree, used as a stabilizer in various food mixtures and confections. Also called **acacia.**

gumbo (US) Literally, "okra"; a Creole soup or stew containing a variety of game, poultry, seafood, and vegetables and with okra or filé (powdered sassafras leaves) used for flavoring and thickening.

gundel (Hu) Thin pancakes filled with chocolate and nuts; flamed.

gunpowder tea (US) A Chinese green tea made from pellets of the smallest and youngest leaves. Also called **pearl tea.**

gur (Ia) Unrefined, honey-brown lump sugar.

gurami (Th) Freshwater bass.

gurda (Ia) Kidney.

guriev kasha (Rs) A dessert made with semolina, cream, fruits, and nuts.

gurka (Sw) Cucumber.

Gurken (Gr) Cucumbers.

Gurkensalat (Gr) Cucumber salad.

gurnard (US) A saltwater fish in the family Triglidae found in Atlantic waters from Norway to the Mediterranean; with firm white flesh; used baked, poached, or fried.

guska (SC) Goose.

güveç (Tr) Individual casseroles of meat and vegetables, served with yogurt.

gvina (Jw–Israel) Cheese.

gwangen (GB–Wales) Shad.

gwaytio (Th) Fresh, soft rice noodles.

gwyniad y môr (GB–Wales) Whiting.

gyokai ryōri (Jp) Fish and seafood dishes.

gyokuro (Jp) "Pearl dew"; superior green tea.

gyro (Gk) Seasoned chopped meat packed with fat on a rotating spit in front of a heat source; slices are cut off and served with pita bread.

gyümölcslé (Hu) Fruit juice.

gyümölcssaláta (Hu) Fruit salad.

gyūnabe (Jp) See **sukiyaki.**

gyūniku (Jp) Beef.

gyūniku no yawatamaki (Jp) Rolls of beef and burdock roots.

H

haaievinnen sop (In) Shark's fin soup.

haarukkaleivät (Fi) Literally, "fork cookies"; cookies made with fork tine patterns by pressing a fork into the dough before baking.

haas (Du) Hare.

Haas avocado (US) An egg-shaped avocado grown in California with purple-black, wrinkled skin and rich, nutty flavor; smaller than the green avocado.

haba (Sp) Fava bean; broad bean.

habas con longanizas (Sp) Broad beans cooked with white pork sausages.

habas verdes (Sp) Green beans.

habbah sawda (Ar), Black caraway.

hacher (Fr) To chop, usually meat.

hachis (Da) Hash made with leftover beef roast or ground beef, onion, and pickled gherkins; served with fried eggs and sugar browned potatoes.

hackat (Sw) Chopped.

hackat kött(Sw) Ground beef.

Hackbraten (Gr) Meat loaf.

Hackrahmsteak (Gr) Ground meat patty in browned cream gravy.

haddock (US) A fish, *Melanogrammus aeglefinus*, smaller than the cod but of the same family; lean soft flesh; used poached, steamed, baked, fried, grilled, and smoked.

haggamuggie (Sc) A fish haggis made with fish livers stuffed in a fish stomach, boiled and eaten with potatoes.

haggis (Sc) A Scottish specialty of minced liver, heart, and lungs of sheep mixed with oatmeal, onion, suet, and seasonings packed into pieces of sheep's stomach, simmered in water, and served hot with potatoes, turnips, and Scotch whiskey.

hagyma (Hu) Onions.

hagymamártás (Hu) Onion sauce.

bái jè pí (Ch) Jellyfish.

băi-shēn (Ch) Sea cucumber.

haiver sin patladjan (Bu) Eggplant caviar made with broiled, minced eggplant, garlic, onion, and tomato seasoned with clove, vinegar, and olive oil.

băi-wèi shălà (Ch) Seafood salad.

hai yup yue (Ml) Deep-fried fish chunks served with a sauce of coconut milk and crab.

hake (US) A fish, *Merluccius merluccius*, regarded the best of the cod family; white, lean flesh; used poached, steamed, baked, or fried, and marinated in seviche.

hakkebøf med løg (Da) Minced beefsteak patties topped with onions.

hakket kjøtt (Nw) Chopped meat.

hakusai (Jp) Chinese cabbage (see **bái-tsài**).

hakusai no shizuke (Jp) Chinese cabbage pickled in salt.

halal (Ar) Food allowed by the Koran.

halászlé (Hu) Spicy fish and paprika soup.

haldi (Ia) Turmeric.

haldi jhinga (Ia) Shrimp marinated in spices and colored yellow with turmeric, dredged in finely ground wheat, and deep-fried to acquire a crunchy coating.

half-and-half (US) A combination of milk and light cream in equal quantities; when substituted for milk, the result is richer than if milk is used; if substituted for cream, the effect is less rich.

half shell (US) Either of the halves of a bivalve mollusk, such as a clam, oyster, or mussel. The shell is often used for a container in which to serve the raw or cooked mollusk, or other preparations.

halibut (US) Largest of the flatfish, *Hippoglossus hippoglossus*, sold in steaks and fillets; firm, medium to oily, white flesh; used poached, baked, fried, or grilled.

hallacas (Sp) A Venezuelan dish of tamalelike appetizers or main course foods, stuffed with ground beef, pork, or chicken. The wrapper may be banana leaves or parchment paper rather than corn husks, and the stuffing may also include cheese, olives, capers, and raisins.

hälleflundra (Sw) Halibut.

hallon (Sw) Raspberries.

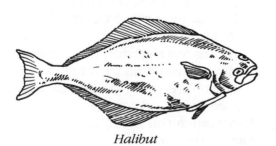

Halibut

Haloumi (Gk) A ewe's milk cheese; ivory color firm texture, sometimes mixed with mint leaves; savory, salty taste; often used sliced and sautéed in butter.

hälsingeost (Sw) A semisoft cheese made of cow's and goat's milk.

haluwa (Af–Swahili) Halva.

halva (US) A sweet confection made from ground sesame seeds; many variations in other ingredients, such as pistachio nuts. Some use fruit or vegetables such as carrots, or rice flour browned in butter and lemon-flavored sugar syrup.

halva (Gk) A molded dessert of farina and pine nuts or almonds mixed with a sugar syrup and served with whipped cream.

ham (US) An animal's hind leg and thigh, usually of a hog in the form of cured bacon. Butt end refers to the upper, meatier part of a ham; shank half, the lower thinner end. Fresh ham means it has not been cured and is used roasted, broiled, fried, or braised. Cured ham is usually served boiled or baked, hot or cold.

hamachi (Jp) Yellowtail tuna.

hamachi tataki (Jp) Yellowtail tuna cooked with scallions.

hamaguri (Jp) Clams.

hamaguri sakani (Jp) Sake-cooked clams.

hamaguri ushiojiru (Jp) Clam broth.

hamantasch (Jw) A three-cornered, yeast-raised pastry with a poppy-seed or prune filling served during the festival of Purim.

hamburger (US) Ground or chopped beef, used in meat loaf, patties, and other dishes.

ham hock (US) The lower part of a hog's foreleg, often served with horseradish or sauerkraut.

Hammelbraten (Gr) Roast mutton.

Hammelfleisch (Gr) Mutton.

Hammelkeule (Gr) Roast leg of lamb or mutton.

Hammelkotelett (Gr) Grilled mutton or lamb chop.

hamur (Ar) An Arabian Gulf grouper with flesh similar to sea bass.

hanagatsuo (Jp) Dried bonito shavings, used as a condiment.

hand pies (US) Small, crescent-shaped pastries with various savory fillings including, pork and apple, beef and kidney, and lamb with chutney. Also called **finger pies.**

handsel (Sc) A piece of bread eaten before breakfast, part of Hogmanay (December 31) tradition.

Hangtown Fry (US) Oysters dipped in an egg and bread crumb mixture, fried, then added to an omelet; cooked until firm; served with bacon; named for Hangtown, California before it was renamed Placerville.

hanhi (Fi) Goose.

hanim göbĕgi (Tr) Literally, "lady's navel"; a round form of baklava with a dimple in the center.

hanjuku tamago (Jp) Soft-boiled eggs.

hanne tamago (Jp) Soft-boiled eggs.

hapanimeläkastike (Fi) Sweet-and-sour sauce.

hapankaalikeitto (Fi) Sauerkraut soup.

hapankerma (Fi) Sour cream.

hapankermakastike (Fi) Sour cream salad dressing.

hapanleipä (Fi) Dark sour rye bread.

hapu'u (Pl) Black sea bass.

hara dhania (Ia) Coriander leaves.

häränhäntäliemi (Fi) Oxtail soup.

hardal (Tr) Mustard.

hardali (Af–Swahili) Mustard.

hard gekookte eieren (Du) Hard-boiled eggs.

hårdkogte æg (Da) Hard-boiled egg.

hårdkokta ägg (Sw) Hard-boiled egg.

Härdöpfelstock (Gr–Swiss) Mashed potatoes.

hard sauce (US) A cold sauce made with butter, sugar (powdered, confectioners' or brown), and a flavoring such as vanilla, rum, brandy, or fruit served on cake or pudding.

hardshell clams (US) A group of quahog clams that includes the categories of littlenecks, cherrystones, and chowder clams.

hardtack (US) A hard biscuit or flat bread baked in a form; made with flour and water and without salt, shortening or yeast. Also called **sea biscuit, pilot biscuit.**

hare (US) A mammal related to the rabbit in the family Leporidae but with a darker color and more powerful back legs. Larger, a wild hare can weigh up to 14 pounds. Stronger in taste and with darker meat than rabbit, it is usually marinated and roasted. A farm-raised hare is less gamey. See **jugged hare.**

haree mirch (Ia) Green chili pepper.

hareng (Fr) Herring.

hareng saur (Fr) Salted and smoked red

herring; used soaked in milk, then broiled.

haresteg (Da) Roast hare.

haricots (Fr) Beans in the species *Phaseolus*; may be oval, round, long, or kidney-shaped, with colors ranging from white, red, brown, and black.

haricots de mouton (Fr) Mutton and white bean stew.

haricots de Soissons (Fr) White beans, preferred for cassoulet.

haricots flageolets (Fr) Small, pale green beans.

haricots larges (Fr) Broad beans.

haricots verts (Fr) Green string beans.

haricots verts à la maitre d'hôtel (Fr) Green beans tossed with butter, parsley, and lemon juice.

haricots verts sautés au beurre (Fr) Green beans sautéed in butter.

harina de maíz (Sp) Cornstarch.

haring (Du) Herring.

haringa (SC) Herring.

haringsla (Du) Herring salad.

harira (Ar) Lamb soup with lemon and cinnamon.

harissa (Ar) A spicy hot condiment made with a purée of dried red chili peppers, cayenne, garlic, salt, caraway, coriander, and olive oil; served with soups, fish, dry meats, and couscous.

Hartford election cake (US) See **election cake.**

hartgekochte Eier (Gr) Hard-cooked eggs.

harusame (Jp) Literally, "spring rain"; cellophane noodles, translucent noodles made with soybean powder.

Harvard beets (US) Diced or sliced beets cooked in vinegar, sugar, and cornstarch; usually served warm. The color, similar to Harvard's football jerseys, is considered the term's origin.

Hase (Gr) Hare.

Haselnussrahm (Gr) Hazelnut cream.

Hasenkeule (Gr) Leg of hare.

Hasenpfeffer (Gr) Jugged hare marinated in wine, onions, pepper, and spices, then cooked in the marinade. Onions, mushrooms, lemon juice, or sometimes bitter chocolate may be added.

Hasenrücken (Gr) Saddle of hare.

hash (US) Leftover cooked meat heated in seasoned brown gravy.

hashed brown potatoes (US) Grated raw potatoes fried in bacon fat to form a crusty pancake.

hasselnötter (Sw) Hazelnuts.

hasselnøtter (Nw) Hazelnuts.

hasty pudding (US) See **Indian pudding.**

hati ayam asam manis (In) Marinated chicken giblets cooked with vegetables.

háu (Ch) Oysters.

haupia (Pl) Hawaiian coconut pudding.

Häuptelsalat (Gr–Austria) Lettuce.

haute cuisine (Fr) "High cookery"; food prepared with the finest ingredients and following well-established formulas for classic dishes.

háu-yóu (Ch) Oyster sauce.

háu-yóu mwó-gŭ (Ch) Mushrooms braised in oyster sauce.

Havarti (Da) A cow's milk cheese; semi-soft, pale yellow interior with many irregular holes; mild but piquant flavor.

havregrød (Da) Cooked oatmeal.

havregrøt (Nw) Cooked oatmeal.

127

havremel (Nw) Oats.

havuç (Tr) Carrots.

havyar (Tr) Caviar.

haw mok (Th) Spicy dish of steamed, chopped fish in a paste of chilis, onions, garlic, lemongrass, coconut milk, and soy sauce.

hazelnut (US) The nut of any variety of shrubs or trees, genus *Corylus*; used ground or roasted for pastries and desserts. When cultivated, generally known as filberts. See **filbert.**

headcheese (US) A jellied meat loaf made with pieces of meat from a boiled pig's head, onion, herbs, and seasonings. A gelatinous broth forms from the boiling. Served cold. Sheep and cow heads may also be used. Also called **brawn, souse.**

head lettuce (US) Any of the lettuces that form compact leaf balls.

hearts of palm (US) The terminal bud and internal part of the young stem of a palm tree, *Oreodoxa oleracea*; a

Hazelnut

bland, delicate taste; simmered and served with a butter sauce or used in salads.

heavy cream (US) Cream containing about 36–42 percent butterfat. Also called **whipping cream.**

hé-bāudàn (Ch) Poached eggs.

hebi (Pl) A spearfish from Hawaiian waters; firm-textured, sweet-flavored pink flesh that turns white when cooked.

Hecht (Gr) Pike.

hedelmäkakut (Fi) Fruit squares.

hedelmäkukkoset (Fi) Blueberry buns.

Hefe (Gr) Yeast; leaven.

Hefengebäck (Gr) Leavened bread or pastry.

Heidelbeere (Gr) Bilberry; whortleberry; blueberry.

hēi-dòu (Ch) Black beans.

heilbot (Du) Halibut.

Heilbutt (Gr) Halibut.

helado (Sp) Ice cream.

hellefisk (Nw) Halibut.

helleflynder (Da) Halibut.

helt (Da) Whitefish.

helva (Tr) Halva.

hepia (In) Fried shrimp with vegetables.

herbata (Po) Tea.

herbata z mlekiem (Po) Tea with milk.

herb butter (US) A spread made by blending butter with minced herbs, such as chives or parsley, used for bread, fish, meat, and vegetables.

herbes (Fr) Herbs.

herbes de Provence (Fr) A dried herb mixture, a combination of thyme, basil, savory, and fennel seeds.

herbs (US) Plants with little or no woody tissues and with no winter buds above ground. They die down to the ground at the end of the growing season although there may be underground bulbs, rootstocks, or tubers. Herbs are sometimes classified according to specific essential oils that contribute to their aroma.

herb vinegar (US) Vinegar flavored with fresh or dried herbs including tarragon, basil, parsley, marjoram, and rosemary. Fresh herbs are inserted in vinegar; dried herbs are heated in the liquid.

hering (Hu) Herring.

Heringsalat (Gr) Herring salad.

Heringskönig (Gr) John Dory fish.

herkkusienikeitto (Fi) Mushroom soup.

herneitä (Fi) Peas.

hernekeitto (Fi) Split pea soup.

hero (US) A sandwich made with a loaf of French or Italian bread sliced lengthwise and filled with a variety of items including meats, cheeses, lettuce, and peppers. The term is reported to be derived from the heroics needed to eat the large sandwich. Many variations in the name include hoagie, grinder, submarine, wedge, and poor boy.

herrgårdsost (Sw) A cow's milk cheese; ivory to yellow with round holes; mild, nutty flavor; Sweden's version of Swiss Emmentaler.

herring (US) Any of various small, saltwater fish, genus *Clupea*, found in the North Atlantic and North Pacific. With an unusually high fat content, when used fresh, herring are grilled, fried, or baked; more often sold in preparations such as Bismarck herring,
bloater, salt-cured, kipper, pickled herring, and rollmops.

Hervé (Bl) A strong-smelling cow's milk cheese with a red-brown rind and soft, pale yellow interior; pungent, tangy taste.

Herz (Gr) Heart.

Herzoginkartoffeln (Gr) Dutchess-style potatoes—mashed, shaped, and browned in the oven.

hé-táu (Ch) Walnuts.

hideg meggyleves (Hu) Cold sour cherry soup.

hidratos de carbone (Sp) Carbohydrates.

hiekka kakkuja (Fi) Sand tarts; made of butter and egg dough, crushed vanilla wafers, and ground almonds; baked in tiny fluted molds.

hielo (Sp) Ice.

hierbabuena (Sp) Mint.

hierro (Sp) Iron.

higashi (Jp) A kind of dry confection or sweet.

hiivaleipä (Fi) Yeast bread, usually made with rye and barley flours.

hiivapannukakku (Fi) An oven-baked pancake made with yeast batter.

hijiki (Jp) An edible seaweed, *Hizikia fusiforme*, that is brown when fresh, black and stringy when dried. When soaked, it expands to four times its dry volume. Used in stir-fried dishes, soups, salads, and sometimes cooked with onion and tofu.

hikiniku (Jp) Ground beef.

hillo (Fi) Jam.

hilu huli (Pl) Spit roasting.

Himbeeren (Gr) Raspberries.

Himbeergeist (Gr) Raspberry schnapps.

Himbeersaft (Gr) Raspberry juice.

hindbær (Da) Raspberries.

hindi (Tr) Turkey.

hing (Ia) Asafetida, dried gum resin from the roots of a plant in India, used as a spice with fish.

hinojo (Sp) Fennel.

hirame (Jp) Halibut; flounder.

hireniku (Jp) Filet mignon.

Hirschbraten (Gr) Roast stag.

Hirschkeule (Gr) Leg of deer.

Hirschsteak (Gr) Steak of stag.

hirvenliha (Fi) Elk meat.

hitashimono (Jp) Spinach or other greens boiled and dipped in shoyu.

hiyamugi (Jp) Cold, cooked wheat flour noodles served with a dip of sweetened soy sauce.

hjärta (Sw) Heart.

hjerter stegte (Da) Roasted hearts.

hjortron (Sw) See **cloudberry.**

hjortstek (Sw) Venison steak.

hladan čaj (SC) Iced tea.

hlávkový salát (Cz) Lettuce; green salad.

hleb (SC) Bread.

hoagie (US) See **hero.**

hochepot (Bl) A dish of meats, vegetables, and herbs poached in a broth.

Hochwild (Gr) Wild game.

ho'i'o (Pl) Hawaiian fern shoots used in salads.

hoisin (Ch) A creamy, red-brown sauce made of a sweet, spicy mixture of soybeans, garlic, sugar, salt, and hot red pepper; used for duck, spareribs, seafood, and as condiment.

hollandaise, sauce (Fr) A classic lemon-flavored sauce made with egg yolks and clarified butter; served with vegetables and fish.

Hollander Kirschtorte (Gr) A puff pastry crust layered with vanilla cream, sour cherries, and whipped cream and topped with powdered sugar.

hollantilainen kastike (Fi) Hollandaise sauce.

Holsteinerschnitzel (Gr) Pan-fried veal cutlet topped with a fried egg.

holub (Cz) Pigeon.

homar (Hu, Po) Lobster.

homard (Fr) Lobster.

homard à l'américaine (Fr) Pieces of lobster sautéed in oil and butter then simmered with wine, brandy, shallots, and tomatoes; created by a chef Fraisse about 1860 after returning to France from America.

homard à la Newburg (Fr) See **lobster Newburg.**

homard cardinal (Fr) Cooked, diced lobster meat in a sauce containing the red lobster coral, topped with cheese, and broiled quickly to brown.

homard grillé (Fr) Broiled lobster.

homard sauté (Fr) Chunks of lobster sautéed in butter with herbs added.

homard Thermidor (Fr) Cooked, diced lobster meat served in refilled shells with a thick cream sauce containing butter, white wine, and mustard then topped with Parmesan cheese and more butter and reheated to form a gratin.

hominy (US) A corn product made from corn kernels that have been dried and then soaked in lye.

hominy grits (US) See **grits.**

høne (Nw) Hen, chicken.

hongo (Sp) Mushroom.

hongroise, à la (Fr) In the style of Hungary; made with paprika, such as a sauce based on onion, paprika, and white wine.

Honig (Gr) Honey.

Honigkuchen-wurfel (Gr) Honey cake squares.

honing (Du) Honey.

honingkoek (Du) Honey cake.

hønsekødsuppe (Da) Chicken soup with meatballs and dumplings.

høns i peberrod (Da) Stewed chicken in a creamed horseradish sauce.

hönssoppa (Sw) Chicken soup.

hontaka (Jp) A small, red-orange, Japanese dried chili pepper, ranging from hot to very hot in taste.

honu (Pl) Turtle.

Hopfenkäse (Gr) A spicy, hop-flavored cow's milk cheese made without rennet, using sour milk; caraway seeds or cumin may be added.

hoppin' John (US) A traditional American dish of rice and black-eyed peas with diced ham or hog jowls and seasonings. In the deep South, it is a New Year's Day dish that reportedly promises good luck for the new year. The origin of the name is obscure.

hops (US) The fruit of a twining vine, *Humulus lupulus*, a conical, seedlike structure used in brewing. Its bitterness counteracts the sweetness of malt grain. In Europe, hop shoots are used as a salad vegetable or cooked like asparagus.

hořcice (Cz) Mustard.

horcheta (Sp) A beverage made with pulverized melon seeds, lemon or lime juice, and sugar.

hōrensō (Jp) Spinach.

hōrensō no goma ae (Jp) Spinach with sesame dressing.

horiatiki (Gk) "Country" salad; made with lettuce, tomatoes, cucumbers, chicory, scallions, peppers, radishes, anchovies, olives, and feta cheese.

horké kakao (Cz) Hot chocolate.

horn (Nw) Crescent roll.

horned melon (US) See **kiwano.**

hornfisk (Da) See **garfish.**

horno, al (Sp) Cooked in an outdoor oven; grilled.

hors d'oeuvre (Fr) Literally, "outside of work"; an appetizer that may be a canapé, relish, or side dish served at a party or before a meal.

horseradish (US) A plant, *Armoracia rusticana*, member of the cabbage family, with large leaves and a pungently flavored taproot that resembles

Horseradish

131

a thin parsnip; grated for use in various sauces; often served with roast beef or fowl.

horseradish sauce (US) A sauce made with grated horseradish, whipped cream, vinegar, lemon juice, and seasonings; served with roast beef, smoked fish, chicken, and hard-boiled eggs.

hortobágyi palacsinta (Hu) A wafer-thin pancake filled with goose liver pâté.

hotategai (Jp) Clams.

hot cross buns (GB) Yeast rolls flavored with cinnamon, allspice, nutmeg, and cloves marked with a cross in frosting for religious holidays.

hot dog (US) A frankfurter in a split bun. See also **frankfurters.**

houbová omáčka (Cz) Mushroom sauce.

houby (Cz) Mushrooms.

houby s octem (Cz) Pickled mushrooms.

hough (Sc) Shin of beef.

houska (Cz) Braided roll.

houskový knedlík (Cz) Bread dumpling.

hout (Ar) Fish.

hovězí maso (Cz) Beef.

hovězí vývar s játrovými knedlíčky (Cz) Beef broth with liver dumplings.

howtowdie (Sc) Chicken stuffed with bread crumbs, sprinkled with spices and chicken broth, browned in a casserole, and served with a sauce of cream and chicken livers on a bed of spinach.

hrachová polévka (Cz) Pea soup.

hrášek (Cz) Peas.

hrozny vina (Cz) Grapes.

hruška (Cz) Pears.

huachinango (Sp) Red snapper.

Hubbard squash (US) A large, melonlike gourd with a green, blue or orange shell; flesh is orange and mildly flavored.

huckleberry (US) The fruit of a bush, genus *Gaylussacia,* similar to the blueberry with dark blue skin, hard seeds, and tart flesh; eaten raw or cooked.

huevas reales (Sp) Royal eggs; cubes of baked egg custard in a mixture of raisins, sugar, pine nuts, cinnamon, and dry sherry.

huevo (Sp) Egg.

huevo duro (Sp) Hard-boiled egg.

huevo escalfado (Sp) Poached egg.

huevo frito (Sp) Fried egg.

huevo passado por agua (Sp) Soft-boiled egg.

huevo revuelto (Sp) Scrambled egg.

huevos rancheros (Sp) Eggs (scrambled, fried, or poached) with a hot, spicy sauce; usually served with tortillas and covered with a variety of hot sauces.

huevos rellenos (Sp) Fried stuffed eggs.

Huhn (Gr) Chicken.

Hühnerbrühe (Gr) Chicken broth.

Hühnerfrikassee (Gr) Chicken fricassee.

Hühnerpalatschinken (Gr–Austria) Creamed chicken and mushrooms in pancake rolls.

Hühnersuppe (Gr) Chicken soup.

huile (Fr) Oil.

huile de noix (Fr) Walnut oil, sometimes used as a salad dressing.

huitlachoche (Mx) A fungus that grows on the ears of sweet corn. A black juice from the fungus is used in Mexican cooking as a flavoring.

huîtres (Fr) Oysters.

hú-jyāu (Ch) Black pepper.

hull (US) The outer layer of a grain kernel, with no nutritional value.

hummer (Da, Nw) Lobster.

hummer (Sw) Lobster.

Hummer (Gr) Lobster.

hummeri (Fi) Lobster.

hummus (Ar) A puree made with a mixture of chick-peas, lemon juice, tahini, olive oil, and sometimes yogurt; used as a dip for pita bread or vegetables and in sauce for meats and fish.

humr (Cz) Lobster.

hunajaluumut (Fi) Honey-stewed prunes.

hunajapiima (Fi) A buttermilk and honey beverage.

hunayni (Ar) A confection made from ground dates and butter, flavored with cardamom and simmered until nearly stiff.

hundred-year eggs (Ch) See **pi-dàn.**

húng chá (Ch) Black tea that makes a red-orange brew.

húng-lwó-bwō (Ch) Carrots.

húng-shāu li-yú (Ch) Carp simmered in soy sauce.

húng-syí-lwó-bwó (Ch) Radish.

húng-tsài-tóu (Ch) Beets.

bünkâr beğendi (Tr) Literally, "the ruler liked it"; broiled chicken with lightly spiced eggplant purée; created for Sultan Murat IV.

hurka (Hu) A spicy sausage made with blood, liver, and rice.

husa (Cz) Goose.

húsgombóc (Hu) Meat dumplings.

hush puppy (US) A deep-fried dumpling of cornmeal and buttermilk, sometimes with chopped onions or scallions; traditionally served with catfish.

husí játra (Cz) Goose liver.

hutspot met klapstuk (Du) A dish of meats, vegetables, and herbs poached in a broth.

huzarensla (Du) Meat salad.

hvetebrød (Nw) Wheat bread.

hvetemel (Nw) Wheat.

hvidløget (Da) Garlic.

hvid sagosuppe (Da) A soup made with sago, beaten eggs, and sherry.

hvitkål (Nw) White cabbage.

hvitløk (Nw) Garlic.

hvitting (Nw) Whiting.

hwáng-dòu (Ch) Soybeans.

hwáng-gwā Ch) Cucumber.

hwáng-yú (Ch) Sturgeon.

hwā-shēng (Ch) Peanuts.

hwā-shēng-yóu (Ch) Peanut oil.

hwe dup bup (Kr) Slices of raw sea bass and red snapper served with sesame seeds, lightly sautéed seaweed (laver), and hot, steamed rice.

hwéi-syāng-dz (Ch) Aniseed.

hwo-jī (Ch) Turkey.

hwún-dwùn (Ch) Wonton.

hyacinth bean (US) A small bean plant, *Dolichos lablab,* native of India, with edible leaves and pods; pods are often pickled.

hydrates de carbone (Fr) Carbohydrates.

hydrolyzed vegetable protein (US) A protein from corn, wheat, or soybeans obtained by a process called acid hydrolysis. With a meaty taste, it is used as a flavoring in commercial food products such as meat extracts and stock cubes.

hyldebæaersuppe (Da) Elderberry soup.

I

iablochnyi pirog (Rs) Apple pie.

iabloki v kreme (Rs) Apples in custard cream.

iadritsa (Rs) Whole buckwheat groats.

iaichnyi pashtet (Rs) Chopped egg pâté.

i'alawalu (Pl–Hawaii) A local fish (aawa) baked in taro leaves.

iantarnaia ukha (Rs) Amber fish soup with saffron threads and lemon slices.

ice (US) frozen water; freezing point of water 32°F/0°C.

iceberg lettuce (US) See **head lettuce.**

ice cream (US) A rich, frozen dessert made with cream or custard, sugar, flavorings, and often eggs.

ices (US) Frozen desserts made with sugar and flavored water and fruit juice or pureed fruit. Ices are similar to sherbets but contain no dairy products. The term may also include shaved ice flavored with fruit syrup or juice. Also called **water ice.**

ichiban dashi (Jp) Basic Japanese soup stock made with dried kelp and dried bonito flakes.

ichigo (Jp) Strawberries.

icicle pickles (US) Cucumber strips pickled in vinegar, water, sugar, and salt.

icing (US) A sweetened mixture with butter, egg whites, milk or cream, often flavored and colored, and used to cover, fill, or decorate cakes and other sweets. Also called **frosting.**

icing sugar (GB) Confectioners' sugar.

iç pilav (Tr) A pilaf of livers (lamb or goose) fried in butter with rice, pine nuts, raisins, tomato, and onions.

idli (Ia) Steamed round bread made of rice and lentils with coconut or other flavorings; may be sweet or spicy.

idrati di carbonio (It) Carbohydrates.

iers mos (Du) Irish moss; carrageen.

igaguri (Jp) Deep-fried balls of pureed shrimp filled with sweet chestnuts. The balls are rolled in cut noodles before frying to give a thorny appearance.

igname (Fr) Yam.

iguana (US) Tropical American lizard; tail meat may be used like chicken; iguana eggs are also eaten fried or pickled.

ijs (Du) Ice cream; ice.

ika (Jp) Cuttlefish; squid.

ika maruyaki (Jp) Broiled squid.

ikan asam manis (In) Fish in a sweet-and-sour sauce with sugar, vinegar, and spices.

ikan asap (In) Smoked fish.

ikang (Ml) Fish.

ikan goreng (In) Fried fish.

ikan gurita (In) Octopus.

ikan masak kelapa (In) Fish in coconut milk.

ikan pangeh (In) Steamed fish.

ikra (Rs) Caviar.

ikra iz baklazhanov (Rs) Eggplant caviar; a thick mixture of chopped eggplant, tomato puree, and onion simmered in olive oil, served chilled with added lemon juice.

ikura (Jp) Salmon roe rolled in seaweed and vinegared rice.

île flottante (Fr) Literally, "floating is-

134

land"; a dessert of custard cream topped with a meringue of egg whites and sugar; covered with caramel and decorated with almonds. See also **oeufs à la neige.**

ilmalish shurb (Ar) Drinking water.

Imam bayildi (Tr) Literally, "the Imam fainted"; eggplant stuffed with tomato, garlic, onions, peppers, and pine nuts; cooked in generous amounts of olive oil; many variations of stuffing ingredients. One story says that the Imam (or priest) found the dish so delicious that he swooned.

Imbiss (Gr) Snack; light meal.

imellettyperunasoselaatikko (Fi) Potato casserole.

imli (Ia) Tamarind.

imli chatni (Ia) Chutney made with tamarind pulp.

imo-sembei (Jp) Sweet potato and rice cake.

impanato (It) Breaded; covered with bread crumbs.

impériale, à l' (Fr) In the Imperial style; various garnishes with fois gras, mushrooms, cockscombs, kidneys, crayfish tails, and truffles.

imposata (It) A very dry, very smooth ricotta cheese used in making the filling for cannolis.

imu (Pl) An earth-dug pit used as an oven.

inab (Ar) Grapes.

inarizushi (Jp) Rice balls wrapped in fried tofu.

in bianco (It) In white; served plain.

incaciatura (It) Grated cheese as a condiment.

incanestrato (It) Literally, "in a basket"; also, a grating cheese, often a ewe's milk cheese, made in a reed basket, showing the imprint.

in carrozza (It) Literally, "in a carriage"; a cheese baked between bread.

incir (Tr) Figs.

incise, to (US) To make slits in raw food for flavorings such as herbs or garlic to be inserted.

incomplete protein (US) Any protein that lacks one or more of the essential amino acids and generally found in foods of plant origin.

inconnu (Ca) A large freshwater fish, *Stenodus mackenzii*, related to the whitefish, found in Canada and Alaska; oily, white, soft flesh; used in dishes as an alternative to salmon.

indad (Ia) Sweet-and-sour pork curry with tamarind, sugar, and vinegar.

indiána fánk (Hu) A small bun filled with chocolate cream and topped with chocolate icing.

Indian cress (US) See **nasturtium.**

Indian date (US) See **tamarind.**

Indianerkrapfen (Gr) Chocolate doughnuts filled with whipped cream.

indiánky (Cz) A dessert of small sponge cakes layered with whipped cream and topped with chocolate icing.

Indian pudding (US) An American colonial baked pudding reportedly invented by the indigenous tribes of the Northeast; made from corn meal, milk, maple syrup or molasses, and spices. Also called **hasty pudding.**

Indian rice (US) See **wild rice.**

Indian shuck bread (US) Corn meal batter wrapped in corn husks and boiled.

Indian tea (US) A tea substitute brewed

135

from the leaves of the yaupon tree, a holly of the southern United States. Also called **New Jersey tea.**

indienne, á l' (Fr) In the style of India; a curry served with rice.

indiva del Belgia (It) Belgian endive.

induction (US) A method of heating cookware made of magnetic materials. A special stove causes molecules in the pan to heat, cooking the food within.

indushka (Rs) Roast turkey.

infuse, to (US) To steep leaves, herbs, or other items such as ground coffee in a liquid, usually hot, in order to extract flavor.

ingberlach (Jw) A Passover honey candy made with matzo farfel, honey, ginger, walnuts, egg, sugar, lemon juice, and orange juice.

ingefær (Nw) Ginger.

ingefær brød (Da) Gingerbread.

ingefära (Sw) Ginger.

ingemaakte rog (Fi) Pickled ray.

ingen (Jp) String beans.

Ingwer (Gr) Ginger.

inhame (Pg) Yam.

injera (Af) The national bread of Ethiopia, made with a fermented batter of water and a flour from a form of millet (teff).

inkfish (US) Cuttlefish; squid.

inky pinky (Sc) A vinegared hash of leftover roast beef, carrots, and onions.

inlagd fisk (Sw) Poached or fried fish marinated in seasoned vinegar, water, and sugar; served with a sharp sauce of mustard, whipped cream, egg yolk, and lemon juice or vinegar.

inlagd gurka (Sw) Sweet-and-sour cucumber salad.

inlagd sill (Sw) Pickled salt herring.

in padèlla (It) In the frying pan; fried.

insalata (It) Salad.

insalata condita (It) Dressed salad.

insalata di carciofi crudi (It) Raw artichoke salad.

insalata di legumi (It) Vegetable salad.

insalata di melanzane (It) Eggplant salad.

insalata mista (It) Mixed salad.

insalata nizzarada (It) See **salade niçoise.**

insalata russa (It) Salad mold of vegetables and egg.

insalata verde (It) Salad of lettuce and other greens, such as romaine, curly endive, dandelion, and escarole, with oil and vinegar dressing.

instant food (US) Commercial products prepared by dehydration or fine grinding and pulverizing; premixed; precooked; instantly soluble; many foods come in instant form, such as cocoa, coffee, cream, onions, and potatoes.

intercostata di manzo (It) Rib steak of beef.

interlard (US) See **larding, lardoon.**

intestines (US) The alimentary canal of animals; that of pigs most commonly used in cooking, as a casing for sausages and for chitterlings.

intingolo (It) Sauce; gravy; ragout.

intinto (It) Sauce.

in umido (It) Braised; stewed, as in tomato sauce.

invasto (It) Potted.

Inverness gingerbread (Sc) A rich, dark gingerbread made with black treacle and oatmeal, but without eggs.

invert sugar (US) Small-crystal sugar, a mixture of glucose and fructose, which occurs naturally in many fruits and is created in the process of making candies and jellies.

involti di cacio (It) Cheese rolls.

involtini (It) Thinly sliced meat rolled around a filling of cheese, vegetables, or other ingredients, cooked in broth, and served in sauce. Fish such as smoked salmon may also be used as a wrapping.

involtini di vitello (It) Rolls of veal filled with ham and sweetbreads and seasoned with nutmeg.

iodine (US) An element essential for the prevention of goiter; the recommended daily allowance (RDA) is 150 micrograms (mcg) for adults; best dietary sources include iodized salt, seafood, dairy products, and bread.

iodized salt (US) Table salt (sodium chloride) that contains a small amount of potassium iodide to provide a source of the essential nutrient iodine.

iota friulana (It) Bean soup with cabbage or mashed turnips.

ipikike kiasi (Af–Swahili) Describes meat cooked medium.

ipikike sava (Af–Swahili) Describes meat cooked well done.

irachi thoran (Ia) One of the few beef dishes in India; fried shredded beef with grated coconut.

Irish coffee (US) A mixture of sweetened coffee with Irish whiskey; topped with a layer of cream.

Irish moss (US) See **carrageenin.**

Irish soda bread (US) Round loaves of white bread leavened with baking soda and buttermilk and flavored with caraway seeds and raisins.

Irish stew (US) A stew of mutton or lamb, potatoes, and onions.

iritamago (Jp) Scrambled eggs.

irmik çorbasi (Tr) Semolina soup.

iron (US) A mineral essential for human health; vital for the formation of hemoglobin in red blood cells; the recommended dietary allowance (RDA) per day is 10 mg for adults; best natural sources include liver and other organ meats.

irradiation (US) A process, classified as a food additive, in which meat and produce are treated with gamma rays by radioactive cobalt or other sources producing X rays. It is intended to extend the commercial life of fresh foods. The effectiveness of the process remains controversial.

is (Da, Nw, Sw) Ice.

iscas à portuguesa (Pg) Strips of liver in a marinade of wine and vinegar then fried with smoked ham and potatoes.

Ischlertörtchen (Gr–Austrian) Biscuits made with ground almonds and flour, cut in half and layered with red jam, then topped with chocolate.

ise ebi (Jp) Lobster.

ishikarinabe (Jp) Salmon and potato stew.

ising (Da) Dab (fish).

isinglass (US) A gelatin made from the

swim bladders of fish; made in sheets and used in Europe to prepare desserts, such as blancmange. Its use has been replaced by refined forms of gelatin.

isipikike sava (Af–Swahili) Describes meat cooked rare.

iskaffe (Sw) Iced coffee.

iskembe nohutlu (Tr) Tripe stew.

Islay (Sc) A firm cow's milk cheese, similar to Cheddar.

isobe tamago yaki (Jp) An omelet rolled in sheets of nori or laver seaweed and cut into one inch rounds.

isobe zukuri (Jp) Rolls of raw fish fillets wrapped in dried nori and served with a dipping sauce.

iso kuninkaankala (Fi) Redfish; ocean perch.

ispanak (Tr) Spinach.

istákoz (Tr) Lobster.

istarke fritule (SC) Fritters made with white wine.

iste (Sw) Iced tea.

istiridye (Tr) Oysters.

isvand (Da) Ice water.

isvatten (Sw) Ice water.

Italian dressing (US) Salad dressing made with olive oil, wine vinegar, and seasonings.

Italian meringue (US) A meringue made by adding hot syrup to beaten egg whites; does not require cooking.

Italienne, à l' (Fr) Describes any dish served with an Italian pasta sauce usually containing mushrooms; or garnished with pasta or artichokes.

itametamono (Jp) Sautéed foods.

itik (In) Duck.

Ivar's Daughter (Sc) Nettles; used in a soup thickened with oatmeal.

ivoire, à l' (Fr) Served with a white sauce made with chicken stock; used for poultry.

iwashi (Jp) Sardines.

iyi (Tr) Cooked medium (meat).

izgara (Tr) Broiled.

iziumnye sukhariki (Rs) Raisin rusks.

jäätee (Fi) Iced tea.

jäätellö (Fi) Ice cream.

jabali (Sp) Wild boar.

jabali estofado (Sp) Stewed wild boar with onions.

jablko (Po) Apple.

jablko (Cz) Apple.

jablkový závin (Cz) Apple strudel.

jabugo (Sp) A delicate, cured ham from the Seville region.

jabuka (SC) Apple.

jabuke u rumu (SC) A dessert of apples poached in syrup and topped with whipped cream.

jabuticaba (Pg) The sweet, black, cherrylike fruit of a tree native to Brazil and the West Indies; used fresh and in jellies. Also spelled *jaboticaba.*

jachtschotel (Du) A casserole of meat, fried apples, and onions.

Jack cheese (US) A yellow to orange cow's milk cheese classified as a Cheddar; depending on age, varies from smooth and bland to salty and sharp; varieties include Monterey Jack, Sonoma Jack, and Dry Jack.

jackfruit (Ia) A huge, tropical fruit from a tree, *Artocarpus integrifolia,* native to India; sweet, juicy flesh; used as a vegetable, boiled or baked, and in curries. The seeds are also used in cooking. Also called **jak, fenesi, nangka.**

Jacobsmuscheln (Gr) Scallops, coquilles.

já de (Ch) Deep-fried.

jaee (Ia) Oats.

jagaimo (Jp) Potato.

Jägarschnitzel (Sw) Ground veal scallops with mushroom sauce.

Jäger Art (Gr) Hunter's style; usually with mushrooms and a wine sauce.

Jägerbraten (Gr) Roast game.

Jägerbackbraten (Gr) Meat loaf.

jaggery (Ia) A coarse, unrefined brown sugar usually made from the sap of coconut and palmyra palms but may also be made from cane sugar; used as a sweetener in India and Southeast Asia. Also called **palm sugar.**

jagnjetina (SC) Lamb.

jagnjjeća sarma u maramici (SC) Ground lamb and lamb variety meats wrapped in lamb's intestine and baked.

jagntegh (Tr) Beet.

jagode (SC) Strawberries.

jahe (In) Ginger.

jahody (Cz) Strawberries.

jaiba (Mx) Crab.

jaiphal (Ia) Nutmeg.

jailles (Fr) A vinegared stew of pork backbone, apples, and bread crumbs.

jaja (SC) Eggs.

jajegh (Tr) Cucumbers with yogurt.

jajka (Po) Eggs.

jajka jajecznica (Po) Scrambled eggs.

jajka na miękko (Po) Soft-boiled eggs.

jajka na twardo (Po) Hard-cooked eggs.

jajka sadzone (Po) Fried eggs.

jak (Ia) See **jackfruit.**

Jakobmuscheln (Gr) Scallops.

jalapeño (Mx) A short, top-shaped, fiery, green chili pepper used in cheese, sauces, and stews.

jalea (Sp) Jelly.

Jalapeño

jalea de guayaba (Sp) Guava jelly.

jalebi (Ia) Snakelike shapes or coils of deep-fried, sweet batter dipped in syrup flavored with rose water.

jälkiruokavobvelit (Fi) Dessert waffles made with heavy cream.

jallab (Ar) A nonalcoholic drink of mulberry and lemon juices topped with a sprinkling of raisins and pine nuts; may be flavored with carob molasses.

jalousie (Fr) A double-crust, oblong jam tart with narrow slits on the glazed top crust, resembling a window blind.

jam (US) A preserve made by boiling fruit with sugar and sometimes pectin. Flowers, rose hips, chestnuts, green tomatoes, and squash may also be used to make jam.

Jamaica flower (US) The acid, dark-red flower of a hibiscus, *Hibiscus sabdariffa*, used in Mexico to make a syrup for punches.

Jamaica pepper (Cb) See **allspice.**

jambalaya (US) A highly spiced Cajun-Creole rice dish with many variations; ingredients may include ham, pork, sausage, shrimp, crayfish, beans, and other vegetables.

jamberry (US) See **tomatillo.**

jambon (Fr) Ham.

jambon bayonnaise (Fr) Smoked ham from near Bayonne in the Pyrénées.

jambon cru (Fr) Raw cured ham.

jambon de paques (Fr) Ham, eggs, and asparagus in aspic.

jambon fumé (Fr) Smoked ham.

jambon persillé (Fr) Parsleyed ham; strips or large cubes of ham molded with parsley in a deep dish.

jamón (Sp) Ham.

jamón en dulce (Sp) Sugar-cured ham; served cold.

jamón serrano (Sp) An air-dried ham, sliced.

jamu (Jp) Jam.

jamur (In) Mushrooms.

Jamwurzel (Gr) Yam.

Jan Hagel (Du) Small cakes or cookies flavored with cinnamon and topped with almonds and sugar.

jan in de zak (Du) Steamed pudding with molasses.

jänis (Fi) Hare, wild rabbit.

Janssonin kiusaus (Fi) See **Jansson's temptation.**

Jansson's frestelse (Sw) See **Jansson's temptation.**

Jansson's temptation (US) A dish of thin strips of potatoes with anchovies or sprats, cream, and onions. Reportedly named for a Swedish immigrant who founded a nineteenth century religious colony in Illinois.

jan-swèi de nyóu-ròu (Ch) Ground beef.

jantung (In) Heart.

Japanese cucumber (US) A term used for certain extra long varieties of cucumber which may be smooth, ribbed, or prickly. Some Chinese cucumbers are included. See also **cucumber.**

Japanese horseradish (US) See **wasabi.**

Japanese pear (US) See **Asian pear.**

Japanese rice (US) A short-grain variety of rice; moist, firm, sticky when cooked.

Japanese white radish (US) See **daikon.**

japonaise, à la (Fr) With a garnish of a tuber that originated in Japan, similar to the Jerusalem artichoke. It became known as the Chinese artichoke.

jardinière, à la (Fr) Garnished with fresh vegetables, which may be boiled or glazed; served with roast, stewed, or braised meat and poultry.

jarish (Ar) Wheat kernels, soaked, dried, and crushed; used like rice, usually boiled; served with a topping of hot pepper and onion or browned in oil and cooked pilaf-style with meat and vegetables.

Jarlsberg (Nw) A cow's milk cheese with yellow rind and a rich yellow interior with large eyes; mild, delicate, slightly sweet flavor.

järpe (Sw) Grouse.

jarp yun yuk (Ml) Beef chunks marinated in tamarind, coated with a paste of nuts, shrimp and ginger, then simmered in coconut milk and the marinade.

jarret de veau (Fr) Veal shank.

jasmine (US) Any of the climbing shrubs, genus *Jasminum* of the olive family with fragrant flowers used to flavor a Chinese green tea and some dishes.

jasne piwo (Po) Light beer.

jäst (Sw) Yeast.

jastog (SC) Lobster.

játernice (Cz) Offal sausage; boiled or fried.

jat juk (Kr) A soup of rice powder and pine nuts.

játra (Cz) Liver.

játrová paštika (Cz) Liver pâté.

jau (Ia) Barley.

jauhelihapiiras (Fi) Ground beef pie.

jauhelihapihvi (Fi) Ground beef patties.

Jause (Gr) Afternoon tea; coffee break.

javali (Pg) Wild boar.

javitri (Ia) Mace.

jazir (Cz) Sole.

jbin (Ar) Cheese.

Jeff Davis pie (US) A vanilla custard pie with allspice, cinnamon, raisins, and pecans; sometimes topped with meringue. The name derives from American statesman Jefferson Davis, president of the Confederacy during the Civil War.

jegestea (Hu) Iced tea.

jehněčí (Cz) Lamb.

jelitko (Cz) Blood sausage.

jelly (US) A preserve of fruit juice boiled with sugar and sometimes pectin until set and holding its shape.

jelly roll (US) A baked, flat sponge cake rolled around a filling of jelly or jam and, sprinkled with confectioners' sugar; served sliced. Also called **Swiss roll.**

jemný sýr (Cz) Mild cheese.

jenever (Du) Gin.

jèn jyāng tsù (Ch) Wine vinegar.

141

Jerez (Sp) Sherry.

Jerez, al (Sp) Served in a sherry sauce.

jericalla (Mx) A light, baked custard that contains cinnamon sticks.

jerky (US) See **dried meat.**

jeruk (In) Citrus fruits.

jeruk bali (In) See **shaddock.**

jeruk kepruk (In) Tangerine.

jeruk manis (In) Orange.

Jerusalem artichoke (US) A potatolike tuber, *Helianthus tuberosus*, in the sunflower family; light brown to purple; sweet, delicate taste; crisp texture; used boiled, fried, in soup and with sauces. Not related to the globe artichoke. Also called **sunchoke.**

Jerusalem artichoke

jesiotr (Po) Sturgeon.

Jessica (Fr) A garnish of braised artichokes stuffed with morels.

jetra (SC) Liver.

jewfish (US) A term derived from the Italian, *giupesce*, meaning bottom fish; two species are called jewfish: 1. grouper and 2. giant sea bass.

Jewish cuisine (Jw) Cooking influenced by many countries throughout the world. In the United States, the dishes best known are mostly eastern European in origin, such as chopped chicken livers, gefilte fish, and tzimmes. The basic flavor principle in many dishes is of fresh chicken fat and onion. See also **kosher, pareve.**

jhinga (Ia) Prawns; shrimp; lobster.

jhinga do-piaza (Ia) "Two-onion shrimp"; shrimp with a sauce of pureed onions, cumin, and turmeric.

jhinga ka khaja (Ia) Sautéed shrimp in a sauce of onion, coriander, tomato, and curry leaf. See **curry leaves.**

jhinga kari (Ia) Prawn curry.

jhinga saag (Ia) Shrimp in spinach sauce.

jhinga shorsha (Ia) Shrimp with a sauce of cinnamon, cloves, scallions, and mustard paste.

ji (Ch) Chicken.

jibini (Af–Swahili) Cheese.

jibn (Ar) Cheese.

jibu ni (Jp) Duck stew with mushrooms.

jibu ni yoshizen (Jp) Bubbling duck stew.

jicama (Mx) A gray-brown, thin-skinned root vegetable, about the size of a beet, with white flesh; crisp like a water chestnut; slightly sweet taste; used

Jicama

in salads, dips, stir-frys, and with other cooked vegetables.

jī-dàn (Ch) Chicken eggs.

jídla (Cz) Food.

jī ěr yān wō tāng (Ch) See **bird's nest soup.**

jīn-jú (Ch) Kumquats.

jī tāng (Ch) Chicken soup.

jiternice (Cz) A white sausage containing a rice and meat mixture.

jì-yú (Ch) Perch.

jocoque (Sp) A heavy cream.

Jod (Gr) Iodine.

Joghurt (Gr) Yogurt.

Johannisbeerkonfitüre (Gr) Red currant jam.

Johannisbeerkuchen (Gr) Cake made with red currants.

Johannisbrot (Gr) Carob.

John Dory (US) A firm, white-fleshed fish, classic ingredient of bouillabaisse. Originally "doree" in France, then John's doree after an eighteenth century actor. Also called Saint Peter's fish from a legend that the spots on its sides were thumb prints made by Saint Peter when he took money from its mouth.

johnny cake (US) A griddle-baked corn bread or pancake. The name is reportedly derived from "journey cake" because it was a food easily carried by travelers. Also spelled *jonnycake.*

joint (US) Large piece of meat.

Joinville (Fr) A dish of sole fillets arranged in a circle, and garnished with prawns, mushrooms, and truffles, and served with a velouté sauce. The name refers to a son of the French Citizen King, Louis-Philippe.

Joinville, sauce (Fr) A sauce made with prawn or crayfish butter and truffles.

Jonchée (Fr) A cow's, goat's, or ewe's milk cheese; white, soft texture; mild, creamy flavor.

jong (Du) Young; with cheese, the term means mild, soft or fresh.

jong belegan (Du) Somewhat aged, as pertains to cheese.

Jordan almond (US) A large Spanish almond with a hard-sugar coating variously colored and flavored, often with anise.

jordbær (Da, Nw) Strawberry.

jordgubbar (Sw) Strawberries.

jordnøtter (Nw) Peanuts.

jordnötter (Sw) Peanuts.

joulukinkku (Fi) Christmas ham; smoked on a rack in a sauna, then baked, coated with a mixture of sugar, bread crumbs, and mustard and browned in an oven.

joululuumukakku (Fi) Christmas prune cake.

joulutähti (Fi) Literally, "Christmas star"; a pulla yeast bread baked in the shape of a star from twisted strands of dough.

jowar (Ia) A cereal grain, *Sorghum bicolor*, ground for flour used to make flat, unleavened bread.

jow ho yay (Ml) Deep-fried oysters in a crust of egg and bread crumbs.

jowl (US) Pig's cheek meat.

joyanabe (Jp) Thin slices of pork, spinach, and green onions cooked in dashi.

jr-má (Ch) Sesame seeds.

jr-má bing (Ch) Sesame seed cookies.

Juan canary melon (US) A California-grown melon with a firm, bright yellow rind, oval shape, and sweet, creamy flesh.

jŭ de mài-pyàn (Ch) Cooked cereal.

judías (Sp) Kidney beans.

judías blancas (Sp) Haricot bean; white bean.

judías escarlatas (Sp) Red beans.

judías verdes (Sp) Green string beans.

judic (Fr) A garnish of small braised lettuces and stuffed tomatoes or sliced truffles, cockscombs, and kidneys in a ragout. Also, poached fillets of sole with lettuce.

jugged (US) Cooked in a deep, fireproof crock, stoneware jug, or casserole.

jugged hare (US) Pieces of hare fried in fat, then baked in a jug or crock with stock and red wine, onion, vegetables, and seasonings; garnished with the hare's liver.

jugo (Sp) Juice.

jugo de manzana (Sp) Apple juice.

jugurtti (Fi) Yogurt.

juhn kol (Kr) A dish cooked at the table; beef strips marinated in soy sauce, garlic, and sesame seeds with sliced onions, mushrooms, and carrots.

juive, à la (Fr) A dish of braised carp, served cold. Also, stuffed artichokes cooked in olive oil.

jujube (US) Small trees, genus *Zizyphus*, that grow in hot, dry areas; olive-size fruits with brown skin when ripe; white, sweet flesh; often candied or preserved in honey, eaten like dates, and used in both sweet and savory dishes.

julekage (Nw) Christmas bread made with yeast and raisins, candied fruits, and cardamom seeds.

jule risengrød (Da) Christmas rice pudding with almonds.

julienne (Fr) Meat or vegetables cut into matchstick-size, thin strips. The term reportedly comes from a seventeenth century chef named Julien.

jultallrik (Sw) A holiday plate of special dishes, such as lutfisk, reindeer, and rice pudding with cinnamon.

jumble (US) A cookie with walnuts, grated coconut, or almonds in the dough; reported to be among the first of American cookies.

jungjang (Kr) Rice wine.

jungkik (Kr) Table d'hôte.

juniper berries (US) The fruit of an evergreen shrub, *Juniperus communis*; essential oils influence the piquant taste;

used to flavor foods such as sauerkraut, baked beans, marinades, and gin.

junípero (Sp) Juniper.

junket (GB) A dessert made with sweetened milk thickened with rennet, sometimes flavored with brandy and topped with cinnamon or nutmeg. Also called **rennet pudding.**

junk food (US) Describes food and drink considered lacking in nutrition and overloaded with unhealthy amounts of sugar, fats, and salt.

jū-ròu (Ch) Pork.

jū-ròu chău-myàn (Ch) Noodles with pork.

jus (Du, Fr) Natural juices from roasted meats; juice; gravy.

jus de pomme (Fr) Apple juice.

jus de viande (Fr) Gravy from meat.

jussière, à la (Fr) With a garnish of onions, braised lettuce, potatoes, and sometimes with glazed carrots.

jūsu (Jp) Juice.

jú-swun (Ch) Bamboo shoots.

juusto (Fi) Cheese.

juustokukkoset (Fi) Buns filled with cream cheese.

juusto-muna voileipä (Fi) Hot egg and cheese sandwich.

juustoruohosipulitahna (Fi) Cheese and chives paste.

juustotangot (Fi) Cheese sticks; baked strands of a Cheddar cheese and dough mixture.

jyān dàn (Ch) Fried eggs.

jyāng (Ch) Ginger.

jyāng-yóu (Ch) Soy sauce.

jyău-dz (Ch) Boiled dumplings.

jyē-mwò-jyàng (Ch) Mustard.

jyou-jī (Ch) An appetizer of chicken marinated in sweet wine, sesame oil, and soy sauce and served cold.

jyú-dz (Ch) Orange; tangerine.

jyú-dz jēr (Ch) Orange juice.

K

kaakao (Fi) Cocoa, hot chocolate.

kaali (Fi) Cabbage.

kaalikeitto (Fi) Cabbage soup.

kaas (Du) Cheese.

kabab (Ia) Small pieces of meat, sometimes marinated or mixed with other ingredients; often skewered; broiled, fried, or cooked in a tandoor oven. Similar to Middle Eastern kebab.

kabak (Tr) Squash, marrows, zucchini.

kabak dolmasi (Tr) Young zucchini stuffed with onions, raisins, pine nuts, parsley or dill, and seasonings, baked and served cold.

kabak tatlisi (Tr) A dessert of cooked, sweetened pumpkin topped with chopped walnuts.

kaban (Rs) Wild boar.

kabayaki (Jp) Broiled fish or eels dipped in sake and soy sauce.

Kabeljau (Gr) Codfish.

kabeljauw (Du) Codfish.

kabeljauwstaart (Du) The tail end of a large cod, often simmered with lemon juice and served with potatoes and carrots.

kabeljo (Sw) Codfish.

kabob (US) Skewered and grilled pieces of marinated meat alternated with various vegetables and sometimes fruit; many versions. See also **kabab, kebab.**

kabocha (Jp) Squash, pumpkin.

kabu (Jp) Turnips.

kabuto-age (Jp) Literally, "fried armor", describes the shell, such as lobster, in which a mixture of lobster, egg, and vegetables are fried.

kacang (In) Peanuts.

kacang hijau (In) Green beans; mung beans.

kacang panjang (In) Yard-long beans.

kachna (Cz) Duck.

kachumbari (Af–Swahili) Onions in vinegar.

kacsa (Hu) Duck.

kaczka (Po) Duck.

kaddu (Ia) The bottle gourd, *Lagenania siceraria*, used when immature as a vegetable in India; with firm, tender flesh; cooked whole, boiled, stuffed, and baked. Also called **calabash.**

kadin budu (Tr) Ground meat and rice in an oval patty, dipped in egg and fried.

kadin göbeği (Tr) A dessert of small biscuits soaked in syrup.

kaeng masaman (Th) Moslem curry made with chicken or beef cooked in coconut milk and spiced with a mild curry paste.

kærnemælk (Da) Buttermilk.

kærnemælkskoldskål (Da) Cold buttermilk soup made with beaten egg and grated lemon rind; may be garnished with whipped cream or stewed fruit.

kærnemælkssuppe (Da) Buttermilk soup with whipped cream and raisins.

kafa (SC) Coffee.

kāfēi (Ch) Coffee.

kafes (Gk) Coffee.

kaffe (Da, Nw, Sw) Coffee.

Kaffee (Gr) Coffee.

Kaffeekuchen (Gr) Coffee cake.

Kaffee mit Schlagobers (Gr) Viennese-style coffee with whipped cream.

kage (Da) Cake.

kâğit helvasi (Tr) Sweet wafer wrapped in paper.

kâğitta (Tr) Cooked in paper.

kahawa (Af–Swahili) Coffee.

kahve (Tr) Turkish-style coffee made from pulverized coffee beans.

kahvi (Fi) Coffee.

kahwa (Ar) Coffee.

kaibashira (Jp) Scallops.

kail brose (Sc) Broth made with kale or cabbage, oatmeal, vegetables, and meat.

kaimati (Af–Swahili) A sweet pastry shaped like balls.

Kaiserfleisch (Gr) Literally, "meat for the emperor"; a Viennese dish of boiled beef with vegetables and horseradish.

Kaiserschmarren (Gr–Austria) Literally, "Emperor's omelet"; a dessert of shredded, sweet pancakes containing raisins, topped with sugar and served with stewed plums.

kajgana (SC) Scrambled eggs.

kajiki (Jp) Swordfish.

kajmak (SC) Cream cheese.

kajsija (SC) Apricot.

kajzerice (SC) Rolls.

kakao (Nw) Cocoa.

kakao (Tr) Cocoa.

kakap (In) Sea fish similar to sole.

kakavia (Gk) Fish soup or stew; similar to French bouillabaisse.

kake (Nw) Cake.

kakesoba (Jp) Buckwheat noodles served in broth.

kaki (Jp) Persimmon.

kaki (Jp) Oyster.

kakimochi (Jp) Small crackers flavored with soy sauce.

kakku (Fi) Cake.

kakoretsi (Gk) Sausage roasted on a spit.

kål (Da, Nw, Sw) Cabbage.

kalafior (Po) Cauliflower.

kalakeitto (Fi) Fish soup with milk, fish, rye bread, potatoes, and onions and topped with dill.

kalakukko (Fi) Literally, "fish-rooster"; tiny white fish and bacon or fat pork baked in a rye dough crust or a hollowed-out rye bread loaf.

kalamarakia tighanita (Gk) Deep-fried squid.

kalamata olives (US) Large black olives from Kalamata, Greece; usually marinated in olive oil and wine vinegar and served as hors d'oeuvres.

kalasalaatti (Fi) Fish salad.

kalbasà saséski (Rs) Salami sausage.

Kalbfleisch (Gr) Veal.

Kalbsbraten (Gr) Roast veal.

Kalbsfrikassee (Gr) Veal fricassee.

Kalbsgulasch (Gr) Veal goulash.

Kalbshaxe (Gr) Veal shanks; usually braised or roasted and served with boiled potatoes.

Kalbsleber (Gr) Calf's liver.

Kalbsrolle (Gr) Boned, rolled breast of veal.

Kalbsschnitzel (Gr) Veal cutlet.

Kalbssteak (Gr) Veal steak.

Kaldaunen (Gr) Tripe.

kåldolmar (Sw) A baked casserole of cabbage rolls stuffed with minced beef, rice, and seasonings and served with a sour cream gravy.

Kale

kåldolmer (Da) Stuffed cabbage rolls.

kale (US) A variety of curly-leafed, loose-headed cabbage; with green to purple leaves; cooked like other greens.

kaléji (Ia) Liver.

kalfkott (Sw) Veal.

kalfsoester (Du) Veal steak.

kalfsvlees (Du) Veal.

kali (Ia) A long, green gourd with sharp ribs used in vegetarian cooking.

kali mirch (Ia) Black pepper.

kali urad (Ia) Black lentils.

kalkas (Rs) Brill.

kalkan (Tr) Turbot or flounder.

kalkkuna (Fi) Turkey.

kalkoen (Du) Turkey.

kalkon (Sw) Turkey.

kalkun (Nw) Turkey.

kalops (Sw) Small pieces of meat, usually in a beef stew.

kal rulader (Nw) Cabbage leaves stuffed with ground meat; served with cucumbers and dill.

kalsoppa (Sw) Cabbage soup.

kalte pikante Sosse (Gr) Ketchup.

kalte Speisen (Gr) Plates of cheese and cold cuts.

Kaltschale (Gr) Chilled fruit soup made with cherries, apricots, strawberries, or raspberries; sometimes includes other ingredients such as almonds or rice; often flavored with wine.

kalua pua (Pl) A pig cooked in a pit in the ground at a Hawaiian luau.

kalv (Nw) Veal.

kalvebräss (Sw) Sweetbreads.

kalvefilé (Nw) Fillet of veal.

kalvehjerte (Da) Veal heart.

kalvekarbonade (Da) Ground veal cooked like hamburgers.

kalvekjøtt (Nw) Veal.

kalvekød (Da) Veal.

kalvestek (Nw) Roast veal.

kalvkotlett (Sw) Veal cutlet.

kamaboka (Jp) Molded fish paste or cake, served steamed.

kamano lomi (Pl) Salted salmon mashed with tomatoes and onions.

kamasu (Jp) Pike.

kamba (Af–Swahili) Shrimp.

kambing (In) Goat.

kaminarijiru (Jp) "Thunder soup"; made with bean curd and vegetables.

kammooniyya (Ar) An Egyptian dish of baked fish with rice and tomatoes.

kamo (Jp) Duck.

kamo namban (Jp) Duck and thin noodles in soup.

kampela (Fi) Flounder.

kamrakh (Ia) See **carambola.**

kana (Fi) Chicken.

kanakeitto (Fi) Chicken soup.

kanapki z jajkami (Po) Canapés made with hard-cooked eggs.

kanasalaatti (Fi) Chicken salad.

kanelbullar (Sw) Cinnamon buns.

kāng (Ch) Bran.

kangaja (Af–Swahili) Small tangerine.

kangaroo tail soup (Aa) Similar to oxtail soup; made with meat from an Australian marsupial with a long tapered tail.

kani (Jp) Crab.

kanidōfu iridashi (Jp) Balls of a crab and bean curd mixture in broth.

kanin (Nw, Sw) Rabbit.

Kaninchen (Gr) Rabbit.

kanisu (Jp) Vinegared crab.

kanpyo (Jp) Dried gourd.

kanten (Jp) See **agar-agar.**

kapamas (Gk) Stewed pieces of lamb with tomatoes, onions, and garlic; sometimes potatoes.

Kapernsosse (Gr) Caper sauce.

kapormártás (Hu) Dill sauce.

káposzta (Hu) Cabbage.

káposztasaláta (Hu) Cabbage salad; coleslaw.

káposztás kockák (Hu) Cabbage-noodle squares.

káposztás rétes (Hu) Strudel with cabbage filling.

kappa maki (Jp) Cucumber wrapped in seaweed and rice.

kapr (Cr) Carp.

kapusniak (Po) Sauerkraut soup cooked with ham or pork, potatoes and onions.

kapusta (Po) Cabbage.

kapustová polévka (Cz) Cabbage soup.

Kapuzinerkresse (Gr) Nasturtium.

kara age (Jp) Fish, meat, or vegetables lightly dusted with cornstarch and fried in a small amount of oil.

karaciğer (Tr) Liver.

karah (Ar) Butter.

karaj (Hu) Chops.

karalábé (Hu) Kohlrabi.

Karamel (Gr) Caramel.

karamelbudding (Da) Caramel custard.

karashi (Jp) Mustard.

karashina (Jp) Mustard greens.

kardhal (Hu) Swordfish.

Kardone (Gr) Cardoon.

karei (Jp) Sole; turbot; flounder.

kare ikan (In) Fish curry.

karei no sashimi (Jp) Sliced flounder served with grated ginger root or wasabi and soy sauce.

karei rikyū funamori (Jp) Flounder served in edible boat-shaped vegetables.

karela (Ia) See **bitter melon.**

karfiol (Hu, SC) Cauliflower.

karibayaki (Jp) A one-pot cooking method in which guests participate in food preparation, similar to fondue. See **fire pot.**

karides (Tr) Shrimp.

karidopita (Gk) Nut cake.

kari-kari (Ph) Oxtail stew thickened with crushed peanut and rice flour.

karişik (Tr) Mixed.

karişik etler izgara (Tr) Mixed grilled meat.

karjalanpaisti (Fi) A stew with beef, pork, and lamb, onions, carrots, and flavored with black peppercorns and bay leaves; a Karelian specialty.

karjalanpiirakoita (Fi) Baked pasties made with rye dough rolled around a rice or potato filling; a Karelian specialty.

karnabahar (Tr) Cauliflower.

karnabeet makly (Ar) Deep-fried cauliflower.

karnemelk (Du) Buttermilk.

karota (Gk) Carrots.

karoti (Af–Swahili) Carrots.

Karotten (Gr–Austria) Carrots.

karp (Po, Rs) Carp.

karpe (Nw) Carp.

Karpfen (Gr) Carp.

karpuz (Tr) Watermelon.

karpyon (Jw) Carp.

kartoffel (Da) Potato.

Kartoffel (Gr) Potato.

Kartoffelgemüse (Gr) Potatoes in cream sauce.

Kartoffelknödel (Gr) Potato dumpling.

kartoffelmos (Da) Mashed potatoes.

Kartoffelpuffer (Gr) Large potato pancakes, served with apple sauce.

Kartoffelpüree (Gr) Mashed potatoes.

Kartoffelsalat (Gr) Potato salad.

Kartoffelsuppe (Gr) Potato soup.

kaşar (Tr) Yellow cheese.

Käse (Gr) Cheese.

Käsebrot (Gr) Cheese bread.

Kasein (Gr) Casein.

Käseplatte (Gr) An assortment of cheese.

kaše z pohanky (Cz) Buckwheat.

kasha (Rs) A dry porridge or mush made with grain, usually buckwheat groats.

kasha varnishkas (Jw) Cooked buckwheat groats (kasha) mixed with cooked, square noodles. They are heated with spices and onions browned in chicken fat.

kashtanovi pudding (Rs) Chestnut pudding.

kasséri (Gk) A pale yellow sheep or goat's milk cheese with a Cheddarlike texture and a salty, savory taste.

kasséri tiganitó (Gk) Bite-size fried cheese cubes.

Kassie (Gr) Cassia.

Kassler Rippchen (Gr) Smoked pork chops.

kastad (Af–Swahili) Custard.

kastanje (In) Chestnut.

kastanjer (Nw) Chestnuts.

kastike (Fi) Sauce.

kasutera (Jp) Sponge cake.

kasviskeitto (Fi) Vegetable soup.

kasza (Po) Buckwheat groats.

katai roru pan (Jp) Hard bread rolls.

katjang kapri (In) A variety of **podded peas.**

katjang kedele (In) Soybeans.

katjang tanah (In) Peanut.

katkarapusalaatti (Fi) Shrimp salad.

katkaravut (Fi) Shrimp.

katrinplommon (Sw) Prune; French plum.

katsudon (Jp) Pork cutlet served over rice.

katsuo (Jp) Bonito.

katsuobushi (Jp) Dried bonito fish, shaved or flaked; used for flavoring.

kău de (Ch) Baked.

kău myàn-bāu (Ch) Toast.

kău nyóu-ròu (Ch) Roast beef.

kău pái-gŭ (Ch) Barbecued spareribs.

kaurapuuro (Fi) Cooked oatmeal.

káva (Cz) Coffee.

kavayd (Jw) Liver.

kávé (Hu) Coffee.

Kaviar (Gr) Caviar.

kavoorya (Gk) Crabs.

kavring (Nw) Hard biscuit.

kavun (Tr) Melon.

kawa (Po) Coffee.

kaws (Po) Sour, fermented beet juice, used in cooking.

kayisi (Tr) Apricot.

kaymak (Tr) A thick dessert topping made by reducing cream over low heat and whipping during the cooking.

kaymakli elma kompostosu (Tr) Poached apples with whipped cream.

kazu no ko (Jp) Herring roe.

kebab (Tr) Charcoal-grilled pieces of meat or poultry, often lamb, on skewers; usually marinated in olive oil, lemon juice, herbs, and spices. Variations, such as shish kebab, include mushrooms and other ingredients alternated with the meat.

kebeji (Af–Swahili) Cabbage.

kecap (In) Soy sauce.

kēchap (Ml) A Malay spicy sauce served with fish and seafood.

kechap (Af–Swahili) Ketchup.

kechappu (Jp) Ketchup.

kečup (Cz) Ketchup.

kedgeree (GB) A hot breakfast dish of cooked rice, kippers, hard-cooked eggs, cream or butter, and seasonings, which may include curry powder. Originated in India. See also **khichari.**

kedju (Ml) Cheese.

kedlubny (Cz) Kohlrabi.

kefalos (Gk) Mullet.

kefalotiri (Gk) A pale yellow cheese made from sheep's or goat's milk; similar to Parmesan cheese; used for grating.

kefiiri (Fi) Soured milk; kefir.

keftedakia (Gk) Appetizers of little meatballs flavored with ouzo and mint.

keftedes (Gk) Aromatic, fried meatballs made with ground beef or veal, bread crumbs, egg, onion, oregano, mint, parsley, vinegar, and olive oil.

kehrasya (Gk) Cherries.

keitetty (Fi) Boiled.

keitto (Fi) Soup.

keju (In) Cheese.

kēki (Jp) Cake.

keki (Af–Swahili) Cake.

keki ya matunda (Af–Swahili) Cake made with fruit.

kebap (Tr) Meat, often lamb, cooked on a skewer.

kefal (Tr) A fish similar to mullet.

kefir (US) A beverage with a sour, acidic taste made from fermented cow's milk; originated in the Caucasus mountains.

keftedhakia (Gk) Little meatballs.

keitetty muna (Fi) A boiled egg.

kékra (Ia) Crab.

Kekse (Gr) Cookies.

kelapa (In) Coconut.

kelapa sayur (Ml) Vegetables in spicy coconut milk.

kelp (US) A large, brown, coarse-textured seaweed often used in Japanese cooking; eaten raw, cooked, or dried. In powdered form, it is used to flavor and thicken soups and sauces. Processed kelp is used as a source of iodine.

kemény tojás (Hu) Hard-boiled eggs.

kentang goreng (In) Fried potatoes.

kentang panggang (In) Baked potatoes.

kentang rebus (In) Boiled potatoes.

kentang tumbuk (In) Mashed potatoes.

kentjoer (Du) See **zedoary.**

Kentucky burgoo (US) See **burgoo.**

kenyér (Hu) Bread.

kepah (In) Mussels. Also called **remis.**

kepiting pedas (In) Crab in a hot spicy sauce.

kerie (In) Curry.

kerma (Fi) Cream.

kermaviilisilakka (Fi) Herring in a rich yogurtlike sauce.

Kernhem (Du) A round, flat cheese made with cow's milk; red rind; rich, creamy taste.

kernmilk (Sc) Buttermilk.

kerrie kool sla (Du) Curried coleslaw.

kersen (Du) Cherries.

kerupuk (Ml) Shrimp fried in peanut oil. The pieces expand like popcorn.

kesäkeitto (Fi) A thick soup with summer vegetables in milk.

kesäkurpitsa (Fi) Summer squash.

keşkec (Tr) Shredded chicken cooked with cracked wheat and topped with melted butter and paprika.

keşkul (Tr) Custard of ground almonds and rice flour; topped with pistachios and coconut.

ketchup (US) A thick spicy tomato sauce. Also called **catsup.**

ketimun (In) Cucumbers.

ketjap (In) A very sweet soy sauce.

ketovaia (Rs) Red caviar, large red eggs of a Siberian salmon.

ketsup (Du) Ketchup.

ketumbar (In) Coriander.

ketupat (Ml) Rice cakes.

kex (Sw) Crackers.

Key lime pie (US) A pie shell filled with a mixture of condensed milk, lime juice, eggs, and sugar; baked and topped with meringue; served cold. Its origin was in the Florida Keys. Traditionally the juice used is from a small, more acid variety of lime that grows there.

khai cheow (Th) Omelet.

khana (Ia) Food; dinner.

kharcho (Rs) Spicy beef, onion, and tomato soup.

khas-khas (Ia) Poppy seeds.

kheer (Ia) A pudding made with rice.

khichari (Ia) A dish of rice, lentils, dal, onions, and spices cooked in ghee. The Anglo-Indian dish of kedgeree evolved from this basic preparation of India.

khleb (Rs) Bread.

khow muck yue (Ml) Squid fried with pork, bamboo shoots, mushrooms, and other vegetables in soy sauce.

khoya (Ia) Very thick condensed milk.

khtapodhi me saltsa (Gk) Octopus sautéed with olive oil and onions then cooked in red wine and tomatoes.

khubz (Ar) Round, flat bread.

khudar (Ar) Vegetables.

kibbeh (Ar) A dish made with a mixture of ground meat and crushed wheat (burghul); many variations with added ingredients. Also spelled *kibbi.*

kibbeh bissaniyyeh (Ar) Ground lamb patties, stuffed and fried.

kibbeh nayya (Ar) Raw ground lamb

with crushed wheat; served with a mint, black pepper, and olive oil dressing.

kibda (Ar) Liver.

kichel (Jw) Crisp biscuit.

Kichererbse (Gr) Chick-peas.

kid (US) Young goat.

kidney (US) An edible organ from a meat animal; often served braised, sautéed, or stewed.

kidney bean (US) Dark red, kidney-shaped haricot bean; shelled when mature; used in New Orleans cooking, salads, chile con carne, frijoles refritos, and in many Mexican dishes.

kielbasa (Po) Red-cased sausage made with chopped pork and pork fat flavored with garlic; air-dried; served sliced as a cold cut or poached.

kielikampala (Fi) Sole.

kiflik (Hu) Crescent rolls.

kiichigo (Jp) Raspberries.

kiisseli (Fi) Fruit soup made with berries and sugar; served warm or cold.

kiji (Jp) Pheasant.

kiks (Da) Cracker; biscuit.

kikujisha (Jp) Chicory.

kikutane (Jp) Chrysanthemum seeds; used as flavoring.

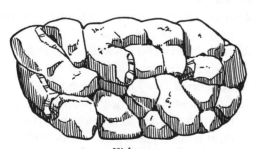

Kidney

kiliç baliği (Tr) Swordfish.

kiliç şiş (Tr) Broiled fish on skewers.

kilohaili (Fi) Sprat.

kimchee (Kr) A Korean specialty, pickled, slightly fermented cabbage flavored with ginger, garlic, and chilies.

kimo (Jp) Chicken liver.

king, à la (US) Served in a cream sauce usually containing pimentos and mushrooms, sometimes sherry or Madeira. The term is attributed to a creamed chicken dish (à la Keene) originated at the Claridge in London; it passed to the Waldorf in New York City, becoming chicken à la king. The sauce is also used with other meats including ham and frogs' legs.

king crab (US) A variety of large crab found along the coast of Alaska; delicate flavor and abundant meat in large claws.

king salmon (US) See **chinook salmon.**

kinkan (Jp) Kumquat.

kinkku (Fi) Ham.

kinywaji (Af–Swahili) Beverage.

kip (Du) Chicken.

kip aan't spit (Du) Broiled chicken.

kipfel (Hu) A small crescent-shaped cookie filled with nuts or thick sweet fruit purees such as apricot or raspberry.

Kipfel (Gr) Crescent-shaped roll.

kippensoep (Du) Chicken soup with vegetables.

kipper (GB) Split fish, usually herring, salted, dried, and smoked; after soaking, usually grilled or baked; often served for breakfast with eggs.

kipper, to (Sc) To cure fish such as her-

153

ring or salmon by salting and smoking.

kirántott hal (Hu) Fried breaded fish.

kirántott sajt (Hu) Fried breaded cheese.

kiraz (Tr) Cherry.

kirjolohi (Fi) Rainbow trout.

Kirsch (Gr) Cherry; cherry brandy; often used in cooking. Also called **Kirschwasser.**

Kirschen (Gr) Cherries.

Kirschwasser (Gr) Cherry water; white cherry brandy.

kirsebær (Da, Nw) Cherries.

kisel (Rs) A dessert made with tart fruit puree.

kisela voda (SC) Mineral water.

kishk (Ar) A soured mixture of wheat and milk dried to a powder for storage; mixed with water when used for cooking.

kishka (Jw) A sausage of beef intestines stuffed with various savory fillings; usually including mashed barley, onions, and chicken; boiled, then baked; served sliced.

kiss (US) A bite-sized pastry or candy.

kisu (Jp) Smelt.

kitsune udon (Jp) Noodles with fried bean curd.

kiwanda (Af–Swahili) Omelet.

kiwano (US) A pear-sized oval fruit, native to New Zealand; yellow, spiky skin and green pulp; similar to passion fruit in taste. Also called **horned melon.**

kiwifruit (US) The fruit of a climbing plant, *Acinidia chinensis*, native to China, with an oval shape and brown, hairy skin; green flesh with tiny, black,

edible seeds; sweet flavor; used as a garnish in salads, made into preserves, and added to sweet or savory dishes.

kiyma (Tr) Chopped meat.

kizandamono (Jp) Chopped.

kizarmis ekmek (Tr) Toasted bread.

kizarmis patlican (Tr) Fried eggplant with green peppers in tomato sauce.

kizartma (Tr) Roast, as for meat.

kizartmasi (Tr) Fried chicken, potatoes, or vegetables.

kjeks (Nw) Crackers, biscuits.

kjøtt (Nw) Meat.

kjøttboller (Nw) Meatballs.

kjøttkaker (Nw) Literally, "meat cakes"; similar to hamburgers.

kjøttpålegg (Nw) Sliced cold meats.

kjøttretter (Nw) Meat dishes.

klarbär (Sw) See **amarelle.**

klare Kraftbrühe (Gr) Consommé.

kletskoppen (Du) Gingersnaps.

klipfisk (Da) A dish of poached dried codfish (first soaked and desalted), garnished with horseradish, hard-cooked eggs, sliced beets, and mustard.

klobása (Cz) Sausage.

klookva (Rs) Cranberries.

Klösse (Gr) Dumplings.

Klosterkäse (Gr) Cloister cheese; a small pungent cheese.

kluski ślaskie (Po) Noodles made from potatoes, potato flour, and eggs.

knäckebröd (Sw) Crisp bread; rusk.

Knackwurst (Gr) A short, plump sausage of smoked beef and pork spiced with cumin and garlic; boiled or grilled. Also called **knockwurst.**

knaidel (Jw) Dumpling; matzo ball.

knead (US) To manipulate or work dough by hand or machine, folding and pressing until air is incorporated and texture is smooth.

knedle (SC) Dumpling.

knedlik (Cz) Dumpling.

knekkebrød (Nw) Thin crisp rye flat bread or cracker.

Knieslück (Gr) Veal shank.

knish (Jw) A dumpling filled with cheese, kasha, or seasoned chopped meat and potatoes; baked, fried, or broiled.

Knoblauch (Gr) Garlic.

knockwurst (US) See **Knackwurst.**

Knödel (Gr–Austria) Dumplings.

knoflook (Du) Garlic.

Knollensellerie (Gr) Celeriac.

knuckle (US) Ankle joint or lower part of the hind leg of a meat animal, usually pork or veal.

kobasice (SC) Sausage.

Kobe beef (Jp) A highly regarded grade of beef from cattle raised in Kobe, Japan; attributed to feeding the cattle beer.

kobliby (Cz) Doughnuts.

kōcha (Jp) Black tea.

kocsonyázott hal (Hu) Fish in aspic.

kocsonyázott sertés (Hu) Pork in aspic.

kød (Da) Meat.

kodok (In) Frog.

koek (Du) Cake; spiced cake.

koekjes (Du) Sweet biscuits; cookies.

koeksisters (Af) South African doughnuts served cold in syrup.

koffie (Du) Coffee.

köfte (Tr) Skewered and grilled balls of ground mutton mixed with bread crumbs, olive oil, and onion.

kofté (Ia) Meatballs.

köfte (In) Ground lamb or mutton meatballs.

kogt oksebryst (Da) Boiled brisket of beef.

kogt skinke med Madeira (Da) Cooked ham in Madeira sauce.

kōhaku namasu (Jp) "Red-and-white" vinegared salad with carrots and daikon.

kōhii (Jp) Coffee.

kohitsuji no niku (Jp) Lamb.

Kohl (Gr) Cabbage.

Kohlenhydrat (Gr) Carbohydrates.

kohlrabi (US) A variety of cabbage, *Brassica oleracea* var. *caulorapa*, with a turnip-shaped, pale green to purple stem and thin leaf stalks; the mild-flavored stem is eaten raw or cooked.

Kohlrabi (Gr) "Turnip-cabbage"; kohlrabi.

Kohlsprossen (Gr) Brussels sprouts.

koi no arai (Jp) Sliced raw carp.

koko iliyo moto (Af–Swahili) Hot chocolate beverage.

kokoretsi (Gk) Kidneys, tripe, and liver of lamb wrapped in intestines and grilled on a spit.

kokt skinke (Nw) Boiled ham.

kokt torsk (Sw) Thick slices of poached cod; served with butter or a white sauce containing chopped hard-boiled eggs.

kol (In) Cauliflower.

kolač (SC) Cake.

koláč (Cz) Pie.

koláčky (Cz) Literally, "little pies"; sweet buns filled with a variety of mixtures of fruit, nuts or poppy seeds.

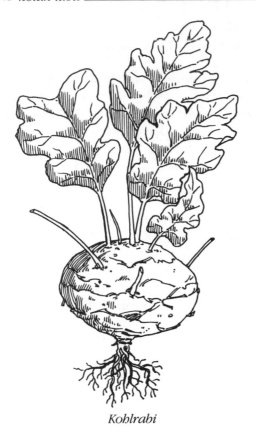

Kohlrabi

kolak labu (In) Pumpkin in a syrup made with coconut.

kolbász (Hu) Sausage.

koldebord (Da) Cold table; a variety of cold dishes such as smoked fish, meats, salads, and many cheeses; may include some hot dishes.

koldtbord (Nw) Cold table; similar to Swedish smörgåsbord.

koliflawa (Af–Swahili) Cauliflower.

kolja (Sw) Haddock.

kolje (Nw) Haddock.

kólliva (Gk) Sweetened boiled wheat mixed with fruit and nuts.

kolozsvári rakott káposzta (Hu) Cabbage layered with pork.

kombosta (Gk) Stewed fruit.

kombu (Jp) A broad-leafed variety of kelp, *Laminaria* species, used in soups and stews and an essential ingredient in dashi.

kome (Jp) Uncooked rice.

köménymagos leves (Hu) Caraway soup.

komijnekaas (Du) A spicy cheese flavored with cumin.

komkommer (Du) Cucumber.

komposto (Tr) Compote of stewed fruits.

Kompott (Gr) Stewed fruit; compote.

kompot z jablek (Po) Apple sauce; a hot beverage of cooked apples, sugar, and cinnamon.

konditorkager (Da) French pastry.

kongesuppe (Nw) Hearty soup with meatballs, onions, carrots, and peas.

Königinsuppe (Gr) "Queen soup"; cream of chicken soup.

Königsberger Klops (Gr) Poached meatballs of beef and pork flavored with anchovies, capers, and onion; served in a spicy sauce of sour cream, lemon juice, anchovies, and capers.

konijn (Du) Rabbit.

konjac (Sw) Brandy; cognac.

konnyaku (Jp) A gelatinous paste or cake made from the root of the devil's tongue or arum plant, genus *Amorphophallus*; used with other foods in cooking.

konyun (Tr) Mutton.

kool (Du) Cabbage.

Kopfsalat (Gr) Head lettuce.

kopi (In) Coffee.

kořeněné (Cz) Spicy.

koření (Cz) Condiments.

156

korf (Sw) Sausage.

korhelyleves (Hu) Literally, "drunkard's soup"; a sauerkraut soup served for a hangover.

korma (Ia) Lamb fillet or chicken breasts braised in a marinade of yogurt, cream, ground almonds, and pureed fruit; served in the sauce.

korn (Nw) Grain.

koromotsuki (Jp) Breaded.

koroptev (Cz) Partridge.

körözött júhtúró (Hu) Sheep's milk cheese (Liptauer), spread with paprika, onion, and caraway.

körsbär (Sw) Cherries.

korstjes (Du) Spiced bread sticks.

körte (Hu) Pear.

korv (Sw) Sausage.

kørvelsuppe (Da) Chervil soup.

kosher (Jw) Describes food prepared or meat killed for consumption according to Jewish dietary laws.

kosher pickle (Jw) Fresh cucumber cured in brine-filled kegs containing garlic, spices, and vinegar.

kosher salt (Jw) A very coarse salt; used to remove blood from meat according to traditional Jewish dietary regulations.

koshihikari (Jp) A flavorful and highly glutinous rice.

koshō (Jp) Pepper.

kota (Gk) Chicken.

kota kapama (Gk) Chicken braised in tomato and cinnamon sauce.

kotasupa (Gk) Chicken soup.

Kotelett (Gr) Chop.

kotelett (Nw) Cutlet, chop.

kotleti (Rs) Fried cutlets made with ground meat, soaked bread, and egg.

kotleti iz rybi (Rs) Cod or pike fish cakes made with milk, bread, and seasonings.

kotlet pane (Tr) Veal cutlet.

kotlety mielone (Po) Pork patties, served with dill.

kotlety wolowe (Po) Ground beef patties.

kotopulo (Gk) Chicken.

köttbullar (Sw) Fried meatballs, served with creamed potatoes.

köttfärsgrotta (Sw) Meat loaf, sometimes stuffed.

köttfärsröra (Sw) Ground meat fried with onions and other vegetables.

koude schotel (Du) Cold cuts.

kouféta (Gk) Candied almonds.

koulitch (Rs) Currant bread traditionally made for the Russian Easter.

kourambiedes (Gk) "Cloud" cookies; delicate butter cookies with a clove pressed in; sprinkled with rose water while still warm.

kousa mahshi (Ar) Stuffed squash with tomato sauce.

kovaksi keitetty muna (Fi) Hard-boiled egg.

krab (Cz) Crab.

krabba (Sw) Crab.

krabbe (Nw) Crab.

Krabben (Gr) Small shrimp, prawns.

kræmmerhuse med flødeskum (Da) Cones shaped from a baked meringuelike mixture, filled with whipped cream, and topped with currant, raspberry, or strawberry preserves.

Kraftbrühe (Gr) Consommé.

Kraftbrühe mit Ei (Gr) Strong beef broth with raw egg.

kräftor (Sw) Crayfish.

157

králík (Cz) Rabbit.

krasata (Gk) Squid sautéed in oil, then simmered in wine with tomatoes and parsley.

kråsesuppe (Da) Soup with goose giblets, apples, and prunes, served with dumplings.

krastavci (SC) Cucumbers.

Kraut (Gr) Cabbage.

kreatopitta (Gk) Triangular, flaky pastries filled with ground meat.

Krebs (Gr) Crayfish; crab.

Krebsschwänze (Gr) Freshwater shrimp.

kreeft (Du) Crayfish; lobster.

krem (Nw) Cream.

krém (Cz) Custard.

kremali (Tr) With a cream filling.

krem od vanile (SC) Custard.

krem şanti (Tr) Whipped cream.

Kren (Gr–Austria) Horseradish.

krentenbrood (Du) Raisin bread.

krentenbroodjes (Du) Raisin buns.

kreplach (Jw) Small triangular dumplings filled with cheese, chicken, liver, or chopped meat; served in soup.

kreps (Nw) Crayfish.

krimu (Af–Swahili) Cream.

kringle (Nw) Pretzel.

kringlor (Sw) Pretzel.

kritharaki (Gk) Tiny grainlike pasta.

krmenadle (SC) Chops.

krocan (Cz) Turkey.

Krokette (Gr) Croquette.

kromeski (Po) Hot appetizers made with various croquette mixtures; wrapped in thin pancakes or bacon and fried.

kromkake (Nw) Crisp cake.

krompir (SC) Potatoes.

kronärtskocka (Sw) Artichoke.

kroppkakor (Sw) Boiled potato dumplings filled with bacon and onion and served with cranberries and cream.

krub (SC) Bread.

kruidkoek (Du) Spiced bread.

krumpli (Hu) Potatoes. Also called **burgonya.**

krumplipüré (Hu) Mashed potatoes.

krumplisaláta (Hu) Potato salad.

krupičná kaše (Cz) Cooked cereal.

krupnik (Po) 1. A barley and vegetable soup made with meat broth. 2. A holiday drink of hot mead, made with honey.

krupuk udang (In) Deep-fried wafers made with dried prawns and manioc or rice flour; puff up when cooked.

krusbär (Sw) Gooseberries.

kruška (SC) Pear.

krustader (Da) Pastry shells or toast slices; croûtes; filled with mixtures such as ham and peas.

krydderier (Nw) Spices.

kryddor (Sw) Spices.

kryddost (Sw) Spiced cheese.

kryddsill (Sw) Spiced, pickled herring.

krydret and (Da) Pickled duck.

kuah (In) Sauce.

kubis (In) Cabbage.

Kuchen (Gr) Cake; coffee cake; tart.

kuchitori (Jp) Hors d'oeuvres and sweet appetizers.

kudamono (Jp) Fruit.

kue dadar (In) Pancakes.

kue kering (In) Pastry.

kue lapis (In) Layer cake.

kufta (Ar) A mix of ground meat, onions, parsley, and spices grilled on skewers.

kufta mabrouma (Ar) Baked roll of

ground meat, onions, and parsley stuffed with pine nuts.

kugel (Jw) Sweet pudding made of rice or noodles with fruits, nuts, eggs, sugar, spices, and chicken fat. A savory kugel is made with potatoes.

Kugelhopf (Gr–Austria) A crown-shaped yeast cake made with raisins or currants and almonds and topped with confectioners' sugar. Also spelled **Gugelhupf.**

ku-gwā (Ch) See **bitter melon.**

kuha (Fi) Pike perch.

kuiken (Du) Squab.

kujira (Jp) Whale.

kuk (Kr) Soup.

kukkakaali (Fi) Cauliflower.

kukki (Jp) Cookies.

kukurjeebhi (Ia) Sole.

kukurydza (Po) Corn.

kuku wa kuchoma (Af–Swahili) Broiled or roasted chicken.

kuku wa kukaanga (Af–Swahili) Fried chicken.

kulebiak (Po) A baked, rolled dough filled with mushrooms, sauerkraut, chopped eggs, and onions.

kulebyaka (Rs) A loaf-shaped envelope of yeast dough or flaky pastry dough, stuffed with meat or fish and garnished with sour cream.

kulfi (Ia) Ice cream made with milk, almonds, pistachios, and rose water syrup.

kulich (Rs) A tall, cylindrical, yeast-raised cake made with saffron, almonds, and fruit; a traditional Easter cake.

kumiss (Rs) A drink made with fermented milk of mares and cows.

kumle (Nw) Raw potato dumpling.

kummel (Sw) Hake.

Kümmel (Gr) Caraway; liqueur flavored with caraway and anise.

kumminost (Sw) Cumin-flavored cheese.

kumquat (US) The fruit of an evergreen tree, *Fortunella* species, which looks like a plum-sized orange and has edible rind and bittersweet, acid flesh; used for marmalades, preserves, and in cooked dishes.

kunde (Af–Swahili) Beans.

kuneli (Gk) Rabbit.

kung pao (Th) Grilled king shrimp with chili peppers and a fish sauce (nam pla).

kùng shui (Ch) Mineral water.

kunsei no nishin (Jp) Smoked herring.

kunyit (In) Turmeric.

kupus (SC) Cabbage.

kura (Po) Chicken.

kurapatka (Rs) Partridge.

kura smażona (Po) Fried chicken.

Kürbis (Gr) Pumpkin.

kurcze z jarzynami (Po) Rolled chicken breast filled with chopped chicken and vegetables and baked in broth.

kuře (Cz) Chicken.

kuri (Rs) Chicken.

kuri (Jp) Chestnuts.

kurkku (Fi) Cucumber.

kurkkukeitto (Fi) Cucumber soup.

kurkkusalaatti (Fi) Cucumber salad.

kurma (In) Dates.

kurnik (Rs) Chicken and rice covered with a pastry crust.

kuro pan (Jp) Dark bread.

kurpitsa (Fi) Pumpkin.

kuru üzüm (Tr) Raisins.

kurz angebraten (Gr) Cooked medium-rare (meat).

kushizashi (Jp) Cooked on a skewer.

kuşkonmaz (Tr) Asparagus.

kuvana jaja (SC) Poached eggs.

kuvano (SC) Boiled.

kuzu (Tr) Lamb.

kuzumanju (Jp) A cake or bun made with soybean and jam.

kuzu pirzolasi (Tr) Lamb chops.

kvass (Rs) A drink made from fermented rye bread or grain in water and sugar; also used as a soup stock.

kveite (Nw) Halibut.

květák (Cz) Cauliflower.

kwark (Du) Skimmed cow's milk cheese; Dutch version of German Quark.

kwaśne (Po) Sour.

kyabetsu (Jp) Cabbage.

kyckling (Sw) Chicken.

kycklinggryta (Sw) Chicken casserole.

kyckling ugnsstekt (Sw) Roast chicken.

kyljys (Fi) Cutlet, chop.

kylling (Nw) Chicken.

kyllinger stegte (Da) Roast chicken, often stuffed with parsley.

kyselé okurky (Cz) Sour pickles.

kyūri (Jp) Cucumber.

kyūri no sumomi (Jp) Vinegared cucumber.

laban zabadi (Ar) Yogurt.

labra (Ia) Mixed vegetable curry including green beans, squash, carrots, and eggplant, and served with coriander leaves.

là-cháng (Ch) Sausage.

Lachs (Gr) Salmon.

Lacrima Christi (It) A dry red or white wine.

lactose (US) A type of sugar that occurs in the milk of mammals. Many persons are unable to tolerate lactose in varying amounts. It is commonly used as an additive in baby foods, as a coating for foods, and in bakery products.

là de (Ch) Peppery in flavor.

là de jye-mwò jyàng (Ch) Hot mustard.

ladyfingers (US) Long, slender biscuits; sweet, crisp; often used as a base in molded desserts. Also called **langue de chat.**

là-gen (Ch) Horseradish.

lagkage (Da) Layer cake.

lagosta (Pg) Spiny lobster.

lagostins (Pg) Scampi.

lágy tojás (Hu) Soft-boiled eggs.

làhana (Tr) Cabbage.

lahm (Ar) Meat.

lahna (Fi) Bream.

lait (Fr) Milk.

laitue (Fr) Lettuce; lettuce salad.

laitue chicorée (Fr) Chicory salad.

laitues braisées (Fr) Braised lettuce, usually Boston lettuce.

là jyàng (Ch) Chili paste.

là jyau (Ch) Hot chili peppers.

lakkoja (Fi) Arctic cloudberries.

laks (Da, Nw) Salmon.

laksørred (Da) Salmon trout.

lam (Nw) Lamb.

lamb (US) The light pink, somewhat fatty meat of sheep, *Ovis aries*, less than one year old. Baby or hothouse refers to milk-fed lambs, less than six weeks; spring lambs, milk-fed and under four months; lamb, weaned and under one year.

lambrópsomo (Gk) A rich spice bread.

lamb's lettuce (US) See **mâche.**

lamb's quarters (US) A wild plant, *Chenopodium album*, with triangular leaves that taste like spinach and have an aroma like lamb; eaten raw or steamed.

lamm (Sw) Lamb.

lammaskaali (Fi) Mutton stew with cabbage.

lammefrikassé (Da) Lamb stew.

lammekotelett (Da, Nw) Lamb chop.

lammestek (Nw) Roast leg of lamb.

Lammfleisch (Gr) Lamb.

lampaanliha (Fi) Mutton, lamb.

lamponi (It) Raspberries.

lamsvlees (Du) Lamb.

Lancashire (GB) A cow's milk cheese; crumbly texture; rich, tangy taste; eaten as a dessert cheese and used in sauces, soups, and rarebit.

langosta (Sp) See **spiny lobster.**

langouste (Fr) See **spiny lobster.**

langoustine (Fr) Prawn; scampi; small lobster.

langue (Fr) Tongue.

langue de boeuf (Fr) Beef tongue.

langue de boeuf gelée (Fr) Beef tongue in aspic.

langue de chat (Fr) Literally, "cat's tongue"; ladyfingers.

lanttu (Fi) Rutabaga.

lanttulaatikko (Fi) Rutabaga casserole served at Christmas.

lapereau (Fr) Young rabbit.

lapin (Fr) Rabbit.

lappi (Fi) A mild cheese.

lapskaus (Nw) Hash.

laranja (Pg) Orange.

laranjada (Pg) Orangeade.

lard (US) White, soft fat; the rendered fatty tissue of the hog.

lard fumé (Fr) Smoked bacon.

larding (US) The insertion of thin strips of fat into meat, poultry, or game using a wooden spike, skewer, or needle.

lardon (Fr) See **lardoon.**

lardoon (US) A thin strip of fat, such as salt pork or bacon, for insertion into meat for larding. Also called **lardon.**

lasagne (It) Broad egg noodles; boiled until tender, then baked in layers with a filling, often meat sauce, ricotta, and mozzarella, between each strip.

lasagne verde (It) Green lasagne flavored with spinach.

lasimestarin silli (Fi) Pickled herring with onions, carrots, and spices.

laskiaispulla (Fi) A bun sometimes topped with marzipan, made for Shrove Tuesday.

lassi (Ia) A diluted yogurt served as a drink, salty, sweetened or spiced.

lathee (Gk) Oil.

latke (Jw) A fried pancake made of grated potatoes, eggs, flour, salt, and pepper; grated cheese or onions may be added. Traditionally served during Hanukkah, the Feast of Lights.

latte (It) Milk.

lättstekt (Sw) Rare (meat).

lattuga (It) Lettuce.

Lauch (Gr) Leek.

làu-myàn (Ch) Lo mein; cooked noodles; served with a sauce or topping.

lavagante (Pg) Lobster.

laver (US) See **nori.**

lax (Sw) Salmon.

lazac (Hu) Salmon.

leather (US) A confection made with a mixture of pureed fruit and sugar or honey, spread in thin sheets; baked slowly and when dried, cut in long strips resembling leather.

lebbencsleves (Hu) A soup made with fried pieces of dough, bacon, onion, and paprika simmered in water; potato slices are added.

leben (Jw–Israel) Yogurt.

Leber (Gr) Liver.

Leberknödelsuppe (Gr) Liver dumpling soup.

Leberwurst (Gr) Liver sausage, precooked and often made with pork and pork liver; usually spreadable and served cold.

Lebkuchen (Gr) A spiced Christmas cake.

leche (Sp) Milk.

leche de manteca (Sp) Buttermilk.

lechem (Jw–Israel) Bread.

leche quemada (Sp) See **arroz con leche.**

lecithin (US) A substance found in all living tissues and in the diet in foods such as nonhydrogenated oils, egg yolks, corn, liver, brains, and soybeans. It is a common food additive used as an emulsifier and an antioxidant.

lecsó (Hu) A sauce made with tomatoes, sweet peppers, onion, paprika, sugar, and bacon.

led (Cz) Ice.

Lederzucker (Gr) Marshmallow.

leek (US) A hardy member of the onion family, genus *Allium*, native to Europe, with green leaves and a white bulbous stalk; eaten as a vegetable, usually boiled.

lefse (Nw) Flat bannock.

légumes (Fr) Vegetables.

legumes (Pg) Vegetables.

Leidse kaas (Du) Cumin cheese from Leiden.

leikkeleitä (Fi) Cold cuts.

leipä (Fi) Bread.

leitão (Pg) Suckling pig.

leite (Pg) Milk.

leite creme (Pg) Custard.

lekvár (Hu) Preserves.

lekváros derelye (Hu) Boiled dough pockets filled with jam and served topped with sugar and cinnamon.

lemon (US) A citrus fruit, *Citus limon*, native to Asia; yellow rind; tangy taste; juice, pulp, and rind used in a wide variety of dishes and desserts.

lemon balm (US) An herb, *Melissa officinalis*, with lemon-scented, mintlike leaves used as a flavoring in fruit salads, beverages, in stuffings for fish and in jellies.

lemongrass (US) A lemon-scented grass, *Cymbopogon citratus*, with white bulbs used often in the cooking of Southeast Asia. Also called **sereh.**

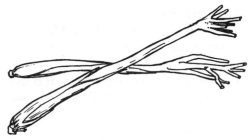

Lemongrass

lencseleves (Hu) Lentil soup.

lenguado (Sp) Sole.

lentejas (Sp) Lentils.

lenticchi (It) Lentils.

lentilhas (Pg) Lentils.

lentille (Fr) Lentil.

lepre (It) Hare.

lesni jahody (Cz) Wild strawberries.

less (US) A food label term as in "less sodium"; applies if the amount of the substance in a product is reduced at least 25 percent; proposed by the U.S. Food and Drug Administration for food labels.

letas (Af–Swahili) Lettuce.

letterbanket (Du) Almond paste.

lettuce (US) Any of a variety of plants, genus *Lactuca*, in particular *Lactuca sativa*, cultivated for its leaves and used in salads. The four main varieties are head lettuce, leaf lettuce, Romaine or Cos, and asparagus lettuce.

leuqkuas (In) See **galangal.**

levadura (Sp) Yeast.

lever (Da, Du, Nw, Sw) Liver.

leverpostej (Da) Liver paste.

levrant (Fr) Young hare.

levrek (Tr) Bass.

levure (Fr) Yeast.

levure de bière (Fr) Brewer's yeast.

liba (Hu) Goose.

libamájas kifli (Hu) Rolls filled with goose liver paste.

libové (Cz) Lean (meat).

licorice (US) A flavoring extracted from the root of a plant, *Glycyrrhiza glabra*, used in the manufacture of candy and liqueurs.

liebre (Sp) Hare.

Liederkranz (US) An ivory- to honey-colored cow's milk cheese of American origin; mild to pungent taste and snappy aroma although not as strong as Limburger.

Licorice

liemi (Fi) Broth.

lievito (It) Yeast; baking powder.

lievito di birra (It) Brewer's yeast.

lièvre (Fr) Hare.

light (US) A food label term that means a product has one-third fewer calories than a comparable product; proposed by the U.S. Food and Drug Administration for food labels.

lights (GB) Lungs of animals; sometimes used in stuffings.

lihajuuresmuhennos (Fi) Beef stew with root vegetables.

lihakaalilaatikko (Fi) Meat and cabbage casserole.

lihakeitto (Fi) A clear meat broth containing meat and vegetables.

lihakohokas (Fi) Meat soufflé.

lihaliemi (Fi) Beef broth.

lihamureke (Fi) Meat loaf.

lihamurekekääryleet (Fi) Stuffed meat rolls.

lihamurekekakku (Fi) Meat loaf cake.

lihamurekepiiras (Fi) Meat pie with a sour cream crust.

lihamurekevoileivät (Fi) A sandwich made with ground beef combined with cream, bread crumbs, egg, onion, salt, and pepper.

lihapyörykät (Fi) Meatballs.

lilikoi (Pl–Hawaii) Passion fruit.

lima bean (US) See **butter bean.**

Limabohnen (Gr) Lima beans.

limão (Pg) Lemon.

limau (Af–Swahili) Lemon.

limba cu misline (Ro) Beef or veal

tongue cooked with vinegar and ripe olives, then baked with a tomato sauce.

Limburger (Gr) A smooth yellow paste-like cow's milk cheese with a yellow to brown rind; strong, pungent aroma and spicy, gamey, piquant taste.

limburský sýr (Cz) Limburger cheese.

lime (US) A small citrus fruit, *Citrus aurantifolia*; several types including Tahiti, Persian, and Bearss; with yellow to green skin and juicy flesh, usually sour; used in similar ways as the lemon: as a flavoring for desserts, fish, and salads; native to Southeast Asia; established in the Florida Keys by the seventeenth century. See also **Key lime pie.**

limon (Fr) Lime.

limon (Tr) Lemon.

limonada (Pg) Lemonade.

limonade (Du) Any fruit drink.

limonata (It) Lemonade.

limone (It) Lemon.

limpa (Sw) Spiced rye bread.

limppukukko (Fi) Fish baked in a bread loaf.

limu (Pl–Hawaii) An edible seaweed used in fish marinades.

lin (Cz) See **tench.**

lingon (Sw) Lingonberries.

lingonberry (US) A red edible berry of a low-growing bush, *Vaccinium vitis*; similar to a cranberry.

lingua (It) Tongue.

lingua di bue (It) Beef tongue.

lingua di vitello (It) Veal tongue.

linguado (Pg) Sole.

linguiça (Pg) Garlic-flavored sausage.

linguine (It) Literally, "small tongues"; a spaghetti that resembles narrow, flat noodles; usually served with a red or white clam sauce.

Linsensuppe (Gr) Lentil soup.

Linzertorte (Gr–Austria) A cake spread with raspberry jam and topped with strips of dough in a lattice shape.

lipeäkala (Fi) A Christmas dish of boiled codfish, first soaked in a lye solution and served with potatoes and a white sauce.

lipid (US) Describes any substance that can be dissolved in a fat solvent such as alcohol, but cannot be dissolved in water. An example is a fatty acid.

liptói körözött (Hu) An hors d'oeuvre made with cheese topped with caraway seeds, paprika, and chives.

liqueur (US) An alcoholic drink sweetened and flavored with fruit, herbs, or other aromatic plant substances.

liquid sugar (US) Sucrose dissolved in sufficient water to keep it fluid.

liquor (US) A general term for a distilled spirit; includes whiskey, brandy, rum, vodka, gin, and cordials.

liquore (It) Liqueur.

lishki (Rs) Literally, "little foxes"; dark ochre chanterelle mushrooms used in stews.

lískové ořechy (Cz) Filberts; hazelnuts.

list (SC) Sole.

litchi (Ch) A fruit, *Litchi chinensis*, native to China and Thailand, commonly with a red, leathery, knobby or spiny skin and juicy, highly scented, grapelike taste when ripe; brown, brittle skin when dried and with a taste like raisins.

lithe (Sc) To thicken a slow-simmering broth; a Scottish cooking term.

littleneck clam (US) Smallest of the hardshell clams; used in soups and sauces, eaten on the half shell, or served stuffed. See **quahog.**

livance (Cz) Pancakes.

Livarot (Fr) A cow's milk cheese with a soft, yellow interior and a red-brown rind, wrapped in reeds; strong flavor, pungent aroma; one of the most esteemed cheeses of France.

liver sausage (US) A cooked sausage made with liver and pork, sometimes smoked; may be flavored with garlic or onion; usually spreadable for sandwiches or appetizers.

lobescoves (Da) A kind of goulash made with large beef chunks; also, a hash made with beef, diced potatoes, and onions in a brown sauce.

lobster (US) A crustacean, genus *Homarus*, with eight legs and two pincers; usually a dark-blue or green that turns red when cooked; rich, lean flesh; eaten boiled, poached, baked, fried, or broiled.

Littleneck

lobster Newburg (US) Chunks of lobster sautéed in butter and served in a cream and egg sauce flavored with paprika and sherry; made famous at Delmonico's in New York.

lobster sauce (US) A sauce to be served or cooked with lobster; made of minced pork, beaten eggs, and scallions.

lobster Thermidor (US) See **homard Thermidor.**

loco moco (Pl) Hawaiian breakfast of fried eggs and a grilled hamburger patty on a bowl of rice.

lody (Po) Ice cream.

løg (Da) Onions.

loganberry (US) A cross between blackberries and raspberries; reported to have been discovered around 1881 by James Logan, a California judge.

lohi (Fi) Salmon.

lohilaatikko (Fi) Salmon casserole.

lohipiirakka (Fi) Salmon pie.

lobz (Ar) Almonds.

lök (Sw) Onions.

løk (Nw) Onions.

löksoppa (Sw) Onion soup.

lokum (Tr) Candy; Turkish Delight.

lombata di vitello (It) Loin of veal; breaded veal chop.

lombo de vitela (Pg) Veal loin.

lombok (In) Hot red pepper.

lo mein (Ch) Cooked noodles made with wheat flour; longer and whiter than egg noodles; resemble spaghetti.

lomi-lomi (Pl–Hawaii) Salted king salmon served with tomatoes and onion.

lomo (Sp) Boneless pork loin; may be stewed with tomatoes and chilis.

London broil (US) A flank steak or similar beef cut; also, an American dish of broiled, marinated flank steak cut into thin slices on an angle; may be served with melted butter and parsley. Origin of the name unknown, other than it derives from the city of London, England.

longan (Ch) A fruit, *Euphoria longana*, related to the litchi, but smaller.

long-billed sturgeon (US) A fish of the Mississippi-Missouri River system; a source of American caviar.

longe (Fr) Loin.

long-grain rice (US) A term applied to a rice grain several or more times longer than wide and that usually cooks with grains separate and not sticky. Carolina rice with a white grain and basmati with a brown grain are examples.

long rice (US) A Hawaiian name for rice stick noodles; thin, white, opaque, and brittle.

lontong (In) Rice cooked in banana leaves.

loquat (US) The edible yellow fruit of an Asiatic evergreen tree, *Eriobotrya japonica*; used for preserves. Also called **biwa.**

löskokta ägg (Sw) Soft-boiled egg.

losos (Cz) Salmon.

losoś (Po) Salmon.

lososina zapechonnaia v fol'ge (Rs) Salmon baked in parchment.

lotte (Fr) Monkfish.

lotte vapeur (Fr) Steamed monkfish.

lotus (US) A plant popularly known as water lilies; about one hundred species, most with edible underwater rhizomes. Lotus roots, leaves, and seeds are often used in the cooking of India, China, and Japan. Roots of the cultivated plant look like turnips with lacy air holes; used raw or cooked, grated, or in salads. The black seeds are roasted, eaten like nuts, or used in soups.

Louis sauce (US) Mayonnaise flavored with chili sauce, whipped cream, chopped green pepper, onions, and lemon juice; created by a chef Louis in San Francisco early in the twentieth century.

loukanika (Gk) Small, coarse-textured, dry pork sausage made with red wine and coriander; may be flavored with orange peel.

loukanikopita (Gk) A puff pastry stuffed with sausage.

loukoumades (Gk) Deep-fried balls of dough soaked in honey.

loup (Fr) Sea bass.

loup de mer au fenouil (Fr) Sea bass grilled and flamed with dried fennel leaves and stalks.

loupáček (Cz) A flaky rolled pastry.

lovage (US) A tall herb, genus *Levisticum*, with dark green leaves like parsley; taste of lemon-flavored celery; used in soups, stuffings, and salads; seeds used in pickling brines and baking.

low-calorie (US) A food label term that means a product contains fewer than 40 calories per serving and per 100 grams of the food in question; proposed by the U.S. Food and Drug Administration for food labels.

low-fat (US) A food label term that

167

means a product contains no more than 3 grams of fat per serving and per 100 grams of the food in question; proposed by the U.S. Food and Drug Administration for food labels.

low in cholesterol (US) A food label term that means a product contains no more than 20 milligrams of cholesterol per serving and per 100 grams of the food in question and no more than 2 grams of saturated fat per serving; proposed by the U.S. Food and Drug Administration for food labels.

low in saturated fat (US) A food label term that means a product contains no more than 1 gram of saturated fat per serving and no more than 15 percent of the total calories come from saturated fat; proposed by the U.S. Food and Drug Administration for food labels.

low-sodium (US) A food label term that means a product contains less than 140 milligrams of sodium per serving and per 100 grams of the food in question; proposed by the U.S. Food and Drug Administration for food labels.

low-sodium milk (US) Whole milk with the sodium reduced and replaced by potassium, more acceptable to people on sodium reduced and restricted diets.

lox (Jw) Smoked salmon; Jewish-American specialty, usually sliced thin and served on a bagel with cream cheese.

luk (Rs) Onions.

lula (Pg) Cuttlefish; squid.

lulu frita (Pg) A Brazilian dish of fried squid.

lumache (It) Snails; also snail-shaped pasta.

lumpfish roe (US) Roe of a marine fish, *Cyclopterus lumpus*; used as caviar; flesh of the lumpfish is oily but may be poached.

luostari (Fi) A cow's milk cheese similar to Port Salut.

luquete (Sp) Zest; orange slice dropped into wine.

lutefisk (Nw) Stockfish soaked in lye.

lutfisk (Sw) Unsalted, air-dried fish (stockfish) soaked in lye; a Christmas specialty.

luumu (Fi) Plum.

lyonnaise, à la (Fr) In the style of Lyons or Lyonnais, a city and province famous for its oustanding cuisine. It is the onion growing region of France, and generally the term refers to dishes prepared with sautéed, chopped onions.

maandazi (Af–Swahili) Sweet pasties; deep-fried breads.

maatjes haring (Du) Herring, caught first of the season, lightly cured; eaten with raw onions and boiled green beans.

maçã (Pg) Apple.

macadamia nut (US) A nut native to Australia, with a white, oily sweet kernel; used in desserts, cakes, jam, and soups. Also called **Queensland nut.**

macaroni (US) Long hollow tube-shaped pasta. Also spelled **maccheroni.**

macaroni and cheese (US) A popular dish of cooked macaroni mixed with cheese sauce; usually served gratin.

macaroons (US) Chewy cookies made with beaten egg white, almond paste or shredded coconut, sugar, and vanilla; may be crushed and used in desserts such as biscuit tortoni.

macarrã (Pg) Macaroni.

macarrones (Sp) Macaroni.

maccheroni (It) See **macaroni.**

mace (US) The red fibrous wrapping (aril) of the nutmeg kernel; dried and ground; used in baking, in chocolate dishes, stuffings, fish sauces, and oyster stew.

macédoine (Fr) Diced and mixed fruit or vegetables, hot or cold, raw or cooked.

macedonia di frutta (It) Fruit salad; fruit cup in wine syrup.

mâche (Fr) A plant, *Valerianella olitoria*, with small oval leaves and a some-

Mace

what bitter taste; used in mixed salads or as a garnish. Also called **corn salad, lamb's lettuce.**

mackerel (US) Any of a large group, some 60 species, of torpedo-shaped fish found on both sides of the Atlantic Ocean. The Atlantic mackerel, *Scomber scombrus*, has firm, oily flesh with a strong, distinctive flavor; used poached, baked, fried, grilled, and soused.

mackerel shark (US) A relatively small, edible shark, family Isuridae; steaks are grilled; may be served with lemon juice. Also called **anequim, mako.**

Madeira (Pg) Fortified wines produced in Madeira; taste ranges from dry to sweet. Dry Madeiras are used in soups, stews, sauces, and braised dishes. Sweet Madeiras are added to desserts.

madeleine (Fr) A small lemon- or

orange-flavored cake baked in a shell-like, ribbed mold.

Maderawein (Gr) Madeira.

madère, sauce au (Fr) A sauce made with Madeira wine.

madrilène (Fr) Clear soup with tomato; served chilled.

magert (Sw) Lean (meat).

maggiorana (It) Marjoram.

magnesium (US) A mineral essential for human health; the recommended dietary allowance (RDA) per day is 300–350 mg for normal adults; best natural sources include leafy, green vegetables, legumes, nuts, and whole-grain cereals.

magro, di (It) A seafood sauce of tuna, anchovies, and herbs.

maguro (Jp) Tuna.

maguro no sashimi (Jp) Sliced raw tuna with grated gingerroot or daikon and soy sauce.

mahi-mahi (Pl) Dolphinfish; found in the semitropical waters of the Pacific and Atlantic oceans; flavorful, tender, lean flesh; used broiled, fried, grilled, poached, or sautéed.

mahlepi (Ar) A spice derived from the black cherry kernel.

ma ho (Th) An appetizer; deep-fried balls of ground pork mixed with coriander root, peanuts, and a shrimp sauce; served with fruit.

mai (Ar) Water.

maiale (It) Pork.

maialino di latte (It) Suckling pig.

maida (Ia) White flour.

mài-dz (Ch) Wheat. Also called **syău-mài.**

Maifisch (Gr) Shad.

maigre, au (Fr) Lean.

maini (Af–Swahili) Liver.

maionese (It, Pg) Mayonnaise.

mài-pyàn (Ch) Cereal.

mais (Fr) Corn.

mais (Nw) Corn.

Mais (Gr) Corn.

maisild (Nw) Shad.

Maismehl (Gr) Cornstarch.

maison (Fr) Literally, "house"; in the style of a restaurant or a recipe exclusive to a restaurant or chef.

maito (Fi) Milk.

maitre d'hotel beurre (Fr) Seasoned butter with fresh parsley and lemon; served with grilled or other foods.

maíz (Sp) Corn.

maize (US) See **corn.**

máj (Hu) Liver.

májas hurka (Hu) Liver sausage.

majfisk (Sw) Shad.

májgombócleves (Hu) Liver dumplings in soup.

maji (Af–Swahili) Water.

maji ya dafu (Af–Swahili) Coconut milk.

maji ya matunda (Af–Swahili) Fruit juice.

majoneesi (Fi) Mayonnaise.

majorana (Sp) Marjoram.

májpastetom (Hu) Chicken liver pâté.

majsild (Da) Shad.

makarna (Tr) Pasta, macaroni, or spaghetti.

makaron (Po) Noodles.

makaroni (Fi) Macaroni.

makaronia me kima (Gk) Pasta, usually spaghetti, with a ground meat sauce.

makarunen (Jw) Macaroons.

makimaki (Jp) See **fugu.**

makizushi (Jp) See **norimaki.**

makkara (Fi) Sausage.

makkhani murgaa (Ia) Chicken cooked in butter and tomato sauce.

mako (US) See **mackerel shark.**

mákos kalács (Hu) Pastry roll with a poppy-seed filling.

mákos metélt (Hu) Sweetened noodles with poppy seed.

makowiec (Po) Poppy-seed roll.

makreel (Du) Mackerel.

makrel (Da) Mackerel.

Makrele (Gr) Mackerel.

makrell (Nw) Mackerel.

makrill (Sw) Mackerel.

makrilli (Fi) Mackerel.

makrut (Th) Kaffir lime, *Citrus hystrix*, a member of the citrus family; highly citrus-scented rind and leaves; used like lemongrass or lemon zest in soups and stews.

maksa (Fi) Liver.

maksalaatikko (Fi) Liver and rice casserole.

malacpecsenye (Hu) Roast suckling pig.

malasol (Rs) Mildly salted varieties of caviar.

maline (SC) Raspberries.

mă-líng-shŭ (Ch) Potatoes.

mă-líng-shŭ shā-là (Ch) Potato salad.

maliny (Cz, Po) Raspberries.

málna (Hu) Raspberries.

malt (US) A material made from a preparation of germinated cereals, usually barley. The process causes enzymes in the grains to turn their starch into certain sugars, maltose and dextrin; used in brewing, distilling, and in some flour and baking.

maltaise, à la (Fr) In the Maltese style; made with orange juice and rind.

maltaise, sauce (Fr) Hollandaise sauce with the juice from blood oranges and grated orange peel; used with asparagus.

malt bread (GB) A sweet, light brown bread made with malt extract, black treacle, and raisins.

malt extract (US) A syrup made from a preparation of germinated barley; used as a sugar substitute.

mămăligá (Ro) Boiled corn meal mush, the national staple of Romania. It is served in a variety of ways, such as with grated cheese, sour cream, or poached eggs, or enriched with butter. It is similar to **polenta.**

mamao (Pg) Papaya.

mame (Jp) Beans.

mämmi (Fi) Rye and molasses pudding flavored with bitter orange; served with cream.

mandariini (Fi) Tangerine.

mandarinka (Cz) Tangerine.

mandarino (It) Tangerine.

mandarin orange (US) A variety of loose-skinned orange with a Chinese origin; a strong orange skin color and sweet, juicy pulp; often used as a dessert fruit. Sold canned in segments. The dried peel is used in Chinese dishes.

mandelbiskvier (Sw) Almond cookies.

Mandelbrezeln (Gr) Almond pretzels.

Mandeln (Gr) Almonds.

Mandeltorte (Gr) Almond torte.

mandlar (Sw) Almonds.

mandler (Nw) Almonds.

mandorla (It) Almond.

mandorla amara (It) Bitter almond.

mandorle tostate (It) Toasted almonds; almond praline.

manestra (Gk) Small, seed-shaped macaroni. Also called **orzo.**

manga (Pg) Mango.

manganese (US) An essential trace element considered by authorities to be adequately supplied in a normal diet; food sources include whole grains, cereal and dairy products, meat, fish, and poultry.

mange-tout (Fr) See **podded peas.**

máng-gwo (Ch) Mango.

mango (US) A fruit, *Mangifera indica*; many varieties, shapes, sizes, colors; leathery skin; orange flesh with an acid-sweet taste when ripe; eaten raw and used in chutney, pickled, and as juice.

mango chutney (Ia) A condiment of mangoes with almonds, citrus peel, raisins, onions, ginger, red peppers, sugar, and vinegar.

Mangold (Gr) Chard.

mangosteen (US) A small orange-sized fruit native to Malaysia; white, juicy, delicious flesh in segments; used in fruit salads or in preserves.

Manhattan clam chowder (US) See **clam chowder.**

Mango

manicotti (It) Large, hollow tubes of macaroni used for stuffing and baking; often filled with cheese and meat and baked in a sauce.

manioc (Fr) See **cassava.**

manitaria (Gk) Mushrooms.

manjarblanco (Sp) Blancmange; for example, one made with guavas, milk, and sugar.

manju (Jp) Rice flour cakes filled with sweet bean paste.

mannagrynspudding (Sw) Semolina pudding.

mannapuuro (Fi) Cream of wheat cereal.

mansikkalumi (Fi) Strawberry-snow dessert.

mansikoita (Fi) Strawberries.

mantar (Tr) Mushroom.

manteiga (Pg) Butter.

mantequilla (Sp) Butter.

mán-tóu (Ch) Steamed bread.

manty (Rs) Lamb dumplings.

màn-yú (Ch) Eel.

manzana (Sp) Apple.

manzo (It) Beef.

manzo arrosto (It) Roast beef.

manzo brasiato (It) Braised beef.

manzo salato (It) Corned beef.

maple syrup (US) The boiled down sap of the sugar maple, *Acer saccharum*, and of the black maple, *A. nigrum*; used on pancakes and waffles and in cooking. Maple sugar is produced from further evaporation.

maquereaux (Fr) Mackerel.

maquereaux au vin blanc (Fr) Mackerel in a white wine sauce.

maquereaux marine (Fr) Pickled mackerel.

marak (Jw–Israel) Soup.

marak perot kar (Jw–Israel) A cold soup of fresh fruit.

marak yerakot (Jw–Israel) Vegetable soup.

maräng (Sw) Meringue.

Maraschino (It) A colorless liqueur made from the fermented juice and crushed pits of the sour marasca cherry and used as a flavoring for sweets and fruits. The large, dyed cherries called Maraschino cherries are preserved in a syrup flavored with real or imitation Maraschino liqueur and used to decorate food or drinks.

marchands de vin, sauce (Fr) Brown sauce reduced with red wine, shallots or onions, garlic, olive oil, oregano, and seasonings.

marchewka (Po) Carrots.

marchewka w sosie (Po) Carrots in sauce.

marelica (SC) Apricot.

margarine (US) A spread invented in the 1860s with ingredients such as beef suet and skim milk. Today a blend of edible oils is used. The wide range of margarines sold can vary in the proportions of saturated and unsaturated fats. The kind recommended by authorities for lowering serum cholesterol levels is labeled "high in polyunsaturates." Various other ingredients such as salt, whey, synthetic flavor, color, and vitamins A and D may be added. Used in cooking and baking as well as a spread.

marguery (Fr) Prepared with a sauce of white wine and stock made from mussels; most often used for fillets of sole.

marhaeröleves (Hu) Beef broth.

marhahús (Hu) Beef.

marhasült (Hu) Roast beef.

maridhes (Gk) Small fish similar to whitebait.

Marienkraut (Gr) Marjoram.

marigold (US) A flower, *Calendula officinalis*, with yellow-orange petals sometimes added to pastas, salads, and poultry dishes to give a pungent, musky flavor and a saffronlike color.

Marille (Gr–Austria) Apricot.

Marillenknödel (Gr–Austria) A dumpling made with a batter-coated apricot stuffed with a sugar lump; first poached, then crisped with bread crumbs and sugar.

marinade (US) A liquid usually with oil, an acid such as lemon juice or wine, and seasonings; or a paste of herbs and spices in which food is soaked to tenderize it or to enrich its flavor.

marinara, alla (It) Fisherman style; with a tomato sauce and basil seasoned with garlic, olive oil, and parsley. Fettucine, clams, and prawns are often prepared this way.

marinata (It) Marinated.

marinate (US) To let food soak or stand in a marinade to tenderize or incorporate flavor from the liquid or paste into the food.

mariné (Fr) Marinated.

marinière, à la (Fr) 1. Mussels and other shellfish with a white wine and onion sauce or broth. 2. Fish cooked in white wine, garnished with mussels.

marinovannye griby (Rs) Pickled mushrooms.

173

marinvota silke (Rs) Fish in tomato marinade.

mariscos (Sp) Shellfish.

maritozzi (It) Sweet buns.

marjolaine (Fr) Marjoram.

marjoram (US) An herb, *Origanum majorana* belonging to the mint family with fragrant aroma and slightly bitter taste; dried leaves and flowers used in casseroles, soups, salads, egg, cheese and vegetable dishes, and with meats.

markjordbær (Nw) Wild strawberries.

Markklösschen (Gr) Dumplings made with pureed beef marrow, egg yolks, and bread crumbs.

marmalade (US) A preserve made with chopped, cooked citrus fruits, usually Seville or bitter oranges, and sugar; boiled until setting point is reached.

marmellata (It) Jam.

marmellata di cotogne (It) Quince jam.

marmelo (Pg) See **quince.**

maroilles (Fr) A soft, tangy cow's milk cheese with a strong aroma; square shape; yellow with a red-brown rind.

marron (Fr) See **chestnut.**

marrons glacé (Fr) Chestnuts glazed in veal stock used as a garnish for roasted meat and game.

marrow (US) 1. Soft, fatty tissue in the hollow, long bones of animals. Beef marrow is used in sauces and soups, as a garnish or filling, and served with broiled or roast meat. 2. The name of a summer squash in England.

Marsala (It) A fortified dessert wine produced in Sicily; often used in cooking.

marshmallow (US) Originally, a thick mucilage extracted from the roots of the marshmallow plant native to Europe; the modern spongy, sweet marshmallow contains gum arabic, egg white, sugar, water, and flavorings such as vanilla.

marsh rabbit (US) A term sometimes used for muskrat, an aquatic rodent; marinated, fried, and served with currant jelly.

mártás (Hu) Sauce.

marul (Tr) Lettuce.

Maryland fried chicken (US) A specialty in the state of Maryland; chicken pieces fried in butter and bacon fat and served with a cream sauce with bacon bits.

marynowane sledzie (Po) Marinated herring in vinegar and olive oil with onions and spices.

marzipan (Fr) A paste of almonds, fine sugar, and egg whites; used to make confections such as flowers and fruit.

masa (Mx) Dough made with a paste of ground corn similar to hominy or with the dry flour, masa harina, mixed with water; used for making tortillas, tamales, and enchiladas.

masa harina (Mx) A white flour made with finely ground, dried corn that has been treated with lime. A blue corn meal masa flour, with a nuttier, richer flavor, is also sold. Used for tortillas, tamales, and enchiladas.

masala (Ia) Spices and seasonings ground together; a liquid may be added to make a paste; used as a base for various sauces.

mascarpone (It) A Lombardy cream cheese made from cow's milk; eaten as a dessert with fruit and spices.

mascotte, à la (Fr) A garnish of artichoke

hearts and small potatoes cooked in butter.

masgoof (Ar) Grilled.

mash (US) 1. Crushed, mixed ingredients such as mashed potatoes; a fermentable, starchy mixture from which alcohol or spirits can be distilled. 2. An alternative term for a pulse, *urd*, used in India for dal.

mash, to (US) To reduce to pulp using an implement or a machine with a wire whisk or paddle.

masline (SC) Olives.

maslo (Po) Butter.

máslo (Cz) Butter.

maso (Cz) Meat.

masové knedlíčky (Cz) Meatballs.

maso z divokého kance (Cz) Wild boar.

Masséna, à la (Fr) A garnishing style for small cuts of meat; artichoke hearts with béarnaise sauce, topped with bone marrow slices.

masu (Jp) Trout.

masur (Ia) A variety of lentil.

mat (Nw) Food.

matcha (Jp) Powdered green tea used in the tea ceremony.

maté (Sp) A slightly bitter, stimulating beverage made from the dried leaves and shoots of a South American holly, genus *Ilex*; contains caffeine but has less tannin than tea. Also called **yerba maté.**

matelote (Fr) A freshwater fish stew made with wine.

matfett (Nw) Lard.

má-tí (Ch) See **water chestnut.**

mäti ja paahtoleipä (Fi) A delicacy of whipped roe combined with whipped cream and onions.

Matjeshering in saurer Sahne (Gr) Pickled herring in sour cream.

matjessill (Sw) Sweet pickled herring; traditional lunch for Midsummer's Day.

matsutake (Jp) Mushrooms with dark brown caps, black gills, and long stems; fragrant with intense flavor; used in soups, stews, with rice, and grilled whole.

matzo (Jw) Unleavened flat bread; crisp, crackerlike; traditionally eaten during Passover but available year round.

matzo balls (Jw) Dumplings made with egg and matzo meal and poached in soup.

matzo brei (Jw) Matzo pieces dipped in beaten eggs and milk; fried like French toast.

matzo meal (Jw) Crumbled matzo used for making dumplings.

Maultaschen (Gr) Oversize pasta pillows filled with meat and vegetables, such as spinach or ham, and served in consommé.

mausteita (Fi) Condiments; spices.

mayai ya kuchemsha yaliyo laini (Af–Swahili) Soft-boiled eggs.

mayai ya kuchemsha yaliyo magumu (Af–Swahili) Hard-boiled eggs.

mayai ya kuvuruga (Af–Swahili) Scrambled eggs.

mayeritsa (Gk) An Easter soup made with lamb offal (the head, heart, lungs, liver, and intestines) and bound with egg and lemon sauce (avgolemono).

mayim (Jw–Israel) Water.

mayonnaise (Fr) A sauce made with egg yolks, olive oil, and vinegar or lemon juice, thoroughly blended.

mazarintårta (Sw) A two-layered cake filled with praline mousse.

maziwa (Af–Swahili) Milk.

maziwa ya kuganda (Af–Swahili) Sour cream.

mazorka de maíz (Mx) Corn on the cob.

mazurek (Po) Literally, a Polish dance; pastry made with a cookie-like crust; topped with various cooked sweetened fruits, nuts, or frostings.

mazurka (Rs) Easter nut cake.

mbaazi (Af–Swahili) Peas.

mchele (Af–Swahili) Uncooked rice.

mchicha (Af–Swahili) Spinach.

mchicha wa nazi (Af–Swahili) Spinach with coconut milk and peanut sauce.

mchuzi (Af–Swahili) Curry.

mchuzi wa kuku (Af–Swahili) Chicken curry.

mchuzi wa nyama (Af–Swahili) Meat curry.

mdzhavai kombosto (Rs) Red cabbage salad.

mead (US) A drink made of honey or sugar in water with yeast and raisins; sometimes flavored with lemon. Also called **sima.**

mealiepap (Af) South African corn meal porridge served with meat and gravy; also served at breakfast with milk and sugar.

meat (US) The flesh of domestic farm animals (cows, sheep, pigs).

meat extender (US) See **textured plant protein.**

mečoun (Cz) Swordfish.

médaillon (Fr) Food cut into a round or oval shape.

médaillons de veau (Fr) Small, round pieces of veal; often pan-fried.

medamayaki (Jp) Fried eggs.

medio crudo (Sp) Rare (meat).

medisterkaker (Nw) Pork patties or cakes.

medivnyk (Rs) Spiced honey cake.

medlar (US) A tree related to the rose family with small, acidic, apple-shaped fruit; eaten fresh or used in preserves. Also called **nespola, loquat.**

mee krob (Th) Fried rice noodles with vegetables, shrimp, pork, and chicken.

Meeresfrüchte (Gr) Seafood.

Meerrettich (Gr) Horseradish.

Meerrettichsosse (Gr) Horseradish sauce.

meggy (Hu) Sour cherries.

meggyes rétes (Hu) Cherry strudel.

Mehlsspeisen (Gr) Flour-based dishes.

mehshi (Ar) Stuffed; eggplants, vine leaves, or cabbage may be stuffed with a ground meat mixture.

mehu (Fi) Juice; a punch made with the juice of raspberries, blackberries, and gooseberries.

mei (Pl) Breadfruit.

méi-dz (Ch) Prunes.

mejillónes (Sp) Mussels.

mel (Nw) Flour.

mela (It) Apple.

melagrana (It) Pomegranate.

melancia (Pg) Watermelon.

mélangée (Fr) Mixed.

melanzane (It) Eggplant.

Melanzani (Gr–Austria) Eggplant.

melão (Pg) Melon.

Melba toast (US) A method of toast preparation devised by Escoffier; very thin sliced toast that is retoasted; named in honor of opera star Dame Nellie Melba.

melcocha (Sp) 1. Molasses. 2. Honey cake. 3. Marshmallow.

mele fritte al rum (It) Fried apples with rum.

melidzanes (Gk) Eggplant.

melidzanosalata (Gk) Puree of baked eggplant mixed with onion, tomato, garlic, olive oil, and vinegar; served cold.

melk (Du, Nw) Milk.

melkbrood (Du) A bread made with milk instead of water.

melktert (Af) A South African cinnamon-flavored custard.

meloa (Pg) Cantaloupe.

melocotón (Sp) Peach.

meloen (Du) Melon.

melokhia (Ar–Egypt) An edible green leaf of a variety of mallow with a flavor like that of spinach or sorrel; used to make a green herb soup.

melon (US) A fruit of a trailing vine, *Cucumis melo*, in the family of cucumbers and gourds; oval or spherical shape; thick skin, usually green or yellow; sweet, juicy green, yellow, or orange flesh; served often in fruit salads. The edible seeds may be toasted and eaten as a snack. Some of the varieties are the cantaloupe, cranshaw, honeydew, muskmelon, and casaba melon.

melon (Fr, Nw, Sw) Melon.

melón (Sp) Melon.

Melone (Gr) Melon; cantaloupe.

melone e prosciutto (It) Melon with ham; an appetizer.

meloun (Cz) Watermelon.

melt, to (US) To liquify, using gentle heat.

menestra (Sp) Stew.

menrui (Jp) Noodle dishes, which may be served hot or cold.

menta (It) Mint.

mentega (Ml) Butter.

menthe (Fr) Mint.

menthe poivrée (Fr) Peppermint.

meriantura (Fi) Sole.

meringue glacée (Fr) Egg whites and sugar beaten together and baked; served with ice cream.

merlan (Fr) Whiting.

merluzzo (It) Fresh codfish.

mermelada (Sp) Jam; preserves; marmalade.

meruňky (Cz) Apricots.

meshimono (Jp) Rice with meat or vegetables.

mesimarja (Fi) A fruit of the Arctic bramble, used in Finnish liqueurs.

meso od divljači (SC) Venison.

metélt (Hu) Noodles.

metsäsieniä (Fi) Wild mushrooms.

metso (Fi) Grouse.

Mettwurst (Gr) A peppery, smoked beef and pork sausage; may be soft and spread on bread. Some is hard and needs to be boiled before eating.

meunière (Fr) 1. Lemon butter sauce. 2. A way of cooking fish by frying lightly floured in butter and sprinkling with lemon juice.

Mexican tea (US) See **epazote.**

mexilhãos (Pg) Mussels.

meyve (Tr) Fruit.

méz (Hu) Honey.

mezedhakia (Gk) Appetizers; canapés.

mézeskalács (Hu) Honey bread.

mezza (Ar) Appetizer.

mezza bishurba (Ar) Lamb shanks with tomato soup.

miasnaia solianka (Rs) Spicy meat soup with ham and vegetables.

míchaná vejce (Cz) Scrambled eggs.

microwave oven (US) An oven with a magnetron tube that transmits short, high-frequency radio waves into the oven cavity. The microwaves are absorbed by food, causing water molecules to vibrate rapidly. The friction produces heat, which cooks the food.

midhia (Gk) Mussels.

midya (Tr) Mussels.

midya dolmasi (Tr) Cold steamed mussels stuffed with rice and pine nuts.

mie goreng (In) Fried noodles with sambal chili sauce, garlic, onion, and shrimp paste.

miel (Fr) Honey.

miele (It) Honey.

mie pangsit (In) Noodle soup with wonton.

mięso (Po) Meat.

mì-gān (Ch) Mandarin orange; tangerine.

mihallabiyya (Ar) An Egyptian cold dessert made with rice flour.

mijoté (Fr) Simmered.

mí jyou (Ch) Rice wine.

mikan (Jp) Mandarin orange; tangerine.

milanese, alla (It) 1. Foods dipped in flour, egg yolk, bread crumbs, and Parmesan cheese, then fried in butter. 2. Prepared with saffron.

Milch (Gr) Milk.

milho (Pg) Corn.

milk (US) Commonly applied to cow's, goat's, and sheep's milk. Cow's milk supplies proteins including a complete protein (casein); carbohydrates from a milk sugar (lactose); minerals such as calcium and phosphorus; and vitamins A, D and B_2. Although raw milk is available in the United States, pasteurized milk is the norm and is usually homogenized (treated so that cream does not rise to the top). Skim milk has almost all fat removed by separation. Milk products include cream, buttermilk, evaporated milk, condensed milk, yogurt, and items from sour milk.

milk powder (US) Refers to whole, skim, or nonfat dry milk. Most nonfat dry milk is fortified with vitamins A and D.

milk substitutes (US) Products made with skim milk solids, fats, and oils or vegetable oils, such as nondairy creamers. Imitation fluid milk may contain derivatives of milk such as casein and whey.

milk, vegetable (US) A liquid, such as coconut milk or soy milk, similar in appearance to cow's milk; used in cooking or as a beverage.

mille-fanti (It) Beef consommé with a beaten mixture of egg, breadcrumbs, and Parmesan cheese poured into it.

mille-feuille (Fr) Literally, "a thousand leaves"; a pastry made of thin layers of puff pastry alternating with vanilla custard and fruit preserves; topped with a fondant icing.

millet (US) Various grasses with small

edible seeds; used as food in many countries, including India, Japan, Africa, and China; ground into flour and made into unleavened bread or boiled as porridge; also fermented into beer.

milt (US) See **roe.**

mimosa (Fr) Green salad with egg yolks.

mince, to (US) To chop food into fine pieces.

mincemeat (US) A cooked filling used for mince pies; many variations but commonly made with minced dried and fresh fruit including apples, raisins, currants, citrus fruit peel and sour cherries; suet; sugar; nuts, spices and brandy; may also contain minced beef as it was made originally.

mince pie (US) A two-crust pie filled with mincemeat, traditionally served at Christmas.

minerálka (Cz) Mineral water.

mineralvann (Nw) Mineral water.

mineralvatten (Sw) Mineral water.

Mineralwasser (Gr) Mineral water.

minestra di verdure (It) A thick vegetable soup; minestrone is a form of minestra.

minestrina (It) Thin clear broth.

minestrone (It) A traditional soup of Italy; made with many diced vegetables seared in pork fat and simmered in beef broth; served with added pasta or rice and topped with Parmesan cheese.

minestrone alla genovese (It) Minestrone Genoese style; flavored with pesto, a sauce of basil, pecorino cheese, garlic, and pine nuts in olive oil.

mint (US) A family of herbs, genus *Mentha*, such as spearmint, peppermint, orange bergamot, and pennyroyal; strong aroma and cool to spicy flavor; spearmint most often used in cooking; used in fruit salads, beverages, stir-fried dishes, chutneys, as a garnish, and with many other dishes.

Minze (Gr) Mint.

miodowo-orzechowy mazurek (Po) A dessert of pastry dough layered with fillings of honey, walnut, and apricot.

miolos (Pg) Sweetbreads; brains.

mirabeau (Fr) A garnish of olives, anchovies, and tarragon leaves; served with meat.

mirabelle (Fr) A small, sweet, yellow plum grown in Alsace; used for jam, stewed, and to make eau-de-vie.

mirepoix (Fr) Diced vegetables such as carrots, onions, and celery cooked in butter, seasoned with thyme and bay leaves; used as a garnish, added to soup, stocks or roasts, and pureed for sauces.

mirin (Jp) Sweet rice wine; used as an ingredient in cooking, such as in teriyaki.

miringhe (It) Meringue.

mirliton (US) See **chayote.**

miroton (Fr) Sliced, boiled beef with sautéed onions and onion sauce, topped with bread crumbs and baked.

mirtillo (It) Blueberry; bilberry.

mirugai (Jp) A type of clam; geoduck.

mì rwan-ji (Ch) Boneless chicken in a honey and oyster sauce; served cold.

mishmishi (Af–Swahili) Apricot.

misir (Tr) Corn.

miso (Jp) A savory paste made from

cooked, fermented soybeans; may be white or colored red; used in soup and as part of a marinade for fish and vegetables.

misoshiru (Jp) A thick soup made with white miso, dried fish, shellfish, seaweed, daikon, and watercress.

misto (It) Mixed.

misto alla griglia (It) Mixed grill.

misto bosco (It) Mixed berries.

misto di verdure (It) Mixed cooked vegetables.

mitili (It) Mussels.

mititei (Ro) Garlic-flavored beef sausages; grilled.

mitsuba (Jp) Aromatic trefoil leaves; a parsleylike garnish.

mitsumame (Jp) Boiled, sweet red beans, gelatin cubes, and fruit in syrup.

mitzutaki (Jp) Chicken or fish and vegetables cooked in boiling dashi.

mix, to (US) To combine two or more ingredients as in a smooth blend or more coarsely such as in a salad.

mixte (Fr) Mixed.

mizu (Jp) Water.

mizutake (Jp) Chicken and vegetables cooked at the table; served with a sauce containing lemon juice and soy sauce.

mjölk (Sw) Milk.

mjuka småfranska (Sw) Soft rolls.

mjukost (Sw) Cream cheese.

mkate na siagi (Af–Swahili) Bread and butter.

mleczko cielece potrawie (Po) Braised sweetbreads.

mleko (Cz, Po) Milk.

mleté hovězí (Cz) Ground beef.

mlevena govedina (SC) Ground beef.

moana (Pl) Red mullet.

mocha (US) Refers to a coffee flavor or a mixture of coffee and chocolate; originally named for a port in Yemen, then center of the world coffee trade.

mochi (Jp) Small rice cakes.

mochi gome (Jp) Sweet, glutinous rice; used for mochi cakes.

mochiko (Jp) Flour made from glutinous rice; used to make sweet tea cakes.

mochonye (Rs) Brined.

mochonye arbuzy (Rs) Brined watermelon.

mock duck (US) Braised chunks of seasoned gluten. Also called **vegetarian duck.**

mock pork (US) A Chinese dish in which fried walnut halves with various spices and seasonings simulate the flavor of pork.

mock turtle soup (US) A soup made with the meat of calf's head, a gelatinous mixture that resembles the flavor of turtle; vegetables and Madeira wine are added. Real turtle soup is rare because green turtles are an endangered species.

moelle (Fr) Beef bone marrow.

mofongo (Sp) Mashed plantains mixed with garlic and pork cracklings and fried or roasted.

mo gwa (Ch) "Hair melon"; a white gourd covered with a hairy skin; used in Cantonese-style dishes.

Möhren (Gr) Carrots.

moído (Pg) Ground.

moje (Sp) Broth; gravy.

moje de ajo (Sp) A sauce made with a paste of ground garlic and lime juice simmered in olive oil.

mokoto (Af) Tripe stew with beef and calf's feet.

molasses (US) A sweetener extracted from sugarcane. Blackstrap molasses comes from the third pressing of the sugarcane and is rich in iron but less sweet.

mold (US) To give food shape in a container or with the hands.

mole (Mx) Sauce; often made with chicken stock, diced bananas, shredded corn tortillas, bitter chocolate, and chilis; many variations.

mole poblano de guajolote (Mx) Cooked turkey simmered in a spicy, bitter chocolate sauce containing three kinds of chilis, poblano (ancho), mulato, and pasilla, and many other ingredients. Variations use chicken or pork. Considered Mexico's national dish.

mole verde (Sp) A sauce of tomatillos, mild pickled chilis, and sour cream; served with meat or poultry.

molho (Pg) Sauce.

molho de salada (Pg) Salad dressing.

molho de tomate (Pg) Catsup.

Molke (Gr) Whey.

mollet (Fr) Medium boiled (eggs).

molletes (Sp) Sweet rolls.

mollusk (US) Any of many soft-bodied invertebrates with a hard outer shell (gastropods and bivalves), such as snails, whelks, clams, and mussels, or the cephalopods without a shell, such as squid and cuttlefish.

molochnyi sup a risom (Rs) Milk and rice soup.

moloko (Rs) Milk.

molusco (Sp) Mollusk.

molusque (Fr) Mollusk.

momo (Jp) Peach.

mondel (Jw) Almond.

monkey bread (Af) A gourdlike fruit of the baobab tree native to Africa; flesh and seeds used in various ways as food.

monkfish (US) A saltwater fish, genus *Lophius*, with a huge mouth in a head almost half the size of the body. The tail flesh, the only part eaten, is lean, white and with a flavor like lobster. Used poached, baked, fried, or grilled. Also called **goosefish.**

monosodium glutamate (US) A sodium salt derived from a seaweed or vegetable protein; used as a flavor enhancer; should be used with discretion as some people get an unpleasant physical reaction with headaches and dizziness. Also called **aji-no-moto.**

mont blanc (Fr) "White mountain"; a dessert made of puréed chestnuts, brandy, and whipped cream.

monte bianco (It) Mont blanc.

Monterey Jack (US) See **Jack cheese.**

montmorency, à la (Fr) Prepared with cherries; most often used with duckling.

Moosbeere (Gr) Cranberry.

moqueca (Pg) A dish of fish or shellfish with palm oil and hot peppers.

morangos (Pg) Strawberries.

morcella (Pg) Spiced pork blood sausage.

morel (US) A mushroom with a brown, pitted, cone-shaped, hollow cap and an earthy flavor; used with pasta, in omelets, soup and as a filling in puff pastry shells. Also called **morille.**

morello cherry (US) Any of several cherries derived from the sour cherry and distinguished from amarelles by their dark skin and juice.

moriawase (Jp) Selected seafood.

morille (Fr) See **morel.**

mornay, sauce (Fr) A cream sauce with cheese added.

moromi miso (Jp) A mixture of soybeans and malted rice; often used in Japanese vegetable dishes.

morötter (Sw) Carrots.

mořské mušle (Cz) Mussels.

morskoi yazyk (Rs) Sole.

mořský okoun (Cz) Sea bass.

mořští mlži (Cz) Clams.

mořští ráčci (Cz) Shrimp.

mortadela (Pg, Sp) Bologna sausage.

mortadella (It) Large sausage popularly known as bologna because of its place of origin, Bologna, Italy; made of pork and beef flavored with white wine, coriander seeds, and myrtle berries.

mortella (It) See **myrtle.**

mortella di palude (It) Cranberry.

morue (Fr) Dried, salted codfish.

mosselen (Du) Mussels.

mostaccioli (It) Small sweet cakes made with chocolate, almonds, and candied fruit; patterned with combs.

mostarda (It, Pg) Mustard.

mostarda di frutta (It) A mustard or relish made from fruits such as cherries, pears, or lemons preserved in mustard oil; served with cold meats and poultry.

mostaza (Sp) Mustard.

mosterd (Du) Mustard.

moučníky (Cz) Desserts.

moules (Fr) Mussels.

moules à la marinière (Fr) Mussels cooked in broth; served with a mixture of broth and melted butter.

moules farcies (Fr) Stuffed mussels.

moulokhiya (Ar) Green leaves from a *moulokhiya* bush, cooked in lamb or chicken stock and served with rice and the meat.

mount, to (US) To add water, wine, or vinegar to a reduction in making one of the butter sauces.

mountain cheese (US) See **Alpkäse.**

mountain oysters (US) A western United States term for sheeps' testicles used as food.

moussaka (Gk) Baked layers of eggplant, lamb, and tomato flavored with oregano and cinnamon with a cheese or cream sauce. Zucchini or potatoes may also be used as a base.

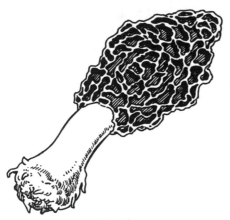

Morel

mousse (Fr) A light, savory or sweet dish made with a base of whipped cream or beaten egg whites; ground or pureed fish, chicken, fruits, chocolate or other ingredients are added to the base; served hot or cold.

mousse de volaille (Fr) Chicken mousse.

mousseline (Fr) A forcemeat made of finely ground meat, poultry, game, fish, or shellfish mixed with cream and egg whites.

mousseline, sauce (Fr) A sauce made by folding egg yolks and heavy cream into hollandaise sauce.

mousseuse, sauce (Fr) A thick, frothy sauce made by combining a thickener composed of butter and flour with salt, lemon juice, and water.

moutarde (Fr) Mustard.

moutarde au poivre verte (Fr) Mustard flavored with herbs or green peppercorns.

moyashi (Jp) Bean sprouts.

mozeček (Cz) Brains.

mozzarella (It) White, elastic, soft cheese made of cow's milk; unsalted; classic topping for pizza; used often in Italian dishes.

mrkev (Cz) Carrots.

mrkve (SC) Carrots.

mshikaki (Af–Swahili) Shish kebab.

mtama (Af–Swahili) Millet.

mtindi (Af–Swahili) Buttermilk.

mtori (Af–Swahili) Plantain and beef soup.

muffin (US) A quick bread.

muhindi (Af–Swahili) Corn.

muhogo (Af–Swahili) Cassava.

muhogo tamu (Af–Swahili) Cassava and beef stew.

muisjes (Du) Anise-flavored sugar used on sliced bread.

muito condimentado (Pg) Spicy.

mù lì chá (Ch) Jasmine tea.

mulligatawny soup (Ia) A popular Anglo-Indian spicy soup with a meat stock base; many variations. The name comes from a term meaning "pepper water."

multer (Nw) See **cloudberry.**

muna ja pekoni (Fi) Eggs and bacon.

munakas (Fi) An omelet.

Münchner Prinzregententorte (Gr) A rich cake named for the prince regent of Munich; five layers of chocolate cake stacked with layers of chocolate cream, then covered with a chocolate and rum icing.

mung beans (US) Smallest of the bean family; used cooked, as sprouts, or ground as flour.

munkar (Sw) Dumplings.

munuaiset (Fi) Kidneys.

mûre (Fr) Blackberry.

murgee (Ia) Chicken.

murgee do pyaza (Ia) Chicken and onion curry.

murg moghlai (Ia) An elaborate saffron-flavored dish in the Mogul tradition; chicken, onions, and a spice mixture are browned in oil and mixed with saffron; served with rice and fried bread.

murg musallam (Ia) Chicken first marinated in yogurt with chilis and onion, then roasted or broiled with peppercorns, gingerroot, garlic, and other spices.

murlins (Ir) A form of brown seaweed, *Alaria esculenta*, used in cooking for its sugary, nutty flavor.

183

muroja (Fi) Dry cereal.

musaka od plavih patlidžana (SC) Moussaka made with eggplant.

Muscheln (Gr) Mussels.

muscoli (It) mussels.

mushi awabi (Jp) Steamed abalone.

mushigashi (Jp) Steamed rice-flour cake.

mushimono (Jp) Steamed foods.

mushita (Jp) Steamed.

mushroom (US) Member of the fungus family; many species, which vary in color, size, shape, and flavor.

Muskatblüte (Gr) Mace.

muskmelon (US) A melon with a creamy netting; small to moderate size; orange flesh; musky odor.

mussel (US) A bivalve mollusk found along seacoasts of Europe and America, and in streams and rivers. The meat within the shell is usually prepared by cooking in wine, wine vinegar, or olive oil. They are featured in dishes such as paella and saltwater species are sometimes eaten on the half shell.

musslor (Sw) Mussels.

musta leipa (Fi) Round, dark brown bread made with graham flour, curds, malt, and sugar.

Mussel

mustár (Hu) Mustard.

mustard (US) An herb, genus *Brassica*, with varieties . producing yellow, brown, or black seeds; when ground to a powder and mixed with a liquid such as wine or water, a pungent condiment is made. Seeds are used whole in some dishes of India.

mustarda (Pg) Mustard.

mustard greens (US) Young leaves of the mustard plant used raw in salads and cooked as a green vegetable.

mustard oil (Ia) Colorless or pale yellow oil made from black mustard seeds.

mustikkapiirakka (Fi) Blueberry pie.

mustikoita (Fi) Blueberries.

mù-syū ròu (Ch) Mu shu pork; shredded pork fried with beaten eggs, green onions, and cloud ear mushrooms; served with little pancakes to hold the mixture.

musztarda (Po) Mustard.

mutton (US) The flesh of sheep and goats.

mutton fish (Aa) Abalone.

muz (Tr) Banana.

myàn-bāu (Ch) Western-style bread.

myàn-bāu jywăn (Ch) Rolls.

myàn-tyáu (Ch) Noodles.

mylta med grädde (Sw) Cloudberry compote with cream.

myrte (Fr) Myrtle.

myrtille (Fr) Blueberry; bilberry.

myrtle (US) An edible, wild plant, *Myrtus communis*, of Mediterranean countries; leaves used for wrapping or stuffing pork or poultry and to flavor bouillabaisse; black berries used like juniper. Also called **arrayán, mortella.**

naan (Ia) A puffy bread made with wheat flour, clarified butter, eggs, curds, salt, and sugar and baked in a tandoori oven.

nabemono (Jp) A type of one-pot cookery in which prepared raw food is simmered in soy sauce at the table; may include mushrooms, cabbage, tofu, and fish.

nabeyaki udon (Jp) Seafood and fishcakes in hot broth.

nabos (Pg) Turnips.

Nach Art des Hauses (Gr) Specialty of the house.

nachinka (Rs) Filling.

nachinka iz gribov dlia zraz (Rs) Mushroom filling for beef rolls.

nachinka iz kapusty (Rs) Cabbage filling; used in pirogi (pies).

nachinka iz luka dlia zraz (Rs) Onion filling for beef rolls.

nachinka iz miasa (Rs) Beef filling; used for pirogi (pies).

nachos (Sp) Grilled tortilla chips topped with cheese; garnished with green chili.

Nachspeisen (Gr) Desserts.

nadívané brambory (Cz) Stuffed potatoes.

naeng myung (Kr) Buckwheat noodles with added potato or cornstarch.

naganegi (Jp) Spring onions.

nagasari (In) Rice cake with bananas.

nage, à la (Fr) Swimming in its own juice; shellfish served in the same broth in which it was cooked.

nahkiainen (Fi) Blackened eel, a delicacy.

nakki (Fi) Frankfurter.

näkkileipä (Fi) Hardtack.

nákyp (Cz) Soufflé.

nalesniki (Po) A pancake folded like an envelope over a filling of cream cheese, sour cream, and strawberry preserves.

nam (Th) Water.

namako (Jp) Sea cucumber; sea slug.

namamono ni shita (Jp) Prepared raw.

nama udon (Jp) Fresh noodles of wheat flour.

nama yuba (Jp) See **yuba.**

nameko (Jp) A tiny wild mushroom similar to the button mushroom.

nam pla (Th) "Fish's gravy"; the basic seasoning of Thailand; a very salty brown sauce made from the fermented liquid of salted fish; used like soy sauce.

nam prik num (Th) Spicy hot chili and tomato sauce or dip.

nam prik ong (Th) Tomato and meat sauce.

nanakusa (Jp) Japanese herbs used in soups.

nanas goreng (In) Pineapple fritters.

nanasi (Af–Swahili) Pineapple.

nangka (In) See **jackfruit.**

nán-gwá (Ch) Pumpkin.

nantaise, à la (Fr) In the style of Nantes; served with a white wine sauce thickened with butter or a garnish for roasts made of peas, potatoes, and turnips.

nantua, sauce (Fr) A reduced béchamel sauce with crayfish or shrimp, tomatoes, and cream; served with egg, fish, and shellfish dishes.

napa cabbage (US) Chinese cabbage.

Napfkuchen (Gr) A yeast cake with raisins.

naphal (Hu) Sole.

Naples medlar (US) See **azarole.**

napój owocowy (Po) A fruit drink.

napój wyskokowy (Po) An alcoholic drink.

Napoleon (Fr) A rectangular puff pastry filled with pastry cream; topped with vanilla icing or confectioners' sugar. Named, not for Napoleon Bonaparte, but for Napolitain bakers in Italy.

Napoléon (Fr) A term meaning cognac is three or more years old.

napolitaine, à la (Fr) In the style of Naples; macaroni or spaghetti served in a tomato sauce and sprinkled with grated cheese.

narancs (Hu) Orange.

narancsiz (Hu) Marmalade.

naranja (Sp) Orange.

naranja agria (Sp) Sour orange.

narazuke (Jp) Gourd or other vegetables pickled in the sediment of sake.

nargesi kofta (Ia) Deep-fried meatballs of ground lamb stuffed with hard-boiled eggs; served with a spicy tomato sauce flavored with ginger and coriander.

naruto (Jp) Steamed fish cakes.

naryal (Ia) Coconut.

nashi (Jp) See **Asian pear.**

nasi (In) Rice, steamed or boiled.

nasi goreng (In) Rice fried with minced pork, shrimp, onions, garlic, hot peppers, and spices; often with strips of beef or chicken; garnished with strips of omelet.

nasi guri (In) Rice cooked in coconut milk with beef, shrimp, cucumber, onion, and spices; garnished with sliced omelet, ground peanuts and mint leaves.

nasi kebuli (In) Spiced, savory rice with crisp, fried chicken.

nasi kuning (In) Yellow rice; cooked in coconut milk and coriander with turmeric for a yellow color.

nastoiki (Rs) Fruit brandies.

nasturtium (US) An annual garden plant, *Tropaeolum majus*; leaves, with cresslike flavor, can be shredded in salads; flowers also used in salads, as a garnish, and in vinegar; seeds can be pickled and used like capers. Also called **Indian cress.**

nasu (Jp) A sweet, tender variety of eggplant.

nasu hasami age (Jp) Deep-fried stuffed eggplant.

nata (Sp) Cream.

natsumikan (Jp) A Japanese summer mandarin orange.

natto (Jp) Whole fermented soybeans, eaten as a garnish with rice.

Natur (Gr) Natural or plain.

Natur Schnitzel (Gr) Sautéed veal chops without breading.

nature (Fr) Served plain; without trim and in its natural state.

na'ud (Ar) Shark meat.

naudanliha (Fi) Beef.

nău-dz (Ch) Brains.

nauris (Fi) Turnip.

naurisraaste (Fi) A salad of grated turnips.

navarin (Fr) A ragout, usually of mutton or lamb, with potatoes, garlic, tomatoes, and sometimes other vegetables; poultry, fish, or shellfish may be used instead of mutton.

navel orange (US) A seedless orange with a dent in the rind that encloses a small secondary fruit.

navet (Fr) Turnip.

navets à la bordelaise (Fr) Turnips cooked in oil with bread crumbs and parsley.

navets au jambon (Fr) Turnips cooked with ham.

nazi (Af–Swahili) Coconuts.

ndimu (Af–Swahili) Limes.

ndizi (Af–Swahili) Bananas or plantains, cooked.

ndizi mbivu (Af–Swahili) Raw, ripe plantains.

neat's foot jelly (GB) Gelatin or jelly made from the shinbone and feet of an ox (neat); also a gelatin for clear aspics.

nectarine (US) The fruit of a tree, *Prunus persica nectarina*, a variety of the peach; with smooth, orange-red skin and rich flavor; used in fruit salads, cooked dishes, and preserves.

nedlagt (Nw) Pickled; preserved.

nefra (Gk) Kidneys.

negi (Jp) Green onions; scallions; leeks.

negimaki (Jp) Thinly sliced beef wrapped around scallions, then sautéed and served with a sauce of sweet rice wine and soy sauce.

neige (Fr) Literally, "snow". 1. Made with egg whites whisked until they form stiff peaks. 2. Made with flakes of pasta in clear soup. 3. A type of sorbet made with red fruit juice and sugar.

Nelke (Gr) Clove.

nem nuong (Vt) Meatballs wrapped in rice paper, then charcoal grilled and dipped in peanut sauce.

Nemours (Fr) Various preparations including a garnish of vegetables, a dish of poached fillet of sole, and a potato soup.

nenas (In) Pineapple.

neper (Nw) Turnips.

nero (It) Black.

neroli (Fr) An orange blossom extract used in confections, small almond pastries, and liqueurs.

nerone, alla (It) In the style of Nero; pressed chicken breasts sautéed in butter and olive oil, blazed with cognac, oven-baked, then blazed with Kirsch; served on a bed of laurel leaves.

neslesuppe (Nw) Nettle soup.

nespola (It) See **medlar.**

Nesselrode (Fr) Various dishes containing chestnut purée including a rum-flavored pudding or sauce made with chestnuts, candied fruits, and whipped cream; named for Count Nesselrode, a nineteenth century Russian diplomat who negotiated the Treaty of Paris.

Neufchâtel (Fr) A soft, creamy, mild cheese, somewhat salty. Also, a version made in the United States.

Newburg sauce (US) Sauce made with egg yolks, sherry, cream, and lobster.

New England boiled dinner (US) A hearty stew made with corned beef, cabbage, potatoes, rutabaga, and carrots seasoned with horseradish or mustard. Other meats or poultry may be used.

New England clam chowder (US) See **clam chowder.**

New Jersey tea (US) See **Indian tea.**

nezhinskie ogurchiki (Rs) Gherkins from Nezhin (a Ukranian city), where the technique of marinating them with the stalks, roots, and leaves of celery and parsley, sweet peppers, and tarragon is said to have originated.

nguru (Af–Swahili) Kingfish.

niacin (US) See **vitamin B$_3$.**

niacinamide (US) An alternative term for nicotinamide.

niboshi (Jp) Dried young sardine or small fish sometimes used instead of dashi in making a basic fish stock for Japanese dishes.

niçoise, à la (Fr) In the style of Nice; with dishes usually including tomatoes, garlic, olives, anchovies, and French green beans; sometimes zucchini and artichokes.

niçoise salad (US) See **salade niçoise.**

nicotinamide (US) A form of niacin that is often used in vitamin supplements.

nid (Fr) Nest; describes an edible bed of deep-fried potatoes or noodles used to hold creamed or small foods.

Niedernaver Kartoffeln (Gr) Potatoes in cream sauce.

nierbroodje (Du) Kidney dumpling or patty.

Nieren (Gr) Kidneys.

Nierenbraten (Gr) Roast loin.

Nierenknödel (Gr) Small dumplings.

Nierenstück (Gr) Loin of veal.

niet te gaar (Du) Underdone or rare (meat).

nigella (US) A species of love-in-a-mist, *Nigella sativa*, with spicy-flavored black seeds in creamy flowers; sometimes mixed with sesame seeds and sprinkled on bread. Also called **quatre épices.**

nigirizushi (Jp) A type of sushi made with frozen shrimp that has been boiled before combining with vinegared rice. See also **sushi.**

nijimasu no karage (Jp) Deep-fried rainbow trout with red ginger and green peppers.

nikomi (Jp) Spareribs.

niku (Jp) Meat.

nikuan udon (Jp) Pork with noodles.

niku-dofu (Jp) Pork with soybean curd (tofu).

niku ryōri (Jp) Meat dishes.

nimame (Jp) Simmered beans.

nimbu achar (Ia) Pickled limes or lemons in oil.

nimbu chatni (Ia) Date and lemon chutney.

nimbu ka chaval (Ia) Saffron rice with cashews, lime, chili pepper, and coriander.

nimki (Ia) A deep-fried pastry; a salted crisp or cracker.

nimono (Jp) Meat, fish, or vegetables simmered in a broth often seasoned with ginger, Japanese or red pepper; the solid foods are served as side dishes.

ning-méng (Ch) Lemon.

ninjin (Jp) Carrots.

ninniku (Jp) Garlic.

Niolo (Fr) A strong ricottalike cheese produced on Corsica that has been allowed to age in brine.

nira (Jp) Chives, scallions.

nishiki tamago (Jp) Steamed, hard-cooked eggs sieved and sweetened with sugar.

nishime (Jp) Cooked vegetable dish.

nishin (Jp) Herring.

nishin no kunsei (Jp) Kippered herring.

nita (Jp) Prepared, cooked.

nitamono (Jp) Boiled or stewed foods.

nitrates (US) Food additives; both potassium and sodium nitrates are used in cured meats as a color preservative. Their use has been controversial because of evidence relating them to substances that cause cancer.

nitrites (US) Food additives; both potassium and sodium nitrites are used as color preservatives in processed meats and other food products. The nitrites also provide antibacterial properties, as in protecting foods against the development of bacteria that cause botulism. Nitrites as well as nitrates can be converted to cancer-causing substances in the digestive tract.

nitrogen (US) An inert gas that is present in the atmosphere. It is used in food processing to displace oxygen, which can cause spoilage such as turning wine into vinegar or making fatty foods rancid.

nitsuke (Jp) Fresh sardines cooked in rice wine and soy sauce flavored with gingerroot.

nivernaise, à la (Fr) With a garnish of glazed small onions and carrots cut into olive shapes; used for braised meat or duck.

niyakko (Jp) Soybean curd with dried bonito flakes.

nizakana (Jp) Simmered fish.

njure (Sw) Kidney.

noce di cocco (It) Coconut.

noce di vitello (It) Sirloin of veal.

noci (It) Nuts; walnuts.

noci del Brasile (It) Brazil nuts.

Nockerln (Gr) Small dumplings used in soups, stews, and broths.

nødder (Da) Nuts.

nogada (Mx) A sauce made with pounded walnuts and spices.

noisettes (Fr) Hazelnuts; also something shaped like hazelnuts, such as small round cuts of meat or vegetables.

noisettes d'agneau (Fr) Boneless lamb chops.

noisettes de chevreuil (Fr) Round or oval-shaped cuts of venison.

noix (Fr) Nut; walnut.

noix d'acajou (Fr) Cashew nut.

noix de coco (Fr) Coconut.

noix du Brésil (Fr) Brazil nuts.

noix muscade (Fr) Nutmeg.

nokedli (Hu) Tiny egg noodles or dumplings; boiled, drained, and fried.

nøkkelost (Nw) Sharp cheese with caraway, cumin, and cloves.

nomimono (Jp) Beverages.

Nonnenfurz (Gr) Deep-fried biscuit.

nonnette (Fr) Small rounds of gingerbread with icing.

nonnutritive sweetener (US) An intensely sweet substance that is not metabolized. Examples include saccharin, cyclamate, and acesulphame-K, which make no caloric contribution to the diet.

nonpareille (Fr) 1. Tiny, colored, granulated sugar beads used for cake decorating. 2. A small chocolate candy covered with white sugar beads. 3. Small pickled capers.

nonvintage (US) Pertaining to wines, the term usually indicates an inexpensive blend of wines from vintages of several years.

nonya (Ml) A variation of a Chinese cooking technique in which packets of chicken are fried in parchment wrappers.

noodles (US) Flat strips of dough made with flour and water, sometimes eggs; various lengths and widths; used fresh or dried.

nopales (Mx) Edible, fleshy, paddle-shaped leaves or pads of the prickly pear cactus, *Opuntia* species. With spines removed, they are steamed, sautéed, or boiled as a vegetable, served in salads, or pickled as appetizers.

nopales con chile pasilla (Mx) Cactus leaves with pasilla chilis, onion, and epazote.

nopales con queso (Mx) Cactus leaves with cream cheese and serrano chilis.

Nordseekrabbencocktail (Gr) Shrimp cocktail.

nori (Jp) An edible seaweed, *Porphyra*; available in green-black sheets that become purple when warmed; used as a wrapping for rice and fish, coated with batter and fried in tempura,

shredded over rice, pasta, or cooked greens, and added to soups, salads, and dumplings. Also called **laver.**

nori chazuke (Jp) Cooked rice topped with toasted nori seaweed and soaked in tea.

norimaki (Jp) Vinegared rice wrapped in seaweed and stuffed with fish or seafood, spinach, egg, gourd shavings, mushrooms, or other ingredients. Also called **makizushi.**

nori sembei (Jp) Rice cake with seaweed.

Normande, à la (Fr) As prepared in Normandy; usually refers to fish or shellfish, apples, or apple by-products such as cider or Calvados.

Normande, sauce (Fr) Cream sauce made with a reduced fish stock and mushrooms; used with fillet of sole.

norrbottensost (Sw) Swiss-type cheese.

no-salt herb blend (US) A mixture of herbs used as flavoring in low-salt diets; may include a variety such as oregano, basil, marjoram, savory, garlic, rosemary, thyme, sage, and pepper.

nosh (Jw) A snack; a food to nibble on.

noten (Du) Nuts.

nötkött (Sw) Beef.

nøtter (Nw) Nuts.

nougat (US) A candy made from nuts such as almonds, honey or sugar, and sometimes egg whites or candied fruits.

nouilles (Fr) Noodles.

nouvelle cuisine (Fr) Literally, "new cookery"; emphasizes top-quality, fresh ingredients prepared and served elegantly and simply without heavy sauces and fats or other elaborate preparations.

nozes (Pg) Walnuts.

nua phad prik (Th) Beef simmered with chilis, garlic, and nam pla.

Nudeln (Gr) Noodles.

Nudeln mit Kümmelkäse (Gr) Noodles with caraway cheese.

Nudelsuppe mit Huhn (Gr) Chicken noodle soup.

nudlar (Sw) Noodles.

nudle (Cz) Noodles.

nueces (Sp) Nuts; walnuts.

nuez del Brasil (Sp) Brazil nuts.

nuoc cham (Vt) A piquant salad dressing made with garlic, chili peppers, the juice and pulp of fresh limes, sugar, and fish sauce (nuoc mam).

nuoc mam (Vt) The basic Vietnamese seasoning; made by layering fish and salt in barrels and allowing the fish to ferment. See also **nam pla.**

Nurnbergerwurst (Gr) A sausage of lean pork, bacon fat, herbs, and seasonings; pan-fried.

Nussauflauf (Gr) Nut soufflé.

Nüsse (Gr) Nuts.

nut (US) Any dry seed or fruit with a hard shell and edible kernel.

nuta (Jp) Shellfish with miso dressing.

nutmeg (US) The kernel of the fruit of the nutmeg tree, *Myristica fragrans*, with a tan color, sweet flavor, and delicate aroma; used grated as a baking spice, in soups, eggnog, puddings, curries, and the garam masala of India.

nutritive sweetener (US) A substance with a sweet taste and which contributes calories to the diet, such as sucrose, corn syrup, honey, molasses, and aspartame.

nyama ya kaa (Af–Swahili) Crab meat.

nyama ya kondoo (Af–Swahili) Lamb.

nyama ya kuchoma (Af–Swahili) Roast beef.

nyama ya mbuzi (Af–Swahili) Goat's meat.

nyama ya ndama (Af–Swahili) Veal.

nyama ya ng'ombe (Af–Swahili) Beef.

nyama ya nguruwe (Af–Swahili) Pork.

nybakt brød (Nw) Fresh bread.

nyóu-pái (Ch) Beefsteak.

nyóu-ròu chīng tāng (Ch) Beef broth.

nyper (Nw) Rose hips.

nyponsoppa (Sw) Rose-hip soup; served with almonds and whipped cream.

nyre (Da) Kidney.

nyrer (Nw) Kidneys.

nysilt melk (Nw) Fresh milk.

nyúlpörkölt (Hu) Stewed rabbit with paprika.

O

oatmeal (US) A meal made from ground or rolled oats, used cooked as a cereal and in baking. See also **oats, rolled oats.**

oats (US) The edible seed of a cereal grass, *Avena sativa*, used in a variety of forms: *oat groat*, the hulled and broken kernel; when broken further it is *pinhead oatmeal*; *rolled oats* are large flakes made when the kernel is flattened with rollers; *quick oats* are flakes cut and rolled thinner to reduce cooking time.

obalované v housce (Cz) Breaded.

obed (Rs) Dinner.

Oberskern (Gr) Cream sauce with grated horseradish.

obiad (Po) Dinner.

obložené chlebíčky (Cz) Open sandwiches as hors d'oeuvres.

Obst (Gr) Fruit.

Obstkuchen (Gr) Fruit tart.

Obstsuppe (Gr) Fruit soup.

oca (It) Goose.

ocean perch (US) An orange-red to bright red member of the rockfish family that has sweet, firm, pink flesh. In Europe the fish is better known by its color, such as redfish or raudfisk.

ocet (Cz, Po) Vinegar.

ocha (Jp) Green tea.

Ochsenbraten (Gr) Roast beef.

Ochsenfleisch (Gr) Beef.

Ochsenlende (Gr) Fillet of beef.

Ochsenmaulsalat (Gr) Literally, "ox snout salad"; a jellied tongue salad served with an onion and vinegar dressing.

Ochsenniere (Gr) Beef kidney.

Ochsenschwanzsuppe (Gr) Oxtail soup.

Ochsenzunge (Gr) Beef tongue.

octopus (US) An edible, shell-less mollusk related to squid; with soft bodies containing an ink sac and eight tentacles, which are the parts favored; white, mild-flavored meat sometimes served in the ink; rubbery texture unless tenderized; eaten boiled or broiled.

odamaki mushi (Jp) Steamed noodles, vegetables, eggs, and fish cakes.

oden (Jp) Stew with vegetables, molded fish paste, fried fish balls, and egg.

odoburu (Jp) Hors d'oeuvre.

oee kim chee (Kr) A mixture of pickled cucumbers with scallions and chilis.

oesters (Du) Oysters.

oeufs (Fr) Eggs.

oeufs à la coque (Fr) Eggs in the shell; boiled eggs.

oeufs à la neige (Fr) A dessert of vanilla-flavored egg custard topped with cooked beaten egg whites and sugar shaped to resemble eggs. Also called **floating island, snow eggs.**

oeufs à la Richelieu (Fr) Eggs served with stuffed tomatoes, mushrooms, and potatoes.

oeufs à la Russe (Fr) Hard-boiled eggs with a mayonnaise sauce of chives, onion, and Tabasco.

oeufs argenteuils (Fr) Scrambled eggs with asparagus.

oeufs au plat (Fr) Fried or baked eggs.

oeufs bénédictine (Fr) A classic dish of eggs over salt cod with a cream sauce.

oeufs Bercy (Fr) Fried eggs with sausages and tomato sauce.

oeufs brouillés (Fr) Scrambled eggs.

oeufs d'alose (Fr) Shad roe.

oeufs de caille au caviar (Fr) Quails' eggs with caviar in pastry shells.

oeufs de poisson (Fr) Fish roe.

oeufs durs (Fr) Hard-boiled eggs.

oeufs farcis (Fr) Stuffed or deviled eggs.

oeufs frits (Fr) Fried eggs.

oeufs mollets (Fr) Soft-boiled eggs.

oeufs pochés (Fr) Poached eggs.

oeufs pochés en gelée (Fr) Poached eggs with strips of ham and tarragon leaves in aspic.

oeufs Rossini (Fr) Eggs with truffles and Madeira wine.

of (Jw–Israel) Chicken.

offal (GB) Discards and entrails of meat animals, including the parts used as edible such as feet, heads, tails, intestines, lungs, hearts, brains, kidneys, and livers. In the United States, called **variety meats.**

of sum-sum (Jw–Israel) Fried chicken coated with sesame seeds.

Offene Torte (Gr) Open pastry tart.

ofu (Jp) Wheat gluten.

ogo (Jp) A form of seaweed pureed as a food drink with an eggnog texture.

ogórek (Po) Cucumber.

ogurtsy solionye v tykve (Rs) Cucumbers brined in a pumpkin.

ohagi (Jp) Confection made with glutinous rice and sweet bean paste.

ohrakyrsä (Fi) A whole-grain bread.

ohraryynipuuro (Fi) Whole barley pudding.

ohukaiset (Fi) Small thin pancakes.

oie (Fr) Goose.

oignon (Fr) Onion.

oignonade (Fr) Stew containing a large amount of onions; also, minced onions cooked in butter or white wine.

oil (US) Fat in liquid form, usually vegetable fat, used for dressing salads and cooking.

oiseau (Fr) Bird.

oiseaux sans têtes (Fr) Literally, "birds without heads"; rolled sliced veal with a stuffing.

oj (US) Abbreviation for orange juice.

oka (Sp) A tuber of a plant, *Oxalis tuberosa*, a kind of yam native to South America; prepared like potatoes.

Oka (Ca) A semisoft, yellow cow's milk cheese with a smooth, piquant taste.

okame soba (Jp) Buckwheat noodles with slices of molded fish paste in broth.

okaribayaki (Jp) Duck with a sauce containing **daikon.**

okashi (Jp) Sweets, pastry, and confections.

okayu (Jp) Rice gruel.

okonomiyaki (Jp) Omelet containing meat and vegetables.

okoun (Cz) Perch.

okowa (Jp) Rice boiled with red beans.

okra (US) A mallow, *Hibiscus esculentus*, with green seed pods used as a vegetable; viscous and sticky when cooked; used to give thickness and flavor to stews and gumbos, often in Creole cooking; also may be deep-fried, baked, and served in sauces.

okroshka (Rs) Chilled vegetable soup with meat or fish and **kvass.**

oksehaleragout (Da) Oxtail stew.

oksekarbonade (Nw) Fried cakes of chopped beef.

oksekjøtt (Nw) Beef.

oksekoedsuppe (Da) Beef soup.

oksesteg (Da) Roast beef.

oksestek (Nw) Roast beef.

okurková omáčka (Cz) Pickle sauce.

okurky (Cz) Cucumbers.

öl (Sw) Beer.

Öl (Gr) Oil.

øl (Nw) Beer.

olaj (Hu) Oil.

olajbogyó (Hu) Olives.

olehneena (Rs) Venison.

olej (Cz) Oil.

óleo (Pg) Oil. Also called **azeite.**

oleomargarine (US) See **margarine.**

olie (Du) Oil.

oliebollen (Du) Doughnuts; fried dumplings.

olijf (Du) Olive.

olio (It) Oil.

olio santo (It) A basil and chili oil mixture.

oliva (It, Pg, Sp) Olive.

olive (US) The fruit of a semitropical tree; many varieties; colors range from green to brown to purple; shapes are round to pointed. Among the kinds are the plum-colored kalamata, the volos, royal, and the alfonso. Olives are used for their oil and eaten green or ripe.

Oliven (Gr) Olives.

olivener (Nw) Olives.

olive oil (US) Oil expressed from olive pulp used in cooking and salad dressings; contains no cholesterol. Olive oil that comes from the first pressing and with an acidity ranging from less than 1 percent to 4 percent includes extra-virgin, superfine, fine, and virgin. A hot pressed type, pure, is from a second or third pressing and is less fruity.

oliver (Sw) Olives.

Olivet (Fr) A cow's milk cheese with a blue or ash-covered skin, a soft, pale interior, and a spicy or fruity taste.

olivette (It) Small pieces of veal cooked in a sauce of white wine with spices. Also called **bocconcini.**

olivi (Fi) Olive.

olivy (Cz) Olives.

oliwa (Po) Oil.

oliwki (Po) Olives.

olja (Sw) Oil.

olje (Nw) Oil.

öljy (Fi) Oil.

olla podrida (Sp) Literally, "putrid pot"; a classic highly seasoned stew cooked in a special pot called an *olla*; varied ingredients include chick-peas, ham, fish, chicken, sausages or other meat, garlic, and vegetables.

øllebrød (Da, Nw) Sweet beer and rye bread soup.

ölsardinen (Gr) Sardines in oil.

olut (Fi) Beer.

omáčka (Cz) Sauce.

omelet (US) An egg dish made by cooking beaten eggs, usually in an omelet pan; served in a variety of ways including plain, garnished, seasoned before frying, or spread with a sweet or savory filling and folded.

omelete (Pg) Omelet.

omelett (Nw) Omelet.

omelette à la confiture (Fr) A dessert omelet with jam.

omelette au foie de volaille (Fr) Omelet with chicken livers.

omelette au fromage (Fr) Cheese omelet.

omelette au jambon (Fr) Omelet with ham.

omelette au lard (Fr) Omelet with bacon.

omelette aux fines herbes (Fr) Omelet with parsley, tarragon, and chives.

omelette aux girolles (Fr) Omelet with mushrooms.

omelette basquaise (Fr) Omelet with peppers, ham, garlic, tomatoes, and mushrooms.

omelette bonne femme (Fr) Omelet with onions and bacon.

omelette nature (Fr) Plain omelet.

omelette norvégienne (Fr) Ice cream covered with meringue, browned in the oven, and served flaming. See also **baked Alaska.**

omelette parmentier (Fr) Potato omelet.

omelette provençale (Fr) Omelet with garlic, tomatoes, onions, and olives.

omeletter (Sw) Omelets.

omena (Fi) Apple.

omenalumi (Fi) Apple-snow dessert.

omenamunakas (Fi) Apple custard.

omenapitko (Fi) Apple-filled pastry strip with a coffee glaze.

omenosilli (Fi) Herring with apples and sour cream.

omlet (Po) Omelet.

omuretsu (Jp) Omelet.

onion (US) An herb, *Allium cepa*, of the lily family with many varieties; edible at all stages of growth from green shoots to mature bulb; most commonly used in the United States is the white or yellow globe onion with a firm, crisp texture and strong aroma and taste.

onion flakes (US) 1. Chopped or cut onion pieces, dried and used as a condiment. 2. Crisp-fried onions used in Asian dishes as a garnish.

onion rings (US) Slices of onions, separated into rings, batter coated, and deep-fried.

ono (Pl) Wahoo mackerel; a large, white-fleshed fish.

ontbijt (Du) Breakfast.

ooka (Rs) Chowder.

ooksoos (Rs) Vinegar.

oolanin kakut (Fi) Fried potato patties with bacon, egg, milk, and onion.

oolong (Ch) A green-brown tea that is partly fermented before it is dried.

ooperavoileipä (Fi) Literally, "opera sandwich"; an open-faced hamburger patty topped with a fried egg.

oostreetsi (Rs) Oysters.

ootka (Rs) Duck.

opékané brambory (Cz) Fried potatoes, home-style.

open-face (US) Without a top crust or bread such as a sandwich or a tart.

operatårta (Sw) Creamy layer cake.

oplagt melk (Nw) Soured or clabbered milk.

orache (US) A tall herb, *Atriplex hor-*

tensis, member of the spinach family with fleshy, green, arrow-shaped leaves; used as a vegetable, in soups, and as a garnish. Popular in France. Also called **bonne-dame.**

orange (US) Any of a variety of trees in the genus *Citrus* bearing round, yellow-red fruit. The juicy, sweet pulp in varieties such as the navel, Valencia, and blood oranges is eaten raw and used for juice. Sour or bitter oranges, known as Seville oranges, are used in marmalade or as a flavoring agent. See also **mandarin orange, tangelo.**

orangeat (Fr) Candied orange peel.

orange drink (US) A beverage artificially colored and flavored to simulate orange juice.

orange juice (US) Juice expressed from an orange.

orange mint (US) Bergamot mint.

orange oil (US) An extract derived from the peel of both bitter and sweet oranges; used for flavoring.

orange pekoe (US) A black tea with long, thin leaves; makes a light-colored brew.

orange roughy (US) A marine fish in the perch family found in waters off New Zealand with orange skin, firm, white, delicate flesh, and bland taste.

ördek (Tr) Duck.

oregano (US) An herb, *Origanum vulgare*, related to marjoram; with pungent flavored leaves, usually dried; used often in Mediterranean and Mexican cooking; in pasta dishes, sausages, and with pork, lamb, eggs, and cheese.

orekhovi pudding (Rs) Walnut pudding.

Oregano

orenji jūsu (Jp) Orange juice.

organen (Du) Giblets.

organic (US) Food prepared without chemical additives and grown without the use of chemicals, such as in fertilizers and insecticides.

orge (Fr) Barley.

orgeat (Fr) An almond-flavored syrup.

origan (Fr) Oregano.

origano (It) Oregano.

ormer (GB) Small European abalones of the genus *Halotis*; cooked and served like the larger species. Also called **See-ohr.**

orobova potica (SC) Raisin and nut pie.

ørred (Da) Trout.

ørret (Nw) Trout.

ortaggio (It) Vegetable.

ortolan (Fr) A small game bird; prepared like quail.

orzechy (Po) Nuts.

orzo (It) Rice-shaped dried pasta made of semolina; used in soup.

os à moelle (Fr) Marrow bone.

oseille (Fr) Sorrel.

osëtra (Rs) A variety of sturgeon that produces a roe prized as caviar; the eggs, green or gold in color, are smaller than beluga.

oshitashi (Jp) Greens cooked in shoyu.

osihtreena (Rs) Sturgeon.

osnovnoi biskvit (Rs) Basic sponge cake.

osnovnoi orekhovyi biskvit (Rs) Walnut sponge cake.

ossenhaas (Du) Fillet of beef.

osso buco (It) Literally, "mouth of the bone"; marrow bone; usually a veal shank braised in white wine, garlic, onions, and tomato sauce; served with pasta or rice.

ost (Da, Nw, Sw) Cheese.

osterit (Fi) Oysters.

østers (Nw) Oysters.

ostión (Sp) Large oyster.

ostkaka (Sw) A puddinglike cheesecake baked in a mold.

ostra (Sp) Oyster.

ostrá hořčice (Cz) Hot peppery mustard.

ostra plana (Pg) Oyster.

ostriche (It) Oysters.

ostrige (SC) Oyster.

ostron (Sw) Oyster.

ostryga (Po) Oyster.

ostrý sýr (Cz) Strong-flavored cheese.

ostsufflé (Sw) Cheese soufflé.

őszibarack (Hu) Peach.

osztriga (Hu) Oysters.

otvarnaia goviadina (Rs) Boiled beef.

otvarnaia osetrina (Rs) Poached sturgeon.

otvarnoi kartofel (Rs) Boiled potatoes.

ou (Ch) Lotus root.

oursins (Fr) Sea urchins.

ouzo (Gk) Anise-flavored alcoholic beverage; turns milky white when mixed with water.

ovčetina (SC) Mutton.

ovnstegt (Da) Oven-roasted.

ovoce (Cz) Fruits.

ovocné knedliky (Cz) Fruit dumplings.

ovos (Pg) Eggs.

ovos com fiambre (Pg) Ham and eggs.

ovos cozidos (Pg) Hard-boiled eggs.

ovos escalfados (Pg) Poached eggs.

ovos estrelados (Pg–Brazil) Fried eggs.

ovos fritos (Pg) Fried eggs.

ovos mexidos (Pg) Scrambled eggs.

ovos pochê (Pg–Brazil) Poached eggs.

ovos quentes (Pg) Soft-boiled eggs.

owsianka (Po) Oatmeal.

oxbringa (Sw) Brisket of beef.

oxfilé (Sw) Fillet of beef.

Oxford sauce (GB) A sauce made of port, orange juice, lemon juice, and red currant jelly, heated, then strained and served cold with game.

oxkött (Sw) Beef.

oxrulader (Sw) Piquant beef rolls.

oxstek (Sw) Sirloin of beef; roast beef.

oxsvanssoppa (Sw) Oxtail soup.

oxtail (US) Tail of an ox, skinned and jointed; used braised, stewed, or in soups.

oyako domburi (Jp) Chicken, eggs, and vegetables served on rice.

oyakodon (Jp) Chicken served over rice.

oyster (US) A marine bivalve mollusk; many species; shell shape, size and taste influenced by the waters in which they grow; lean meat eaten raw in seafood cocktails, baked in the shell, fried or stewed in chowders or soups.

oyster cracker (US) A small, round

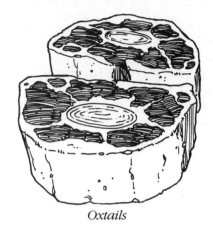

Oxtails

cracker served with soups, chowders, and seafood.

oyster plant (US) See **salsify.**

oyster sauce (US) A Chinese sauce made from oysters cooked in brine and soy sauce; used in stir-fried dishes, with fried rice, and other foods.

oysters Bienville (US) Baked oysters on the half shell with a béchamel sauce containing green pepper, onion, cheese, and bread crumbs. Created by the chef of Antoine's in New Orleans and named for the founder of the city.

oysters en brochette (Fr) Oysters skewered with bacon; may be broiled or grilled.

oysters Rockefeller (US) A dish of oysters on the half shell, broiled or grilled on a bed of rock salt and served with a highly seasoned sauce using watercress, scallions, celery, and anise. The original dish was created at Antoine's restaurant in New Orleans. Another version tops the oysters with anise-flavored spinach puree.

özgerinc (Hu) Saddle of venison.

paahtopaistivoleipä (Fi) Roast beef sandwich.

paalaeg (Da) Literally, "something laid on"; toppings put on buttered bread to make the open-face sandwich.

paan (Ia) Betel leaf stuffed with lime paste, spices, and nuts; served as a digestive after a meal.

paani (Ia) Water.

paapar (Ia) See **pappadam.**

pääsiäisjuusto (Fi) Easter cheese; a breakfast or dessert cheese made in Häme, north of Helsinki.

pääsiäisleipä (Fi) An Easter bread made with cardamom, orange and lemon peel, raisins, and almonds.

pääsiäispasha (Fi) A molded cheeselike Easter dessert flavored with almonds, raisins, lemon peel, fruits, and whipped cream.

pabellón caraqueño (Sp) A specialty of Venezuela; a dish made with steak, plantains, rice, and black beans; topped with fried eggs.

pacalpörkolt (Hu) Tripe stew with paprika, garlic, caraway seeds, onions, tomatoes, and green peppers.

pacolt marhahus (Hu) Sweet and sour beef.

paczki (Po) Jelly doughnuts.

paddlefish (US) A large bony freshwater fish with a paddleshaped snout, the source of a large-grained gray caviar similar to Caspian Sea caviar. Also called **long-billed sturgeon.**

paella (Sp) A classic Spanish dish of saffron-flavored rice with seafood, a variety of meats, fresh vegetables, onions, and garlic; the whole, with varying ingredients, is simmered in olive oil and water in a wide, shallow pan called a paellera.

paellita (Sp) A modified version of paella.

pærer (Nw) Pears.

paezinhos (Pg) Rolls.

paglia e fieno (It) Literally, "straw and hay"; a dish of egg pasta and green spinach pasta; often served in a cream sauce with peas and prosciutto ham.

pah jook (Kr) Rice and beans.

pähkinäkakut (Fi) Almond and walnut cookies.

pai (Jp) Pie.

pái dòu-fú ròu (Ch) White soy cheese made by fermenting bean curd in rice wine and salt.

pái-gǔ ròu (Ch) Chops.

paillard (Fr) A scallop of veal or boned shell steak pounded very thin and cooked quickly; served with melted butter. Named for a Monsieur Paillard, a leading Parisian restaurateur of the nineteenth century.

paillassons (Fr) Literally, "straw mat"; thin, crisp potato pancakes.

paillettes au fromage (Fr) Cheese straws.

pain (Fr) Bread.

pain à cacheter (Fr) Wafer.

painappuru (Jp) Pineapple.

pain aux noix (Fr) Nut bread.

pain bis (Fr) Brown bread.

pain complet (Fr) Whole meal bread.

pain de cuisine (Fr) A loaf made from a molded forcemeat made of fish, meat, poultry, or vegetables; the loaves are called by their main ingredient.

pain d'épice (Fr) Spice bread; gingerbread.

pain des algues (Fr) A composite jelly produced in France from two forms of sugary seaweed, *Laminaria saccharina* and *Chondrus crispus* (Irish moss). Also called **seaweed bread.**

pain de seigle (Fr) Rye bread.

pain grillé (Fr) Toast.

pain ordinaire (Fr) A "peasant-style" bread with a crisp, uneven crust; usually baked in a pottery stew-pan.

pain perdu (Fr) Literally, "lost bread"; comparable to what is called French toast in the United States.

paistettu kala (Fi) Fried fish coated with a rye-flour batter.

paistettu metsälintu (Fi) Braised game bird, such as pheasant, grouse, or partridge.

paistettu sianselka (Fi) Roast pork with prunes.

paistettu silakka (Fi) Batter-covered herring fried and served with lemon and dill.

paiusnaia (Rs) Caviar of any species of sturgeon pressed so that 5 pounds of raw caviar becomes 1 pound of commercial product with concentrated taste and nutrients.

paj (Sw) Pie.

pak choy (Ch) Chinese cabbage. Also spelled **bok choy.**

paketti (Fi) Squares of pastry with two opposite corners folded toward the center and dotted with jam where the corners meet.

pakora (Ia) A small snack; a deep-fried fritter made of chick-pea flour, onion, and other ingredients, such as minced chicken and spices.

palačinky (Cz) Rolled pancakes with a filling.

palacsinták (Hu) Thin pancakes rolled around a sweet filling or a savory filling made with paprika.

palacsintametélt (Hu) Strips of pancakes used in soup.

palak (Ia) Spinach.

palak bhurgi (Ia) Marinated spinach with black mustard seeds and garlic.

palak murgh (Ia) Chicken in a creamy spinach sauce.

palak paneer (Ia) A ricottalike cheese pressed into a cake, cubed and served with pureed spinach sauce.

palak raita (Ia) Spinach with spicy yogurt.

palapaisti (Fi) Beef ragout.

Palatschinken (Gr) Austrian-style thin pancakes rolled around various sweet fillings, such as fruit, jam, or nuts; sometimes served with a savory filling, such as minced veal, onions, and herbs.

palée (Fr) A type of whitefish.

paling in't groen (Bl) A Flemish dish of eels with potherbs.

palline al cioccolato (It) Chocolate balls.

palmier (Fr) A puff pastry cut into strips and twisted to form layers.

palm oil (US) A vegetable source of cholesterol-raising saturated fatty acids.

palm sugar (US) See **jaggery.**

palócleves (Hu) Lamb soup with potatoes, string beans, and sour cream, flavored with paprika, caraway seeds, and garlic; named for the Paloc people.

paloma (Sp) Pigeon.

palourdes (Fr) Clams.

paltus s zelionym sousom (Rs) Halibut with green sauce.

pambacitos (Sp) Tiny bread rolls stuffed with a mixture of chopped chorizo sausage, onion, egg, refried beans, and tomato sauce.

Pampelmuse (Gr) Grapefruit.

Pampelmusensaft (Gr) Grapefruit juice.

pamplemousse (Fr) Grapefruit.

pamushki s chesnokom (Rs) Yeast-dough buns with an oil and garlic dressing; often served with borscht.

pan (US) A cooking or baking utensil made of metal or another heat-resistant material.

pan (Jp, Sp) Bread.

panaché (Fr) Two or more kinds of foods combined, such as mixed fruit.

panaché au Roquefort (Fr) A mélange of mushrooms, bean sprouts, and watercress with Roquefort cheese.

panade (Fr) 1. A flour paste used to bind and thicken forcemeats; eggs may be added for poultry and fish forcemeats. 2. A kind of soup made with bread, stock, butter, and milk or water, and sometimes eggs or sugar.

panado (Pg) Breaded.

panais (Fr) Parsnip.

panbroil (US) To broil in a pan with just enough fat to keep food from sticking.

Pan broil

pancake (US) A flat, batter cake baked on a griddle, usually made of eggs, milk, flour, and with or without leavening; served in a variety of ways, such as hot with butter and syrup, filled and rolled, or cold as in Scotland.

pancar (Tr) Beet.

pancetta (It) A kind of bacon; usually fatty, cured with salt and spices, and air-dried instead of being smoked.

pancit (Ph) Diced pork, chicken, and sausage with noodles in fish sauce.

pancit guisado (Ph) Fried noodles with chopped meats, seafood, and vegetables.

pancit molo (Ph) A turnover with spiced pork and shrimp.

pan de bigos (Sp) Fig loaf made with sun-dried black figs ground with spices.

201

pan de centeno (Sp) Rye bread.

pandekager (Da) Pancakes often filled with fruit or jam and served with whipped cream.

pan de maíz (Sp) Corn bread.

pan di spagna (It) "Spanish bread"; sponge cake used as a basis for other desserts, such as layered with fruits and whipped cream.

pandorato (It) "Golden bread"; bread dipped in milk and egg and fried in olive oil.

pandowdy (US) See **apple pandowdy.**

pan dulce (Sp) Sweet pastries.

pane (It) Bread.

pané (Fr) Breaded.

pane a caponata (It) Marinated bread salad.

pane caldo (It) Hot bread.

panecillo (Sp) Bread roll.

pane integrale (It) Whole-grain bread.

panela (Sp) 1. Corn cake. 2. Brown sugar.

panelle (It) Bread or fritters made with chick-pea flour and fried in olive oil.

paner (Fr) To cover with bread crumbs.

panerat (Sw) Breaded.

pane tostato e marmellata (It) Toast and jam.

panettone (It) A specialty of Milan; fruitcake made with fine flour, eggs, sugar, butter, and candied fruit peel; sometimes orange flavored.

panfish (US) Any fish suitable for frying; usually refers to a hand-caught fish.

panforte di Siena (It) Dried fruit and nut cake or gingerbread popular in Siena, Italy.

panfry (US) To fry in a pan with little fat.

pan giallo (It) A fruitcake with pine nuts.

pangsit goreng (In) Fried wonton.

páng-syè (Ch) Crab.

panier de crudités (Fr) A basket of prepared raw vegetables to be dipped in a sauce.

paniert (Gr) Breaded.

panini (It) Rolls or buns.

panini di pasqua (It) A sweet, raised bread of yellow corn meal with raisins and lemon flavor; an Easter specialty.

panini imbotiti (It) Stuffed rolls.

panino gravido (It) Sandwich.

panir (Ia) A freshly made cheese curdled with lemon juice or sour yogurt; drained and pressed of liquid; used primarily to add protein to vegetarian dishes.

panir tikka (Ia) Fresh cheese roasted in a special oven called a tandoor.

panko (Jp) Dried bread crumbs.

panna (It) Cream.

panna cotta (It) A satiny, very rich caramel custard made with thick cream.

panna montata (It) Whipped cream.

pannato (It) Breaded.

pannbiff med lök (Sw) Chopped steak and onions.

pannekaka (Nw) Pancake.

pannekoeken (Du) Pancakes.

pannequets (Fr) Large, thin pancakes rolled around a stuffing.

pannkakor med sylt (Sw) Pancakes with jam.

pannukakku (Fi) Oven-baked pancake.

panocha (Sp) A coarse brown Mexican sugar. Also spelled *panoche.*

panquecas (Pg) Pancakes.

pan roasting (US) A method of cooking in which only enough fat is used in a nonstick skillet to keep the food from sticking; the residue of preheating oil is poured out before meat is added.

pansotti (It) A ravioli-like dumpling filled with spinach, chopped eggs, and grated cheese; served with a sauce.

pantothenic acid (US) See **vitamin B₅**.

pantua (Ia) A deep-fried sweetmeat made from cottage cheese (channa) and soaked in sugar syrup.

panuchos (Sp) Small tortillas covered with black bean paste and a pork mixture in hot sauce.

panzanella (It) A salad of dried chunks of bread with tomatoes, cucumbers, onions, basil, and olive oil and topped with anchovies and capers.

pão (Pg) Bread.

pão branco (Pg) White bread.

pão escuro (Pg) Dark bread.

pao yü (Ch) Dried abalone.

pãozinhos (Pg) Rolls.

pap (Du) Cooked cereal or other soft or semisolid food.

papa (Sp) A term used in South America for potato.

papa (Af–Swahili) Shark.

papa de cereal (Pg) Cooked cereal.

papai (Af–Swahili) Papaya.

papain (US) A protein-digesting enzyme derived from the juice of unripe papayas and used as a meat tenderizer.

papaja (SC) Papaya.

papas chorriadas (Sp) A Colombian dish of potatoes with cheese sauce.

papas rellenas (Mx) Deep-fried potatoes stuffed with ground meat, egg, and chili peppers.

papatzul (Sp) A Yucatan appetizer of tortillas stuffed with chopped eggs, hot chilis, and tomato sauce.

papaw (US) An alternative spelling for pawpaw.

papaya (US) The fruit of a plant, *Carica papaya*, with an elongated melonlike shape; size varies with species; yellow skin when ripe; soft, juicy, salmon-pink flesh with a taste like a mixture of peaches and strawberries; eaten raw and used in fruit salads. Also called **pawpaw.**

papillote, en (Fr) Cooked in a packet or bag made from a sheet of oiled paper or parchment. The bag expands with steam during cooking.

pappa al pomodoro (It) A traditional Florentine dish of bread soaked with tomatoes, garlic, basil, and olive oil in chicken or meat broth; served with grated cheese.

pappadam (Ia) Very thin, large wafers made from lentil flour; fried in oil until crisp; eaten like bread, whole or crushed over food. Lentil flour may be mixed with chick-pea flour or sometimes with chilis and spices to contrast with bland food. Also called **paapar.**

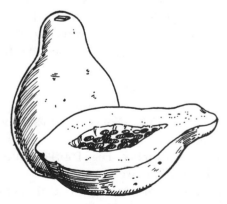

Papaya

203

pappardelle (It) Lasagne prepared with a game sauce and served with duck or hare.

pappardelle con lepre (It) A Tuscan dish of hare served with broad noodles. The pieces of hare are marinated in red wine, seared and cooked in the marinade to make a sauce.

pappardelle con porcini (It) Wide noodles in a mushroom sauce made with funghi porcini (*Boletus edulis*).

pappilan hätävara (Fi) "Parsonage emergency dessert"; a sweet similar to a trifle made with berries, bread crumbs, and whipped cream.

paprika (US) A red-orange powder made from dried and ground varieties of sweet pepper without the pungent heat of chili peppers. The seeds and core are usually removed before drying. Considered the best, Hungarian paprika is an essential part of many dishes such as goulash and paprikás.

paprika butter (US) Butter sauce colored and flavored with paprika.

Paprika Hüner (Gr–Austria) Chicken cooked with paprika.

paprikas (Du) Peppers.

paprikás (Hu) A term for any dish, usually a stew with chicken or veal, containing paprika and sour or fresh cream.

paprikás burgonya (Hu) Potatoes stewed in paprika sauce.

paprikás csirke (Hu) Chicken stew with paprika and cream.

paprikás mártás (Hu) Paprika sauce.

paprike (SC) Green peppers.

paprikový salát (Cz) Green pepper salad.

paquette (Fr) A female lobster with fully formed eggs; considered at the peak of succulence.

paradajz (SC) Tomatoes.

Paradeiser (Gr–Austria) Tomatoes.

Paradeissuppe (Gr–Austria) Tomato soup.

paradicsom (Hu) Tomatoes.

paradicsommártás (Hu) Tomato sauce.

Paraguay tea (Sp) An alternative name for maté.

Paranuss (Gr) Brazil nut.

paratha (Ia) A textured, slightly crisp flat bread of unleavened whole wheat, cooked on a griddle; sometimes stuffed with a filling of pureed vegetables; often served with curries.

parboil (US) To boil food for a short time before changing to another cooking method.

parch (GB) To make hot and dry, as in toasting or roasting; the term is usually applied to exposure of corn, peas, or similar foods to great heat.

parcha (Sp) Passion fruit.

parchment paper (US) A tough, usually translucent, paper for lining baking pans or wrapping foods to be prepared en papillote.

parcook (US) To simmer food for a short time before changing to another cooking method.

pare (US) To strip away outside layers.

pare-pare (In) Bitter melon.

pareve (Jw) Pertaining to a neutral product that does not violate Jewish dietary laws; made without milk, meat or any product derived therefrom.

parfait (Fr) A dessert made with ice cream, gelatins, puddings, or whipped toppings, alternating with fruits, jams, or jellies.

parilla, a la (Sp) Grilled.

pariloituvasikankaaryleet (Fi) Pan-broiled veal rolls.

Paris-Brest (Fr) A large cream puff made to resemble a bicycle wheel filled with praline buttercream, topped with almonds and whipped cream. Created and named by a nineteenth century chef to celebrate a bicycle race on the route between Paris and Brest.

Parisienne, à la (Fr) In the style of Paris; poultry or meat dishes garnished with small potato balls sautéed in butter and coated with thick veal stock.

Paris-Nice (Fr) A pastry dessert made like a Paris-Brest but filled with Saint-Honoré cream rather than buttercream and also without almonds.

Parker House rolls (US) A folded bread roll originated at Parker House in Boston.

parkins (Sc) Oatmeal biscuits or cakes spiced with ginger and cinnamon and sweetened with treacle.

párky (Cz) Pairs of long, thin frankfurters.

parlies (Sc) Thin and fiery ginger cookies said to have been popular with members of the old Scottish Parliament.

parma (Cz) See **barbel.**

Parma ham (It) See **prosciutto.**

Parmentier (Fr) Any dish in which potatoes are the main ingredient or garnish; a term in tribute to the French agronomist Antoine-Augustin Parmentier who popularized the use of the then-disdained potato for its nutri-

tional value during the late eighteenth century.

Parmesan (US) A hard, granular cheese, spotted with light yellow color and aromatic in flavor; used for grating. See also **Parmigiano-Reggiano.**

parmigiana, alla (It) Chicken, veal, or eggplant dishes prepared with Parmesan cheese; may also contain tomato sauce and mozzarella cheese.

Parmigiano-Reggiano (It) The original Parmesan cheese, one of the world's most widely imitated; a cow's milk grana cheese with a rich, spicy taste. See also **Parmesan.**

päron (Sw) Pears.

parposz (Po) Shad.

parsley (US) An herb, genus *Petroselinum*, with several varieties commonly used: curly leaf, celery leaf, fern leaf, and plain leaf or Italian parsley, which is the preferred variety for cooking. Used as garnish and to flavor stuffings, sauces, egg dishes, and soups.

parsley root (US) A member of the parsley family; tastes like a blend of parsley and celery or celery root; used in soups.

parsnip (US) An herb with yellow flowers and a pale yellow root cultivated as a garden vegetable. The sweet edible root is boiled, baked, sautéed, or steamed.

partan (Sc) Large edible crab.

partridge (US) A small upland game bird, strongly flavored with most of the meat in the breast. Also called **bobwhite.**

parwal (Ia) A small, green gourd similar

205

Parsnip

to a cucumber; eaten when young and immature.

Pascal celery (US) A variety of green celery grown for its crisp leafy stalks; served with soups and fish dishes.

pasha (Fi) Cheesecake of Russian origin.

pashtet iz pechonki (Rs) Calf's liver pâté.

pashtet iz ryby (Rs) Fish forcemeat.

pasilla (US) A thin, long pepper; turns from dark green to dark brown when mature.

paskha (Rs) A traditional pyramid-shaped cheesecake made with pot cheese, eggs, cream, almonds, and candied fruits; served at Easter.

passas (Pg) Raisins.

passion fruit (US) The tropical fruit of certain species of passionflower, *Passiflora*, with a pulp and flavor like that of a peach. Two main varieties are the yellow passion fruit, introduced into Hawaii from Australia, and the purple passion fruit grown in India. In addition to its use in fruit salads and custards, passion fruit juice is often added to commercial blends of orange and other fruit juices.

pasta (Tr) Cake.

pasta (It) Paste, dough. Most pasta is made from semolina and water; eggs and coloring such as spinach, may be added. Many shapes have been devised. May be boiled or baked.

pasta al forno (It) Pasta precooked in salted water before other ingredients are added, then mixture is oven baked.

pasta alla frutta (It) Fruit tart.

pasta all'uovo (It) Pasta made with eggs in flour dough.

pasta asciutta (It) Macaroni flavored with sauce.

pasta con tonno (It) Pasta with tuna.

pasta e fagioli (It) Soup made with macaroni, beans, and pork.

pasta filata (It) Literally, "spun paste"; a step in the manufacture of mozzarella cheese in which the curd is stretched.

pasta frolla (It) Shortcrust pastry.

pasta in brodo (It) Pasta, such as tiny shells, in broth or soup.

pasta reale (It) Small balls of dough used in soup.

pasta sfoglia (It) Puff pastry.

paste (It) Pastry.

paste (US) Any of various smooth, blended preparations such as almond paste, a dough used for pastry, a puree of fruit or vegetables, and a spread of meat or fish for toast.

pastéis (Pg) Danish-style pastry.

pastel (Sp) Pie, tart, cake, or pastry.

pastel de choclo (Sp) Literally, "overshoe"; a Chilean pie of spiced meat and corn.

pastel de merluza (Sp) Poached cod or hake molded into a cake; served cold.

pasteles (Sp) A Puerto Rican dish of pork, raisins, olives, and chick-peas rolled in plantain leaves.

pastelitos de boda (Mx) "Wedding cookies"; a popular cookie coated with confectioner's sugar.

pastèque (Fr) Watermelon.

pasternak so smetanoi (Rs) Braised parsnips with sour cream.

pasteurization (US) The sterilization or destruction of bacteria in milk or other foods by heating followed by rapid cooling. The process, discovered in the 1850s, was named for its French inventor, Louis Pasteur.

pasticciata (It) Baked strips of egg dough seasoned with meat sauce, mozzarella, flour paste, or cream.

pasticcio di maccheroni (It) Macaroni and cheese casserole.

pastiera (It) Ricotta cake.

pastij (Du) Pie or tart.

pastille (Fr) A round, flat, sugared, and fruit-flavored confection.

pastini (It) Little cookies.

pastirma (Tr) Pastrami.

pastitsio (Gk) A casserole of macaroni, ground beef, or lamb, grated cheese, tomatoes, onions, wine, and flavored with oregano and cinnamon.

pastoules (Gk) Almond cookies.

pastramá (Bu) Cured meat.

pastrami (US) Salted, spiced, smoked beef; boiled.

pastrmka (SC) Trout.

pastry (US) A pastelike dough made with flour, fat, and water; variations are made with the addition of eggs, milk, sugar, and leavening agent. Pastry is usually rolled out on a floured surface with a rolling pin.

pastry cream (US) A creamy preparation made with eggs, sugar, milk, and flour; various flavorings; used as a filling in pastries or as a garnish in some desserts. Also called **confectioners' custard.**

pasty (GB) A flaky pastry turnover filled with meat, potatoes, and other vegetables; served hot or cold. Also called **Cornish pasty.**

pasulj (SC) Beans.

pa sze ping kuo (Ch) Literally, "apples like spun silk"; apple pieces cooked in peanut oil, then coated with sugar syrup and sesame seeds, and plunged into ice water to fan out the threads of sugar glaze.

paszteciki (Po) Filled pastries.

patakukko (Fi) A baked casserole of freshwater fish and salt pork with a rye crust.

patata (It, Sp) Potato.

patata al forno (It) Baked potato.

patata bollita (It) Boiled potato.

patate (Fr) Sweet potato.

patate fritte (It) Fried potatoes.

patates (Gk) Potatoes.

patates püresi (Tr) Mashed potatoes.

pâté (Fr) Dough, pastry; originally applied only to a meat or fish dish enclosed in a pastry and baked; now it may describe any dish of ground meat or fish baked in a mold that has been lined with bacon strips.

pâte à pâté (Fr) The pastry usually made for a pâté en croûte; may use lard or butter or be puff pastry or brioche dough.

207

pâté brisée (Fr) Flaky, sweet pastry dough; puff pastry.

pâté de campagne (Fr) Coarse pâté, country style.

pâté de foie (Fr) A pâté containing 15 percent pork liver and 45 percent fat.

pâté de foie gras (Fr) Although originally invented by the ancient Egyptians, the exotic French pâté made from the livers of force-fed geese and flavored with wine and truffles was introduced in 1772.

pâté en croûte (Fr) A preparation of meat, game, or fish cooked in a pastry crust; served hot or cold.

pâté en terrine (Fr) A preparation of finely ground or chopped meat, game, or fish with seasonings, baked in a mold or dish (terrine) lined with bacon; served cold. Also called **terrine.**

pâté maison (Fr) A pâté unique to a particular restaurant.

pâté molle (Fr) Soft cheese.

pâté pressée (Fr) Pressed cheese.

pâtes (Fr) Pasta.

pâtisserie (Fr) Pastry.

patina (It) Tiny pieces of noodle dough.

patka (SC) Duck.

patlican (Tr) Eggplant.

patlican kebabi (Tr) Stew of lamb, eggplant, and tomatoes.

patlicanli kebap (Tr) Barbecued meat and eggplant on skewers.

pato (Pg, Sp) Duck.

pat prik king (Th) Stir-fried chicken with vegetables and herbs.

patrijs (Du) Partridge.

pattypan (US) A summer squash, *Cucur-*bita pepo*; disk-shaped with a central bulge and a scalloped edge; light skin and flesh both used cooked. Also called **cymling.**

pau (Ia) A Goan bread.

pauhi (In) Abalone.

pauhi tjha (In) Sautéed abalone.

paupiettes (Fr) Rolls of veal or beef stuffed with chopped meat and vegetables, wrapped in bacon, browned, and braised.

paupiettes de sole (Fr) Slices of sole, rolled and stuffed.

pavese (It) Broth with poached egg on fried bread.

pavot (Fr) Poppy seed.

pawpaw (US) See **custard apple, papaya.**

paximadakia (Gk) Sweet biscuits.

payasam (Ia) Sweet creamed rice, made with basmati or long-grain rice, milk, cream, sugar, raisins, almonds, cardamom, and rose water.

payousnaya ikra (Rs) Pressed caviar; less mature sturgeon eggs pressed into small tubs.

payrot (Jw–Israel) Fruit.

paysanne, à la (Fr) In the peasant style; with onions, carrots, and bacon.

pea (US) The small, green, podded fruit of a climbing plant, *Pisum sativum*; many varieties; eaten raw in salads or used in cooked dishes. Dried peas are sold as whole green peas and as yellow or green split peas. See also **podded peas.**

peach (US) The fruit of a deciduous tree, *Prunus persica*, native to China; many varieties. Most are globular in shape with slightly fuzzy, cream to orange skin; sweet, juicy, white or yellow flesh; and a rough central stone. There are two main varieties: *clingstone* with firm flesh that clings to the pit; and *freestone* with a softer flesh that separates from the pit. Eaten raw, in fruit salads, cooked, and as preserves.

peanut butter (US) A spread made of ground peanuts, salt, vegetable oil, and dextrose (a form of sugar); sold commercially in various styles.

peanut oil (US) Oil extracted by pressing peanuts; used as a cooking oil.

pear (US) A fleshy tree fruit of the genus *Pyrus* with a distinctive pyramidal shape, tapering toward the stalk. There are many species of pears and numerous varieties. Some of the common varieties are Anjou, Bartlett (sweet, golden), Bosc, Comice, Seckel, and Vermont beauty.

pearl barley (US) See **barley.**

pearl sago (US) See **sago.**

pearl tea (Ch) See **gunpowder tea.**

pease porridge (GB) A thick soup of green split peas, simmered with cloves and other spices and put through a sieve.

pebernødder (Da) Christmas cookies called pepper nuts.

pečen (SC) Baked.

pečené (Cz) Baked, roasted.

pečené hovězí (Cz) Roast beef.

pečené na rožni (Cz) Grilled.

pêche (Fr) Peach.

pêches cardinal (Fr) Stewed peaches on strawberry ice cream topped with red currant jelly.

pêches Melba (Fr) Peaches steeped in vanilla syrup served over vanilla ice cream, topped with raspberry puree; an 1894 creation of Escoffier in honor of opera singer Nellie Melba.

pechuga de pollo (Sp) Breast of chicken.

pecivo (SC) Pastry.

pecorino (It) Salty, piquant cheese made of sheep milk.

pectin (US) A carbohydrate found in the cellular walls of plants. Pectin provides a semisolid material for jellies and jams and is obtained by boiling fruit peels, cores, or off-grade fruit; the heat and fruit acids combine to release the substance that helps form a white neutral gel in the presence of sugar.

pečurke (SC) Mushrooms.

peel, to (US) To cut away skin a strip at a time.

peel oil (US) An essential oil extracted from tiny glands in citrus fruit peel and used to impart a citrus flavor or taste to other foods.

peertjes (Du) Pears.

peixe (Pg) Fish.

peixe assado (Pg) Baked fish.

peixe frito (Pg) Fried fish.

pekmez (SC) Jam.

Pelkartoffeln (Gr) Potatoes boiled in their skins.

pemmican (US) Dried strips of beef, venison, or other meats, pounded into a paste with fat, suet, raisins, or dried berries. A nutritious food with a minimum spoilage risk, pemmican was developed originally by native Americans and adapted by voyageurs, hunters, and pioneers.

penne (It) Literally, "quill pen"; hollow pasta, cut diagonally.

penne all' arrabbiata (It) Macaroni in a spicy tomato sauce with a name that translates as "angry," made hot with red peppers and garlic and flavored with Romano cheese.

pennyroyal (GB) An aromatic herb of the mint family, *Mentha pulegium*, sometimes used as a substitute for spearmint.

pepe (It) Pepper.

peper (Du) Pepper.

peperonata (It) Appetizers (antipasti) of sliced peppers, onions, and tomatoes.

peperoni (It) Capsicum peppers.

pepino (Pg) Cucumber.

pepino (Sp) Cucumber.

pepitas (Sp) Seeds, such as green pumpkin seeds, used in cooking.

peppar (Sw) Pepper.

pepparkakor (Sw) Gingersnap cookies; ginger cakes.

pepparrot (Sw) Horseradish.

pepper (Nw) Pepper.

pepper, black (US) The unripe, dried berries of a vine, *Piper nigrum*; on drying, the skin becomes black and wrinkled; a volatile, pungent flavor; should be freshly ground.

peppercorns, green (US) The immature berries of the pepper vine, *Piper nigrum*; prepared pickled, canned or freeze-dried; pungent flavor; used with meat, poultry, or fish.

pepperrot (Nw) Horseradish.

pepper, white (US) The ripe berries of a vine, *Piper nigrum*, with the skin and pulp removed; the white inner seed is dried and bleached in the sun; a milder flavor and less aroma than black pepper; used in white sauces and other dishes in which the black color is not wanted.

pepř (Cz) Pepper.

pera (Af–Swahili) Guava.

pera (It) Pear.

pêra (Pg) Pear.

perca (Pg) Bass.

percebe (Sp) A species of barnacle; the stalk is cooked and served cold with lemon juice; popular in tapas bars.

perche (Fr) Perch.

perdiz toledana (Sp) Stewed partridge.

perdreau (Fr) Partridge.

pere (It) Pears.

perigourdine (Fr) With foie gras and truffles.

periwinkle (GB) See **winkle.**

perkedel (In) Deep-fried soft fritters made from flour, mashed potatoes, or corn, mixed with vegetables, meat, or seafood.

perna de carneiro (Pg) Leg of lamb.

perník (Cz) Gingerbread.

pernuce (It) Partridge.

perogen (Jw) Ground beef pies.

persico (It) Perch.

persika (Sw) Peach.

persil (Fr) Parsley.

persilja (Sw) Parsley.

persillade (Fr) Chopped parsley, usually mixed with garlic.

persille (Nw) Parsley.

persillesovs (Da) Parsley sauce.

persimmon (US) The orange-colored plumlike fruit of trees of the genus, *Diospyros*. An American variety, sometimes called Date-plum, is very astringent but becomes sweet after exposure to frost. A Japanese variety, Hachiya, is used in frozen purees, ice creams, and puddings.

peršun (SC) Parsley.

perú (Pg) Turkey.

perzik (Du) Peach.

pesca (It) Peach.

pescado guisado (Sp) Fish stew.

pesce (It) Fish.

pesce spada (It) Swordfish.

pesciolino (It) Whitebait.

pêssego (Pg) Peach.

pesto (It) Pounded; ground in a mortar.

pesto Genovese (It) A sauce of olive oil, garlic, basil, and pine nuts.

pesto Romano (It) A sauce of olive oil, garlic, chopped basil, parsley, lemon juice, and egg yolks.

petcha (Jw) Jellied calves feet with onions, garlic, vinegar, and lemon juice. Also spelled **ptcha.**

Petersille (Gr) Parsley.

petit-beurre (Fr) Butter cookie.

petite marmite (Fr) Clear soup made with meat, poultry, marrow bones, stockpot vegetables, and cabbage; usually served with toast and sprinkled with grated cheese.

petit-lait (Fr) Whey.

petit mont blanc (Fr) A dessert made with chestnuts and whipped cream.

petit pain (Fr) Roll.

petits pois (Fr) Young peas eaten shelled, without the pods.

petrezselyem (Hu) Parsley.

peya (Af–Swahili) Pear.

peynir (Tr) Cheese.

peynirli pide (Tr) Cheese bread.

Pfannkuchen (Gr) A pancake, usually folded around a filling of cooked fruit.

Pfeffer (Gr) Pepper.

Pfeffernüsse (Gr) Literally, "pepper nuts"; whisked egg dough cookies with almonds and spices.

Pfifferling (Gr) Chanterelle mushroom.

Pfirsich (Gr) Peach.

Pflaumen (Gr) Plums.

Pflaumenmuss (Gr) Prune preserve.

phalon ka pullao (Ia) Pine nut pilaf with fruit.

pheasant (US) An upland game bird with a flavor resembling that of chicken. The legs and thighs are the choice parts of the bird. Domestic pheasants may have a mild, unflavorful taste.

pho (Vt) A soup of beef stock with thin slices of beef, rice noodles, and scallions; dish may include shrimp.

phoa (Ia) Deep-fried rice that has been pounded into flakes; eaten as a snack.

phosphates (US) Chemicals used in food processing to improve firmness of the product and to reduce moisture loss.

phyllo (Gk) Leaf-thin sheets of dough made from flour and water; used layered with sweet or savory fillings; similar to **mille-feuille.** Also called **brik, filo, yukka.**

picadinho (Pg) Chopped meat.

picado (Pg) Chopped.

picante vinaigrette (US) A spicy dressing of cider vinegar, tomatillo sauce, white wine, lemon and lime juice, cilantro, and salad oil.

piccadillo (Sp) Chopped steak simmered with green peppers, onion, garlic, tomatoes, olives, capers, and raisins; served with black beans and rice.

piccalilli (US) A relish made of chopped vegetables, including peppers, tomatoes, celery, onions, and cabbage, layered in salt, vinegar, mustard, and turmeric.

piccante (It) Piquant.

piccioncini con risotto (It) Squabs prepared on a spit; served with rice.

piccione (It) Pigeon, squab.

pichi (Af–Swahili) Peach.

pickled mustard (Ch) Turnips preserved with Szechuan peppers and served in steamed dishes or sour and hot soups.

pico de gallo (Sp) Literally, "rooster's beak"; a condiment of diced tomatoes, chopped red onions, minced jalapeño peppers, and cilantro. It is used with poultry, meat, and seafoods.

pi-dàn (Ch) Duck eggs preserved in a special clay bound with strong tea for about three months. The eggs acquire a greenish brown color and a sulfuric taste. Also called **hundred-year eggs, thousand-year eggs.**

pie (US) A sweet or savory mixture in a pie pan or other container and baked with a bottom crust of pastry or a top crust or both; may also have crumb crusts or be topped with meringue.

pie à la mode (US) Pie, often apple pie, served with ice cream, usually vanilla.

pièce de résistance (Fr) The high point of a meal; the specialty of a menu or of a particular chef.

pieczeń wołwa (Po) Roast beef.

pieds de porc (Fr) Pig's feet; commonly prepared by grilling.

piemontese, alla (It) With a sauce containing truffles and nutmeg.

pie plant (US) A popular name for rhubarb.

pieprz (Po) Pepper.

pigeon en cocotte (Fr) Casserole of pigeon or squab.

pigeonneau (Fr) Squab.

piggvar (Nw, Sw) Turbot.

pigments (US) Chemicals that contribute distinguishing color characteristics to foods. Natural pigments include anthrocyanin, which gives blood oranges a red flesh color, and carotenes and xanthophylls that account for tangerine colors.

pignoli (It) Pine nuts.

pignon (Fr) Pine nuts.

piimä (Fi) A kind of buttermilk.

piirakka (Fi) Pasties or pies.

pike (US) A sharp-nosed, duck-billed fish, genus *Esox*, found in nontropical Northern Hemisphere lakes and streams; firm, white meat; cooked or prepared in any of the ways commonly used for fish.

pikkels (Nw) Pickles.

pilaf (Tr) A modern Turkish word for a rice dish that originated in the Middle East and migrated to many countries with the Moguls. In the basic dish the rice is browned in butter with onion and always spiced, sometimes with saffron; vegetables, meat, or fish may be added. There are many variations of ingredients with regional differences in the dish and what it is called, such as *pilaff, pilav, pilaw* and *pilau.* See **pullao.**

pileća čorba (SC) Chicken soup.

piletina (SC) Chicken.

piliç fırında (Tr) Roast young chicken.

pilipili manga (Af–Swahili) Pepper.

pilipili shamba (Af–Shwahili) Large red or green pepper.

pilot biscuit (US) See **hardtack.**

Pilze (Gr) Mushrooms.

piman (Jp) Green pepper.

pimenta (Pg) Pepper.

pimenta do reino (Pg) Black pepper.

pimenta verde (Pg) Green pepper.

piments (Fr) Pimentos.

pimiento (Sp) Heart-shaped chilis sold canned in the United States, soft, sweet flesh of the capsicum pepper. Also spelled *pimento.*

pimiento de Jamaica (Sp) Allspice.

pinaattiobukaiset (Fi) Spinach pancakes.

pineapple (US) The fruit of a plant, *Ananas comosus*, native to Brazil; now widely cultivated in tropical areas, such as Hawaii. Its appearance is like a tapered cylinder with a rough, honeycomb, yellow, green, or red skin. The flesh is yellow, juicy, and fibrous; used in desserts, preserves, and sweet or savory dishes. Raw pineapple prevents setting of gelatin. Also called **abacaxi, ananas, ananasso, ananász.**

pine nuts (US) The edible seeds of the pine tree; small, white, oval and slightly oily in flavor; used in pesto, other sauces, in soup, salads, main courses, and desserts. Also called **pignoli, pignon, piñón.**

ping-gwo (Ch) Apple.

ping-yú (Ch) Turbot.

pinnekjøtt (Nw) Steamed, salt-cured mutton chops.

piñón (Sp) See **pine nuts.**

pinole (Mx) A finely ground powder or flour made from parched maize (corn); used sweetened.

pinto bean (US) A legume, *Phaseolus vulgaris*, of the kidney bean family; brown-pink skin; common in Spain and Latin America; used like the red kidney bean in stews and with rice.

piononos (Sp) Deep-fried plantain fritters filled with ground beef.

pip (US) Small seeds found in fruits such as grapes, oranges, and apples.

pi-pá (Ch) See **loquat.**

pipèrade (Fr) Omelet with peppers, tomatoes, garlic, ham, and onions.

pipián (Sp) A sauce made with ground nuts or seeds. It may be red, *colorado*, with sesame seeds or green, *verde*, with green pumpkin seeds.

pippuri (Fi) Pepper.

pirinač (SC) Rice.

pirogi (Rs) Pasties; pies.

piroshki (Rs) Small pies or patties with varied fillings, such as meat, cabbage, rice, potatoes, or fruit; used as an appetizer or served with borsch.

pirzola (Tr) Chops; usually lamb.

pisang goreng (In) Fried banana.

piselli (It) Green peas.

pissenlits (Fr) Dandelion greens.

pista (Ia) Pistachio.

pistaches (Fr) Pistachio nuts.

pistachio nuts (US) The green seeds with cream-colored shells of a tree, *Pistacia vera*; related to the cashew family; a resinous taste; sold roasted and salted as a snack; used in stuffings, pilafs, and in sweetmeats.

pisto manchego (Sp) A mixed vegetable dish with pieces of ham, bound with eggs; not quite an omelet; many variations.

pistou (Fr) 1. A French sauce of tomatoes, garlic, olive oil, Parmesan cheese, and crushed basil leaves. 2. Name for a vegetable and vermicelli soup.

pisztráng (Hu) Trout.

pit (US) A fruit stone.

pita (SC) Pie.

pita sa orasima (SC) Walnut pie.

pi-táu-kàn (Ch) Raisins.

pitepalt (Sw) Potato dumplings stuffed with pork.

pith (US) The white, spongy layer beneath the rind of citrus fruits.

pito-ja-joulupuuro (Fi) A pudding of whole grain barley and rose hip or raisin puree cooked in milk.

pivo (Cz, SC) Beer.

pizza (It) A round, flat, open pie of yeast dough baked with varied toppings, including cheese, black olives, anchovies, sausages, tomato sauce, and seasonings.

pizzaiola (It) Pizza style; served with mozzarella cheese and tomato sauce; often with steak.

plaice (US) A flatfish, *Pleuronectes platessa*, most important in European fisheries; used whole or in fillets; with lean white flesh; served poached, steamed, baked, fried, or grilled.

pla kung (Th) Grilled shrimp with lime juice.

planking (US) A method of serving foods on a hot wooden plank; sometimes food finishes cooking on the plank.

plantain (US) A tropical herbaceous plant (*Musa paradisiaca*) with a green fleshy fruit resembling the banana. Yellow plantain is firm and mildly sweet while black plantain is soft and intensely sweet.

plátano (Sp) Banana; plantain.

plàteau de fromages (Fr) Choice of cheese.

plättar (Sw) Small pancakes.

platýs (Cz) Halibut.

Plätzchen (Gr) Cookies.

pletionka s makom (Rs) Braided white bread.

pleurote (Fr) A kind of mushroom served with fish.

plísňový sýr (Cz) Blue cheese.

pliushki (Rs) Cinnamon crescents.

pljeskavica (SC) Spicy meat patty, grilled.

plommer (Nw) Plums.

plommon (Sw) Plums.

plommonpudding (Sw) Plum pudding.

plommonspäckad fläskkarré (Sw) Pork loin with prunes.

plum (US) A round, sweet, fleshy fruit of the *Prunus domestica* tree. Although grown in many varieties, the common plum, also called Italian prune, has a purple skin, yellow pulp, and flat pointed stone. The plum was first introduced into Europe around 65 B.C. by Roman troops returning from campaigns in Syria. The Damson plum was similarly introduced into France in 1204 by knights of the Fourth Crusade returning from Syria. Most American varieties of plums are descended from Japanese imports.

plump, to (US) To soak dried fruits in warm water until softened.

plum sauce (US) A Chinese tart sauce made from dried plums, apricots, sugar, and spices; thick and sweet, used with roast duck, pork, egg rolls, and other foods. Also called **duck sauce.**

poach (US) To cook in a simmering liquid just below the boiling point.

poached eggs (US) Eggs cooked in a simmering liquid until firm but not hard.

poché (Fr) Poached.

pocherade ägg (Sw) Poached egg.

pocheteau blanc (Fr) Skate.

pod (US) The outer seed shell of fruits and vegetables, usually applied to legumes.

podded peas (US) Pea varieties of which the seed shell is eaten as well as the small, almost undeveloped seeds; prepared and cooked as for green beans; used in Oriental dishes. Also called **sugar peas, snow peas, mange-tout, sywě-dòu, katjang kapri.**

podvarku (SC) Baked sauerkraut.

poêle, à la (Fr) Fried.

poffertjes (Du) Fritters.

pohovan (SC) Breaded.

poi (Pl) A paste made from the tubers of the taro plant.

point, à (Fr) Cooked to a medium doneness (meat).

point d'asperges (Fr) Asparagus tips.

poire (Fr) Pear.

poire à la Condé (Fr) Pear served on vanilla-flavored rice.

poireaux (Fr) Leeks.

poires belle Hélène (Fr) Poached pears served on vanilla ice cream with hot chocolate sauce.

pois (Fr) Peas, all forms: fresh, dried, shelled and podded.

pois à la francaise (Fr) Peas cooked with lettuce and onions.

pois cassés (Fr) Split peas.

pois chiche (Fr) Chick-peas.

pois et riz (Fr) A Haitian dish of peas and rice.

poisson (Fr) Fish.

poisson d'eau douce (Fr) Freshwater fish.

poisson de mer (Fr) Saltwater fish.

poitrine (Fr) Breast.

poitrine de veau farcie (Fr) Stuffed breast of veal.

poivrade (Fr) A peppery sauce.

poivre (Fr) Pepper.

poivre vert (Fr) Green pepper spice.

poivron (Fr) Green bell pepper.

polenta (It) Yellow corn meal mush.

polenta e osei (It) Yellow corn meal mush garnished with small roasted birds and gravy.

polévky (Cz) Soups.

Polish sausage (US) See **kielbasa.**

pollack (US) A flavorful saltwater fish and member of the cod family. Also spelled *pollock.*

pollo (It) Chicken.

pollo (Sp) Chicken.

pollo ai ferri (It) Broiled chicken.

pollo a la chilindrón (Sp) Sautéed chicken with peppers, tomatoes, and olives.

pollo alla cacciatore (It) Chicken cooked "hunter style."

pollo al vino bianco (It) Chicken in white wine.

pollo arrosto (It) Roast chicken.

pollo asado (Sp) Roast chicken.

pollo fritto (It) Fried chicken.

Polonaise sauce (Fr) A topping of buttered bread crumbs, chopped hard-cooked eggs, and parsley; served over cooked vegetables.

polpetta (It) Croquette.

polpette (It) Meatballs.

polpettone (It) Meat loaf.

polpo (It) Octopus.

pølse (Nw) Sausage.

polvo (Pg) Octopus.

polyunsaturated fats (US) Food fats such as cottonseed, corn, and soybean oils that contain polyunsaturated fatty acids.

polyunsaturated fatty acids (US) Fatty acids that consist of chains of carbon atoms with two or more points in the chain where hydrogen atoms can be added. A fatty acid with additional hydrogen atoms generally becomes more fluid. Thus, liquid vegetable oils are usually rich in polyunsaturated fatty acids. Linoleic acid is a polyunsaturated fatty acid and is termed an essential fatty acid because it must be supplied in the diet.

pomarańcza (Po) Orange.

pombe (Af–Swahili) Beer.

pombo (Pg) Pigeon.

pome fruits (US) Fruits that have the flavor and aroma characteristics of apples.

pomegranate (US) A large round fruit of the *Punica granatum* tree grown in Asia and Africa. It has a tough rind and a juicy reddish pulp with many seeds. The pulp is eaten raw or made into a juice or syrup. Also called *Chinese apple.*

pomelo (US) See **shaddock.**

Pomegranate

pomeranč (Cz) Orange.

pomidory (Po) Tomatoes.

pomme (Fr) Apple.

pommes de terre (Fr) Literally, "apples of the earth"; potatoes.

pommes de terre à l'huile (Fr) Potato salad with vinaigrette sauce.

pommes de terre duchesse (Fr) Sieved potatoes mixed with butter, salt, and pepper; served as is or put through a pastry bag to make a border.

pommes frites (Fr) Fried potatoes.

pommes gaufrettes (Fr) Apple waffles.

pommes purée (Fr) Mashed potatoes.

pomodori (It) Tomatoes.

pomodori ripieni (It) Stuffed tomatoes.

pomodoro, al (It) Prepared with tomato sauce.

pomorandža (SC) Orange.

pompano (Sp) Any of several species of tropical saltwater fish with a delicious and delicate flavor and texture found in the South Atlantic and Caribbean waters. A small blue to green pompano is found along the Pacific Coast.

pompano en papillote (Fr) Pompano baked with white wine, butter, and seasonings inside a parchment bag.

pompelmo (It) Grapefruit.

pompelmoes (Du) Grapefruit.

ponty (Hu) Carp.

poori (Ia) Deep-fried unleavened bread rounds made with whole wheat and clarified butter. Also spelled **puri.**

popover (US) A muffin made from a poured flour-egg-milk batter.

poppy seeds (US) Small seeds of the opium poppy, *Papaver somniferum*, that when ripe lose the opium alkaloid; black and light varieties; nutty taste; used on breads and cakes, in curries and sauces.

porc (Fr) Pork.

porchetta (It) Whole suckling pig, salted, spiced, and roasted.

porcini (It) See **boletus.**

pôrco (Pg) Pork.

porgy (US) Generic name for many species of small saltwater food fish of the Sparidae family found along the Atlantic Coast, in the Gulf of Mexico, and the Mediterranean. Examples include scup and sheepshead.

pork and beans (US) Pea beans or navy beans simmered with salt pork, onions, tomato sauce, molasses, and brown sugar.

Porree (Gr) Leek.

porri (It) Leeks.

porridge (GB) A soft food made by stirring oatmeal or other cereal in hot water or milk. The term is derived from *pottage*.

portakal (Tr) Orange.

porterhouse steak (US) A cut of meat from the short loin of beef, including parts of the tenderloin.

Porto (Pg) Identifies Portuguese port wine.

Port Salut (Fr) A mild, creamy, semisoft dessert cheese originally produced by Trappist monks at Port du Salut abbey.

port wine (US) A sweet wine made from grapes grown in the Oporto region of Portugal, fortified with brandy. Four main types are ruby, with a sweet, fruity taste; tawny, older and less sweet; vintage, aged up to 20 years with a sediment called "crust"; white port, a drier apertif made from white grapes.

posillipo, alla (It) With a seafood sauce containing tomatoes and herbs.

posset (GB) A hot beverage of milk with wine or ale, flavored with sugar and spices.

postej (Da) Paste; pâté.

potage (Fr) Soup.

potage clair (Fr) Clear soup.

potage crécy (Fr) Purée of carrot soup.

potage crème (Fr) Cream soup.

potage crème de céleri (Fr) Cream of celery soup.

potage crème d'épinards (Fr) Cream of spinach soup.

potage de betterave (Fr) Beet soup; borscht.

potage Dubarry (Fr) Purée of cauliflower soup.

potage germiny (Fr) Soup of puréed peas, chicken stock, and heavy cream.

potage parmentier (Fr) Purée of potato soup.

potage St. Germain (Fr) Green pea soup.

potage tortue (Fr) Turtle soup.

potajes de garbanzos (Sp) A soup made with chick-peas, garlic, potato, red peppers, and olive oil.

potassium (US) A chemical element and essential mineral in human nutrition; a recommended dietary allowance (RDA) has not been established but an intake of 2–6 grams per day has been suggested by some authorities; best natural sources include leafy, green vegetables, oranges, potatoes, and bananas.

potatis (Sw) Potatoes.

potatismos (Sw) Mashed potatoes.

potato (US) An elongated, ball-shaped tuber of a plant, *Solanum tuberosum*, in the nightshade family, native to South America; many varieties; skin color varies from light brown to red. The starchy, white or cream-colored flesh may be waxy or floury in texture, which determines the most satisfactory cooking method or use made. For example, waxy potatoes become gummy when mashed. Floury ones have more starch. Potatoes are rich in vitamin C and potassium. Used boiled, baked, fried, and combined in many dishes.

potato bread (US) A bread developed in Europe by bakers who found that adding mashed potatoes to bread dough helped bread retain freshness; also, before the development of compressed yeast, potatoes could contribute a leavening effect. Commercial potato bread contains about 6 percent potato flour.

potato buds (US) A form of dehydrated mashed potatoes; granules or nuggets that require a minimum of stirring for reconstitution.

potato chips (US) Very thin slices of potato deep-fried in oil and salted. Potato chips were invented at Saratoga Springs, New York, in 1853. Also called **Saratoga chips.**

potato flour (US) A flour made from a coating of mashed potatoes spread on a hot rotating drum. The resulting thin sheet of dehydrated potatoes is then finely ground in a hammer mill.

pot-au-feu (Fr) French version of the boiled dinner.

poteter kokte (Nw) Boiled potatoes.

poteter ovnstekte (Nw) Baked potatoes.

poteter stekte (Nw) Fried potatoes.

potetpuré (Nw) Mashed potatoes.

potkas (Sw) Pot cheese.

pot liquor (US) The liquid remaining in a pot after being used to prepare a meal of meat and greens. Also spelled *potlicker, potlikker*.

pot luck (US) Pertaining to the luck of an uninvited guest as to what might be in the dinner pot of a hostess.

pot pie (US) A crusted meat pie usually containing chopped vegetables and pieces of chicken, beef, or pork.

pot-posy (Sc) A bunch of herbs for flavoring soups and stews; like the French *bouquet garni*.

pot-roasting (US) Braising a whole, large piece of meat.

pots de crème au chocolate (Fr) Rich chocolate pudding.

pottage (GB) Literally, anything that is in a pot; usually vegetables, with or without meat, boiled to the consistency of a thick soup.

pouding (Fr) Pudding.

poudre, en (Fr) Powdered.

poulard à la hongroise (Fr) Roast chicken stuffed with rice and flavored with paprika.

poulard à la vapeur (Fr) Steamed chicken.

poule au pot (Fr) Chicken stewed with vegetables.

poulet (Fr) Chicken.

poulet à la Marengo (Fr) A method of cooking a chicken created by Napoleon's personal chef after the general's successful battle against the Austrians at Marengo in 1800; he browned the chicken in oil, added wine, and served it with a garnish of fried eggs, mushroom, and crawfish. In a modern version, the chicken is served with crawfish eggs.

poulet chasseur (Fr) Literally, "hunter's chicken"; chicken sautéed with mushrooms, shallots, white wine, and tomatoes.

poulet de Bresse (Fr) A meal prepared with a highly prized and specially fed chicken from the French district of Bresse.

poulet en cocotte (Fr) Chicken roasted in a casserole.

poulet froid (Fr) Chicken served cold.

poulet rôti à l'estragon (Fr) Roast chicken with tarragon.

poulette sauce (Fr) A meat or fish-flavored velouté sauce containing onions and lemon juice.

poulpe (Fr) Small octopus.

poultry (US) Any domestic bird used for food, including chicken, turkey, Rock Cornish game hen, duckling, and goose.

pound cake (GB) A traditional British butter cake for which all the ingredients, including flour, sugar, butter, and eggs, were weighed to the pound.

poussin (Fr) Young chicken.

powdered sugar (US) See **confectioners' sugar.**

pozole (Sp) Soup made with pork, hominy, and hot chili peppers.

prairie oysters (US) Calves' testicles, soaked in salt water, dipped in bread crumbs, and fried in bacon drippings.

praline (US) A confection of almonds or pecans boiled in a sugar mixture that hardens when cooled. Originally a French almond candy, eighteenth century Louisiana colonists changed the recipe to utilize native pecans and brown sugar.

pranzo (It) Meal.

pranzo di manzo (It) Vegetable platter.

prawn (US) A large marine crustacean of the Palaemondidae family, resembling a shrimp with large claws.

preclík (Cz) Pretzel.

preeo (Th) Sour.

preheat (US) A cooking technique of rai-

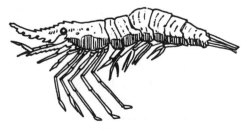

Prawn

219

sing the temperature of an oven or skillet up to that needed for cooking a food before adding the food.

Preisselbeere (Gr) A cranberrylike fruit.

preliv za salutu (SC) Salad dressing.

preserved eggs (Ch) See **pi-dàn, syán-dàn.**

preserves (US) A fruit spread made of berries or pieces of fruit cooked with sugar. The term is also commonly applied to jams.

pressed caviar (US) See **paiusnaia.**

Presskopf (Gr) Headcheese.

pressòkàvè (Hu) Espresso coffee.

press peach (US) Popular name for cling peach.

pressure cooker (US) An airtight utensil for quick-cooking or preserving by steaming food under pressure.

presunto (Pg) Cured ham.

pretzel (US) A crisp salted biscuit or roll usually baked in the shape of a knot, but also prepared as tiny sticks, wafers, or other shapes. Origin credited to seventh century monks who gave them as a reward to children who learned their prayers. Also spelled **bretzel.**

prezzemolo (It) Parsley.

prianiki tyl'skie (Rs) Spice or gingerbread cakes with designs pressed into a glazed surface.

prickly pear (US) The edible, spiny-skinned fruit that grow along the edges of the flat pads of *Opuntia* cactus; color varies from yellow to purple; with a high water and sugar content, the flavor is mild and sweet; usually eaten raw. Also called **cactus pear.**

prik (Th) Pertaining to fiery, spicy foods, including chilies and green peppercorns.

prik haeng (Th) Dried red chilies.

prik kee noo (Th) Very hot, tiny, bird chilies, red or green.

prik mum (Th) See **banana pepper.**

prima colazione (It) Breakfast or first refreshment of day.

primeiro almoĉo (Pg) First luncheon; breakfast.

primeurs (Fr) Early or spring vegetables.

primo piatto (It) First course of a meal after antipasto.

primost (Nw) Whey cheese.

printanière, à la (Fr) Garnished with a variety of vegetables.

přírodní řízek (Cz) Cutlet, unbreaded.

prixuelos (Sp) A thin pancake.

prodel (Rs) Medium buckwheat groats, usually served with milk or butter as a side dish.

profiterole (Fr) Small cream puffs filled with a savory or sweet filling such as a puree, custard, or jam.

profiteroles glacées au chocolate (Fr) Small cream-filled pastries with chocolate frosting.

proja (SC) Corn bread.

proof (US) A measure of the alcoholic strength of a product. Each degree of proof represents 0.05 percent of alcohol; thus, 100-proof straight whiskey is 50 percent alcohol.

prosciutto (It) Italian ham, air-dried and spiced but not smoked. Also called **Parma ham.**

prosciutto cotto (It) Cooked ham.

prosná kaše (Cz) Millet.

proteases (US) Protein enzymes used in cheese making and meat-tenderizing products.

protein (US) Any of a large group of organic compounds containing carbon, hydrogen, nitrogen, and oxygen; found in meat, fish, fowl, and certain vegetables such as soybeans, rice, and other cereals; needed for growth, work, or repair of cells vital to life. Authorities suggest that at least 13 grams of protein consumed each day should consist of the essential amino acids. See also **complete protein.**

proustille (Fr) A confection of praline, chocolate cream, and orange rind, named for French author Marcel Proust.

provençale, à la (Fr) With tomatoes, garlic, olives, and eggplant.

provola (It) Fresh cheese similar to mozzarella.

Provolone (It) A cow's milk cheese with a light yellow interior sold in various shapes; gold to brown rind; mild to sharp taste depending on age.

pršuta (SC) Smoked ham.

prugna (It) Plum.

prugne cotte (It) Stewed prunes.

prugne secche (It) Prunes, dried plums.

pruim (Du) Plum.

prune (US) Plum; the dried fruit of the plum tree, usually _Prunus domestica,_ eaten raw or stewed, or used as a source of juice or nectar.

pruneau (Fr) Prune.

pruneaux du pichet (Fr) Prunes in Port and red wine.

prune butter (US) A spread of sweetened prune puree flavored with cinnamon and cloves.

prune juice (US) A breakfast beverage made from a water extract of the soluble parts of dried prunes.

prünellen (Gr) Prunes.

prune whip (US) A dessert of strained prune puree, sugar, and egg white.

pržen (SC) Fried.

pržena jaja (SC) Fried eggs.

psaria ke thalasina (Gk) Fish and seafood.

psarosupa (Gk) Fish soup.

pšeničný chléb (Cz) Wheat bread.

psito sto furno (Gk) A pot roast of veal with onions, tomatoes, garlic, and wine.

pstruh (Cz) Trout.

psyllium (US) A high-fiber cereal grain grown in India and added to foods to reduce cholesterol levels.

ptcha (Jw) See **petcha.**

pua'a (Pl) Pork.

puchero (Sp) A hot-pot stew of beef, pork, chicken and assorted vegetables; served in two portions, the liquid used as a soup, followed by the meat and vegetables as the entrée.

pudding (US) A soft, creamy, or custardlike baked or boiled mixture, using a base of flour, corn meal, or other ground cereal. Fruit, milk, eggs, or other ingredients may be added. The term may also be applied to certain baked, boiled, or steamed foods, such as Yorkshire pudding.

pudim (Pg) Pudding.

pudim flan (Pg) Caramel custard.

pudin de centollo (Sp) Fish loaf with king crab.

pudink (Cz) Pudding.

pudin ya mayai (Af–Swahili) Egg pudding.

pu erh (Ch) A smoky dark fermented tea.

puerro (Sp) Leeks.

puff pastry (US) A pastry dough made light and flaky when baked by kneading and rolling many layers of dough together with butter.

puikot (Fi) Cookie sticks.

puits d'amour (Fr) Small rounds of puff pastry filled with jam or flavored pastry cream.

pulgogi (Kr) Barbecued beef.

pulla (Fi) A sweet yeast bread, usually braided and wreath shaped; flavored with cardamom seeds and almonds.

pullao (Ia) A dish that is traditional in Indian cuisine, made with highly seasoned saffron rice, often basmati, fried in clarified butter (ghee); then steamed with stock and nuts. Other ingredients may be added, such as vegetables, lamb, shrimp, chicken, or Indian-style cottage cheese (channa). Also called **pilaf.**

pullao dilbahaar kajoo (Ia) Pilaf of broccoli and cashew nuts with cumin.

pullet (US) A female chicken less than a year old.

pulpeta (Sp) A baked slice of veal browned in olive oil; topped with hard-boiled egg, garlic, olives, parsley, and sherry.

pulpo (Sp) Octopus; often fried with garlic.

pulse (US) Legume seeds such as beans and peas.

pultost (Nw) A rennet type of sour-milk cheese.

pumelo (US) See **shaddock.**

Pumpernickel (Gr) A dark, sour, rye bread.

pumpkin (US) Any of the fruits of the vines of the genus *Cucurbita;* usually a large, orange gourd; the flesh is used as a vegetable, in salads and soups, and made into pie or preserves; seeds may be roasted and salted for a snack.

pumpkin pie spice (US) A blend of ground cinnamon, cloves, and ginger, used for flavoring cookies, pies, and sweet potatoes.

punajuuret appelsiikastikkeesa (Fi) Beets cooked in orange juice.

punajuurikaalikeitto (Fi) Beet and cabbage soup.

punajuuri salaatti (Fi) Beet salad with potatoes, apples, carrots, onions, and dill pickles.

punaviinisilakka (Fi) Herring in garlic sauce.

punch (US) An iced beverage made with fruit juices, cut pieces of fruit, carbonated water, and often sparkling wine.

punjene paprike (SC) Green peppers stuffed with ground meat.

punsch (Sw) A liqueur of fermented rice, molasses, and spices.

puntas de filete (Sp) Cubed beef filet in red chili and tomato sauce with cheese, red onions, and green chili slices.

punto, al (It) Cooked medium (meat).

puré de batatas (Pg) Mashed potatoes.

puré di patate (It) Mashed potatoes.

purée (Fr) A thick, smooth-textured paste, sauce, or soup.

purée de pois (Fr) Thick pea soup.

purée de pommes de terre à l'ail (Fr) Mashed potatoes flavored with garlic.

purée, to (US) To reduce to a smooth-textured paste by mashing, putting through a sieve, or processing in a blender.

puri (Ia) See **poori.**

purjo (Sw) Leeks.

purjokeitto (Fi) Leek soup.

purpoo mulligatawny (Ia) Curried lentil soup.

puss pass (Nw) A stew of mutton, potatoes, carrots, and cabbage.

pú-táu (Ch) Grapes.

Putenbraten (Gr) Roast turkey.

putera (SC) Butter.

putu (In) A dessert of steamed sweet cake.

puuroa (Fi) Hot, cooked cereal, such as oatmeal or farina.

puževi (SC) Snails.

pweza (Af–Swahili) Lobster.

py mei fun (Th) Thin rice stick noodles.

pyridoxine (US) See **vitamin B$_6$.**

pytt i panna (Sw) Literally, "tidbits in the pan"; hash; diced leftover meat, potatoes, and onions fried together; served with pickles and fried eggs.

qabargah (Ia) A Kashmir dish of cooked, dried lamb.

qamar ad-din (Ar) A beverage made from sheets of dried, pressed apricots that are pureed with water.

qamardin (Ar) A sweetmeat made from apricot puree.

qar' (Ar) A large yellow-fleshed squash used in Middle Eastern dishes.

qarnoun machi (Ar) An Algerian dish of artichoke hearts stuffed with a ground meat mixture.

qatayif (Ar) Tiny pancakes stuffed with chopped nuts or cheese and served with syrup.

qishtah (Ar) Clotted cream.

qorma (Ia) A thick spiced curry sauce used with rice and lamb.

qua (Vt) Fruit.

quaddid (Ar) Preserved or dried meat.

quadrucci (It) Small squares of pasta.

quaglia (It) Quail.

quagliata (It) 1. A goat cheese. 2. A dish of junketlike curdled milk.

quaglie alla fiorentina (It) Quails cooked in butter, olive oil, and white wine with parsley, bay, and thyme.

quaglie alla piemontese (It) Roast quails in a cream sauce with truffles and Marsala wine.

quaglie arrosto con polenta (It) Roast quails with fried polenta.

quaqliette di vitello (It) Rolled veal "birds" with ham, onion, and sage leaves on skewers, cooked on a spit.

quaglio (It) Rennet.

quahog (US) A round, hard-shelled clam, *Mercinaria mercinaria*, indigenous to the Atlantic coast of the United States. Depending on their size from small to large, they are known as littleneck clams, cherrystones, and chowder clams. They can be used in most clam recipes. Also spelled *quahaug*.

quail (US) A small migratory European game bird, *Coturnix coturnix*. The bird that is native to America, called a quail because of its resemblance to the European bird, is a bobwhite, *Colinus virginianus*. Served stuffed, with a sauce, or in an aspic.

quandong (Aa) A native fruit of Australia, similar to the peach in shape and size, but only the seed (quandong nut) is the edible part. Also spelled *quandang, quantong*.

Quargel (Gr) An Austrian sour-milk cheese with a red-brown skin, yellow to white inside, and a sharp, acid flavor.

Quark (Gr) Curds; a low-fat, fresh cottage cheese with a slightly sour taste; used in cooking.

Quarkauflauf (Gr) A cottage cheese soufflé.

Quarkklösse (Gr) Sweet dumplings of cottage cheese or pot cheese.

Quarkkuchen (Gr) Cream cheese cake.

Quark mit Früchten (Gr) Cottage cheese with fruit.

Quarkpfannkuchen (Gr) Sour cream pancakes.

quarter (US) One-fourth part of a meat

carcass, including a leg, the forequarter, or hindquarter. Quarter alone usually means the hindquarter.

quartirolo (It) A smooth, cream-colored cow's milk cheese made in Lombardy.

quarto de carneiro (Pg) Shoulder of mutton.

quasi (Fr) A thick piece from a loin end, often of veal.

quassia (Du) A flavoring in bitters, derived from the bark, root, or wood of a tropical tree, *Quassia amara*; used in tonic waters and apéritifs.

quatre épices (Fr) A mixture of four spices, usually ginger, nutmeg, cloves, and cinnamon; many formulas for the mixture and often more than four spices are used. The term is sometimes applied to the allspice berry and to the seeds of nigella.

quatre mendiants (Fr) An old-fashioned dessert plate of fruits and nuts, including dried figs, raisins, filberts, and almonds. The name comes from the four chief orders of the mendicant friars.

quatre-quarts (Fr) A cake with ingredients in four equal parts, similar to pound cake.

quattro stagioni (It) Describes a pizza with four filled sections representing the seasons: one of seafood, one of anchovies and tomato, one of cheese, and one of tomato, anchovies, capers, and oregano.

qubqub (Ar) A slender but succulent crab taken from the Arabian gulf.

queen conch (US) Helmet shellfish of tropical coasts; flesh used in chowders, seafood cocktails, and stews.

queen of puddings (GB) A baked pudding made with a bread crumb and custard base; spread with jam and topped with browned meringue.

queen olive (US) A variety of large Spanish olive with an elongated pit; usually pickled while green and used for eating, not in making olive oil.

queen scallop (GB) See **quin.**

Queensland nut (Aa) See **macadamia nut.**

queijadas (Pg) Small pastries with a filling like cheesecake.

queijinhos do ceu (Pg) Small confections similar to macaroons made with almonds, egg yolks, and sugar; rolled in powdered sugar.

queijo (Pg) Cheese.

queijo de minas (Pg) A bland, white cheese similar to mozzarella.

queijo de nata (Pg) A soft, creamy, fresh cheese.

queijo londrino (Pg) A dessert of egg yolks and sugar.

quelites (Sp) Greens.

quelites con chile ancho (Mx) Cooked greens with pureed ancho chili, onions, and garlic sauce.

quenelles (Fr) Dumplings made with minced fish or meat; bound with eggs and fat; poached; used in a variety of ways including as an entrée, a garnish, and in soups.

quenelles de brochet (Fr) Dumplings of finely minced, creamed pike.

quenelles de veau (Fr) Dumplings of minced veal.

quente (Pg) Hot.

quesadilla (Mx) Deep-fried or grilled tortillas folded in tubes or crescents;

filled with cheese and chili sauce or meat and beans; served as a main course or as a snack.

quesadillas de huitlacoche (Mx) Tortillas with a filling of a type of edible fungus from green corn.

quesadillas de pollo (Mx) Tortillas stuffed with chicken and cheese.

queso (Sp) Cheese.

queso al horno (Sp) Grilled cheese.

queso añejo (Mx) A strong flavored, white cheese made with skimmed cow's milk.

queso blanco (Sp) Any of fresh, white cheeses made from cow's milk. Also called **queso fresco.**

queso de almendra (Mx) A soft, almond-flavored cheesecake.

queso de cerdo (Sp) Headcheese.

queso del pais (Sp) A Puerto Rican white, semisoft pressed cheese.

queso de prensa (Sp) Pressed cheese; cottage cheese with the whey removed by pressure.

queso enchilado (Mx) 1. A sharp, aged, cow's milk cheese coated with red chili powder. 2. An enchilada made with cheese and red chilis.

queso fresco (Mx) See **queso blanco.**

queso fundido (Sp) Roasted cheese and chorizo on a corn tortilla and covered with salsa.

queso gallego (Sp) A medium soft cheese made in Galicia, Spain.

queso manchego (Sp) Ewe's milk cheese, a specialty of La Mancha, Spain.

queso rallado (Sp) Grated cheese.

quetsche (Fr) A sweet plum with yellow flesh used to make an Alsatian clear, colorless eau de vie and for cooking.

Quetschenkuchen (Gr) A tart made with quetsche plums.

queue (Fr) Tail.

queue de boeuf à l'auvergnate (Fr) Oxtail cooked in the style of Auvergne; braised in white wine and served with chestnuts and glazed onions.

queue d'écrevisses gratinée (Fr) Crayfish tails in an onion and cheese sauce.

queue de homard (Fr) Lobster tail.

queue de porc (Fr) Pig's tail; used in jellied and stewed dishes for its gelatin.

quiabo (Pg) Okra.

quibebe (Pg–Brazil) Stewed pumpkin with cured meat.

quiche (Fr) A pastry shell filled with a savory custard and other added ingredients; baked and served hot, as a first course or often as an hors d'oeuvre. Some dessert tarts are also called quiche.

quiche Alsacienne (Fr) Quiche made with onions.

quiche de jambon (Fr) Quiche made with ham.

quiche Lorraine (Fr) Quiche made with eggs, cream, cheese and bacon; said to have originated in Lorraine, France.

quick bread (US) See **soda bread.**

quick freeze (US) A food preservation process; rapid freezing forms ice crystals too small to damage cells so that color, flavor, and texture are retained.

quignon (Fr) Wedge-shaped piece of bread, usually the end crust.

quillet (Fr) A small sponge cake filled with an almond syrup and vanilla flavored cream and topped with an icing.

quimbombo (Cb) Okra.

quin (GB) A small, bivalve mollusk, *Chlamys opecularis*, of the scallop family; eaten raw or cooked. Also called **queen scallop.**

quince (US) A hard, acid, apple or pear-shaped yellow fruit of a small tree, *Cydonia vulgaris*; needs to be cooked to be edible; used in preserves or liqueurs. Also called **coing, marmelo, Quitte.**

quindims (Pg) A kind of coconut candy.

quinine (US) A bitter extract from the bark of a South American *Chinchona* bush; used in tonic water and other flavorings.

quinnat (US) See **chinook salmon.**

quinoa (Sp) A small, high-protein grain, *Chenopodium quinoa*, of the Andes; similar to millet in appearance with a bland, nutty flavor; used like barley or rice in porridge and bread.

quinquina (Fr) An apéritif of wine flavored with quinine.

quintal (Fr) A variety of cabbage.

quintoniles con chile mulato (Mx) Cooked greens with sauce of puréed mulato chilis, onion, and garlic; often garnished with hard-boiled eggs.

quisquillas (Sp) Shrimp.

Quitte (Gr) Quince.

Quittenkonfekt (Gr) Quince confection.

qursan (Ar) A lamb and vegetable mixture baked with alternate layers of bread.

raakapihvi (Fi) Beef tartare.

raastelautanen (Fi) Grated raw vegetables in salad.

raavilohi (Fi) Raw salted salmon.

rabacal (Pg) Ewe's milk cheese; soft, oily, pastelike.

rabakoz halkolbasz (Hu) Fish sausage stuffed in casings for grilling or boiling, or rolled in egg and crumbs and fried.

rabanetes (Pg) Radishes.

rábano (Sp) Radish.

rábano picante (Sp) Horseradish.

rabarbaro (It) Rhubarb.

rabarber (Sw) Rhubarb.

rabarbersuppe (Da) Rhubarb soup.

rabarbra (Nw) Rhubarb.

rabbit (US) A small mammal, member of the family Leporidae, including the cottontail, *Sylvilagus*; may be wild or domesticated; used fried, braised, stewed, and roasted. See also **hare.**

râble (Fr) The saddle or meaty part of the shoulder to tail of small animals such as rabbit and hare.

râble de lapereau (Fr) Saddle of young rabbit.

rabo de toro (Sp) Braised oxtail.

rabo sueco (Sp) Swede turnip, rutabaga.

racasse (Fr) A Mediterranean hogfish used in boullibaisse.

raccoon (US) A small mammal, *Procyon lotor*; the young sometimes eaten in the southern United States; prepared like rabbit and usually roasted.

račići (SC) Shrimp.

rack (US) The rib section or neck and forequarter of meat, particularly lamb and mutton.

rack of lamb (US) The entire rib section of lamb from which the crown roast and rib chops are obtained; may be roasted in one piece and cut into portions at the table.

rack steaming (US) A type of wet steaming in which food is placed on a perforated tray or rack a few inches above a pot of boiling water.

raclette (Fr) 1. A dish of Swiss origin in which a cut section of cheese is exposed to heat; the melted cheese is scraped onto a heated plate; served with boiled potatoes, chopped onions, and pickles. 2. The cheese used to prepare the dish.

racuszki (Po) Potato puffs; served with sour cream.

radicchio (It) A vegetable, *Cichorium endiva*, member of the endive family; looks like a small red cabbage; slightly bitter taste; used in salads and as a garnish.

radicchio di Treviso (It) A narrow, tu-

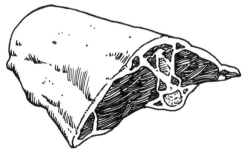

Rack of veal (double)

228

liplike chicory with pinkish, satiny leaves that taste like Belgian endive.

radicchio rosso di Verona (It) A red chicory eaten cooked or raw in salads. It is crisp, bittersweet, and resembles a small head of red cabbage.

Radieschen (Gr) Radishes.

radiki (Gk) Boiled greens served cold with a dressing.

radikia me ladi (Gk) Boiled dandelion greens.

radis (Fr) Radish.

radis beurre (Fr) Radishes with butter and salt.

radish (US) A pungent root vegetable, *Raphanus sativus*, with edible leaves; many varieties; color varies from white to red to black; small to huge in size; used in salads, cooked and creamed, as a relish, and as a garnish.

rädisor (Sw) Radishes.

rafano (It) Radish; horseradish.

rågbröd (Sw) Sour rye bread, sometimes with caraway seeds.

raggmunker (Sw) Potato pancakes.

ragi (Ia) A coarse millet grown in India and Africa; used in breads and other cereal dishes.

ragi dosas (Ia) Pancakes made with a batter of fermented millet.

ragnons de veau (Fr) Veal kidneys.

ragoût (Fr) A thick, highly seasoned stew made from browned pieces of meat, poultry, or fish; vegetables may be added.

ragoût chipolata (Fr) Stew of braised chestnuts, onions, mushrooms, and chipolata sausages in a wine sauce.

ragoût des pattes et boulettes (Fr) A stew of pig's knuckles and meatballs.

ragù (It) Meat stew or sauce with tomatoes, garlic, and herbs.

ragù di fegatini (It) Sauce with chicken livers.

rahkapiirakat (Fi) Cheese-filled buns.

rahkapiirakka (Fi) An open pie made with a sweet yeast dough (pulla) and a filling of curds, eggs, milk, and sugar.

rahkatorttu (Fi) Cheese torte made with lemon juice and jam or fruit.

Rahm (Gr) Cream.

raie (Fr) See **skate.**

raie au beurre noir (Fr) Skate fish poached in court bouillon; served with a black butter sauce containing capers.

raie fritte (Fr) Deep-fried skate.

raifort (Fr) Horseradish.

raifort sauce (Fr) A sauce made with horseradish, bread crumbs, cream, and vinegar.

rainbow trout (US) Food and game fish of Pacific coast streams. See **trout.**

raisin bark (US) Raisins embedded in sheets of bittersweet chocolate.

raisin sec (Fr) Dried grapes; raisins.

raisins (US) Sun-dried grapes; many varieties; used in baking, in salads, cooked dishes, and as a kind of fruit candy. See also **sultana.**

raisins (Fr) Grapes.

raisu (Jp) A modern Japanese word for rice. The traditional Japanese word is **gohan.**

raita (Ia) Thick yogurt usually spiced with cumin, coriander, and pepper and mixed with a chopped vegetable, such as cucumber, eggplant, spinach, or potato. Raita can also be made with a variety of fruit with mint. Served with curries or bread. Also spelled **rayta.**

raiton (Fr) Small ray (fish); usually skinned, floured, and fried.

raja gladka (Po) Skate.

rajas con crema (Sp) A dish made with strips of poblano chilies, cheese, cream, and onions.

rajas dalna (Ia) Red kidney beans with tomatoes, sour cream, and spices.

rajas de chili poblano (Sp) Strips of poblano chilies with cheese and tomato.

rajma dal (Ia) Curried red beans.

rajská omáčka (Cz) Tomato sauce.

rak (SC) Crab.

räkor (Sw) Shrimp, prawns.

rakørret (Nw) Fermented salmon trout; eaten with aquavit.

räksallad (Sw) Shrimp salad.

rakott burgonya (Hu) Casserole of layered potato slices and hard-boiled eggs topped with sour cream and bread crumbs.

rakott káposzta (Hu) Layered sour cabbage, ground pork, smoked sausage and onions; topped with sour cream and baked.

rakott metélt (Hu) Baked noodles with eggs, sour cream, cottage cheese, white raisins, nuts, and jam; served as a dessert.

ral-la (Ar) Fruit.

rambutan (In) A bright red tropical fruit, *Nephelium lappaceum*, similar to a lychee but with dense tendrils.

ramekin (US) A small lidless individual casserole.

ramen (Jp) Instant noodles; usually precooked wheat flour noodles.

ramequin (Fr) A toasted cheese snack; a small tart filled with cheese.

ramps (US) A North American wild onion, *Allium tricoccum*, similar to scallions in size, with flat leaves like leeks but which taper to a point; with a garlic flavor; used in fried eggs.

ranchero sauce (US) A barbecue or picante sauce made with chunks of salt pork, chopped tomatoes, onions, green peppers, and hot green chilies.

rancidity (US) A change in flavor and odor of a fatty food caused by exposure to oxygen in the air. The oxygen molecules combine with those of the fatty acids, changing their composition. Color changes in foods often accompany rancidity.

rane (It) Frogs.

rane in guazetto (It) Frogs' legs in a stew with garlic and tomatoes.

rántotta (Hu) Scrambled eggs.

rántotta zöldpaprikával (Hu) Omelet with green peppers.

rántott ponty (Hu) Fried carp dipped in egg and bread crumbs.

rántott sértes borda (Hu) Fried breaded pork chops.

rapa (It) Turnip.

rapanelli (It) Radishes.

rapaperikiisseli (Fi) Rhubarb soup.

rapa svedese (It) Swede turnip, rutabaga.

rape (US) A member of the cabbage family, *Brassica napus*, with edible leaves used like cress; the seeds are the source of rapeseed oil used in cooking and for salad dressings.

rape (GB) A wine vinegar made from the

Rape

grape cluster stalks and other refuse (pomace) of earlier wine making.

rapphöna (Sw) Partridge.

rapphøns (Nw) Partridge.

rapukeitto (Fi) Crayfish soup.

rårakor (Sw) Lacy potato pancakes made with grated raw potatoes and chives fried in butter.

rare (US) Meat that is not thoroughly grilled or roasted; meat cooked at a temperature of about 60°C (140°F).

rarebit (US) See **Welsh rabbit.**

rasam (Ia) A South Indian thin, hot-spiced lentil consommé; served with rice.

rascasse rouge (Fr) A silvery-rose Mediterranean fish, *Scorpaena scrofa*, considered an essential part of an authentic bouillabaisse. Also called **scorpion fish.**

rasgulas (Ia) A dessert of cottage cheese balls poached in syrup flavored with rose water.

rasher (GB) A slice of bacon or ham.

rasomalai (Ia) Sweetened cottage cheese balls served in a cream sauce flavored with almonds and rose water.

raspberry (US) The red, black, purple, or yellow fruit of a prickly shrub, genus *Rubus*, related to the blackberry; delicate flavor; eaten raw, in cobblers, pies, puddings, sorbets, syrup, and jam.

rasstegai (Rs) Literally, "unbuttoned"; a round meat pie with a hole in the center of the top crust so the filling is seen.

rasstegai s ryboi (Rs) A pie with a fish filling.

rassypchataia grechnevaia kasha (Rs) Fluffy buckwheat kasha.

rassypchatoe testo (Rs) Short pastry.

ratafia (GB) A liqueur used for flavoring made with an infusion of fruit kernels and bitter almonds.

ratafias (It) Small almond-flavored biscuits, like little macaroons.

ratatouille (Fr) Sautéed mixture of eggplant, zucchini, tomatoes, onions, green or red peppers, garlic, basil, rosemary, and thyme in olive oil; served hot or cold.

Rauhreif (Gr) A chilled dessert of grated raw apple and whipped cream.

rauwe biefstuk (Du) Raw beef; steak tartare.

rauwe haring (Du) Raw herring, eaten with onions.

rauwkostsla (Du) Raw vegetable salad.

rava idli (Ia) An egg-shaped cake made with coriander-flavored millet; filled with carrots and coriander leaves.

ravani (Gk) A cake made with semolina and honey.

ravenelli (It) Small radishes.

231

ravigote (Fr) A highly seasoned dressing or sauce: either a vinaigrette with capers and served with salads or cold meats; or a hot sauce with veal velouté in white wine and vinegar, served with meats, poultry, and fish.

ravioli (It) Small, usually square, pasta pockets filled with mixtures of meat, cheese, or vegetables; boiled and served with sauce or grated cheese; also used in soup.

ravut (Fi) Crayfish.

rawon (In) Diced beef in spicy black sauce.

ray (US) A boneless fish similar to the skate.

rayta (Ia) See **raita.**

razmaznia (Rs) A thin porridge of cereal and milk.

ražnjići (SC) Skewered spiced pork; kebab without vegetables.

razor clam (GB) A long narrow marine bivalve of the genus *Solen* with a curved shell. Also called *razor fish.*

rebā (Jp) Liver.

rebarbara es eper lekvar (Hu) Rhubarb and strawberry jam.

Rebhuhn (Gr) Partridge.

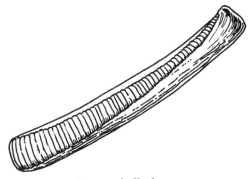

Razor-shell clam

Rebhuhner mit Weintrauben (Gr) Roast partridge with grapes.

Reblochon (Fr) A cow's milk cheese; golden-brown rind; light yellow paste, creamy texture; savory, semistrong taste.

reçel (Tr) Jam.

recheio (Pg) Stuffing; filling.

rečni rak (SC) Crayfish.

reconstitute (US) To bring food back to a natural or normal state, usually by adding water or liquid.

red bean (US) See **kidney bean.**

red bean sauce (US) A Chinese sauce made from mashed soy beans colored with red miso; used in poultry and meat dishes.

red beans and rice (US) A traditional Louisiana dish of red beans, onions, and bacon drippings boiled together and served over rice. Some of the beans are mashed to thicken the mixture.

red cabbage (US) A cruciferous vegetable of the *Brassica* genus with thick reddish leaves. It is cooked, eaten raw in salads, or used in pickling.

red cooked (US) A Chinese cooking method in which food is simmered in soy sauce until the liquid evaporates, leaving a reddish tinge on the food.

red currant (GB) The red fruit of a shrub (*Ribes rubrum*) that grows throughout Europe and North America. The fruit is used in jellies, jams, puddings, and beverages.

reddik (Nw) Radish.

red-eye gravy (US) A gravy made from the browned particles of a previously cooked ham steak in the bottom of a skillet. Water is added to the ham particles and the mixture is boiled briefly. Coffee may be added to darken the gravy.

redfish (US) A saltwater fish, red drum or channel bass, with a copper color.

red flannel hash (US) Cooked corned beef mixed with potatoes, beets, onions, and bacon drippings and cooked in a skillet until browned on both sides.

red herring (GB) Salted and smoked herring, giving it a red color.

ředkvička (Cz) Radishes.

red miso (Jp) A salty mixture of soybeans and rice allowed to ferment naturally for one to three years. The result is a deeply fragrant sweet protein food ranging in color from russet to dark reddish brown.

red snapper (US) A saltwater fish, genus *Lutjanus*, with a distinctive red skin; delicious white flesh; usually served broiled or baked with one or more kinds of citrus juice. A Chinese technique, called five-spice smoking, soaks the snapper in a spicy marinade before deep-frying.

reduce (US) To evaporate part of the water in a sauce or other liquid in order to thicken the fluid or concentrate the flavor.

reduced-calorie (US) A food-label term meaning a product has one-third fewer calories than comparable food preparations; proposed by the U.S. Food and Drug Administration for food labels.

reduced-fat (US) A food-label term that applies to foods with no more than half of the fat of a comparable product; proposed by the U.S. Food and Drug Administration for food labels.

reduced-sodium (US) A food-label term for a product that contains no more than half of the sodium of comparable food preparations; proposed by the U.S. Food and Drug Administration for food labels.

reduction (US) The product resulting from reducing the volume of a liquid, usually spiced, when making a sauce.

red wines (US) Wines that result when the crushed grape skins, pulp, and seed of red or purple grapes are allowed to remain with the juice during the fermentation period. The longer the fermenting juice remains with the skins, pulps, and seeds, the deeper the color of the wine. See also **rosé.**

refined (US) Pertaining to cooking oils, fats that have been treated with chemicals such as antioxidents, preservatives, and stabilizers. The oils can be used at higher temperatures than other oils without smoking.

refined cereal (US) A cereal grain that is mainly the starchy portion that remains after the outer layers containing the vitamins and minerals have been removed.

refined sugar (US) Table sugar, the portion remaining after the nonedible parts of beet sugar, sugarcane, or other natural sources of the sweetener have been removed.

reerug (Du) Venison.

refogado (Pg) Sautéed or served in an onion and tomato gravy.

refresh (US) To cool hot food quickly

by putting it in ice water or under running water; prevents overcooking.

refried beans (US) A Mexican dish of boiled beans, usually pinto beans, mashed and fried in oil. When leftover beans are served again, they are "refried" with a dry, nutty flavor and texture.

refritos (Mx) Refried, as with cooked, mashed, refried beans.

réglisse (Fr) Licorice.

Rehbraten (Gr) Roast venison.

Rehrücken (Gr) Saddle of venison.

Rehrücken mit Rotwein Sose (Gr) Saddle of venison with red wine sauce.

rehydrate (US) To restore fluids to foods.

Reibekuchen (Gr) Potato pancakes in the Rhineland.

Reiberdatschi (Gr) Potato pancakes in Bavaria.

reikaleipa (Fi) Sour rye bread with a hole in the middle so loaves can be strung on a pole for storage.

reine (Fr) A large chicken.

reine-claude (Fr) Greengage plum.

reine de saba (Fr) Cake of chocolate, rum, and almonds.

Reis (Gr) Rice.

rejer (Da) Shrimp, prawns.

reker (Nw) Shrimp, prawns.

relevé (Fr) The dish that replaces the soup or fish; usually precedes the entrée.

relevée, sauce (Fr) Ketchup.

religieuse (Fr) A cake made with cream-filled eclairs arranged in a pyramid on a pastry base; topped with a cream puff and piped with whipped cream.

relish (US) A condiment of highly fla-vored chopped pickles and raw vegetables served with a meal or used as an appetizer.

rellenong alimango (Ph) Stuffed crabs in the shells.

remis (In) Mussels. Also called **kepah.**

remis besar (In) Clams.

rémol (Sp) Brill.

Remoladensosse (Gr) Rémoulade sauce; also, tartar sauce.

rémoulade (Fr) A mayonnaise-based sauce with gherkins, capers, parsley, onions, tarragon, chervil, and anchovy; many variations; may include hard-cooked egg yolks, oil, vinegar, and sometimes mustard; used as a dressing for fish, shellfish, and salads.

rempah (In) Coconut fritters.

rempah-rempah udang (In) Shrimp and bean-sprout fritters.

rempejek (In) Peanut wafers or fritters.

rempejek bayam (In) Spinach fritters.

rempejek kedele (In) Soybean fritters.

renaissance, à la (Fr) A garnish of small mounds and groups of vegetables; usually arranged around roast meat or poached chicken; served with a sauce.

render (US) To melt solid animal fats with gentle heat.

renkon (Jp) Lotus root.

rennet (US) A preparation from the stomach lining of an unweaned calf or other animal that curdles milk; used in making curds and whey, cheese, and junket.

rennet pudding (GB) See **junket.**

rennin (US) An enzyme that curdles milk and makes it easier to digest. It is present in the stomachs of human infants and some young domestic animals. See also **rennet.**

rensdyrstek (Nw) Roast leg of reindeer.

renstek (Sw) Reindeer steak.

repa s sousom iz malagi (Rs) Turnips with Malaga wine sauce.

repôlho (Pg) Cabbage.

rétesh (Hu) Strudel.

Rettich (Gr) Radish.

retasu (Jp) Lettuce.

reteges sonkatorta (Hu) Boiled ham torte in puff pastry.

retinol (US) See **vitamin A.**

retsina (Gk) A Greek wine with a resin flavor, as from pine sap. The flavor evolved from a practice by Greek peasants of topping their containers of wine with pine pitch as a preservative.

Reuben sandwich (US) A sandwich of pumpernickel or rye bread with a filling of Swiss cheese and corned beef.

revani (Gk) A cake made with farina, orange juice, and almonds; topped with a lemon syrup.

revbensspjäll (Sw) Spareribs.

reveň (Cz) Rhubarb.

reverdine (Fr) A flavoring made with the angelica herb; used as an ingredient in certain brandies and liqueurs.

revithosupa (Gk) Chick-pea and onion soup.

rezanci (SC) Noodles.

Rhine wines (Gr) Very dry white wines produced along the northern Rhine River of Germany. The dryness is attributed to climatic conditions that restrict the level of sugar development in the local grapes.

Rhône wines (Fr) Wines produced from grapes grown in the Rhône River valley between Lyons and Avignon. The lighter wines are produced in the northern part of the region and the heavier types from southern vineyards.

rhubarb [US] The leaf stem of a plant, *Rheum rhaponticum*. The broad green leaves contain oxalic acid and are not eaten. The tart-flavored pink to red stalks are used as a fruit in pie, sauces, puddings, marmalade, and other dishes.

riabchiki pechonye v gline, na okhote (Rs) Grouse baked in clay.

rib chops (US) Good quality lamb or veal chops cut from the rack section.

rib eye (US) A small beef steak cut from the chuck section.

riboflavin (US) See **vitamin B$_2$.**

ribollita (It) A traditional soup of white beans, cabbage, chard, potatoes, and other vegetables with olive oil, cheese, and toasted bread.

rib roast (US) 1. Any part of the beef rib first cut with the bones intact, roasted

Rhubarb

235

or broiled. 2. One-half of a rack of lamb or veal for roasting. See also **rolled rib.**

ricciarelli (It) Almond cookies.

riccio (US) Sea urchin.

rice (US) A staple grain, *Oryza sativa*, with thousands of varieties. It was cultivated in China seven thousand years ago, introduced into Europe by armies of Alexander the Great, and brought to the Americas by Spanish explorers. Natural rice, also known as brown rice, is more nutritious and flavorful than polished white rice, which may also be enriched with otherwise missing nutrients. Soft rice varieties tend to become soft and expansive when cooked while hard varieties remain firm. Converted rice retains some of its bran while parboiled rice has been subjected to steam or water before milling. Wild rice (*Zezania aquatica*) is really not a rice but the seed of an aquatic grass. See also **long-grain rice, short-grain rice.**

rice miso (Jp) One of the three basic types of miso, classified according to the basic raw material, rice, barley, or soybeans. More than 80 percent of miso is made with rice.

ricer (US) A cooking utensil with small holes through which soft foods are extruded in bits the size of rice grains.

rice vinegar (US) A mild, slightly sweet vinegar, dark or light, used in Asian cooking for pickling, preserving, and souring.

rice wines (Jp) Alcoholic beverages made in China, Japan, and Hawaii by fermenting rice. Japanese rice wine (sake) is about 15 percent alcohol and is usually served warm with food. Two types of Chinese rice wines, yellow and white, are sweet, strong, and similar to sherries.

ricotta (It) A fresh, unripened cheese, white when fresh; originated in Italy as a whey by-product of provolone, mozzarella, or pecorino; now produced throughout the world and may contain whey from other cheeses.

ricotta salata (It) Ricotta that has been salted and dried until it is very firm.

rieska (Fi) Unleavened barley bread.

Riesling (Gr) A German dry white wine.

rigaglie (It) Giblets.

rigani (Gk) Oregano.

rigatoni (It) Large, ribbed macaroni.

rigatoni al forno col ragù (It) Rigatoni baked with a meat sauce.

rigatoni con salsiccia (It) Rigatoni with sausage, mushrooms, tomato, and cheese sauce.

Rigó Jancsi (Hu) A chocolate mousse cake named for a famous leader of a Gypsy band.

riisi (Fi) Rice.

riisimakkara (Fi) Rice and liver sausage.

riisipuuro (Fi) Creamed rice with an almond in it; the finder is the next to be married; a Christmas dish.

riivinkropsu (Fi) Grated potato casserole.

rijst (Du) Rice.

rijstpap (Du) Rice pudding with saffron.

rijsttafel (Du) Literally, "rice table"; an

Indonesian feast with a vast array of meat, fish, chicken, eggs, and vegetable side dishes using many herbs and spices and served with rice.

rillauds (Fr) Cubed pieces of fat pork from the belly or shoulder, salted and cooked in lard; served hot or cold; a specialty of Angevin.

rillettes (Fr) A spread made with pork, goose, rabbit, or poultry; cooked in lard, seasoned, and pounded to a smooth paste; sealed in small jars; served cold as an hors d'oeuvre on toast or on a sandwich.

rilletes d'oie (Fr) Goose spread.

rilletes de porc (Fr) Fried chopped pork intestines; chitterlings.

rillons (Fr) Pieces of pork belly or shoulder cooked like rilletes with the addition of caramel; a specialty of Touraine.

rimmad skinka (Sw) Salted ham.

Rinderrouladen (Gr) Rolled fillets of beef.

Rindfleisch (Gr) Boiled beef.

Rindfleischkochwurst (Gr) An air-dried sausage of minced lean beef with pork fat, coriander, and seasonings; boiled before eating.

Ringelblume (Gr) Marigold.

ringo (Jp) Apple.

riñones (Sp) Kidneys.

riñones al Jerez (Sp) Kidneys sautéed with Sherry.

riñones de ternera (Sp) Veal kidneys.

rins (Pg) Kidneys.

rins de vitela (Pg) Veal kidneys.

Rioja (Sp) A Spanish table wine.

ripa (Sw) Grouse.

ripieni (It) Describes food with a stuffing.

ripieni di castagna (It) Chestnut stuffing.

ripieno (It) Stuffed; stuffing.

rips (Nw) Red currants.

ris (Da, Nw, Sw) Rice.

ris (Rs) Rice.

ris de veau (Fr) Veal sweetbreads.

ris de veau archiduc (Fr) Veal sweetbreads prepared in a paprika and cream sauce.

risgrynsgröt (Sw) Rice pudding.

risi e bisi (It) Thick rice soup with peas, onions, bacon, and ham; sprinkled with Parmesan cheese; also, rice and peas with shredded lettuce.

riso (It) Rice.

riso al limone (It) Rice with lemon and cheese.

risotto (It) Rice sautéed with onion, then cooked by gradually adding broth; dishes vary with region.

risotto a Barolo (It) Rice cooked with Barolo red wine, meat stock, onion, butter, and Parmesan cheese.

risotto alla milanese (It) The most famous risotto; rice cooked in white wine with beef marrow and onions, flavored with saffron; chicken stock and chicken livers are sometimes substituted.

risotto al limone (It) Rice with lemon.

risotto con le seppie (It) Small squid cut in long strips and cooked in their own ink with rice onions, garlic, and fish stock.

risotto con scampi (It) A rice dish with prawns.

risotto e funghi (It) Rice with mush-rooms.

risotto marinaio (It) Rice with seafood.

risotto tortino (It) A rice cake filled with Gorgonzola and fontina cheeses.

risovye kotlety (Rs) Rice patties.

rissóis (Pg) Shrimp pies.

rissole (Fr) Sweet or savory turnovers of pastry with various fillings; usually deep-fried; served hot as appetizers, small entrées, or garnishes. Rissoles for desserts are prepared similarly but are garnished with jams, marmalades, or stewed fruit.

rissoler (Fr) To brown food slowly.

ristet brød (Nw) Toast.

ristras (Sp) Handstrung ropes of dried chilis, onions, and garlic cloves.

riz (Fr) Rice.

riz à l'impératrice (Fr) Molded Bavarian cream with candied fruits, rice, and Kirsch.

riz étuvé au beurre (Fr) Steamed and buttered rice.

riža (SC) Rice.

rizi (Gk) Rice.

rizogalo (Gk) Rice pudding served with milk and honey.

rizs (Hu) Rice.

rizsfelfújt (Hu) Rice soufflé.

roast (Fr) To make food ready for eating by exposure to heat, in an oven or before an open fire, usually with little or no moisture added.

roaster (US) A chicken, usually more than 13 weeks old, weighing 4 to 7 pounds, with tender flesh.

robalo (Pg) Sea bass.

robata (Jp) Open-fire cooking on a Japa-nese charcoal burner, usually with skewers.

robatayaki (Jp) Grilled food.

Robert sauce (Fr) A brown sauce with onion, white wine, and mustard; served with goose, pork, and venison; created by Robert Vinot, a seven-teenth century saucemaker.

robiola (It) Cheese made of sheep or goat's milk.

Rock Cornish hen (GB) A miniature chicken with a good quality of meat produced as a crossbreed between a Plymouth Rock and a British strain of Cornish hens.

rocket cress (US) See **arugula.**

rockfish (US) An edible fish of the bass family, *Morone saxatilis*, found in both the Atlantic and Pacific oceans; with lean, white flesh. Also called **striped bass.**

rockling (Aa) A small gadoid fish found in Australian waters.

Rock Point (US) A small salty oyster found on the Pacific Northwest coast.

rocky road (US) A confection flavor composed of chocolate, marshmal-low, and chopped nuts; applied in var-ious ice creams, candies, cakes, cookies.

rodaballo (Sp) Turbot.

rodbedesalat (Da) Beet salad.

rødbeter (Nw) Beets.

rödbetor (Sw) Beets.

rodekool (Du) Spiced red cabbage with red currants.

rode wijn (Du) Red wine.

rødgrød med fløde (Da) A pudding of boiled and strained red currants and raspberries, thickened with potato flour, flavored with vanilla and almonds, and served with sugar and cream.

rødgrøt (Nw) Fruit pudding.

rodovalbo (Pg) Turbot.

rödspätta (Sw) Plaice.

rødspette (Nw) Plaice.

rödvin (Sw) Red wine.

rodzynki (Po) Raisins.

roe (GB) The spawn of female fish or the milt of male fish. Also, the eggs contained in the ovarian membrane of a female fish, the swollen ovaries, or the expelled eggs. Milt is sometimes identified as soft roe and the eggs as hard roe. The roe of some species, such as the sturgeon, is prized as caviar. The roe of a lobster is called coral.

roereieren (Du) Scrambled eggs.

rogan josh (Ia) A North Indian lamb curry made with yogurt flavored with spices such as cardamom and cinnamon and sprinkled with coriander leaves.

roggebrood (Du) Rye bread; dark pumpernickel.

rognon (Fr) Kidney.

rognoncini trifolati (It) Sliced, sautéed veal or lamb kidneys.

rognoni (It) Kidneys.

rognoni di vitello (It) Veal kidneys.

rognons de veau (Fr) Veal kidneys.

rognons de veau à la moutarde (Fr) Veal kidneys with mustard sauce.

roblík (Cz) Crescent roll.

robliky (Jw) Crescent-shaped salt and caraway yeast rolls.

Robwurst (Gr) Smoked, cooked sausage.

rojoes comino (Pg) Braised pork with coriander, cumin, lemon, and white wine.

røket laks (Nw) Smoked salmon.

rollatini (It) Veal or chicken pounded thin, rolled, and prepared various ways.

rollatini di vitella al pomodoro (It) Stuffed veal rolls with tomato sauce.

roll, to (US) 1. To roll out with a rolling pin. 2. To roll a flat food into a tight, compact cylinder. 3. To coat.

rolled Boston butt (US) A boneless rolled ham roast from the shoulder butt.

rolled double sirloin roast (US) A special cut of veal made from two boneless sirloins rolled and tied.

rolled lamb shoulder (US) A deboned shoulder cut, rolled, shaped, and tied.

rolled oats (US) Oat flakes produced by steaming and rolling the groats with the hulls removed. Rolled oats usually refers to oatmeal. Chopped or coarsely milled whole oats may be identified as "steel cut," "oat grits," or "Scotch oatmeal."

rolled rib (US) A fully trimmed beef rib roast that has been rolled and tied.

rolled rump (US) A lean beef roast from the hip end of a round; commonly used for pot roasts.

rollmops (Gr) Butterfly fillets of herring, rolled around a stuffing of onion, gherkin, and spices; marinated in vinegar.

roll-ups (US) Any mixture of meat or vegetables or both with spreads and seasonings; rolled up in a tortilla.

rolpens (Du) Sliced pickled beef and tripe sautéed in butter; served with apple and red cabbage.

roly-poly pudding (GB) Sausage-shaped pudding made with suet-crust pastry; spread with jam and rolled; steamed or baked.

rom (Sw) Roe.

Romadur (Gr) A cow's milk cheese with brown or red rind, white, semisoft inside, and a strong taste.

romagnola, alla (It) Served with a tomato, garlic, and parsley sauce.

romaine (US) Crisp, long-leafed lettuce, used in salads. Also called **cos lettuce.**

romana, alla (It) Served with a seasoned meat sauce.

Romano (It) A somewhat sharp cheese, used most often for grating; originally produced around Rome.

Romanello (It) Literally, "little Romano"; an Italian grana, or grating cheese.

romarin (Fr) Rosemary.

rombo chiodato (It) Turbot.

rombo liscio (It) Brill.

romeritos (Sp) Greens.

romescu (Sp) A tangy sauce of wine vinegar, olive oil, almonds, tomatoes, and chili peppers.

rømmergrøt (Nw) A cream pudding made with flour, butter, milk, sugar, and a flavoring such as cinnamon.

rompope (Sp) An eggnog with ground almonds.

rookvlees (Du) Smoked beef.

room (Du) Cream.

roomsoezen (Du) Cream puffs.

rooz (Ar) Rice.

ropa vieja (Mx) Literally, "old clothes"; shredded beef cooked with onions, poblano peppers, garlic, black peppercorns, and lard; served in rolled flour tortillas.

Roquefort (Fr) A semisoft ewe's milk cheese; an ivory interior color marked by blue-green veins of mold; a sharp, salty but creamy taste.

Roquefort gougères (Fr) Cheese puffs made with Roquefort in egg dough pastry.

røræg (Da) Scrambled eggs.

rosbif (Fr, It, Sp) Roast beef.

rosbife (Pg) Roast beef.

rosca (Pg) Rusk.

rosca de los Reyes (Mx) Three Kings' bread; a traditional Mexican cake served on Twelfth Night, January 6; circular shape; garnished with candied fruits and nuts. Also called *kings' ring*.

rosé (US) See **rosé wine.**

rose hips (US) The fruit of the wild rose (*Rose canina*). Mildly sweet and tangy, the fruits are used in jelly, bakery products, and cooking.

rosemary (GB) An herb with a resinous aroma and piny taste; used sparingly fresh or dried in lamb, chicken, or veal dishes and with potatoes.

rosenkål (Nw) Brussels sprouts.

Rosenkohl (Gr) Brussels sprouts.

rose petals (US) Both wild and cultivated varieties of roses used in salads and main dishes; an infusion of petals sometimes used in desserts.

rosette (It) Soft, crusty rolls.

rosette de Lyons (Fr) Dry, mild, sweet but meaty French sausages; eaten uncooked.

rose water (US) A diluted essence of

Rosemary

roses used in desserts and sweets, particularly in the Middle East and India.

rosé wine (Fr) A generally dry and pink wine. It may be made from pink-fleshed grapes or from red grapes by allowing the wine to ferment on the red skins for a few days, then drawing off the liquid when the wine has absorbed the right shade of color from the skins.

rosin (Nw) Raisin.

rosmarino (It) Rosemary; often used to flavor lamb.

rosól (Po) Chicken.

rosolli (Fi) Beet and herring salad.

rosollikastike (Fi) A dressing of whipped cream colored with beet juice.

Rossini (Fr) Any of numerous dishes, including soups, named for the Italian composer; most are garnished with thin slices of sautéed foie gras and truffles.

rosso (It) Red.

rostat bröd (Sw) Toast.

rostbiff (Nw, Sw) Roast beef.

Rostbraten (Gr) Roast beef.

rösten (Gr) Broiling.

rostelyos (Hu) Braised, stuffed rolled beef.

Rostkartoffeln (Gr) Fried potatoes.

rösti (Gr–Swiss) A fried cake made from parboiled, shredded potatoes with onions or bacon. Also spelled _roesti_.

rosto (Gk, Tr) Roast.

roston (It) Braised veal or fowl with a sauce containing porcini mushrooms.

rōsuto bifu (Jp) Roast beef.

Röte Grutze (Gr) A cold dessert of stewed red berries such as raspberries with tapioca, whipped cream, and vanilla sauce.

roti (In) Bread.

roti (Ia) Unleavened tandoor-baked bread.

rôti (Fr) Roast.

roti bolu empuh (In) Soft rolls.

roti bolu keras (In) Hard rolls.

rôti de porc au lait (Fr) Roast pork with milk.

rôti de veau vinaigrette (Fr) Roast veal tenderloin, glazed, with a vinaigrette sauce.

roties (Fr) Buttered toast served at breakfast or with tea.

roti hitam (In) Dark bread.

roti putih (In) White bread.

rotisserie (Fr) Literally, one who roasts meats; a rotating spit for roasting meats or poultry.

Rötkohl (Gr) Red cabbage.

Rötkohl mit Apfeln (Gr) Red cabbage cooked with apples.

241

rotmos (Sw) Mashed turnips.

rotoli di manzo (It) Rolled fillets of beef.

rotoli di vitello (It) Rolled fillets of veal.

rotselleri (Sw) Celery root.

Rotwein (Gr) Red wine.

ròu (Ch) Meat.

ròu-bāu (Ch) Steamed pork-filled buns.

rouelle de citron (Fr) Round slice of lemon.

rouelle de veau (Fr) Fillet of veal.

rouget (Fr) Mullet.

rouget à la Bordelaise (Fr) Grilled red mullet; served with Bordelaise sauce containing white Bordeaux wine, shallots, and mushrooms.

rouget de roche (Fr) Mediterranean red mullet.

rouille (Fr) Literally, "rust"; a sauce with red peppers, garlic, bread crumbs, basil, olive oil, stock, and sometimes saffron; served with fish and seafood such as baked oysters.

roulade (Fr) Thin slices of veal rolled and stuffed with a variety of fillings and garnishes.

Rouladen (Gr) Rolled, stuffed slices of beef; often veal, braised.

round of beef (US) The leanest cut of the hind quarter of a beef carcass. The entire round may weigh 70 to 80 pounds, including the rump, which is separated from the top of the whole round. The remainder is divided into six sections: a top round, eye round, bottom round, top sirloin, shank, and heel.

ròu-pyàn (Ch) Cutlets.

ròu wán (Ch) Meatballs.

roux (US) A blended mixture of melted fat or butter and flour used to thicken gravies and sauces; may be white, blond, or dark depending upon the amount of time it is cooked; and thin, medium, or thick depending upon the amount of liquid added.

rovita jaja (SC) Soft-boiled eggs.

rowanberry (GB) The tart-tasting berry of the mountain ash, sometimes used in jellies and as a flavoring for game. Also called *ashberry*.

royal (Gk) A variety of Greek olive.

Royal Brabant (Bl) A Belgian cheese similar to Limburger.

royale, á la (Fr) Any of several types of garnishes for soups, often in the form of a molded custard.

rozbif (Tr) Roast beef.

rozbratie z cebula (Po) Sliced beef with onions.

roze (Ar) Rice.

Rube (Gr) Turnip.

rubiyan (Ar) A fat, pink shrimp from the Arabian Gulf.

rubra (It) Catsup.

ruby port (GB) A port wine that is usually of one vintage kept in a cask until it has become mellow, but sometimes may be a blend of several vintages.

rue (GB) A strong scented evergreen shrub with bitter leaves used as an ingredient of bitters and occasionally to flavor soups and stews.

Rüebli (Gr–Switzerland) Carrots.

rugbrød (Nw) Rye bread.

rŭ-gē (Ch) Squab.

Rübreier (Gr) Scrambled eggs.

ruiskorppu (Fi) Sour rye rusk.

rujak (In) A hot, spicy fruit and vegetable salad with a chili sauce.

rum (GB) An alcoholic beverage distilled from molasses or sugar cane juice. Raw rum is colorless but caramelized sugar or flavorings may result in various shades of yellow or brown.

rumbledethumps (Sc) A variation of Scottish colcannon made with mashed potatoes, diced cabbage, chives, and Cheddar cheese.

rump roast (US) A lean roast cut from the tail section of a beef round muscle.

runderrollade (Du) Rolled fillets of beef.

rundstykke (Nw) Hard roll.

rundvlees (Du) Beef.

runner bean (US) A string bean that is larger than the French snap bean. The pods are sliced and cooked along with the seeds. Also called *pole bean, scarlet runner*.

rusalda (Sp) Potato and leek soup with salt cod.

rusk (US) Slightly sweet, bread slices that are baked, dried, and rebaked until golden brown; zweiback is a rusk.

ruskistettua (Fi) Sautéed.

russel (Jw) Fermented beets; used in soup.

russet (US) A reddish or yellowish brown color. The term is sometimes used to identify a winter apple or a potato with that color.

Russian dressing (US) Salad dressing similar to Hollandaise sauce, made with mayonnaise, chili sauce, and a tangy ingredient such as horseradish or pickle. The traditional recipe called for caviar as an ingredient but this item is rarely included today.

russin (Sw) Raisin.

rusty dab (US) Flounder.

rutabaga (US) A turniplike root vegetable (*Brassica napobrassica*) with a strong taste. It is usually yellow to orange in color but one variety has white flesh. Also called **swede,** *Swedish turnip*.

rūz (Ar) Rice.

rūz abbyabd (Ar) White rice.

rūz billabun (Ar) Rice pudding.

ryba (Rs) Fish.

rybí filé (Cz) Fish fillet.

rybiz (Cz) Currants.

rybnaya ikra (Rs) A dish of mackerel or herring roe with lemon and salt.

ryby (Po) Fish.

ryby duzone w smietani (Po) Fish in sour cream.

rye flour (US) Flour made with rye; sold in four grades: *light rye*, pale flour that contains no bran; *dark rye*, contains bran and has a stronger flavor; *me-*

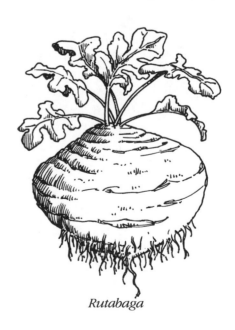

Rutabaga

243

dium rye, a mixture of light and dark rye. *Pumpernickel rye* contains more bran than dark rye.

rye whiskey (US) A whiskey made at least partly from rye grain mash. If the mash contains 51 percent or more, the product may be labeled "straight rye" whiskey.

rype (Da, Nw) Grouse.

ryyppy (Fi) Cold aquavit or vodka.

ryytikalasalaatti (Fi) A dressed salad of marinated fish, onions, beets, cucumbers, potatoes, and capers.

ryż (Po) Rice.

ryz do legumin (Po) A dessert made with rice, egg yolks, sugar, vanilla, and butter.

rýže (Cz) Rice.

rzodkiewka (Po) Radishes.

saag (Ia) Greens.

Saanen (Gr) A hard yellow Swiss cow's milk cheese.

saba (Jp) Mackerel.

sábalo (Sp) Shad.

sabanegh (Ar) Spinach.

saba no misoni (Jp) Stewed mackerel with soybean paste.

saba no suzuke (Jp) Pickled mackerel.

sabayon (Fr) See **zabaglione.**

sablé (Fr) Biscuits made with a rich, buttery dough.

sablefish (US) A large, fatty fish found off Alaska and Canada; white, buttery flesh.

sabljarka (SC) Swordfish.

sabores (Pg) Flavors.

sabzi (Ia) Vegetables.

sabzi bora (Ia) Vegetable croquettes.

sabzi ké katlét (Ia) Vegetable patties or cutlets.

sabzi kitchuri (Ia) Baked rice and lentils.

sabzi kofta kalia (Ia) Vegetable ball curry.

sacalate (US) A small flavorful panfish found in southern U.S. waters, dipped in milk and flour and fried or broiled.

sacarina (Pg) An artificial sweetener.

saccharin (US) A nonnutritional sweetener approximately five hundred times sweeter than cane sugar.

saccoula (Gk) Yogurt with all liquid drained through a fine sieve until it acquires the consistency of softened cream cheese.

Sachertorte (Gr) A rich, chocolate cake layered with apricot jam and covered with chocolate icing; named for its creator, Franz Sacher, who owned the Hotel Sacher in Vienna.

sack (GB) Originally a name used to identify white wines from Jerez, Spain, the term is now used interchangeably with sherry.

sacristain (Fr) A small almond flavored puff pastry tea biscuit.

saddle (US) A large cut of meat, often lamb or rabbit, including the unsplit back and the whole loin from each side of the animal.

sadziki (Gk) A dip made with chopped cucumber, garlic, dill, olive oil, vinegar, and yogurt.

safarjel (Ar) Quince.

safflower oil (US) An oil containing polyunsaturated fatty acids, made from the seeds of the safflower plant, *Carthamus tinctorius*; often mixed with other oils.

saffron (US) The dried, yellow-red stigmas of the flower, *Crocus sativus*; used, particularly in dishes of Spain and India where the flower grows, to give foods a pleasant briny taste and a strong, yellow color; because it is costly, turmeric is often used as a substitute.

safran (Fr) Saffron.

Safran (Gr) Saffron.

Saft (Gr) Juice, gravy.

Saftbraten (Gr) Beef stew.

Saftig (Gr) Juicy.

Saga Blue (Da) A cow's milk cheese; Brie with a blue mold; mild, piquant taste.

saganaki (Gk) An appetizer of floured fried cheese; served with lemon.

sage (US) An herb, *Salvia officinalis*, of the mint family; grey-green leaves when dried; pungent flavor; used to season pork, some fish dishes, salad dressings, cheese, and marinades.

Sage Derby (GB) A pale orange cow's milk cheese, marbled with green sage leaves.

sago (US) A dried, granulated starch prepared from the pith of several tropical palms of the *Metroxylon* family; used as a thickener in foods, such as pudding or soup. Also called **pearl sago.**

sago croquettes (US) A fried Creole fritter batter mixture with rice and sago marmalade.

sagu (In) Sago; tapioca flour.

sahlab (Ar) A hot milky drink flavored with nuts and coconut.

Sahne (Gr) Cream.

Sahnekäse (Gr) Cream cheese.

Sahnemeerrettisch (Gr) Horseradish.

Sahnenkuchen (Gr) A cream tart.

saignant (Fr) Bloody; lightly cooked, rare meat.

saigneux (Fr) Neck or scrag end of veal or lamb.

saim foogath (Ia) Green beans with grated coconut.

saimin (Pl) A Hawaiian stew of pork, raw shrimp, and noodles.

saim rasa (Ia) Green bean curry.

Sainte Maure (Fr) A goat's milk cheese; log-shaped with a slightly blue or white rind and smooth white interior; fresh, mild to piquant taste.

Saint-Germain, à la (Fr) In the style of Saint-Germain near Paris; with peas in the dish such as a thick, green pea soup; also, a garnish of pureed green peas.

Saint-Honoré (Fr) An elegant cake with cream (Chiboust or Chantilly) filling and a ring of small, sugar-glazed cream puffs.

St. John's Bread (US) See **carob.**

Saint Otho (Gr) A mild soft-textured, low-fat cow's milk cheese made in Switzerland.

Saint Peter's fish (US) See **John Dory.**

Saint-Pierre (Fr) See **John Dory.**

saisir (Fr) To sear, fry, or broil quickly.

saith (Sc) A soup made with young coalfish or codfish.

saithe (US) A dark variety of pollock (*Pollachius virens),* a distant relative of the cod.

saive (Ia) A savory or sweet snack made from vermicelli.

sajt (Hu) Cheese.

sajur (In) Vegetables.

sakana no teriyaki (Jp) Marinated broiled fish.

sakana ushojiru (Jp) Fish stock flavored with soy sauce, scallions, and rice wine.

sakana yaki (Jp) Broiled fish.

sake (Jp) Salmon. Also spelled **shake.**

sake (Jp) A colorless alcoholic drink called rice wine but more closely related to beer; usually served warm in tiny cups; also used as a tenderizer and flavoring in foods.

sake no oyakomushi (Jp) Steamed salmon with salmon roe.

sake-zushi (Jp) Boiled rice flavored with

sake; served with seafood and vegetables.

sakhar (Rs) Sugar.

sakurambo (Jp) Cherries.

sakuramochi (Jp) Bean-paste cake wrapped in a cherry leaf.

sal (Sp, Pg) Salt.

salaad (Ia) Lettuce.

salaatinkastike (Fi) Salad dressing.

salaatti (Fi) Lettuce; green salad.

salad (US) A dish often made with marinated vegetables and dressed greens; meats, eggs, seafood, cheese, or fruit may also be used. Many salads are not dressed, using only pungent or acid-tasting herbs. The word is derived from the Latin for salt, *sal*, the original dressing.

salada (Pg) Salad.

salada mista (Pg) Mixed salad.

salada praz (Bu) A salad or relish of chopped leeks, cooked mashed green peppers, and mashed black olives in a dressing of olive oil, paprika, and vinegar.

salada verde (Pg) Green salad.

salad burnet (US) An herb, *Sanguisorba minor*; green leaves taste of cucumber; used in fruit drinks and desserts.

salad dressing (US) A dressing usually based on mayonnaise, oil, vinegar, lemon juice, or yogurt.

salade (Fr) Salad.

salade de cresson (Fr) Watercress salad.

salade d'endive aux noix (Fr) Salad with endive and nuts.

salade d'épinards aux champignons (Fr) Spinach salad with mushrooms.

salade de fonds d'artichauts (Fr) Globe artichoke salad.

salade de pissenlits (Fr) Salad of dandelion greens.

salade de saison (Fr) Seasonal salad.

salade haricots verts (Fr) String bean salad.

salade mimosa (Fr) Green salad with sieved eggs, herbs, and a vinaigrette dressing.

salade niçoise (Fr) A salad of lettuce, eggs, black and green olives, green beans, anchovies, and sometimes tuna, tomatoes, and capers with an oil and vinegar dressing. Also called **insalata nizzarada.**

salade panachée (Fr) Mixed vegetable salad.

salade verte (Fr) Green salad.

salado (Sp) Salty, salted.

salad oil (US) An edible triglyceride oil that remains unclouded and pourable at temperatures slightly above freezing. It is usually made from a cooking oil by removing the portion that would become solid or crystalline at low temperatures.

salaka (Rs) Baltic herring.

salam (In) Laurel leaves; bay leaves. Also called *daun salam*.

salam (Tr) Sausage; salami or bologna.

salame (It) A variety of sausages; spiced pork sausage.

salame di fegato (It) Liverwurst.

salamette (It) Salami links.

salami (It) An air-dried, uncooked Italian sausage made of chopped beef or pork, or both, and flavored with red wine, garlic, and peppercorns. Most typical of the various salamis is the Genoa salami. Similar sausages are produced in other countries but most are smoked and less highly spiced. Also spelled **salame.**

salammbô (Fr) A small cake made of choux pastry filled with a Kirsch-flavored pastry cream; frosted with green fondant sprinkled with chocolate bits on one end.

salamoia (It) Brine; pickle.

salamon (Ar) Salmon.

salat (Nw) Lettuce or prepared salad.

Salat (Gr) Salad; lettuce.

salata (Ar) Salad.

salata (Tr) Salad.

salata (Po) Lettuce.

salata (Gk) Salad; often a mixed salad with greens, tomatoes, cucumbers, feta cheese, onions, green peppers, black olives, vinegar, and oil.

salataat (Ar) Dips, usually creamy.

salatagurker (Nw) Dill pickles.

salata khadra (Ar) Mixed salad of greens.

salátaleves (Hu) Lettuce soup with sour cream, vinegar, garlic, and dill.

salatalik (Tr) Cucumber.

salata melitzanes (Gk) Eggplant salad.

salata od morske ribe (SC) Seafood salad.

salata od piletine (SC) Chicken salad.

salátaöntet (Hu) Salad dressing.

salatet bataatis (Ar) Potato salad.

salatet tamaatis (Ar) Tomato salad.

salatet tayheenah (Ar) Sesame salad.

salat og tomater (Nw) Lettuce and tomatoes.

salátová marináda (Cz) Salad dressing.

salát z rajských jablíček (Cz) Tomato salad.

Salbei (Gr) Sage.

salça (Tr) Sauce, often tomato.

salchichas con judias (Sp) Small sausages with kidney beans.

salchichas en hojasd de maiz (Sp) Corn-husk sausages.

salchichón (Sp) Large sausage.

salchisa (Sp) Sausage.

salciccia (It) Sausage.

salcissa (It) Salami.

sale (It) Salt.

salé (Fr) Salted.

salep (Tr) A sweetened milk drink.

salers fromage (Fr) An untreated whole cow's milk cheese with a firm curd and strong flavor made in the Auvergne region of France.

salgado (Pg) Salted, salty.

salicoque (Fr) Prawn.

Salisbury steak (US) A large fried or broiled patty of ground beef mixed with egg, bread crumbs, onions, and seasonings. Named for a nineteenth century physician who advocated lean meat diets.

salladsås (Sw) Salad dressing.

Sally Lunn (GB) A bun leavened with yeast; split and layered with thick cream or butter; reportedly named for a girl who devised it and sold the bun on the streets of Bath, England.

Salm (Gr) Salmon.

salmagundi (GB) An elaborate salad with a colorful arrangement of pickled herring, chicken, beef, and various vegetables; served with a dressing of oil and vinegar.

salmagundi (US) A dish of chopped meat, eggs, anchovies, and onions served on lettuce with vinegar and oil.

salmao (Pg) Salmon.

salmi (Fr) Meat, often game, partially roasted, then stewed in wine.

salmi de canard sauvage (Fr) Salmi of wild duck.

salmigondis (Fr) A ragout of several reheated meats in a sauce.

salmon (US) A salt- and freshwater fish found in both the Atlantic and Pacific oceans, in rivers and landlocked lakes; with firm flesh, a rich distinctive flavor and a moderate amount of fat; the flesh color reflects the content of its diet. There are five different species of Pacific salmon: chinook with white to orange flesh; chum and humpback with pink flesh; sockeye with red flesh; and coho with red flesh but less fat content than sockeye. The Baltic salmon has a very light flesh color and a high fat content. Salmon is served in a variety of ways including poached, smoked, in quenelles, mousseline, and teriyaki.

salmon (Sp) Salmon.

salmonberry (US) A salmon-colored raspberry (*Rubus spectabilis*) that grows wild on the Northwest coast of the United States. It is related to the orange cloudberry (*Rubus chamaemorus*) that grows in the same area.

salmone (It) Salmon.

salmone affumicato (It) Smoked salmon.

salmon en salsa verde (Sp) Salmon with cilantro sauce.

salmonete (Pg) Red mullet.

salmonetitos (Sp) Fried baby red mullet.

salmon trout (US) A species of trout, *Salmo trutta*, in the salmon family with freshwater and saltwater varieties; prepared as for salmon.

salmuera (Sp) Brine.

salpicão (Pg) Smoked ham roll.

salpicon (Fr) Finely diced meat, fish, poultry, vegetables, or fruit bound with a sauce, syrup, or cream; used in small croustades, barquettes, and tartlets; as garnishes; and as stuffings for fish, game, and poultry.

salpicon de lengua (Sp) Cold tongue with vegetables.

salpicon de pescado (Sp) Red snapper hash cooked with pico de gallo.

salsa (It, Sp) Sauce.

salsa (Pg) Parsley.

salsa (Mx) Sauce; many variations combining fresh tomatoes, chilis, avocados, and other ingredients; most have a spicy heat; used with enchiladas, tamales, tacos, tortillas, meat, fish, chicken, and vegetables.

salsa alla milanese (It) A sauce of ham and veal cooked in butter with fennel and wine.

salsa bianca (It) White sauce; melted butter.

salsa borracha (Mx) Literally, "drunken sauce"; a sauce made with wine or other alcoholic beverage.

salsa casera (Mx) A mildly piquant sauce of tomatoes and chilis.

salsa cruda (Mx) Uncooked tomato sauce.

salsa d'acciughe (It) Anchovy sauce.

salsa d'aglio (It) Olive oil dressing.

salsa de chile guero (Mx) Cooked green chili sauce.

salsa de chile rojo (Mx) Cooked red chili sauce.

salsa di burro al gorgonzola (It) A sauce with Gorgonzola cheese and melted sweet butter.

salsa di carne (It) Meat sauce.

salsa di funghi (It) Mushroom sauce.

salsa di pignoli (It) A cream sauce with pine nuts.

salsa di pomodori (It) Tomato sauce.

salsa inglesa (Sp) Worcestershire sauce.

salsa tonnata (It) Tuna sauce sometimes served with cold veal.

salsa verde (It) Green sauce; usually made with parsley, garlic, capers, olive oil, and vinegar; served with fish or boiled meats.

salsa verde (Mx) Green sauce; usually made with tomatillos, fresh coriander, and serrano chilis.

salsicce (It) Highly spiced, cooked pork sausage.

salsicha (Pg) Sausage.

salsifis frits (Fr) Fried salsify.

salsify (US) A vegetable, *Tragopogon porrifolius*, related to lettuce; with long, fleshy, edible white roots; taste resembles oysters; used raw, boiled as a vegetable or used in savory dishes.

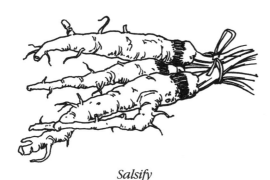

Salsify

Young leaves may be eaten in salads. Also called **oyster plant.**

salt (US) Sodium chloride; a condiment or food flavoring. Table salt, fine grained, contains a chemical, magnesium carbonate or calcium phosphate, to prevent absorption of moisture. Iodized salt has potassium iodide added; used for iodine deficiency. Sea salt, coarse grained, is produced from evaporating sea water. Kosher salt is fine grained sea salt. Pickling salt is pure salt without additives. Rock salt is large grained and unrefined. Flavored salt has herbs or other ingredients added such as garlic.

salt (Nw, Sw) Salt.

salteado (Pg) Sautéed.

saltfiskballer (Nw) Seafood fishballs.

salt-free (US) See **sodium-free.**

saltimbocca (It) Literally, "jump-in-the-mouth"; a dish with rolls of thinly sliced veal and ham, cooked in butter with fresh sage; then simmered in wine.

saltpeter (US) Crystalline potassium nitrate, a salty tasting food preservative sometimes used to treat processed meats.

salt pork (US) A cured belly cut of the hog; used primarily for flavoring and shortening.

salt-rising bread (US) A bread that is not leavened with yeast but depends instead on the fermentation of a mixture of salt, milk, flour, sugar, and corn meal.

sàltsa (Gk) Sauce.

salty dog (US) A cocktail of grapefruit juice, vodka, and salt.

salva (Pg) Sage.

salvia (It, Sp) Sage.

Salz (Gr) Salt.

Salzbrühe (Gr) Brine.

Salzburger Mozart Kugel (Gr) A confection of dark and light nougats and dark chocolate over a marzipan center; produced in Salzburg, Austria, to honor the eighteenth century composer.

Salzburger Nockerl (Gr) An Austrian dumpling.

Salzgebäck (Gr) Salty cracker; pretzel.

Salzgurken(Gr) Dill pickles.

Salzkartoffeln (Gr) Boiled potatoes.

samak (Ar) Fish.

samaki (Af–Swahili) Fish.

samaki wa changu (Af–Swahili) Bream.

samak meshwi (Ar) Grilled, marinated fish.

samak moosa (Ar) Sole.

sambal (In) A thick, fiery mixture of chili peppers and spices; used in sauces and dishes of meat, fish, eggs, chicken, or vegetables. Also spelled **sambol.**

sambal goreng daging sapi (In) Fried beef with sambal.

sambal goreng udang (In) Fried shrimp with sambal.

sambhar (Ia) Lentil or chick-pea (dal) dishes with a blend of ground hot spices, such as asafetida, cayenne pepper, fenugreek, and mustard.

sambol (In) See **sambal.**

sambusa (Af–Swahili) Meat patties.

sambusek (Ar) Small savory pies, usually filled with cheese and onions.

samek (Ar) Fish.

samfaina (Sp) A Catalan sauce of mixed vegetables, similar to ratatouille.

şam fıstığı (Tr) Pistachio nuts.

samin (Ar) Butter.

samneh (Ar) Clarified cow's or sheep's butter with a somewhat rancid flavor.

samosa (Ia) Deep-fried pastries filled with meat or vegetable mixtures. Also called **singara.**

samp (US) Coarsely ground corn meal; hominy grits.

samphire (US) An aromatic marine plant (*Crithmum maritimum*) with fleshy leaves, used in making pickles.

sampi (Fi) Sturgeon.

sämpylä (Fi) A roll.

Samsøe (Da) A Swiss-like cow's milk cheese originally produced on the Danish island of Samsoe.

sand bakkelse (Sw) Sand tarts of rich pastry in fluted tins; filled with custard, jam, and whipped cream.

sand cake (GB) A dry Madeira cake; a rich butter, sugar, flour, and egg cake with two layers of candied citron peel. It was created originally to be served with Madeira wine.

sande (Pg) Sandwich.

sandesh (Ia) Cheese fudge.

sandia (Sp) Watermelon.

sandkage (Da) Sand cake; pound cake.

Sandkuchen (Gr) Madeira cake.

sand pear (US) See **Asian pear.**

sandra (Fr) A pike perch. Also called **zander.**

sandwich (GB) A portable meal on bread named for John Montagu, 4th Earl of Sandwich, and said to be originated by his chef.

sandwich (US) A thin cut of beef steak from the sirloin, round, or chuck, for pan broiling.

251

sang, au (Fr) A sauce made from the blood of the animal used.

sangaree (US) See **singaree.**

sang chu (Kr) A traditional Korean dish of rice, tofu or meat, vegetables, and spices, wrapped in a lettuce leaf.

sanglier (Fr) Wild boar.

sangrento (Pg) Rare (meat).

sangria (Sp) A fruit-flavored wine punch; usually made with red wine but white wine may also be used.

sangrita (Sp) A cold drink of orange, tomato, and lemon juices, spiced with hot pepper sauce and green onions.

sangsun hwe (Kr) A Korean form of sashimi.

sangue (It) Rare (meat).

sanguinaccio (It) Blood sausage.

San Pedro (Sp) St. Peter's fish; John Dory.

sansai (Jp) Wild mountain vegetables.

sansho (Jp) A fragrant, brown-green pepper made from the seed pods of the sansho tree, native to Japan.

santaka (Jp) A small, hot to very hot, Japanese dried chili pepper, orange to red in color.

santan (In) Coconut milk.

santaraa (Ia) Orange.

santen (In) Coconut milk.

santola (Pg) Spider crab.

santola gratinada (Pg) Deviled crab.

saos (In) Sauce.

sap (Du) Juice.

sapodilla (US) An apricot-size fruit with brown flesh. Also called **sawo.**

saporoso (It) Relish.

Sapsago (Gr) A hard greenish Swiss grating cheese made from skimmed cow's milk. The green tint is attributed to a special clover fed the cows. Also called **Schabzieger.**

sapsis (US) A bean porridge.

sapucaya nut (Pg) A sweet oily nut produced by a South American tree (*Lecythis sabucajo*). It is related to the Brazil nut and used in candy making.

Saracen corn (US) See **buckwheat.**

sarada yu (Jp) Salad oil.

Sarah Bernhardt cookie (US) A macaroon with a filling of cream and chocolate and coated with chocolate.

sarang burang (In) See **bird's nest.**

şarap (Tr) Wine.

sarapatel (Pg) Liver and bacon.

Saratoga chips (US) See **potato chips.**

Saratoga chops (US) Deboned, rolled lamb shoulder chops.

sarcelle (Fr) Wild duck; teal.

sard (Fr) A saltwater fish related to the sea bream.

sarda (Pg) Mackerel.

sardalya (Tr) Sardines.

sardalya tavasi (Tr) Fried sardines.

sardeen (Ar) Sardine.

Sardellen (Gr) Anchovies.

sarden (In) Sardines.

sardheles (Gk) Sardines.

sardiini (Fi) Sardine.

sardin (Sw) Sardine.

sardine (It) Sardines.

Sardinen (Gr) Sardines.

sardiner (Nw) Sardines.

sardines (US) A number of small, silvery, soft-boned fish including herring, sprat, pilchard, and alewife.

sardinha (Pg) Sardine.

sardinhas de caldeirada (Pg) Boatman's stew.

Sardo Romano (It) A Romano-type cheese produced in Sardinia.

sardynka (Po) Sardine.

sárgabarack (Hu) Apricot.

sárgadinnye (Hu) Cantaloupe.

sárgarépa (Hu) Carrots.

šargarepe (SC) Carrots.

sarma (SC) Stuffed cabbage.

sarmi (Bu) Small meat-stuffed cabbage rolls.

sāroin (Jp) Beef sirloin.

sarriette (Fr) See savory.

sarsaparilla (Sp) A carbonated drink made with an extract of the roots of a tropical American woody vine (*Smilax*).

sarson kaa saag (Ia) Mustard greens.

sås (Sw) Sauce.

sashimi (Jp) Literally, "pierced fish"; bite-size cuts of raw fish or seafood dipped in soy sauce; served with grated daikon or wasabi.

sassafras (US) A small North American tree (*Sassafras albidum*) with aromatic roots, leaves, and bark. Sassafras bark is the source of safrole flavoring agent, and the leaves are dried and powdered to make filé, a Creole seasoning.

sassafras mead (US) A Creole summer drink made from sassafras roots, honey, molasses, cream of tartar, and soda water.

sassefrica (It) Salsify.

satay (In) See **saté.**

saté (In) National dish of Indonesia; skewered strips of meat or fish coated with spices and grilled; served with a spicy-sweet peanut sauce. Also spelled **satay.**

saté ajam (In) Broiled spicy chicken cooked and served on skewers.

satō (Jp) Sugar.

satoimo (Jp) Taro root.

satsuma (US) A small orange with loose skin, grown in the southeastern United States.

satsuma age (Jp) Fried patties of ground fish, wheat flour, carrots, burdock root, and sake.

satsuma imo (Jp) Sweet potato.

saturated fat (US) A food fat composed of saturated fatty acids. As a rule of thumb, a fat that is solid at room temperature is a saturated fat. Most animal fats, butter, and margarine contain saturated fatty acids.

saturated fatty acid (US) See **fatty acids.**

Saubohnen (Gr) Broad beans.

sauce (US) Any liquid or soft food preparation intended to be served with other foods as a garnish. It may contain meat, vegetable, or fruit and is commonly identified with a main ingredient, such as cheese sauce or egg sauce.

sauce piquante de soya (Fr) Soy sauce.

saucijsjes (Du) Sausages.

saucijzenbroodje (Du) Sausage patty in a pastry roll.

saucisse (Fr) Very small sausages.

saucisses au vin blanc (Fr) Sausages with white wine.

saucisson (Fr) Large sausage; sliced for serving.

saucisson à l'aioli (Fr) Garlic sausage.

Sauerampfer (Gr) Sorrel.

Sauerbraten (Gr) Braised marinated beef; various marinades are used, such as red wine and vinegar, beer, or lemon and sour cream; other ingredients may be added, such as gingersnaps or dried fruits and nuts; often served with dumplings and red cabbage.

Sauerkraut (Gr) Chopped cabbage that has undergone lactic acid bacteria fermentation in a mixture of salt and spices. The natural sugars in the cabbage leaves are converted to lactic and acetic acids, ethyl alcohol, and carbon dioxide. The acids prevent the growth of organisms capable of food spoilage.

Sauerkraut mit Schweinebauch (Gr) Sauerkraut with pig's belly.

Sauermilchkäse (Gr) An Austrian low-fat firm cheese.

sauge (Fr) Sage.

saumon (Fr) Salmon.

saumon d'Ecosse fumé (Fr) Smoked Scottish salmon.

saumon en gelée (Fr) Salmon in aspic.

saumon fumé (Fr) Smoked salmon.

saumon glacé (Fr) Salmon in aspic; served cold.

saumon poché (Fr) Poached salmon.

saumure (Fr) Brine.

saunamakkara (Fi) Literally, "sauna sausage"; sausages cooked in foil in the sauna.

saunf (Ia) Anise; fennel.

Saure Rahmsauce (Gr) Sour cream sauce.

Saure Sahne (Gr) Sour cream.

sauro (It) Sorrel.

saus (Nw) Sauce.

saus (Du, In) Sauce.

sausage (US) A finely ground mixture of pork and other meats stuffed in cas-

ings; highly seasoned; used fresh or cured.

saussiski v tomate (Rs) Sausages with tomato sauce.

sauté (US, Fr) To fry quickly over a moderately high heat in a little butter, oil, or other fat, turning frequently.

sautérat (Sw) Sautéed.

sautiert (Gr) Sautéed.

sauvage (Fr) Wild, undomesticated.

savanyú káposzta (Hu) Sour cabbage; sauerkraut.

savarin (Fr) Rich yeast cake soaked in liqueur-flavored syrup; many variations; served hot or cold.

sável (Pg) Shad.

savoiardi (It) Ladyfingers.

savory (US) Food that is not sweet.

savory (US) An herb with an aroma resembling both mint and thyme. Two main varieties are summer savory, used in cooking, and winter savory,

Savory

used in marinades and flavorings. Also called **sarriette.**

savouries (GB) Appetizers; snacks; antipastos.

savoyarde (Fr) Pertaining to egg dishes and others involving a gratin of potatoes with milk and cheese.

savoy biscuits (GB) Small sponge cakes.

savoy cabbage (Fr) A dark green cabbage with curly leaves.

savu (Fi) Smoked.

savukala (Fi) Smoked fish.

savukalasalaatti (Fi) Smoked fish salad.

savusiika (Fi) Smoked whitefish.

savusilakka (Fi) Smoked Baltic herring.

sawi (In) Chinese cabbage; white cabbage.

sawo (In) See **sapodilla.**

saya éndo (Jp) A variety of podded peas.

sayoo chatni (Ia) Apple chutney.

sayur (In) Vegetables.

sayur kuning (In) Spicy vegetable and meat stew colored yellow with turmeric.

sazené v mléku (Cz) Poached.

sbanikh (Ar) Spinach.

sbrinz (It) A hard Swiss cheese that is aged for two to three years. It is basically a Parmesan-type grating cheese but shaving it onto buttered black bread is also a popular use.

sbrisolona (It) A cake of white and corn flour, flavored with chopped almonds.

scadán (Ir) Herring.

scald (US) 1. To bring milk up to temperature of 82°–85°C (180°–185°F) to kill microorganisms. 2. To pour boiling water over a food. 3. To heat almost to boiling.

scallions (US) Small green or spring onions; or shoots of immature white onions; used as a garnish or in soups, salads, and stir-fry dishes.

scallop, to (US) To oven-cook vegetables in milk or béchamel sauce.

scalloped veal (US) Small, very thin slices of boneless veal, generally cut from the leg, rib, loin, or shoulder.

scallops (US) Bivalve mollusks with fan-shaped shells; many species including the bay, sea, and calico scallops. The cream-colored adductor muscle is most commonly eaten; the red "coral" or "tongue" is included in Europe. Used broiled, marinated in wine, baked, grilled, or eaten raw.

scaloppine (It) Thin slices of meat, usually veal cutlets.

scaloppine al funghi (It) Veal cutlets with mushrooms.

scaloppine al sedano (It) Veal cooked in butter with prosciuto and celery.

Scamorze (It) A water buffalo's milk cheese sold in white or yellow ovals; chewy, mild, slightly salty; sometimes

Scallop

255

smoked; served sliced in olive oil. It may be made from cow's milk.

scampi (It) Large prawns prepared in many styles and served in soups and sauces.

scampi (US) A term used for shrimp cooked in garlic sauce.

scampi fra diavole (It) Shrimp in a spicy tomato sauce.

Scanno (It) A buttery-textured Italian sheep's milk cheese.

scarola (It) Escarole.

scarpariello, alla (It) "Shoemaker style"; sautéed with sausage.

scarzetta (It) Zest.

scate (Sc) Poached codfish served with mustard sauce and parsley.

Schabzieger (Gr) See **Sapsago.**

Schalotten (Gr) Shallots.

Schaltiere (Gr) Shellfish.

schapevlees (Du) Mutton.

scharf (Gr) Spicy.

Schaschlik (Gr) Kabobs.

Schaum (Gr) Foam, froth, mousse.

Schaumrollen (Gr) Puff pastry rolls filled with whipped cream.

Schaumwein (Gr) Champagne, sparkling wine.

Schellfisch (Gr) Haddock.

schelvis (Du) Haddock.

schelviskuitjes (Du) Haddock roe.

schelvislever (Du) Haddock milt.

schiacciata (It) Crushing; a kind of flat cake or bread.

Schildkrötensuppe (Gr) Turtle soup.

Schinken (Gr) Ham.

Schinkenfleckerl (Gr) Ham and eggs with baked pasta.

Schinkenomelette (Gr) Ham omelet.

Schlachtplatte (Gr) Boiled meats or liver sausage with dumplings and sauerkraut.

Schlag (Gr) Cream; usually whipped.

Schlagobers (Gr–Austria) With whipped cream.

Schlagsahne (Gr) Whipped cream.

Schlegel (Gr) Drumstick.

Schlesisches Himmelreich (Gr) Literally, "Silesian heaven"; pork with dried fruits.

Schlosser Buben (Gr–Austria) Literally, "locksmith's boys"; a sweet made with chocolate and sugar coated dough stuffed with almond and dried plums.

Schmalz (Gr) Melted fat, lard.

Schmalzgebackenes (Gr) Lard-fried pastries.

Schmandschinken (Gr) Ham cooked with onions and sour cream.

Schmarrn (Gr) Omelet.

Schmierkäse (Gr) A cream cheese that may or may not be rich in cream.

Schmorfleisch (Gr) Spiced meat.

Schnäpel (Gr) Trout.

Schnaps (Gr) Alcoholic spirits; gin, brandy, liqueur.

Schnecken (Gr) 1. Snails. 2. Coiled yeast buns topped with cinnamon.

Schneenockerln (Gr) Sweet dumplings with egg custard.

Schnittbohne (Gr) French bean.

Schnitte (Gr) A chop or steak.

Schnittlauch (Gr) Chives.

Schnitz (Gr) Slice, cut, chop, steak.

Schnitzel (Gr) Cutlets.

Schnitzel Holstein (Gr) Veal cutlet with fried egg and anchovies.

Schnitz und Gnepp (Gr) Dried apples and raised dumplings. Also spelled *Schnitz un Knepp*.

Schnupfnudel (Gr) A large noodle.

Schokolade (Gr) Chocolate.

Schokoladeneis (Gr) Chocolate ice cream.

schol (Du) Flounder.

Scholle (Gr) Sole.

Schöpsenschlegel (Gr) Roast leg of lamb.

Schotensuppe (Gr) Fresh green pea soup.

Schrotbrot (Gr) Whole wheat bread.

Schüblig (Gr) A sausage.

schuimpjes (Du) Meringue.

Schulter (Gr) Shoulder.

Schupfnudeln (Gr) Thick noodles.

Schutzenkäse (Gr) An Austrian cheese type between Brie and Limburger.

Schwämme (Gr–Austria) Mushrooms.

Schwärtelbraten (Gr) Roast leg of pork.

Schwarzbrot (Gr) Black bread.

Schwarzer Kaffee (Gr) Black coffee.

Schwarzfisch (Gr) Carp.

Schwarzsauer (Gr) Goose giblet stew.

Schwarzwälder Kirschtorte (Gr) Black Forest cherry cake.

Schwarzwürste (Gr) Black sausage.

Schwarzwurzeln (Gr) Salsify; oyster plant.

Schweinebauch (Gr) Pork belly.

Schweinebraten mit einer Kruste (Gr) Roast pork in a crust.

Schweinebrust mit Apfeln (Gr) Breast of pork with apples.

Schweinefleisch (Gr) Pork.

Schweinefleisch im bier (Gr) Pot roast of pork in beer.

Schweinekeule (Gr) Leg of pork.

Schweinekotelett (Gr) Pork chop.

Schweineohren (Gr) Pig's ears, usually stewed with sauerkraut.

Schweinepfeffer (Gr) Spicy pork.

Schweinerippchen (Gr) Pork spareribs.

Schweinerucken (Gr) Pork tenderloin.

Schweineschenkel (Gr) Roast pork leg.

Schweinsfilets mit Saure Sahne (Gr) Fillets of pork in sour cream.

Schweinsjungfernbraten (Gr) Roast young pig.

Schweinskarre (Gr) Smoked pork chops.

Schweins sulz (Gr–Austria) Pork aspic; often served cubed.

Schweizerkäse (Gr) Swiss cheese.

Schwertfisch (Gr) Swordfish.

sciroppo (It) Syrup.

scone (Sc) A small cake made with flour, bicarbonate of soda, and buttermilk; often flavored with spices and molasses; cooked on a griddle; served with butter and jam.

score (US) To cut narrow slits on the surface of a food.

scorpion fish (US) See **racasse rouge.**

scorzonera (Sp) An herb, *Scorzonera hispanica*, with long, slender black-skinned roots; white flesh; used like salsify or parsnips. Also called **black salsify.**

Scotch broth (Sc) A soup of barley, mutton, and chopped vegetables. Also called *Scots broth.*

Scotch eggs (Sc) Hard-cooked eggs encased in sausage, rolled in cracker crumbs, and fried. Also called *Scots eggs.*

Scotch tender (US) A roasting filet from the center section of a beef chuck.

Scotch woodcock (Sc) Thickened egg yolk and cream mixture poured over anchovy toast.

scottadito (It) Literally, "burnt fingers";

grilled lamb cutlets, eaten as finger food.

scramble (US) To cook eggs while mixing yolks and whites.

scrapple (Gr) A chilled mixture of pork, corn meal, and spices, cut into slices and fried.

scripture cake (US) A cake made with ingredients cited in the Bible, such as "butter . . . Psalms 55:21."

scrod (US) A name used for any small or young nonoily white fish of the cod family; a delicate flavor and often poached.

sculpin (US) Any of a variety of small scaleless saltwater fishes.

scungilli (It) Conch, a shellfish; may be boiled and served with a hot sauce.

scup (US) See **porgy.**

scuppernong (US) 1. A sweet yellowish-green muscadine grape. 2. The name of a wine made from the grape.

sea bass (US) See **black sea bass.**

sea bean (GB) A small shellfish.

sea biscuit (US) Hardtack.

sea-bob (US) Shrimp.

sea bream (US) Several species of fish with gold or silvery scales; served whole or in fillets; broiled, roasted, steamed, or poached. Also called **daurade, tai.**

sea cucumber (US) A marine animal with a long wormlike body (*Holothuroidea*) found in coastal waters and used in Oriental cooking. Also called **bêche de mer, sea slug.**

sea dates (It) Small date-shaped shellfish found on the Italian coast.

sea ear (US) See **abalone.**

sea fennel (US) See **samphire.**

seafood (US) Any marine aquatic foods, including fin fish, shellfish, and vegetable matter, such as seaweed.

sea kale (US) A cruciferous family herb that grows along the European coast. Its shoots are cooked like asparagus and the edible leaves are used in salads.

sea moss (US) Irish moss.

sea pie (US) A beef stew with dried apples, molasses, and a suet crust.

sear (US) To brown the surface of a food using a small amount of fat in the pan or using intense or direct heat.

sea salt (US) A table salt produced by evaporating sea water.

sea slug (US) See **sea cucumber.**

seasnails (US) A group of marine gastropods, including conches, tritons, and whelks, used in chowders.

seasoned salts (US) Salts made with powdered vegetables or spices, such as celery salt.

seasoning (US) Herbs, spices, salts, or other flavorings added to foods to make them tastier.

sea swallow (GB) See **flying fish.**

sea tongue (US) A red seaweed, *Gigartina corymbifera*, with a good flavor and texture; often fried in batter.

sea trout (US) See **weakfish.**

sea urchin (US) An edible spiny creature of the Atlantic Ocean; its orange ovaries are eaten, usually in omelets or lemon juice.

seaweed (US) Any marine vegetable, such as dulse, sea tongue, carragheen, and laver.

seaweed bread (US) See **pain des algues.**

seb chatni (Ia) Apple chutney.

sebze (Tr) Vegetables.

sebze çorbasi (Tr) Vegetable soup.

sec (Fr) Dry.

šećer (SC) Sugar.

séché (Fr) Dried.

séco (Pg) Dried.

sedano (It) Celery.

sedano-rapa (It) Celeriac.

seeg (Rs) Smoked fish.

seekh kabab (Ia) A meat preparation threaded on an iron skewer or rod called a seekh.

Seekrabben (Gr) Crabs.

Seelachs (Gr) Smoked coalfish.

See-ohr (Gr) Ormer; abalone.

seesehr (Tr) Chick-peas.

seesehri aghtsan (Tr) Chick-pea salad.

Seezunge (Gr) Sole.

sefrina (Ar) Beef stew with chick-peas, saffron, and ginger.

şeftali (Tr) Peach.

segala (It) Rye.

sehr (Tr) Cream.

şehriye çorbasi (Tr) Vermicelli soup.

seigle (Fr) Rye.

sekahedelmakeitto (Fi) Dessert soup of mixed dried fruits.

sekahedelmakiisseli (Fi) Cold fruit pudding.

sekaná pečeně (Cz) Meat loaf.

sekané (Cz) Chopped.

şeker (Tr) Sugar; candy.

sekihan (Jp) Red beans and rice.

seksu (Ar) Couscous.

Sekt (Gr) Champagne, dry wine.

sel (Fr) Salt.

sel'd' (Rs) Herring.

selderie (Du) Celery.

seleek (Ar) Lamb stewed with milk, onions, and rice.

self-rising flour (US) Flour that is premixed with salt and baking powder so the dough will rise during the baking process.

selha chawal (Ia) Converted rice.

selino avgolemono (Gk) Cooked celery with egg and lemon sauce.

selinon me ladi (Gk) Knob celery (celeriac) fried in olive oil and lemon juice, then simmered.

Selkirk bannock (Sc) A pastry made of baker's dough, butter, lard, sugar, seedless raisins, and candied citrus peel.

selle (Fr) The saddle of an animal, from the last rib to the leg.

selle d'agneau (Fr) Saddle of lamb.

selle de pre-salé desosée (Fr) Saddle of boned lamb.

selleri (Nw) Celery.

selleri (Fi) Celery.

Sellerie (Gr) Celery.

Selleriesalat (Gr) Celery salad.

Selles-sur-Cher (Fr) A generally piquant French goat's milk cheese.

selodka (Rs) Salt herring.

selters (Nw) Mineral water.

seltzer (US) Ordinary water that has been carbonated with carbon dioxide. Also called **soda water.**

selvaggina (It) Game; venison.

sém (Ia) Green beans.

sembei (Jp) Rice wafers; often named for their assumed shapes and according to ingredients added, such as seaweed or egg.

sëmga (Rs) Salmon.

semi di melone (It) Tiny pasta shapes called melon seeds; used in soup.

semifreddo (It) Literally, "half frozen"; frozen desserts.

semifrio (Sp) Semifreddo.

semillas (Sp) Seeds.

semillas tostados de calabaza (Sp) Roasted pumpkin seeds, popular snack food.

semimoist foods (US) Foods that contain moderate levels of moisture, generally less that 50 percent, and can be stored without refrigeration.

semisweet chocolate (US) A form of chocolate with a minimum chocolate liquor content of 35 percent and less than 12 percent milk solids.

semlor (Sw) Buns made with almond paste eaten during Lent.

semmel (US) Pennsylvania Dutch breakfast roll.

Semmelklosse (Gr) Bread dumplings.

Semmelknodel (Gr) Bavarian dumplings.

semolina (US) A flour or meal of finely ground inner kernels of durum wheat; used commercially for pasta including Greek orzo and North African couscous. When cooked it has a texture like porridge. Coarsely ground rice or corn flour is sometimes called semolina.

semur (In) Smothered.

semur ayam (In) Chicken in soy sauce.

semur lidah (In) Boiled tongue in soy sauce.

semur terong (In) Eggplant in soy sauce.

senap (Sw) Mustard.

senape (It) Mustard.

senf (SC) Mustard.

Senf (Gr) Mustard.

Senfgurken (Gr) Yellow cucumber pickles.

sennep (Da, Nw) Mustard.

sepia (Sp) Cuttlefish, squid.

seppie (It) Cuttlefish, squid.

seppie al pomodoro (It) Cuttlefish in tomato sauce.

sequestrant (US) A food additive that helps remove trace metals, such as iron and copper, that cause off-color reactions in foods.

ser (Po) Cheese.

šerbet (SC) Sherbet.

şerbet (Tr) A fruit drink.

sereh (In) See **lemongrass.**

serendipity berry (US) An edible African red berry that is hundreds of times sweeter than sugar.

sergevil (Tr) Quince.

sergevili anoosh (Tr) Quince jam.

sergevili bastegh (Tr) Quince candy.

sergevili osharag (Tr) Quince sherbet drink.

seri (Jp) Japanese parsley; watercress.

seroendeng (In) Fried coconut with peanuts.

serpenyös rostelyos (Hu) Pot roast with beef, tomatoes, potatoes, green peppers, onion, garlic, caraway seeds, and paprika.

Serrano chile (Mx) A small tapering chili, usually less than 1½ inches long; rich waxy green changing to red as it matures; very hot.

serrucho en escabeche (Sp) Kingfish braised in a marinade of onions, peppers, olives, olive oil, and vinegar; served cold.

sertésborda parasztosan (Hu) Braised

pork chops with potatoes, onions, and bacon.

serundeng (In) Grated coconut, roasted.

serviette, à la (Fr) Any food presented served in a folded napkin.

Serviettenklöss mit Birnen und Bohnen (Gr) Dumplings folded up like a napkin and served with pears and beans.

seryi skat (Rs) Skate.

sesame oil (US) The colorless oil pressed from sesame seeds; used as a flavoring in stir-fried dishes and as a salad dressing. A dark sesame oil is made from toasted sesame seeds and used as a seasoning. It is high in polyunsaturated fats.

sesame seeds (US) The seeds of an herb, *Sesamum indicum*; usually toasted to bring out a nutty flavor; used on salads, desserts, baked products, and as a base for dips and spreads, such as tahini. Also called **benne seeds.**

se smetanou (Cz) With cream.

sesos de ternera (Sp) Calves' brains.

set, to (US) To allow a food to become settled in a finished state, as when gelatin becomes firm by standing.

setas (Sp) Mushrooms.

setas sobre las parillas (Sp) Grilled mushrooms.

setrup (In) Syrup.

sevaee (Ia) Vermicelli; a snack made with sweet vermicelli, raisins, almonds, and pistachio nuts.

seviche (Sp) See **ceviche.**

seviche de vieiras (Sp) Scallops seviche.

Seville orange (US) The fruit of the sour orange tree *Citrus aurantium*; a rough, dark-orange skin; somewhat bitter, astringent pulp; used in making marmalade. Also called **bitter orange, sour orange.**

sevruga (Rs) Small sturgeon roe; caviar.

sfarjal (Ar) Quince.

sfeeha (Ar) Meat pies.

sfingi (It) Cookies or small cakes.

sfogato (Gk) Meat loaf made with squash.

sfogliatelle (It) Layered, flaky pastry similar to strudel; filled with sweetened ricotta and candied fruit.

sfogliatine di crema (It) Flaky pastry with cream.

sformato (It) Food cooked in a mold.

sformoto di tonno (It) Tuna pudding.

sgombro (It) Mackerel.

shābetto (Jp) Sherbet.

shabu-shabu (Jp) A meal in which a raw meat and vegetable assortment is served around a pot of boiling broth. The food is cooked by dipping it into the broth with chopsticks, then into a mixture of soy sauce, rice wine, and sugar or sesame oil. The broth is served as a soup.

shad (US) The largest member of the herring family native to both sides of the Atlantic Ocean; a flavor similar to pompano and salmon; many fine bones but delicate flesh with a mild oiliness; often broiled or stuffed and baked.

shaddock (US) Largest of the citrus fruits; resembles a huge grapefruit and has a similar taste; usually pink juice capsules; brought to the Caribbean from Southeast Asia by a Captain Shaddock. Also called **jeruk bali, pomelo, pumelo.**

shad roe (US) Unfertilized eggs of the

shad; may be sold with the fish or separately; considered a delicacy; served sautéed, simmered in butter, poached, or with watercress or sorrel in a white sauce.

shahbahr (Ar) Small porgy.

shakarkand (Ia) Sweet potatoes.

shake (Jp) Salmon. Also spelled **sake.**

shakuwlaata (Ar) Chocolate.

shā-là jyàng (Ch) Salad dressing.

shaljam (Ia) Turnips.

shaljam bharta (Ia) Turnip puree.

shaljam rasa (Ia) Turnip curry.

shallot (US) An onion variety, *Allium ascalonicum*; sometimes called green onion; has a smaller bulb and a milder flavor.

shammehm (Ar) Melon.

shamme kabab (Ia) Fried patties of ground meat, yellow peas, and spices.

shammoama (Ar) Melon.

shamouti (US) A Jaffa orange.

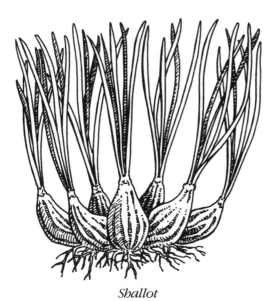

Shallot

shàn-bèi-ké (Ch) Scallops.

shandy (GB) Beer or ale mixed with lemonade.

shandygaff (GB) Beer mixed with ginger beer.

shank (US) The extreme end of a leg of lamb.

shao (Ch) Braising.

shao mài (Ch) Steamed pork dumpling.

sharbat (Ia) A chilled fruit, flower petal, or nut mixture, which may be thin enough to drink or thick enough to eat with a spoon; the original sherbet.

sharbati (Af–Swahili) Sherbet.

shareeyee (Ar) Orzo.

shark (US) Any of a genus (*Selachii*) category of nearly 250 sea creatures, of which a few are a source of delicious steaks, fillets, and meat chunks. The few include the mackerel shark and mako shark of the Atlantic Ocean and the bonito shark of the Pacific Ocean. The mako and bonito shark meats are similar to the flesh of the more expensive swordfish.

shark's fin (US) A Chinese delicacy used in soup.

shashlik (Rs) Shish kebab; skewered, grilled pieces of meat, often lamb and sheep's kidneys, with mushrooms and onions.

shataavar (Ia) Asparagus.

shawirma (Ar) Finely sliced spiced grilled meat.

shchi (Rs) Fresh cabbage soup with sauerkraut, carrots or parsnips, onions, and sour cream.

she-crab soup (US) A thick bisque made with the meat and eggs of a female crab.

sheepshead (US) The popular name for three different species of related (*Archosargus*) popular game and food fish found along the Atlantic coast from Canada to Florida. They range up to three feet in length with firm rich flesh. Also called *casbourgot*.

shehrieh (Tr) Browned noodles.

sheldrake (GB) A large wild European duck.

shelisheli (Af–Swahili) Breadfruit.

shell bean (US) Any bean used for the seed rather than the pod.

shellfish (US) Any aquatic animal with a shell, such as a clam, crab, crayfish, or lobster.

shell steak (US) A cut of meat from the short loin of beef.

shēng tsài (Ch) Lettuce.

shepherd's pie (GB) A traditional mashed potato-topped pot pie with minced lamb and gravy.

shepherd's purse (US) A cruciferous herb with pouchlike pods.

sherbet (US) A frozen dessert containing less than 2 percent milk fat and relatively low levels of other milk solids. They are mainly water, sugar, and tart fruit flavorings. The product is granular and may contain beaten egg white or gelatin.

sheriya miftoon (Ar) Steamed noodles with meat.

sherry (Sp) A still white wine originally made near Jerez, Spain, in the Andalusia region. The production of sherry wines is strictly controlled. All sherries are completely dry when first made and fortified by the addition of brandy. Variations in strength and sweetness are made later to suit the demand.

shé-tóu (Ch) Tongue.

shī (Ar) Hot tea.

shi bilabun (Ar) Tea with milk.

shi binayna (Ar) Tea with mint.

shichimi (Jp) Seven-flavor spice; a blend of spices and herbs used to garnish rice and noodle dishes.

shiitake (Jp) Japanese mushrooms, *Cortinellus shiitake*, called tree mushrooms because they are grown on logs soaked in water; dark color, strong flavor; sold dried or fresh.

shikaar kaa gosht (Ia) Game.

shi metallig (Ar) Iced tea.

shinmei (Jp) Moist new rice; used for special dishes.

shio (Jp) Salt.

shio sembei (Jp) Rice crackers flavored with soy sauce.

shioyaki (Jp) A Japanese cooking method in which fish is rubbed with salt to seal the fat beneath the skin before broiling.

shiozuki (Jp) Vegetables pickled in salt.

ship biscuit (US) Hardtack.

ship caviar (US) The roe of a hybrid sturgeon.

shiraita kombu (Jp) An edible food wrapper made from the kombu seaweed leaf.

shirataki (Jp) Literally, "white waterfall"; long translucent threads of gelatinous starch extracted from the tuber of the devil's tongue plant, a yam of the arum family.

shiratamako (Jp) A mixture of rice cake (mochi) and rice flour.

shiriyyi (Ar) Vermicelli.

263

shiro (Jp) Albacore tuna.

shiro miso (Jp) White miso from fermented soybeans.

shirona (Jp) A form of chard.

shirred eggs (US) Eggs topped with butter or cream and seasonings and baked in individual molds or muffin tins.

shirring (US) Oven cooking in a shallow casserole, usually eggs in cream, butter, and crumbs.

shiruko (Jp) A dessert soup made with sweetened red beans; served with dumplings or rice cakes.

shirumiso (Jp) Soup made with miso.

shirumono (Jp) Soups, usually served with finely cut pieces of vegetables, soybean paste, or tofu.

shish kabob (US) A skewered meat dish similar to the Turkish şiş kebab; many variations but commonly pieces of marinated meat alternated with mushrooms, chunks of green pepper, and onion; grilled or broiled.

shiso (Jp) Highly flavored leaves and berries of a plant native to Japan; beefsteak plant; used as a seasoning.

shoat (US) A piglet that has been weaned but is less than one year old.

shoga (Jp) Fresh gingerroot; brown and gnarled.

shoga sembei (Jp) A rice biscuit coated with ginger-flavored sugar.

shokishoki (Af–Swahili) Rambutans or lychees.

shomin (Tr) Spinach.

shomini aboor (Tr) Spinach soup.

shoofly pie (US) A rich open-face Pennsylvania-Dutch pie with a molasses or brown sugar filling and a topping of butter, flour, and sugar. It was originally created as a fly trap rather than as a food.

shooshma (Tr) Sesame seed.

shooshmayov bahts (Tr) Sesame bread sticks.

shooshmayov pleet (Tr) Sesame cookies.

shorba (Ar, Ia) Soup.

shorbet ads (Ar) Lentil soup.

shorbet basal (Ar) Onion soup.

shorbet ferakh (Ar) Chicken soup.

shorbet khudahr (Ar) Vegetable soup.

shorbet lahmah (Ar) Beef broth.

shorbet samak (Ar) Fish soup.

shorbet shreeya (Ar) Noodles in broth.

shore dinner (US) A seafood meal.

shortbread (Sc) A hard flat cake or cookie made of flour, sugar, and large proportions of butter or shortening. The edges are notched by pinching with the fingers before baking. For Scottish holidays, such as Hogmanay, shortbread is made larger and thicker and decorated with citron peel and almonds.

shortcake (US) A thin flat sponge cake, often multilayered, served with strawberries or other fruit, and whipped cream.

shortening (US) A fat used to "shorten" or tenderize foods. They make pastries rich, flaky, brittle, and likely to crumble because the high percentage of fats in the mixture prevents the proteins and carbohydrates from cooking into a hard mass.

short-grain rice (US) A type of rice that is literally shorter than other varieties. It is also richer, wetter, and stickier than long-grain varieties.

short loin (US) Small sirloin steaks cut from the middle of the sirloin section of the loin.

shortnin' bread (US) See **shortbread.**

short ribs (US) The bony part of the end of the rib and plate meat of beef.

shorva (Ia) Soup.

shoulder (US) A lean part of the beef chuck used for roasts and steaks.

shoulder of pork (US) The butt section of the hog, used for roasting.

shoyu (Jp) See **soy sauce.**

shproti (Rs) Sprats.

shr-dz (Ch) Persimmon.

shred (US) To cut or rip into small thin slivers.

Shrewsbury cake (US) A small cake made with butter, sugar, eggs, mace, and flour.

shrimp (US) Any member of the *Crangon* genus of slender, long-tailed marine crustaceans used as food. Shrimp are closely related to prawns, which generally measure up to 6 inches in length, as marketed, while shrimp are seldom larger than 2 inches. Neither shrimp nor prawns are sold alive in the United States or Europe and, except for size, both are handled like crayfish for cooking purposes. Also called **crevette.**

shrimp paste (US) See **bagoong, trassi.**

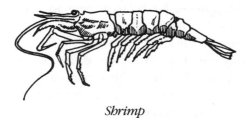

Shrimp

shuànyángròu (Ch) A Mongolian hot-pot of meat, seafood, and poultry cooked with spices in a communal caldron.

shuck (US) To remove the outer layer of a food item, such as a corn husk or oyster shell.

shukti (Ia) Oysters.

shukto (Ia) A vegetable combination that includes bitter melon.

shummam (Ar) A long cantaloupe.

shungiku (Jp) Edible chrysanthemum leaf (*Chrysanthemum spatiosum*); roots and flowering buds are discarded; used in soups and other foods to give a pleasant fragrance; raw in salads; sometimes used to wrap rice.

siadle mleko (Po) Clabber.

sianliha (Fi) Pork.

sids (Sc) The inner husks of oat grain, regarded as the most nutritious part of the cereal; prepared as a porridge served with cream or milk.

sieniä (Fi) Mushrooms.

sienimuhennos (Fi) Creamed mushrooms.

sienisalaatti (Fi) A salad of minced mushrooms and onions with a sour cream sauce.

siero di latte (It) Whey.

sieve (US) A utensil with a perforated bottom used to separate coarse pieces of food from fine, and as a strainer of liquids.

sift (US) To separate and remove lumps or coarse pieces of food from fine by shaking through a sieve.

sig (Rs) Whitefish.

sigara böreği (Tr) Layers of thin pastry filled with cheese.

265

sig̃ir (Tr) Beef.

sigtebrød (Da) Light, sweet rye bread, like Swedish limpa.

siika (Fi) Whitefish.

sik (Sw) Whitefish.

sikampouri kabab (Ia) Broiled or deep-fried balls of minced lamb mixed with chick-pea flour, green chilis, and ginger root.

siki (Af–Swahili) Vinegar.

sikotakia tiganata (Gk) Pieces of lamb's liver sautéed in oil with lemon juice and oregano.

silakka (Fi) Baltic herring, smaller than other herring.

silakkalaatikko (Fi) A casserole of Baltic herring, potatoes, and onions with an egg and milk sauce.

silakkapihvit (Fi) Fried Baltic herring with dill.

silakkarullat (Fi) Rolled up fillets of Baltic herring cooked in a spicy sauce.

silcock (Sc) A small saltwater fish dipped in salted oatmeal and fried in butter.

sild (Nw) Herring.

sild (Da) Baltic herring.

sildeboller (Nw) Herring croquettes.

sildeflyndere (Da) Fried stuffed smelts, sardines, or small herring fillets.

sildegryn (Nw) Herring soup.

sildesalat (Nw) Herring salad.

sill (Sw) Any herring except Baltic.

sillbullar (Sw) Herring croquettes.

sillgratäng (Sw) Casserole of herring, potatoes, onions, and cream.

silli (Fi) Herring; served with potatoes, bread, and butter.

sillisalaatti (Fi) Herring salad.

sillock (Sc) The fry or young of a fish similar to cod.

sill polsa (Sw) Warm herring dish.

sillsalat (Sw) Herring salad with fruit and vegetables.

silq (Ar) Swiss chard.

silvano (It) Chocolate meringue.

silver and gold leaf (Ia) The tissue-thin squares of pure, beaten metal used to decorate sweets and rice dishes on special occasions.

silverside (GB) A cut of beef.

silverside (GB) A European species of sand smelt.

sima (Fi) See **mead.**

simit (Tr) Bread sprinkled with sesame seeds.

simlaa mirch (Ia) Green pepper.

simmaq (Ar) Ground sumac seeds.

simmehm (Ar) Quail.

simmer (US) To cook food in a liquid over low heat just below the boiling point.

simnel (GB) An Easter or Mother's Day cake; a light fruitcake layered with almond paste; topped with a marzipan chicken and egg. The name is believed to be derived from the Latin *simnila*, a Roman word for fine flour.

simpukat (Fi) Mussels.

simsim (Ar) Sesame seeds.

sinaasappel (Du) Orange.

sinaasappelsap (Du) Orange juice.

sinappi (Fi) Mustard.

sinappisilakka (Fi) Herring in a mustard sauce.

singara (Ia) See **samosa.**

singaree (US) A winter drink of warm claret flavored with sugar, cloves, allspice, cinnamon, and nutmeg. Also called **sangaree.**

singe (US) To burn off hairs from poultry.

sini kufteh (Tr) Layers of meat and wheat.

sinsullo (Kr) The Korean version of the Chinese fire pot; thin sliced meat and vegetables cooked in a broth by each diner.

sippee (Ia) Clams.

sippets (US) Croutons.

sipuli (Fi) Onion.

sipulikeitto (Fi) Onion soup.

sipulipihvi (Fi) Beefsteak with onions.

sir (SC) Cheese.

sirće (SC) Vinegar.

sirke (Tr) Vinegar.

sirloin (US) A loin end of beef or hip roast or steak. Sirloin is also used to identify cuts from the loin muscles of hogs, lambs, and veal.

sirloin chops (US) Lamb chops cut from the rump end of the loin.

sirloin roast (US) A lamb roast cut from the rump end of the loin.

sirloin tip (US) A side of beef round that can be cut into roasts or steaks.

sirnaya (Rs) A cottage cheese and egg pudding.

sirniki (Rs) Small, flat patties made with pot cheese and eggs; deep-fried.

sirop (Fr) Syrup.

şişe suyu (Tr) Bottled water.

şiş kebab (Tr) Shish kabob; pieces of grilled marinated mutton or lamb alternated with mushrooms, chunks of green pepper, and onion; served on a rice pilaf, sometimes with a tomato sauce.

sitron (Nw) Lemon.

sitronfromasje (Nw) Lemon pudding.

sitruuna (Fi) Lemon.

sitruunakohokas (Fi) Lemon soufflé.

siyah havyar (Tr) Black caviar.

siyah şarap (Tr) Red wine.

sjelé (Nw) Jelly.

sjokolade (Nw) Chocolate.

sjömansbiff (Sw) "Sailor's stew" with potatoes, beef, and onions.

sjøørret (Nw) Salmon trout.

skaldjurssallad (Sw) Seafood salad.

skaldjursstuvning (Sw) Creamed lobster, shrimp, crabmeat, or other shellfish.

skansko potatis (Sw) Creamed potatoes with dill.

skärbönor (Sw) Green beans.

skarpsås (Sw) Sharp mustard sauce.

skarpsill (Sw) Sprat.

skate (US) A flat, scaleless fish with "wings" and a tail; used fried, simmered, and served with a sauce. See **stingaree.**

skembe (Gk) Tripe.

škembići (SC) Tripe.

skewer, to (US) To impale foods on a long wooden or metal spike; to hold rolled foods in shape with a toothpick or thick pin; to close the cavity of poultry with pins.

skim (US) To clear a liquid of matter floating on the surface.

skim milk (US) Milk from which the cream content has been removed. Because fat-soluble vitamins A and D are removed along with the fat globules, the vitamins are usually replaced before the product is marketed.

skinka (Sw) Ham.

skinkbullar (Sw) Ham and potato balls.

267

skinke (Da) Ham.

skinke med røræg (Da) Ham with scrambled eggs.

skinke og egg (Nw) Ham and eggs.

skinklada (Sw) Ham omelet.

skirlie (Sc) Oatmeal cooked in chopped suet or fat drippings.

skirret (US) An herb with sweet and tender tuberous roots that are cooked like salsify.

skirt steak (US) A steak cut from the side of the plate section of the beef carcass.

sköldpadda (Sw) Turtle.

sköldpaddssoppa (Sw) Turtle soup.

školjke (SC) Clams.

skopové maso (Cz) Mutton.

skordalia (Gk) A sauce or dip made with garlic, vinegar, and olive oil thickened with potatoes, bread crumbs, or nuts; served with fried codfish, cooked vegetables, and in fish soups.

skordalia me pignolia (Gk) Garlic sauce with pine nuts.

skorpor (Sw) Rusks; baking soda biscuits.

skoumbria (Gk) Mackerel.

skummet melk (Nw) Skim milk.

sla (Du) Salad; lettuce.

slab bacon (US) Unsliced bacon, usually cut from the belly of the hog.

sladké (Cz) Sweet.

sladoled od vanilije (SC) Vanilla ice cream.

slagroom (Du) Whipped cream.

slaked lime (US) Calcium hydroxide, a white crystalline chemical used as a firming agent in making pickles.

slanina (SC) Bacon.

slapjack (US) A pancake made with corn meal, milk, and eggs.

sla saus (Du) Salad dressing.

slatrokka (Sw) Skate.

slaw (GB) A shortened form of *salade*. See **coleslaw.**

sled (Cz) Herring.

sledz (Po) Herring.

sledz marynowany ze smietanom (Po) Marinated herring with sour cream.

šlehačka (Cz) Whipped cream.

slepiči polévka (Cz) Chicken soup.

slethvarre (Da) Brill.

slettvar (Nw) Brill.

slice (US) A relatively flat broad piece of substance cut from a larger portion of the same material.

sling (GB) An alcoholic beverage served in a tall glass and garnished with fruit, such as a lemon sling.

sliver (US) A splinter or small slice.

slivovitz (SC) A plum brandy popular in the Balkans.

šljive (SC) Plums.

slodkie (Po) Sweet.

sloe (GB) A small wild blackthorn fruit related to the plum used to flavor sloe gin. A similar native plum in the United States is used to make jams, jellies, and preserves.

sloke (GB) Laver cooked in butter, cream, and lemon juice.

sloppy joe (US) Ground beef with tomato sauce and seasonings, served on a split bun.

slotssteg (Da) Pot roast made with anchovies, brandy, vinegar, sweetening, and seasonings.

slottsstek (Sw) Pot roast.

slumgullion (US) Any simple low budget meal of hash or stew.

slump (US) A cooked fruit dessert served with cream.

småbröd (Sw) Cookies; small cakes.

småfranska (Sw) Rolls.

småkage (Da) Danish cookies.

småkaker (Nw) Cookies.

smaker (Sw) Flavors.

små köttbullar (Sw) Small meatballs.

småländsk ostkaka (Sw) A specialty of Småland; curd cake.

smallage (US) A variety of celery with seeds used for seasoning.

småltsill (Sw) "Melted" sill herring.

smasill (Sw) Pilchard, a sardine.

småvarmt (Sw) Hot hors d'oeuvres that may accompany a smorgasbord.

smažená vejce (Cz) Fried eggs.

smažené (Cz) Fried.

smelt (US) Any of a number of herringlike fish, genus *Osmerus*; the flesh is firm and may be lean or oily; poached, steamed, fried, or grilled. Also called **éperlan.**

smen (Ar) Rancid butter.

smetana (Rs) A mixture of sour cream and sweet cream. Also called **smitane.**

smetanick (Rs) Sour cream and jam pie.

smid (Ar) A coarsely ground flour.

śmietanka (Po) Cream.

smitane (Fr) See **smetana.**

Smithfield ham (US) A cured, salted, and smoked ham from hogs fattened on peanuts.

smoke (US) A method of preserving meat or fish by exposing it to the drying effect of a wood chip fire. The choice of wood affects the flavor of the smoked product. The meat or fish to be smoked may also be immersed in brine to further retard spoilage.

smoked butt (US) A boneless smoked pork roast cut from the shoulder of the hog.

smokies (US) Smoked cooked links of spiced beef or pork sausages.

smokve (SC) Figs.

smör (Sw) Butter.

smør (Da, Nw) Butter.

smørbrød (Nw) Bread and butter; open-face sandwich array.

smörgåsar (Sw) Open-face sandwich.

smörgåsbord (Sw) Literally, "sandwich table"; a large array of hot and cold fish and meat dishes, salads, cheeses, fruits, and desserts.

smørkage (Da) Rich Danish pastry.

smørrebrød (Da) Elaborate array of open-face sandwiches.

smult (Nw) Lard.

smultron (Sw) Wild strawberries.

smyrnaika (Gk) Meat patties of beef, veal, or pork; simmered in spicy tomato sauce.

snails (US) Slow-moving land gastropods with a spiral protective shell. Some species are a popular food item in Europe where the escargots, in particular, are allowed to feed on the leaves of grape vines. They are usually cooked in a garlic butter sauce with white wine.

snap bean (US) Any of the many varieties of green beans or yellow wax beans. They may be grown especially for use of the pods in cooking. Also called *string beans.*

sneeuwballen (Du) Literally, "snow-balls"; deep-fried, puffy, sweet ball-shaped cakes.

snegelhus (Nw) Cinnamon buns.

snijbonen (Du) French beans; haricots.

snipe (GB) A marsh game bird slightly smaller than a woodcock; served roasted. Also called **bécassine.**

snittbønner (Nw) String beans.

snitter (Da) Small open-face sandwiches often served at lunch.

snoek (Du) Pike.

snöripa (Sw) Ptarmigan.

snow eggs (US) See **oeufs à la neige.**

snow peas (US) See **podded peas.**

so (SC) Salt.

só (Hu) Salt.

soak, to (US) To cover a food with liquid for a length of time.

soba (Jp) Thin, buff-colored, buckwheat noodles made in flat sticks; served in broth or salads or with a spicy sauce and nori seaweed.

socker (Sw) Sugar.

socivo salata (SC) Lentil salad.

soda (US) See **bicarbonate of soda.**

soda bread (US) A bread leavened with bicarbonate of soda or baking powder. Also called **quick bread.**

soda water (US) See **carbonated water, seltzer.**

sodium-free (US) A term meaning a food product contains less than 5 mg of sodium per serving; proposed by the U.S. Food and Drug Administration for food labels. Also called **salt-free.**

šodó (Cz) Frothy dessert custard; zabaglione.

sødsuppe (Da) A Danish specialty; a sweet soup thickened with barley, sago, or tapioca and containing fruit such as raisins, plums, dried apples, and pears.

soepen (Du) Soups.

soffritto (It) 1. Spicy sauce of tomatoes and pork, sautéed. 2. Sauce of onions fried in butter.

sofrito (Sp) A Puerto Rican sauce of onions, garlic, cilantro, oregano, seasonings, and sometimes tomatoes ground together and sautéed; other vegetables may be added. It is added to many stews and soups.

soft-serve (US) A frozen dessert with a milk fat content of between 3 percent and 6 percent , compared to a range of 8 percent to 14 percent for plain ice cream.

soğan (Tr) Onion.

sogliola (It) Sole.

sogliole alla marinara (It) Fried pickled sole.

soğuk et (Tr) Cold sliced meats.

sohk (Rs) Juice.

sohl (Rs) Salt.

Soissons (Fr) See **haricots de Soissons.**

sokeri (Fi) Sugar.

sokh (Tr) Onion.

sokhov tutoom (Tr) Squash with onions.

sok od narandže (SC) Orange juice.

sól (Po) Salt.

sola (Po) Dover sole.

solbær (Nw) Black currants.

sole (US) A name for many species of flatfish with sweet, tender flesh that may be prepared similarly. The Dover sole, *Solea solea,* is considered one of the finest of all flatfish.

sole à la bonne femme (Fr) Sole, first

poached, then baked in white wine with mushrooms; served in its own sauce.

sole à la dieppoise (Fr) Sole poached in mussel stock, then covered with béchamel sauce and garnished with mussels.

sole à la dugléré (Fr) Sole baked in a herbed liquid and served with a velouté sauce.

sole à la normande (Fr) Sole poached in white wine, covered with a cream and egg normande sauce; garnished with mussels, mushrooms, and truffles.

sole à la meunière (Fr) Sole sautéed in butter; served with lemon and the pan butter.

sole cardinal (Fr) Sole served with a lobster butter sauce.

sole colbert (Fr) Sole fried with an egg and bread crumb coating.

sole Marguery (Fr) Fillets of sole poached in white wine with shrimp and oysters or mussels.

soles de douvres (Fr) Dover sole.

sólet (Hu) Beans, barley, smoked meat, onions, and paprika mixed together and baked.

solianka (Rs) A thick soup of fish or meat with salted cucumber, onion, and olives.

solid fat index (US) A measure of the solidity of fats at various temperatures; the percentage of a fat that is crystalline rather than a melted oil at a given temperature.

sologa (Sw) A snack of chopped anchovies, raw egg, and onions.

solomillo (Sp) Loin of pork.

somen (Jp) Thin, white, wheat-flour noodles, similar to vermicelli; usually eaten cold and served with salads.

somlói galuskas (Hu) Layered sponge cake in three flavors, vanilla, walnut, and chocolate; filled with egg custard, nuts, and white raisins; soaked in rum; served with chocolate sauce and cream.

sondesh (Ia) A soft candy made from cottage cheese mixed with sugar, cardomom, and pistachio nuts.

sonhos (Pg) Literally, "dreams"; a dessert of pieces of deep-fried butter and egg dough sprinkled with sugar and spice.

sonka (Hu) Ham.

sonkás metélt (Hu) Noodles with ham.

sonkás palacsinták (Hu) Ham crepes.

sonkás rétes (Hu) Strudel with ham filling.

sood manti (Tr) Stuffed shells.

soon (In) Bean threads.

soong (Tr) Mushroom.

soongi aghtsan (Tr) Mushroom salad.

soop (Rs) Soup.

soorj (Tr) Demitasse coffee.

sop (In) Soup.

sopa (Sp, Pg) Soup.

sopa à alentejana (Pg) Bread and egg soup.

sopa al jerez (Sp) Beef broth with sherry.

sopa al queso (Sp) Cheese soup.

sopa borracha (Sp) Tipsy cake, a sponge cake made with muscatel wine and meringue.

sopa de albóndigas (Sp) Soup with meatballs.

sopa de ameijoas (Pg) Clam soup.

sopa de batata e agrião (Pg) Potato and watercress soup.

sopa de camarão (Pg) Shrimp soup; shrimp bisque.

sopa de fideos (Sp) Noodle soup.

sopa de feijão (Pg) Red bean and cabbage soup.

sopa de frijol negro (Sp) Black bean soup.

sopa de grão (Pg) Chick-pea, onion, and tomato soup.

sopa de hortaliça (Pg) Vegetable soup.

sopa de legumbres con huevos (Sp) Vegetable soup with eggs.

sopa de mariscos (Pg, Sp) Shellfish soup, such as mussels and clams in tomato and clam broth.

sopa de mexilhão (Pg) Mussel, potato, and rice soup.

sopa de tomate à alentejana (Pg) Tomato, garlic, onion, egg, and bread soup.

sopaipillas (Sp) Fritters; puffy, deep-fried, sweetened breads; often served with honey and butter.

sopaipillas chilenitas (Sp) Squash fritters.

sopa seca (Sp) "Dry soup"; rice, pasta, or tortillas cooked in a broth until the liquid is absorbed.

sopa seca de fideos (Sp) Dry soup of spaghetti.

sopa transmontana (Pg) Pork and vegetable soup.

sopes (Sp) Enchiladas, tortillas, or tostada shells filled with refried beans, cheese, onion, and cilantro; served with sausage.

sopita (Sp) A light soup.

sopón de garbanzos con patas de cerdo (Sp) Chick-pea soup with pigs' feet.

sopp (Nw) Mushroom.

soppstuing (Nw) Creamed mushrooms.

sör (Hu) Beer.

soramame (Jp) Lima beans.

sorbet (Fr) Sherbet or fruit ice, sometimes containing liqueurs; may be served between courses to refresh the palate.

sorbet au cassis (Fr) Sherbet flavored with a black currant liqueur.

Sorbett (Gr) Sherbet.

sorbetto (It) Sherbet; fruit ice; soft ice cream.

sorbitol (US) A sweet white alcohol in crystalline form. It occurs naturally in some fruits and is used as a sugar substitute and as a humectant to control moisture in soft candies.

sorghum flour (US) A flour made from a cereal grain, *Sorghum bicolor*, a staple in India and Africa.

sorghum syrup (US) A syrup made from the juice of the stem of the sugar sorghum (sorgo) plant; similar to molasses.

sorrel (US) An herb, genus *Rumex*, similar to spinach; with green, lance-shaped leaves; sour flavored; wild varieties are edible as well as cultivated kind; used in salads, purees, soups, sauces.

sorvete (Pg) Sherbet; ice cream.

sos (Po, Tr) Sauce.

sosaties (Af) Lamb kebabs in a curry-flavored sauce.

sosej (Af–Swahili) Sausage.

sôsëji (Jp) Sausage.

sosis (Tr) Sausage.

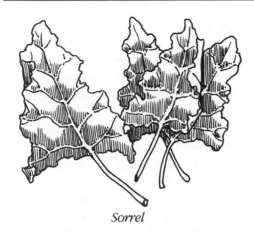

Sorrel

Sosse (Gr) Sauce; gravy.

søsterkage (Da) Raisin cake.

sōsu (Jp) Sauce.

sos z jaj do ryby (Po) An egg sauce for fish dishes.

sotirano (SC) Sautéed.

soto (In) Thick stew.

soto ayam (In) Thick, spicy chicken stew.

sött (Sw) Sweet.

sottaceti (It) Literally, "under vinegar"; pickled vegetables.

søtunge (Da) Sole.

soubise (Fr) Puree of onions and rice served with meats or eggs; also, a cream sauce with onion puree added.

soubise, sauce (Fr) A cream sauce with onion puree added.

sou boereg (Tr) Cheese bake.

souci (Fr) Marigold.

soufflé (Fr) A delicate, baked, custardlike dish made with pureed ingredients, thickened with egg yolks and stiffly beaten egg whites; many varieties; may be made with vegetables, fruit, fish, meat, nuts, or liqueurs; served as an appetizer, a main dish, or a dessert.

soufflé ambassadrice (Fr) Soufflé made with macaroons and blanched, rum-soaked almonds.

soufflé aux épinards (Fr) Spinach soufflé.

soufflé aux fraises (Fr) Strawberry soufflé.

soufflé ze śledzia (Po) Herring soufflé.

soup (US) Any of a variety of dishes with a liquid stock as a base and often containing some solid food. Examples include bouillon, consommé, broth, chowder, bisque, vegetable soup, and cream soup.

soupa avgolemono (Gk) Soup made with lamb broth, rice, eggs, and lemon.

soupe (Fr) A thick, peasant-style soup.

soupe à la reine (Fr) Chicken soup with rice.

soupe à l'oignon (Fr) Onion soup.

soupe au pistou (Fr) Vegetable soup with garlic, basil, and cheese.

soupe aux congres (Fr) Eel soup.

soupe aux marrons (Fr) Chestnut soup.

soupe bonne femme (Fr) Potato and leek soup made with milk.

soupe de jour (Fr) Soup of the day.

sour cherry (US) See **amarelle.**

sour cream (US) A pasteurized cream thickened and soured usually by natural lactic acid fermentation; it is higher in fat and heavier in consistency than cultured buttermilk. The citric acid in lemon juice will also produce sour cream. Many Russian, Hungarian, and other European dishes use sour cream.

sourdough (US) A natural leavener or bread starter made with fermented

273

flour and water, making use of wild yeast; commercial yeast may also be used. Sourdough bread is a specialty in San Francisco because of a unique starter.

sour orange (US) See **Seville orange.**

soursop (US) See **custard apple.**

souse (US) See **headcheese.**

soused (GB) Describes pickled or brined mackerel or herring; served cold.

sous la cendre (Fr) Cooked in the coals.

Southern fried chicken (US) A specialty in the southern United States; coated with seasoned flour and browned in fat, the chicken pieces have a firm crust; served with a cream gravy.

souvlakia (Gk) Kebabs; lamb, veal, or pork marinated in lemon juice and olive oil; grilled on skewers.

soybean (US) A legume, *Glycine max*, from eastern Asia. The bean, with a less appealing flavor and texture than other beans, is used most often as a basis for products such as soy sauce, soybean curd (tofu), miso, tempeh, and soy flour.

soybean curd (US) A thick, soft, cheeselike preparation made from a milky liquid processed from soybeans; may be fried, mashed in a sauce, and stewed with fish or vegetables. Also called **tofu.**

soy sauce (US) A condiment, with dark and light varieties, made from fermented soybeans, toasted wheat, barley, salt, and water; used in Chinese, Japanese, and Southeast Asian recipes. Also called **shoyu.**

spagety (Cz) Spaghetti.

spaghetti (It) Long, solid rod of pasta; usually served with oil-based sauces, shellfish sauces, and tomato sauces.

spaghettini (It) A thin spaghetti.

spalla di vitello al forno (It) Roast veal shoulder.

spanać (SC) Spinach.

spanakopitta (Gk) Triangular phyllodough pastries filled with spinach and feta cheese.

spanakorizo (Gk) Spinach stewed with rice and dill or bay leaves.

španělští ptáčci (Cz) Meat rolled around a filling.

Spanferkel (Gr) Roast suckling pig.

spanischer Pfeffer (Gr) Capsicum pepper, paprika.

sparagio (It) Asparagus.

spárga (Hu) Asparagus.

spárgaleves (Hu) Asparagus soup.

Spargel (Gr) Asparagus.

Spargelkohl (Gr) Broccoli.

špargle (SC) Asparagus.

sparris (Sw) Asparagus.

spatula (US) A broad, flexible knife used for lifting foods.

Spätzle (Gr) Tiny noodlelike dumplings made with an egg and flour mixture, pressed through a colander into boiling water.

Speck mit Eiern (Gr) Bacon and eggs.

speculaas (Du) Spiced cakelike cookies pressed into a decorative wooden mold before baking.

spegesild (Da) Pickled herring.

spegepølse (Da) Salami.

speilegg (Nw) Fried egg.

spek (Du) Bacon.

spekekjøtt (Nw) Dried, smoked leg of mutton.

speldings (Sc) Small saltwater fish related to cod.

spenat (Sw) Spinach.

spenót (Hu) Spinach.

spersiebonen (Du) String beans.

spetsiotiko (Gk) Fish baked with tomatoes, olive oil, white wine, and garlic; covered with a layer of bread crumbs.

spettakaka (Sw) Tall cake baked on a spit.

spezzatino di vitello (It) Veal stew.

spice (US) Any of a variety of aromatic roots, bark, seeds or fruit of plants, such as cinnamon, pepper, nutmeg, and cloves; used to add flavor to baked goods, entrées, desserts, and pickles.

spickgans (Gr) Pickled, smoked breast of goose.

spiedini (It) Sliced Italian bread topped with mozzarella and anchovies and fried.

Spiegeleier (Gr) Fried eggs.

Spieseeis (Gr) Ice cream.

spiess (Gr) Skewered.

spigola (It) Bream; sea bass.

spinach (US) A vegetable, *Spinacea oleracea*, native to Asia; loose cluster of thick stalks with crinkly, oval or triangular green leaves; eaten both cooked and raw.

spinach beet (US) See **chard.**

spinaci (It) Spinach.

spinaci alla romana (It) Spinach with raisins and pine nuts.

spinat (Nw) Spinach.

Spinat (Gr) Spinach.

spinazie (Du) Spinach.

spiny lobster (US) A large crustacean, *Palinurus elephas* and other species, variously colored and with a meaty tail but without large claws; prepared as for lobster. Also called **langosta, langouste.**

spitisies hilopites (Gk) Wide egg noodles.

sponge cake (US) A light, butterless cake made rich with beaten eggs.

spoon bread (US) See **batter bread.**

sporacciona, alla (It) "Dirty spaghetti"; with tomatoes, garlic, and Gorgonzola cheese.

spotted dog (GB) Steamed suet pudding with raisins or currants; resembles the spots of a Dalmatian dog.

sprat (US) A small fish in the herring family found along the Atlantic coast from Norway to the Mediterranean; sold as brisling and Swedish anchovies.

Springerle (Gr) Molded, decorated anise-flavored Christmas cookies.

spring roll (US) See **egg roll.**

spritsar (Sw) Spritz ring cookies.

Spritzgeback (Gr) Pressed hazelnut cookies.

Spritzkuchen (Gr) Deep-fried crullers.

sprot (Du) Sprat.

Sprotte (Gr) Sprat.

sproty (Cz) Sprat.

spruce beer (US) A beverage made by fermenting boiled spruce sprigs with yeast and molasses.

spruitjes (Du) Brussels sprouts.

spud (US) A popular term for potato.

spuitwater (Du) Soda water.

spuma (It) Foam; mousse; a type of custard.

spuma di banane (It) Banana whip.

spumone (It) A rich, frothy ice cream

made with egg whites and whipped cream; variously flavored, colored, and filled with fruits and nuts; often molded.

squab (US) Formerly a game bird, now cultivated. Squabs are young pigeons (*Columba livia),* about four weeks old. Because they are fat, squabs are usually roasted or broiled. After they become mature pigeons, the birds are too tough to be marketed.

square cut shoulder (US) An untrimmed lamb shoulder roast.

squid (US) A member, genus *Loligo,* of the cephalopod group of mollusks; many species; with a torpedo-shaped body, a transparent inner shell, eight arms and two tentacles; used poached, baked, or fried. The body is often served stuffed or cut into rings.

squirrel (US) Any of a family of tree-dwelling rodents commonly eaten in the United States. The white meat is similar to that of rabbit and prepared according to the rabbit recipes.

srce (SC) Heart.

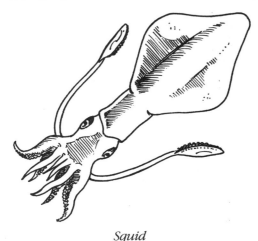

Squid

srdce (Cz) Heart.

średnio (Po) Rare (meat).

srnčí maso (Cz) Venison.

srpski sir (SC) Feta cheese.

stabilizers (US) Gums, starches, dextrins, and other additives used to thicken foods by combining with water to form gels.

stafilia (Gk) Grapes.

stalk (US) 1. An individual piece, as in a stalk of celery. 2. A long narrow peduncle of some animals.

standing rump (US) The rump end of a veal leg roast.

stap (Sc) Boiled haddock heads and livers.

star anise (US) The star-shaped fruit of a tree, *Illicium verum*; the dried, brown slices are similar to anise in flavor; used in Chinese cooking and in spice mixtures.

star fruit (US) See **carambola.**

stark senap (Sw) Hot mustard.

starkt kryddat (Sw) Spicy.

šťáva z masz (Cz) Meat juice or gravy.

steak au poivre (Fr) Steak cooked with crushed black peppercorns and served with a tomato and wine sauce.

steak tartare (Fr) Uncooked ground meat seasoned with salt and pepper; served with a raw egg yolk on top and with capers, chopped parsley, and onion.

steam, to (US) To cook by contact with steam in a covered container or a perforated container placed over hot water.

stebghin (Tr) Carrot.

stebghini aghtsan (Tr) Carrot salad.

Steckrube (Gr) Rutabaga.

steep (US) To infuse; to extract the flavor from a substance into a liquid by allowing it to stand in hot liquid.

stefado (Gk) Spiced braised beef with onions.

stein wines (Gr) Literally, "stone" wines, a group of light-flavored wines produced in northern Germany.

stek (Nw) Roast.

stekt (Sw) Fried.

stekt på spett (Sw) Cooked on a skewer.

stekt sill eller stromming (Sw) Fried herring fillets with dill.

stellini (It) "Little stars"; pasta usually served in soup.

steur (Du) Sturgeon.

stew, to (US) To simmer food in a small amount of liquid.

stiacciata (It) A flat cake; bun.

štika (Cz) Pike.

stikkelsbær (Nw) Gooseberries.

stikkelsbærgrød (Da) Gooseberry pudding.

Stilton (GB) A cow's milk cheese; crusty rind with blue-veined, creamy, Cheddar-like interior; rich, piquant taste.

stingaree (US) The stingray, a fishlike vertebrate related to the shark. The wings are boiled and eaten with a butter sauce.

Stinte mit saurer Sosse (Gr) Smelts with sour cream gravy.

stir, to (US) To mix ingredients together, usually with a circular motion, by means of a spoon, a wooden paddle, or by using a slow speed on a machine with a paddle.

stirred custard (US) See **crème anglaise.**

stoccafisso (It) Stockfish; unsalted, air-dried cod or haddock.

stoccafisso accomodato (It) Soaked, dried cod prepared with milk, olive oil, anchovies, and black olives.

stock (US) Broth in which meat, poultry, bones, or fish have been cooked; used as a base for gravies, sauces, and soups.

stockfish (US) Any of a group of fish, such as cod, haddock, or hake; split, cleaned, and hung in the open until air-dried hard without salt.

stockpot (US) A pot used for preparing soups or stews.

Stollen (Gr) Large yeast bread made with fruit, traditional at Christmas.

stör (Sw) Sturgeon.

stør (Da, Nw) Sturgeon.

storione (It) Sturgeon.

storskate (Nw) Skate.

stracchino (It) A soft, mild cheese made of cow's milk; from Lombardy.

stracciatella (It) Broth with beaten egg and Parmesan cheese.

stracotto (It) Beef stew.

strain, to (US) To pass foods through a sieve to remove large particles; to pour liquids through a cloth to clear them.

Straussburg sausage (US) A veal and liver sausage flavored with pistachio nuts.

straw mushrooms (US) Dark mushrooms, *Volvariella volvacea*, cultivated on rice straw; meaty texture; sold canned or dried.

Streuselkuchen (Gr) Cake with crumb topping.

striped bass (US) See **rockfish.**

strip steak (US) A boneless short loin, T-bone, or shell steak.

strömming (Sw) Small Baltic herring.

štruca od mesa (SC) Meat loaf.

Stückchen (Gr) Zest.

stufato (It) Stew.

stufato di manzo (It) Beef stew.

sturgeon (US) A freshwater and saltwater fish, genus *Acipenser*, with white to pink flesh; strong flavor often compared to veal; a fish so valued once considered the property of only a royal family; used roasted, broiled, stewed, and in chowders.

sturgeon roe (US) Caviar.

su (Tr) Water; juice or broth.

su (Jp) Rice vinegar.

suar kaa maans (Ia) Pork.

sucadekoek (Du) A breakfast spice cake with raisins.

succo (It) Juice.

succo d'arancio (It) Orange juice.

succo di frutta (It) Fruit juice.

succotash (US) A traditional American dish of sweet corn kernels and lima beans cooked together.

sucées (Fr) A small cake.

suchar (Cz) Cracker.

suco (Pg) Juice.

suco de laranja (Pg) Orange juice.

sucre (Fr) Sugar.

sudak (Rs) Pike perch.

sudako (Jp) Vinegared octopus.

suero de la leche (Sp) Whey.

suet (GB) The fat from around the loins and kidneys of sheep, cattle, and other meat animals. It is used in cooking.

suffle (It) Soufflé.

sufle (Tr) Soufflé.

sugar (US) A usually sweet crystalline form of the saccharose or glucose cat-egories of carbohydrates. The various kinds include beet sugar, cane sugar, corn sugar, milk sugar, and maple sugar. It is sold as granulated, super-fine castor, coffee crystals, cubes, refined brown, raw demerara, and dark brown Barbados sugars.

sugar-free (US) A term meaning a food product contains less than 0.5 g of sugar per serving; proposed by the U.S. Food and Drug Administration for food labels.

sugar peas (US) See **podded peas.**

sugo (It) Sauce; gravy; meat juices.

suika (Jp) Watermelon.

suiker (Du) Sugar.

suimitsu (Jp) Peach.

suimono (Jp) A clear soup made with meat, fish, or vegetable stocks; usually flavored with shoyu and dashi.

suji malpua (Ia) Saffron pancakes in syrup.

sukari (Af–Swahili) Sugar.

sukhdor (Tr) Garlic.

sukhdori tahtsan (Tr) Garlic and nut sauce.

sukhdori yev (Tr) Garlic and yogurt sauce.

suki (Jp) Flat iron pan.

sukiyaki (Jp) Literally, "roasted on a plough"; sliced beef or chicken and vegetables simmered at the table in soy sauce, rice wine, and sugar. Also called **gyūnabe.**

sukkar (Ar) Sugar.

sukker (Nw) Sugar.

sůl (Cz) Salt.

süllö (Hu) Pike perch.

sultana (US) Seedless white raisins,

originally produced in Turkey but now grown throughout the world, including the United States.

sülün (Tr) Pheasant.

sumashijiru (Jp) Stew; soup; usually with meat, fish, or chicken in dashi stock.

summer pudding (GB) A British dessert made from raspberries and red currants, which mature in the same midsummer weeks, stale white bread, and whipped cream.

summer sausage (US) Any dry sausage, such as cervelat, that is hopefully expected to require no summer refrigeration.

sumomo (Jp) Plums.

sumpoog (Tr) Eggplant.

sumpoogi aboor (Tr) Eggplant and chick-pea soup.

sumpoogi leetsk (Tr) Stuffed eggplant.

sumpoogi tahtsan (Tr) Eggplant sauce.

sumpoogi yev loligi aghtsan (Tr) Eggplant and tomato salad.

sumpoogov yev meesov pancharegan (Tr) Meat and eggplant casserole.

sunchoke (US) See **Jerusalem artichoke.**

sundae (US) An ice cream dessert with a topping of fruit or syrup. It was reportedly invented to circumvent Sunday Blue Laws prohibiting the sale of beverages on the Sabbath. The sundae is basically an ice cream soda without the soda water.

Sunderland pudding (US) A quick-baked mixture of eggs, flour, cream, and nutmeg; served with a sweet sauce.

sun drying (US) An ancient method of preserving foods, still used in many parts of the world, including the United States. Raisins, prunes, dates, figs, and apricots are among foods dried in the sun to reduce the moisture content that would otherwise lead to spoilage.

sunflower oil (US) A cooking and salad oil expressed from seeds of the sunflower plant. It is favored for some Oriental recipes, such as miso.

šunka (Cz, SC) Ham.

sunomono (Jp) A salad of raw or cooked vegetables and pieces of seafood marinated in vinegar.

suola (Fi) Salt.

suolasilakka (Fi) Salted, whole herring packed upright in brine.

suomuurain (Fi) A Finnish liqueur made from cloudberries.

supa avgholemono (Gk) Rice cooked in chicken stock with added egg and lemon juice.

suppe (Nw) Soup.

Suppe (Gr) Soup.

suppli (It) Croquettes made with mortadella sausage and mozzarella cheese.

suppli di riso (It) Fried balls of rice stuffed with cheese or meat.

suppon (Jp) Snapping turtle.

supreme sauce (Fr) A delicate white sauce made from clear poultry stock, mushroom cooking liquor, cream, and butter.

suprêmes de volaille à blanc (Fr) Chicken breasts poached in butter with a wine and cream sauce.

supu ya kuku (Af–Swahili) Chicken soup.

supu ya mboga (Af–Swahili) Vegetable soup.

suquet de peix (Sp) A Catalan fish stew.

sur commande (Fr) To your special order.

sur grädde (Sw) Sour cream.

surimi (Jp) Literally, "formed fish"; artificial crab or lobster meat made by forming pieces of fin fish, then flavoring and coloring them with extracts of crab and lobster.

surkål (Nw, Sw) Sauerkraut.

sur melk (Nw) Sour milk.

surströmming (Sw) Fermented salmon trout; a popular, strong smelling dish.

sušené švestky (Cz) Prunes.

sušenky (Cz) Cookies.

sushi (Jp) Hand-shaped balls of vinegared rice topped with Japanese horseradish (wasabi), a slice of raw fish, egg, or seafood; served as an appetizer or in a selection as a complete meal. Also called **nigirizushi, zushi.**

sushi-meshi (Jp) Vinegared rice.

Süsstoff (Gr) Artificial sweetener.

süt (Tr) Milk.

sutēki (Jp) Steak.

sütve (Hu) Baked.

suutarinilohi (Fi) Baltic herring, onions, and peppers marinated in vinegar; called "shoemaker's salmon."

suve šljive (SC) Prunes.

suvlas (Gk) Spit-roasted lamb.

suzuke (Jp) Vegetables pickled in vinegar.

suzuki (Jp) Sea bass.

suzuki shioyaki (Jp) Salt-grilled sea bass.

svamp (Sw) Mushrooms.

svarta vinbär (Sw) Black currants.

svecia ost (Sw) A Gouda-type cheese.

sveitserost (Nw) Swiss cheese.

švestky (Cz) Plums.

svíčková na smetaně (Cz) Sauerbraten.

svinekjøtt (Nw) Pork.

svinemørbrad (Da) Braised pork tenderloin, stuffed with apples and prunes.

svinjetina (SC) Pork.

svisker (Nw) Prunes.

svoja (SC) Halibut.

swàn (Ch) Garlic.

swān-syǎu-tsài (Ch) Pickles.

sweat (GB) The appearance of juices exuding from food being cooked. Also called *fat steaming.*

swede (GB) A large firm yellow-orange turnip. Also called *Swedish turnip.*

sweet-and-sour (US) Pertaining to dishes or sauces with both sweet and sour flavors, usually based on sugar and vinegar. Other sweet-and-sour ingredients may include chocolate, raisins, and soy sauce.

sweetbread (US) The soft, rounded thymus or pancreas, usually from young animals, calves, or lambs; used poached, sautéed, broiled, and braised. Also, animal testicles used for meat; usually from the ram, lamb, and bull.

sweet chocolate (US) Chocolate that contains at least 15 percent milk chocolate, 10 percent bittersweet chocolate, and 15 percent chocolate liquor.

sweet cicely (GB) An aromatic herb used in stews and salads. Also called **cerfeuil.**

sweet corn (US) Any of several varieties of field corn (*Zeya mays*) harvested in the unripe milky stage when the kernels are rich in sugar rather than starch. Green sweet corn loses its sugar content rapidly after harvesting. Unless refrigerated, sweet corn loses more than half its sugar content in 72 hours.

sweet pepper (US) A green pepper, *Capsicum annuum*, with varieties that ripen to yellow, red, or almost black; somewhat square shape, fist-sized; crisp, firm texture; usually sweet, mild taste; eaten raw or cooked, in salads, fried, stuffed, baked and combined in many dishes. Also called **bell pepper.**

sweet potato (US) The tuber of a plant, *Ipomoea batatas*; the skin may be white, red, or purple. One of the main types has dry, mealy, yellow flesh. Another is white-fleshed, softer, and sweeter. Most often baked.

sweet rice flour (US) See **glutinous rice flour.**

Sweet potato

sweetsop (Cb) A custard apple with a thick yellow-green skin.

Swiss chard (US) See **chard.**

Swiss cheese (US) A cow's milk cheese with many versions worldwide; with a sweet nutty flavor and holes, or eyes, both due to the presence of an organism, *Propionibacterium shermanii* that causes fermentation of the lactic acid. The original Swiss cheese is **Emmentaler.**

Swiss roll (GB) See **jelly roll.**

Swiss sausage (US) A fresh sausage similar to bockwurst.

Swiss steak (US) A tenderized slice of beefsteak, floured on both sides and braised in an onion-tomato sauce.

swizzle (GB) An alcoholic drink of bitters, lime juice, and sugar; further identified by the alcoholic spirit used, such as gin swizzle.

swordfish (US) A saltwater game fish with tasty firm flesh, sold in steaks and fillets, and baked, broiled, or sautéed.

syán-dàn (Ch) Preserved eggs.

syāng-jyāu (Ch) Banana.

syāng-tsài (Ch) Parsley.

syāng-yóu (Ch) Sesame seed oil.

syǎu-mài (Ch) Wheat. Also called **mài-dz.**

syǎu-nyóu-ròu (Ch) Veal.

syǎu-syār (Ch) Shrimp.

syǎu-yáng-ròu (Ch) Lamb.

sybo (Sc) Spring onion.

sydän (Fi) Heart.

syī-gwā (Ch) Watermelon.

syìng-dz (Ch) Apricot.

syìng-rén (Ch) Almonds.

syìng-rén dòu-fú (Ch) Almond jelly.

syllabub (GB) A mixture of milk or cream and wine, cider, or other acidic beverage, whipped to a froth. Also spelled *sillabub*.

sylt (Sw) Jam.

sylte (Da) Head cheese.

syltesild (Da) Pickled herring.

syltetøy (Nw) Jam.

sýr (Cz) Cheese.

syrniki (Rs) Sweet cakes made of cheese or cottage cheese, browned in butter and sprinkled with powdered sugar.

syrup (US) A thick sweet liquid, particularly one containing a high concentration of sugar. A syrup may be sweet, sour, or neutral, depending upon its acid content. The term is derived from an Arabic word for wine, *sharab* or *shurb*.

sywě-dòu (Ch) Snow peas. See **podded peas.**

szalonnás gombóc (Hu) Bacon dumplings.

szalonnás súlt (Hu) Beef cooked in paprika-flavored bacon.

szardinia (Hu) Sardine.

szarvas (Hu) Venison.

Sz-chwān hú-jyāu (Ch) A reddish brown, spicy aromatic pod with a tiny black seed used in highly spiced Szechuan-style Chinese cooking. Also called **Szechuan pepper.**

Sz-chwān jyău-dz (Ch) Dumplings in Szechuan-style sauce made with chilis and peanut oil.

Szechuan cooking (Ch) A style of cooking associated with the western region of China; usually deep-fried, steamed, or smoked and highly-spiced dishes.

Szechuan pepper (Ch) See **Sz-chwan hú-jyāu.**

székelygulyás (Hu) Pork goulash with sauerkraut and sour cream.

székely sertésborda (Hu) Pork chops simmered with onions, paprika, garlic, and caraway seeds; then braised with sauerkraut, sour cream, and dill.

szeletek (Hu) Cutlets.

szilva (Hu) Plums.

szilvalekvár (Hu) Plum jam.

szilvás gombóc (Hu) Plum dumplings.

sziv (Hu) Heart.

szölö (Hu) Grapes.

szparagi (Po) Asparagus.

szpinak (Po) Spinach.

szprot (Po) Sprat.

sztufada (Po) Braised beef.

taartjes (Du) Pastries.

taateleita (Fi) Dates.

taazaa (Ia) Fresh.

tabasco (Sp) A variety of the tropical *Capsicum* pepper family, which also includes paprika, chili, and pimiento peppers, named for the Tabasco state of Mexico.

Tabasco sauce (US) A trademark for a commercial bottled condiment using very hot tropical red peppers, vinegar, and salt. It is usually served with shellfish and other seafood.

tabbouleh (Ar) A traditional Arabic salad of burghul mixed with chopped parsley, mint leaves, onion, and tomatoes; dressed with lemon juice and olive oil; served with vine leaves to use as spoons. Also spelled *tabooley, tabouli.*

tabboun (Ar) A Middle-Eastern oven with terra-cotta walls used for baking. The term also refers to a tightly covered, clay cooking pot used as an oven within an oven.

tabeet (Jw) A Sephardic passover dish of stuffed chicken cooked with rice and onions.

table cream (US) Light cream containing 18–30% milkfat.

table d'hote (Fr) A communal table at which diners are served; also, a complete meal of several courses offered at a fixed price.

table salt (US) A refined sodium chloride suitable for use in cooking and at the table. It is treated with some chemical compounds such as magnesium phosphate or calcium phosphate to prevent caking.

table water (US) Mineral water or other bottled water that may be provided with a meal.

table wine (US) Any wine, red, white, or rosé, but usually of light alcohol content, served with food.

tablier de sapeur (Fr) Literally, "sapper's apron"; pieces of tripe dipped in egg and bread crumbs, then fried or broiled.

Tàche (Fr) A smooth, full-bodied red Burgundy table wine.

tacchino (It) Turkey.

tacchino ripieno (It) Stuffed turkey.

Táchira (Sp) A type of rich, acidy coffee produced in Venezuela.

tack (GB) A term originally applied to food with "substance and stability," such as **hardtack** biscuits.

taco (Mx) A small tortilla, either soft or crisp-fried, that is folded or rolled around a filling of meat, cheese, refried beans, and other ingredients.

tacon (Fr) Young salmon.

tacos de pescado (Mx) Fish tacos.

tacos de pollo asado (Mx) Roast chicken tacos.

tädinkakut (Fi) Crescent-shaped sugar cookies.

tädin kalavuoka (Fi) Smoked fish casserole.

Tafelbirne (Gr) A dessert pear.

Tafelspitz (Gr) A traditional Austrian boiled beef dish with dozens of variations, usually including potatoes, root vegetables, and horseradish.

Tafelwein (Gr) Table wine.

Taffel (Da) A common Danish cow's milk cheese.

Taffelost (Nw) A mild semisoft cheese with a piquant flavor.

taffy (US) A chewy candy made from boiled brown sugar or molasses and butter. While still soft, it is pulled into long strands and shaped. Also called *toffee*.

taffy (GB) A sweetmeat of sugar or treacle, butter, and flour and mixed with chopped nuts. Also spelled *toffee*.

Tafi (Sp) A South American cow's milk cheese similar to traditional French Cantal.

Tagessuppe (Gr) Soup of the day.

tagine (Ar) Chicken stew with olives, ginger, paprika, and bulgur. Also spelled **tajine.**

tagin orz (Ar) Baked rice with chicken livers. Also spelled **tajine.**

tagliarini (It) Very narrow egg noodles.

tagliatelle (It) The term in Bologna for thin egg noodles; broader pasta than linguine. Also called **fettucine.**

tagliatelle al ragù (It) Noodles, with meat sauce.

tagliatelle verde (It) Green egg noodles, made by mixing spinach with the dough.

tahari (Ia) Rice and peas flavored with turmeric and herbs.

taheenov dzaghgagaghamp (Tr) Cauliflower with sesame seed paste.

taheenov gargantag (Tr) Cake with sesame seed paste.

taheenov jajegh (Tr) Swiss chard salad.

taheen yev rube (Tr) A spread of honey and sesame seed paste.

tahina (Ar) Pureed chick-peas and sesame seed paste.

tahini (Ar) Sesame-seed paste or thick oil of ground sesame seeds; used in Greek and Arab cooking. Also spelled *tahine*.

tahiyn (Ar) Flour.

tahn (Tr) A buttermilk derived from yogurt.

tahtsan (Tr) Sauce.

tahu (In) Soybean curd; tofu.

tahu campur (In) Salad made with soybean curd and wafers.

tai (Jp) Sea bream.

taiglach (Jw) Little balls of dough cooked in hot honey with chopped nuts, fruit, and spices which stick to the dough.

tailor (US) Popular name for bluefish.

tails (US) The tails of young steers; a flavorful dish when carefully prepared. Sometimes erroneously identified as "ox tails," the tail of a mature ox would be too tough to eat.

taimen (Fi) Trout.

taimeshi (Jp) Sea bream cooked with rice.

tai nam (Vt) Shredded beef brisket and thinly sliced steak in hot broth.

tai no sashimi (Jp) Sliced raw sea bream served with grated gingerroot or wasabi (Japanese horseradish) and soy sauce.

tai tempura (Jp) Fried sea bream in batter.

tajine (Ar) A meat or poultry and vegetable casserole with many variations; often with olives, ginger, paprika, quince, and burghul; the pot used is also called tajine. Also spelled **tagine.**

tajine ez zitoun (Ar) A casserole with veal and olives.

takenoko (Jp) Bamboo sprouts; delicate flavor; used often with pork and mushrooms.

takenokomeshi (Jp) Bamboo sprouts cooked with rice.

take out (US) Food bought ready-to-eat and taken away by the customer, such as deli foods, hamburgers, fried chicken, and pizza.

taki (Jp) Turkey.

takikomi-gohan (Jp) Brown rice with mushrooms and miso.

taklia (Ar) Garlic and coriander sauce.

tako (Jp) Octopus.

tako kushisashi (Jp) Grilled octopus on skewers.

takrai (Th) See **lemongrass.**

takuan (Jp) Dried Japanese white radish pickled in brine.

takuan maki (Jp) Pickled Japanese white radish wrapped in seaweed and rice.

takuan zuke (Jp) A salad of shredded Japanese white radish pickled in brine.

tala bua (Ia) Fried, deep-fried.

talas (In) Taro root.

Taleggio (It) A buttery cow's milk cheese with a piquant flavor; a soft cheese in the United States but original Italian version is runny.

tali machchi (Ia) Fried fish.

tallarines (Sp) Noodles.

Tallyrand (Fr) A savarin cake made with chopped pineapples soaked in syrup and covered with apricot glaze, named for the epicurean French statesman Charles Maurice de Tallyrand. His name is also associated with numerous other French dishes, including Tallyrand sauce, omelette Tallyrand, and anchovy fillets Tallyrand.

talmouse (Fr) A small cheese tart served as an hors d'oeuvre.

tamaatim (Ar) Tomatoes.

tamago (Jp) Egg.

tamagodōfu (Jp) Egg custard.

tamagodon (Jp) Egg served on rice.

tamago toji udon (Jp) Noodles with egg.

tamagoyaki (Jp) Omelet.

tamal de cazuela (Mx) Pork chops baked between layers of corn meal and flavored with chili sauces.

tamale (Mx) Steamed corn meal dough wrapped around a filling of ground meat seasoned with chili and other spices. Tamales were originally cooked and served in corn husks.

tamale pie (US) A baked dish made with layers of corn meal, ground beef, tomatoes, and onions.

tamalitos (Mx) Little tamales.

tamalitos de elote (Mx) Small sweet corn tamales.

tamanegi (Jp) Onions; dried onion.

tâmaras (Pg) Dates.

tamari (Jp) A type of shoyu (Japanese soy sauce) that is darker, richer, and more flavorful than ordinary shoyu. It is regarded as a "natural shoyu," made almost entirely from soybeans and with a minimum amount of wheat.

tamarind (Ia) The seed pod of the tamarind tree, *Tamarindus indica*, with brown, sticky pulp usually diluted with water and strained; used to add tang to soups, stews, curries, dressings, sauces, and chutneys. Also called **Indian date.**

tamattar (Ia) Tomato.

tamattar chatni (Ia) Tomato chutney.

Tambo (Aa) A mild Australian cow's milk cheese.

Tamié (Fr) A cow's milk cheese produced by Trappist monks in the Savoy area of France.

tamis (Fr) A cloth for straining sauces and other liquids. Also called **tammy cloth.**

tammy (US) See **tamis.**

tampala (Ia) Chinese spinach.

Tandil (Sp) A Cantal-type cow's milk cheese produced in Argentina.

tandir kebab (Tr) The process of baking an entire sheep or lamb in a pit of charcoal.

tandoor (Ia) A charcoal-fire heated, clay oven shaped like a barrel and buried in sand or soil; used to roast meat and fish and bake some breads.

tandoori (Ia) Roasted; baked.

tandoori murg (Ia) Baked, marinated chicken.

tandoori roti (Ia) Whole wheat flat bread, oven-baked in a tandoor.

táng (Ch) Sugar.

tāng (Ch) Soup.

tángcù liji (Ch) Sweet-and-sour boned pork.

táng-dz (Ch) Candy.

tangelo (US) A hybrid citrus fruit created from a cross of grapefruit, orange, and tangerine; lumpy with a yellow skin. Also called **ugli fruit.**

tangerine (US) A variety of sweet, loose-skinned orange that came from North Africa through Tangiers; deep orange skin and pulp.

tang kwah ah jad (Th) A condiment of sliced cucumber and hot red chilis; served with curries.

tangmiàn (Ch) Noodles in soup.

tango (Af–Swahili) Cucumber.

tangor (US) See **temple orange.**

tanmen (Jp) A type of noodle.

tanner (US) A species of crab.

tansansui (Jp) Mineral water.

tanuki jiru (Jp) A soup of barley miso, burdock root, and carrot.

tanuki soba (Jp) Buckwheat noodle.

tanuki udon (Jp) Noodles with tempura batter crusts.

Tanzenberger (Gr) A Limburger-type cheese produced in Austria.

taoge (In) Bean sprouts.

Tapachula (Sp) A good quality native Mexican coffee bean.

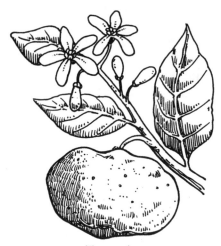

Tangerine

tapada de pollo (Mx) A chicken and pork stew flavored with raisins, olives, almonds, and spices.

tapai (In) Fermented cassava; eaten as a dessert.

tapang baka (Ph) Cured beef.

tapang baboy (Ph) Pork.

tapas (Sp) Canapés and small dishes served in Spanish bars; said to mean a "lid" or cover; fills in before a full meal.

tapenade (Fr) A condiment of desalted anchovies, capers, and black olives ground together with olive oil, garlic, lemon juice, and brandy.

tapinette (Fr) A curdled milk tart.

tapioca (US) The tiny balls or flakes made from the dried paste of grated cassava root; a starchy food; used for cereal, puddings, in soups, and for thickening in pies; may also be ground into flour.

täpläsilli (Fi) Shad.

taquitos (Mx) Small folded and fried tortillas with meat or other filling.

tara (Jp) Cod.

Tara (GB) A firm, bland Irish cheese.

tarako (Jp) Cod roe.

taramasalata (Gk) A caviar appetizer or spread; a mixture of carp roe (pink), olive oil, lemon juice, garlic, and soaked, mashed bread.

taratoor (Tr) A sauce of garlic, olive oil, lemon juice, and crushed walnuts, almonds, or filberts.

tarator (B1) A soup made with grated cucumber, yogurt, milk, lemon juice, garlic, and parsley; served cold.

taratur (Ar) A sesame seed sauce.

tarbooz (Ia) Watermelon.

tarhana çorbasi (Tr) Soup made with yogurt, tomatoes, and peppers.

tarhonya (Hu) Egg barley; dried pellets made with a mixture of flour and eggs; boiled and used in soup, or baked.

tari (Ia) Gravy.

tarka (Ia) Food preparation in which spices or flavorings are cooked separately before adding to the main ingredients for further cooking.

tarkari (Ia) Mixed vegetable curry.

taro (US) A starchy, potatolike tuber, *Colocasia esculenta*, with hairy, brown skin; the nutty flavored flesh varies in color from white to violet; commonly used in dishes of the tropics and the Orient, such as poi and dasheen.

tarragon (US) An aromatic herb with a flavor similar to anise. It is used on fish and poultry as well as in sauce béarnaise.

tarragon butter (Fr) Fresh tarragon pounded in a mortar, mixed with butter, strained through a fine sieve, and chilled. Also called **beurre d'estragon.**

tart (US) A small pastry shell usually containing a fruit, custard, or jam filling, but it may also have a filling of meat,

Taro

287

fish, or poultry, with or without a top crust. Also a sharp, sour, acidulous taste.

tarta (Sp) A tart.

tårta (Sw) Cake.

tartare (Fr) A cold sauce of mayonnaise, hard-cooked egg yolks, chopped onions, capers, pickles, lemon juice, or vinegar. Also spelled *tartar*.

Tartare (Fr) A Neufchátel-type cow's milk cheese flavored with herbs.

tartar med æg (Da) An open-face sandwich of raw chopped beef and onions, topped with raw egg.

tartar sauce (US) See **tartare.**

tartar steak (US) An open-face sandwich of raw chopped beef, sometimes topped with raw egg.

tarte (Fr) Tart, flan.

tarte à l'oignon (Fr) A creamy onion tart or pie.

tarte alsacienne (Fr) An apple flan with cinnamon added to the custard.

tarte aux fruits (Fr) Fruit tarts; small pastries filled with custard; topped with glazed fruits.

tarte des demoiselles Tatin (Fr) An upside-down apple tart, baked with the pastry on the top while a bottom layer of sugar carmelizes into a sweet crust. The tart is inverted for serving after it is baked. An ancient recipe, it was made famous by the Tatin sisters who operated a French restaurant at the end of the nineteenth century.

tartelette (Fr) A small tart.

tartelette Agnes (Fr) A tart similar to a quiche; a pastry shell filled with bacon strips fried in butter and alternate layers of slices of Gruyère cheese, baked in an oven.

tartelette à la Florentine (Fr) A tartlet crust filled with Parmesan cheese, grated truffles, and diced crayfish tails.

tartelette au Eglefin (Fr) A tartlet crust filled with a mixture of poached haddock and curry sauce.

tarteletter med hummer og asparges (Da) Small tarts filled with lobster and asparagus.

tarte liègeoise (Fr) A Belgian fruit tart with filling that includes juniper berries and whipped cream.

tartina (It) Tart.

tartines (Fr) Slices of buttered bread with jam or other spreads.

tartufi (It) Truffles.

tarwe brood (Du) Wheat bread.

Tascherin (Gr) Literally, "pockets" of dough, filled with meat, cheese, or fruit preserves.

tas kebob (Tr) Potted lamb.

tassergal (Fr) See **bluefish.**

tataki gobō (Jp) A salad of crushed burdock root with sesame dressing.

tatli (Tr) Sweet; desserts.

Tätschii (Gr) Potato pancakes in Switzerland.

tatti (Fi) See **boletus.**

tatties (Sc) Potatoes.

Taube (Gr) Pigeon.

Tauben in Specksauce (Gr) Pigeon or dove in bacon sauce.

taucheo (Ml) Soy sauce.

taucho (In, Th) Soy Sauce.

táu-dz (Ch) Peach.

tauşan (Tr) Hare.

tausi (Ph) Soy sauce.

tautog (US) A popular shallow water game fish found along the Atlantic Coast. Its flesh is good, white, and juicy.

tavada (Tr) Fried.

tavola fredda (It) Literally, "cold table"; cold buffet.

tavuk (Tr) Chicken.

tavuk çorbasi (Tr) Chicken soup.

tavuk izgara (Tr) Grilled chicken.

tavuk suyu (Tr) Chicken broth.

tay (Tr) Tea.

täytekakku (Fi) A layer cake filled or topped with berries, whipped cream, or other sweets.

tă-yú (Ch) Sole.

taze sebze (Tr) Fresh vegetables.

T-bone steak (US) A cut of beef taken from the center of the short loin next to the porterhouse. It contains parts of the loin and the tenderloin along with a T-shaped bone.

te (Da, Nw, Sw) Tea.

tè (It) Tea.

té (Sp) Tea.

tea (US) The leaves of a flowering evergreen of the camellia plant family, *Camellia sinensis*, grown mainly in China, India, Japan, Taiwan, Sri Lanka, and Africa. The major types of tea are green, black, and oolong. Black tea is produced from leaves withered by hot air and rolled to bruise them and release fermentation enzymes. Green tea is not fermented so the leaves remain green and mild. Oolong leaves are semifermented. Many commercial teas are blends, like English Breakfast tea, or flavored, like Earl Grey tea. Caf-

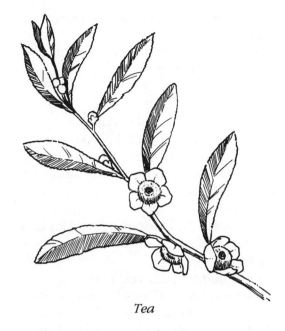

Tea

feine content of teas ranges from 2.0 percent for Japanese Green tea to 3.35 percent for India Black.

teaberry (US) A plant (*Gaultheria procumbens*) with leaves and fruity berries used in herbal teas.

teal (US) A freshwater game bird and smallest of the wild ducks. Also called **sarcelle.**

tebrød (Nw) Tea cake.

tee (Fi) Tea.

Tee (Gr) Tea.

teen (Ar) Figs.

teeri (Fi) Black grouse.

teesri (Ia) Clams.

teetar (Ia) Partridge.

teff (Ia) A variety of millet; used to make a flat bread.

tefteli (Rs) Braised meatballs.

teb (In) Tea.

289

Téiggemüse (Gr) Dishes with macaroni.

tej (Hu) Milk.

tejfeles úburgonya (Hu) New potatoes with sour cream.

tej patta (Ia) Bay leaf.

tejszines (Hu) With cream.

tekaka (Sw) Tea cake; crumpet.

tekka miso (Jp) An all-purpose condiment of fermented soybean curd and finely shaved burdock root sautéed in sesame oil.

tél (Ia) Oil.

tel beneer (Tr) String cheese with caraway seeds.

teleci (Cz) Veal.

teleci kotleta (Cz) Veal cutlet.

Teleme (Gk) A Greek/Romanian brine-cured cheese made with the milk of cows, goats, and/or sheep. Various Teleme products have been compared to feta, mozzarella, and Monterey. While popularly known as a "pickled" cheese, Teleme sold in the United States is not pickled.

Teleme Jack (US) An American cow's milk cheese produced by the manufacturers of Monterey Jack. Although named for the European Teleme by Greek immigrants, the products are not related.

teletina (SC) Veal.

tel khadayeef (Tr) Shredded pastry with walnut filling.

tellin (US) A variety of clam.

telur (In) Eggs.

telur goreng (In) Fried eggs.

telur rebus (In) Hard-cooked eggs.

telyatina (Rs) Veal.

temesvári sertésborda (Hu) Pork chops simmered with tomatoes, green beans, onion, sweet peppers, and bacon.

tempe (In) Fermented soybean cake. Also spelled *tempeh*.

temper (US) To bring food to the proper texture or consistency by moistening and kneading.

Temple orange (US) A spicy, thick-skinned hybrid fruit (*Citrus nobilis*) produced as a cross between the orange and tangerine. Also called **tangor.**

tempura (Jp) Fish, seafood, vegetables, and other ingredients coated in batter and deep-fried in oil; served with a dipping sauce.

tempura soba (Jp) Fried shrimp in batter served with buckwheat noodles in broth.

tench (US) A European freshwater fish, *Tinca tinca*: an important food fish in some areas. Also called **lin.**

tende (Af–Swahili) Dates.

tenderette (US) A cubed individual round steak.

tenderloin (US) The most tender part of the loin of beef or other meat animal, lying under the short ribs of the hind quarter. It is usually the most tender part of the animal because the psoas muscle, from which the cut is made, is seldom used. Steaks cut from the tenderloin may be labeled as **chateaubriands**, cut from the center, or **filet mignons** or **tournedos,** thick round cuts wrapped in bacon.

tendon (Jp) Deep-fried shrimp and vegetables coated in batter; served over rice.

tendron de veau (Fr) Braised breast of veal.

tengeri rák (Hu) Crab.

tentsuyu (Jp) A dipping sauce.

tepertös pogácsa (Hu) Biscuits with bacon cracklings.

tepid (US) Slightly warm.

teppenyaki (Jp) Beef, fish, or chicken and vegetables broiled on a steel plate at the table.

tequila (Mx) An alcoholic beverage made from the fermented juice of the agave plant. It is used in Margarita cocktails.

tereyaği (Tr) Butter.

teri (Jp) Glaze.

terik ayam (In) Chicken in macadamia nut sauce.

terik tempe (In) Fermented soybean cake in macadamia nut sauce.

teriyaki (Jp) Fish, meat, or poultry marinated in a soy-sherry-ginger sauce and broiled or grilled on skewers.

ternera (Sp) Veal.

ternera al jerez (Sp) Veal in sherry.

ternera borracha (Sp) Literally, "drunken veal"; veal strips in white wine flavored with cinnamon.

ternera en agujas (Sp) Breaded veal with ham and bacon; skewered and roasted.

ternera jardinera (Sp) Veal with vegetables.

terrapin (US) A North American freshwater turtle whose meat is used in highly flavored stews.

terrine (Fr) Finely chopped meat, fish, or fowl, baked in a dish called a terrine; served cold. Also called **pâté en terrine.**

terrine de caneton (Fr) Terrine of duckling.

terrine maison (Fr) An individual pâté of a restaurant made or served in a terrine.

tertanoosh (Tr) A many layered pastry with walnut filling.

Tête de Moine (Fr) Literally, "monk's head," a firm Swiss cheese originally produced by tenant farmers five hundred years ago as a means of paying rent. The cow's milk cheese, with the flavor of local herbs, is now produced by local dairies.

tête de veau (Fr) Calf's head, boiled and served with a vinaigrette or sauce à l'huile.

tetrazzini (It) A dish of meat, usually poultry, noodles, mushrooms, and cream sauce, topped with Parmesan cheese and browned in the oven. It was named for Italian soprano Luisa Tetrazzini.

Teufelsdreck (Gr) Asafetida.

textured plant protein (US) The isolated and flavored protein of plants, such as soybeans, peanuts, and wheat, used to extend or create other food products; resembles meat when processed; nutritious and high in protein. Also called **meat extender.**

thali (Ia) A large tray containing a vegetarian assortment in separate bowls with rice, chutney, and yogurt dips.

thalj (Ar) Ice.

thandai (Ia) A milk-based beverage flavored with almonds, sugar, and spices.

thé (Fr) Tea.

thé à la menthe (Fr) Mint tea.

thee (Du) Tea.

thee complet (Du) Tea with pastries.

theobromine (US) A chemical cousin of caffeine present mainly in chocolate; its effects on the body are similar to those of caffeine.

theophylline (US) A substance in tea leaves that is related to caffeine and has similar effects on the body.

thermidor (Fr) Originally applied to the *therme* (hot) month (July-August) of the French Revolutionary Calendar, *Thermidor* became the title of an 1894 play, which was honored by creation of the seafood dish of lobster cubes mixed with Bercy sauce and mustard and served in the lobster shells.

thiamine (US) See **vitamin B₁.**

thicken (US) To increase the density of a soup, sauce, or pudding by adding a substance such as flour, cornstarch, arrowroot, or tapioca. Also, food may be thickened by applying heat to cause moisture to evaporate.

thickener (US) A substance added to foods during processing, such as egg yolks, vegetable gums, cellulose derivates, or starches.

thimbleberry (US) A thimble-shaped fruit, such as a raspberry or blackberry.

thit (Vt) Meat.

Thompson seedless (US) A small sweet green seedless grape.

thon (Fr) Tuna.

Thousand Island dressing (US) A dressing made with mayonnaise, chili sauce, chopped peppers, and olives.

thousand-year eggs (US) See **pi-dàn.**

thread (US) A candy-making stage in which lifting a spoon of boiling syrup leaves a 2-inch thread.

Thunfisch (Gr) Tuna fish.

Thunfischsalat (Gr) Tuna fish salad.

Thuringer (Gr) A German pork sausage that may contain some beef or veal and may be sold either fresh or smoked.

thym (Fr) Thyme.

thyme (US) An herb (*Thymus vulgaris*) with a pungent mintlike aroma native to southern Europe. The ancient Greeks favored honey made by bees from thyme blossoms. Thyme is commonly used in Creole cuisine and, with bay leaf and parsley, is the basis of the French *bouquet garni*. It is complementary to seafood and poultry dishes.

Tia Maria (Sp) A coffee-flavored liqueur.

tibid (Da) A light snack.

tien mien jiàng (Ch) A sweet wheat flour and soybean paste.

Thyme

tif-fah (Ar) Apple.

tiger lily buds (US) Pale yellow, stringy buds of the tiger lily; used in Southeast Asian cooking. Also called **golden needles.**

tiges (Fr) A type of sausage.

tighanites (Gk) Fritters.

Tignard (Fr) A French blue cheese made from goat's milk.

tikki (Ia) Cutlet.

tikki chana dal (Ia) Cutlets made with chick-peas, eggs, and spices.

tikvice (SC) Zucchini.

til (Ia) Sesame seeds.

ti leaves (US) Oblong, shiny leaves of the ti plant, native to Hawaii and other Pacific islands; used to wrap food for cooking or to decorate.

tilefish (US) A saltwater fish found at the edge of the Continental Shelf of the Atlantic coast. It has good flavor, firm flesh, and is usually steamed, baked, or used in chowders, but may also be available as a smoked fish.

Tillamook (US) An American yellow Cheddar-type cheese made from raw milk. It has a pungent but mild flavor and is also made in a salt-free variety.

tilli (Fi) Dill.

tillikastike (Fi) Dill sauce.

tilliliha (Fi) Boiled veal or lamb with dill sauce.

tillisilakka (Fi) Herring in a dill sauce.

tilltug (Sw) Appetizer.

Tilsit (Gr) A cow's milk cheese with many cracks in a yellow interior; may or may not have a rind; pungent flavor and aroma.

timbale (Fr) Literally, "kettledrum"; round, molded cakes or pastries that may enclose meats, vegetables, cheese, seafood, or combinations.

timballo abruzzi (It) A three-layered casserole; chicken, meatballs, and cheese baked in a double crust.

timballo di riso con salsicce (It) Baked rice mold with a sausage filling.

tim joke (Ch) Sweet bean curd sticks, made with sugar cane.

timo (It) Thyme.

tinda (Ia) An East Indian gourd.

tini (Af–Swahili) Figs.

Tintenfisch (Gr) Squid.

tippaleivät (Fi) A May Day pastry made with a thin egg and milk batter drizzled into hot fat to form a cruller that resembles a bird's nest.

tipsy cake (GB) Layers of sponge cake soaked in whiskey or brandy with a custard in between layers; garnished with almonds.

tiram (In) Oyster.

tiramisù (It) Literally, "pick-me-up"; ladyfingers soaked in espresso and covered with powdered chocolate and sweet Mascarpone cheese.

tiri (Gk) Cheese.

Tirolen Eierspeisen (Gr) A casserole of hard-cooked eggs, potatoes, and anchovies.

Tiroler Knödeln (Gr) Dumplings with bacon.

tiropeta (Gk) Puffy cheese pie made with phyllo pastry filled with feta cheese, ricotta, eggs, and parsley.

tirotrigona (Gk) Phyllo pastry triangles stuffed with feta cheese.

tisane (Fr) A tea or light drink, often made with dried herbs.

titori bhujia (Ia) Bean sprout curry.

tlačenka (Cz) Head cheese.

tlami (Ar) A round, flat bread.

tmar (Ar) Dates.

tmar michi (Ar) A date confection stuffed with pistachios.

toad-in-the-hole (GB) Sausage meatballs baked in batter.

toast (US) To parch or brown bread or other food by heating it thoroughly.

tocino (Sp) Bacon.

tocino de cielo (Sp) Literally, "bacon from heaven"; thick caramel custard.

tocopherols (US) A group of substances that are technically alcohols but which have vitamin E activity. They occur naturally in wheat germ and other grains, vegetables, and fruits.

toddy (GB) A beverage of hot water and sugar flavored with whiskey or other spirits.

tofu (Jp) See **soybean curd.**

togan (Jp) A melon with firm white flesh.

togarashi (Jp) Hot pepper.

tohm (Ar) Garlic.

tojás (Hu) Eggs.

tojáskocsonya (Hu) Pieces of egg custard for soup.

tokány (Hu) Strips of beef or veal cooked in their own juice with onion, black pepper, and paprika; lamb or pork may be used.

Tokay grape (US) A large sweet grape used in the production of Hungarian dessert wine. The term also is applied to a Flame Tokay grape grown in California for wine blends.

tökebal (Hu) Cod.

tökfőzelék (Hu) Strips of fried squash dressed in lemon juice and yogurt.

Toll House cookie (US) A chocolate chip cookie named after the Toll House Inn in Massachusetts where the recipe was created.

töltött (Hu) Stuffed.

töltött káposzta (Hu) Cabbage stuffed with ground meat, usually beef or pork, onions, and rice; served with sour cream.

töltött paprika (Hu) Sweet peppers stuffed with ground meat, rice, and onions.

töltött paradicsom (Hu) Stuffed tomatoes.

tomaatti (Fi) Tomato.

tomaattimehu (Fi) Tomato juice.

tomaattisilakka (Fi) Herring in a tomato sauce.

tomalley (US) The liver of the lobster, a delicacy that turns green when cooked.

Tom and Jerry (GB) A drink made of hot rum and brandy with sugar, beaten eggs, water or milk, and nutmeg.

tomat (Da) Tomato.

tomate (Pg, Sp) Tomato.

Tomaten (Gr) Tomatoes.

Tomatensalat (Gr) Tomato salad.

tomatensap (Du) Tomato juice.

Tomatensuppe (Gr) Tomato soup.

tomater (Da, Nw, Sw) Tomatoes.

tomates farcies (Fr) Stuffed tomatoes.

tomatillo (Mx) A green, somewhat tart fruit, *Physalis ixocarpa*, of the tomato family; about the size of a walnut with parchmentlike skin that is stripped away to expose the fruit; very dense pulp with tiny seeds; used in guacamole, jams, chutneys, and other dishes. Also called **jamberry.**

tomato (US) A pulpy, usually red, juicy

berry of a solanaceous plant (*Lycopersicon esculentum*), and a member of the nightshade family. The tomato was originally a native of tropical America but is now cultivated throughout the world.

tomato juice (US) The juice expressed from raw prime tomatoes. Because the raw flavor components of a tomato are in chemicals concentrated in the pulp and skin, the expressed juice usually does not taste like a raw tomato. Salt and other flavorings including other vegetable juices may be added.

tomato paste (US) A thick concentrate made from cooked tomatoes; usually unflavored except for salt.

tomato puree (US) A thick liquid made of unseasoned cooked tomatoes strained for uniform consistency.

tomato sauce (US) A sauce made of puréed tomatoes seasoned with salt and usually other spices and herbs.

tomatsaft (Nw) Tomato juice.

tomatsås (Sw) Catsup; tomato sauce.

tomber (Fr) To cook watery vegetables such as spinach in their own liquid over low heat without fat.

Tom Collins (US) A cocktail made of gin, lime or lemon juice, soda water, and sugar, served over crushed ice. The drink, which has many variations depending upon the ingredients, is reportedly named for a bartender who created it.

Tomino del Monferrato (It) A cow's milk cheese with a smooth, easy to slice texture and a mild, milky taste.

Tomme (Fr) A term for two groups of cheeses in the Pyrénées and Savoie, one made from ewes' or goats' milk and the other from cows' milk. Both are pressed and uncooked and include many different types. Most are mild-flavored and are good for snacks. In some rural regions, the word tomme is used to mean cheese. Also spelled *Tome*.

Tomme au raisin (Fr) Describes a cheese covered with dried grape seeds.

Tomme de chèvre (Fr) A small goat's milk cheese.

Tomme de Savoie (Fr) A semisoft cheese made in the Savoie region of France.

tom sot cay (Vt) Shrimp sautéed with chilis, onion, ginger, tomato, and vinegar.

tonfisk (Sw) Tuna.

tong (Du) Sole.

tongue (US) The fleshy organ from the head of a meat animal, usually beef, sometimes lamb, pork, or veal; used boiled, pickled, smoked, baked, and in aspic.

tongue and blood loaf (US) A sausage of calves' tongues, pork fat, pork skin, and beef blood.

tonhal (Hu) Tuna.

tonic water (US) See **quinine.**

tonija (Du) Tuna.

tonka bean (Pg) A fragrant almond-shaped seed of a Brazilian tree, used in imitation vanilla flavorings.

tonkatsu (Jp) Pork cutlet.

tonnato (It) In a sauce made from tuna; often used on veal.

tonnikala (Fi) Tuna.

tonno (It) Tuna.

tonno, al (It) With a seafood sauce of tuna, garlic, tomatoes, and capers.

tonno e fagioli (It) Tuna fish and white beans in a garlic-flavored vinaigrette.

tonno sott' olio (It) Tuna fish in olive oil.

toorshee (Tr) Pickled vegetables.

top butt (US) The boneless tender center of a beef sirloin.

Topf (Gr) Stew.

Topfengolatschen (Gr) An Austrian specialty of puff pastry filled with cottage cheese, eggs, vanilla, and grated lemon peel.

Topfenknodel (Gr) Cream cheese dumplings; served with stewed fruit.

Topfenpalatschinken (Gr) Pancakes made with cottage cheese.

topig (Tr) Chick-pea appetizer.

topinambour (Fr) Jerusalem artichoke.

topinka (Cz) Toast.

top loin chop (US) A center cut loin chop.

top of chuck (US) A chuck steak.

top round (US) The best section of the whole round of beef for both roasts and broiled steaks.

top sirloin (US) The lean and tender side portion of the beef round, used for roasts and broiled steaks.

tordi allo spièdo (It) Small birds (thrush) roasted on a spit.

tordo (It) Thrush.

toriganni (Jp) Chicken balls.

tori hoban (Jp) Fried rice with chicken, bamboo shoots, mushroom, and soy sauce.

toriniku (Jp) Chicken.

toriniku tatsuta age (Jp) Deep-fried marinated chicken.

tori no nimono (Jp) Simmered chicken and vegetables.

tori no sashimi (Jp) Sliced raw chicken served with grated gingerroot or Japanese horseradish and soy sauce.

torkad frukt (Sw) Dried fruits.

tørkage (Da) Cake.

torma (Hu) Horseradish.

tormamártás (Hu) Horseradish sauce.

toronja (Pg, Sp) Grapefruit.

tororoimo (Jp) Grated yam or taro root.

tororo kombu (Jp) A variety of seaweed, kombu leaves soaked in vinegar and cut into threads.

tororo soba (Jp) Noodles with yam paste.

torpedo (US) Hoagie.

torrada (Pg) Toast.

tørrekaker (Nw) Cookies.

tørret frugtsuppe (Nw) Dried fruit soup, served hot or cold.

torrfisk (Da, Nw, Sw) Stockfish.

torrijas (Sp) Bread squares dipped in milk and eggs; fried and then baked with honey.

torrone (It) Nougat candy made of honey, almond, and nuts.

torsk (Da, Nw, Sw) Codfish.

Tororoimo

torsk med eggesaus (Nw) Poached codfish served with a sauce containing chopped eggs, tomato, parsley, and chives.

torta (Ph) A fried pancake of ground pork, eggs, tomato, and onion.

torta (SC) Cake.

torta (Pg) A rolled, filled cake; pie.

torta (It) Tart, pie, cake.

torta con formaggio (It) Cheesecake.

torta di macedonia di frutta (It) Tart or cake made with mixed fruit.

torta di ricotta (It) Cheese cake.

torta di tagliatella (It) Noodle cake made with almonds, sugar, macaroons, and noodles in a pastry shell.

torta pasqualina (It) Thin layers of dough, or dough pockets, stuffed with green vegetables, cheese, and eggs.

Törtchen (Gr) Small tarts.

Torte (Gr) 1. A very light, delicate cake baked in round layers and filled with whipped cream, fruit, chocolate, other icings, jams, or jellies. 2. A flan or tart with a filling.

torte (US) A variation of the German torte; a cake in which the flour has been replaced by bread crumbs or cookie crumbs or finely ground nuts.

tortellata crema (It) Cream tart.

tortellini (It) Literally, "little twisted ones"; meat (or other) stuffed, twisted pasta.

tortellini alla bolognese (It) A specialty of Bologna; small pockets of dough filled with minced meat, such as chicken and sausage, eggs, cheese, and spices; served in broth or meat sauce.

tortiglione (It) Almond cake

tortilha de mariscos (Pg) A shellfish omelet.

tortilla (Mx) The traditional unleavened, round, flat bread of Mexico; made of corn or wheat flour; used toasted, fried, cut up and made into chips, rolled, folded, and filled with other ingredients.

tortilla de huevos (Mx) Omelet.

tortina (It) Small tart.

tort iz meringi (Rs) Meringue cake made with cream, walnuts, and brandy; topped with nuts and chocolate.

tortoni (It) See **biscotto tortoni.**

tortue (Fr) Turtle.

toscane, à la (Fr) Dishes prepared with Parmesan cheese and ham.

Toscano (It) A firm but soft Pecorino-type Italian cheese made with sheep's milk.

toscatårta (Sw) A cake with almonds.

toso (Jp) Sweet sake flavored with herbs and served on ceremonial occasions, such as New Year's Day.

toss (US) Mix by gently turning ingredients, such as salad greens, over several times.

tossed salad (US) A green vegetable salad thoroughly mixed with the dressing by turning it over several times. Tossing also prevents soggy greens due to accumulation of the dressing.

tostadas (Mx) Corn tortillas fried crisp, then topped with various combinations of meat, poultry, fish, cheese, beans, or vegetables.

tostato (It) Toast.

tosti na jamu (Af–Swahili) Toast and jam.

to-su (Ch) A red herb of the mint family (*Perilla nankinesis*) with a combined flavor of parsley, coriander, and cumin. It is commonly used in Oriental cooking.

tōsuto (Jp) Toast.

totani (It) Small squid.

totopos (Mx) Small, crisply-fried triangles of tortillas.

toucinho (Pg) Smoked slab bacon.

toucinho de céu (Pg) Literally, "bacon from heaven"; egg yolks and almonds baked in syrup.

toulousaine, à la (Fr) A garnish for certain dishes such as roast poultry or vols-au-vent.

tourin (Fr) A French onion soup made with milk and egg yolks.

tournedos (Fr) A small, round, thick slice of beef tenderloin; usually sautéed or grilled.

tournedos de veau (Fr) Medallions of veal.

Tournedos Rossini (Fr) Tournedos sautéed in butter and arranged on toast; topped with a slice of foie gras and truffles and covered with a sauce.

tourte (Fr) Sweet tart.

tourtelettes (Fr) Small tarts.

toute-épice (Fr) Allspice.

tra (Vt) Tea.

tracciole d'agnello (It) Lamb cooked on skewers, like shish kebab.

trace elements (US) Minerals such as selenium or vanadium required daily by the body in microscopic amounts. They serve mainly as cofactors for metabolic functions.

tragacanth (US) A shrub that is the source of a white tasteless vegetable gum used in candies and other confections.

tranche (Fr) Slice.

tranebær (Nw) Cranberry.

Trappiste (Fr) A cheese made by Trappist monks in France.

Trasch (Gr) An apple-pear liqueur made in Switzerland.

trassi (In) A pungent, fermented shrimp paste; thick, brown and salty; used fried or roasted and added to the spices in the recipe. Also called **balachan.**

Trauben (Gr) Grapes.

travailler (Fr) Literally, to be industrious; in French cuisine, to blend or smooth ingredients.

treacle (GB) A by-product of sugar making. Black treacle is molasses. A lighter, refined molasses may also be called treacle, as may golden syrup.

tree ear (US) See **cloud ear.**

trefoil (US) A type of three-leaved clover used for color and flavoring.

trenette (It) Fine pasta, matchstick-thin and cut in long pieces.

trenette con pesto (It) Long noodles with a sauce of garlic, olive oil, herbs, and pine nuts.

Trenton cracker (US) A light round oyster cracker.

trepang (GB) See **sea cucumber.**

treska (Cz) Cod.

třešně (Cz) Cherries.

trešnje (SC) Cherries.

trifle (GB) A traditional dessert made with sponge cake soaked in sweet sherry, covered with an egg custard, and topped with whipped cream. There are many variations that may include fruit, jelly, chocolate, and other flavorings.

trifli (Da) Trifle; sponge cake soaked in wine or liqueur, with macaroons, jam, and whipped cream.

triglie (It) Red mullet.

triglie alla livornese (It) Mullet seasoned with garlic, parsley, and celery; cooked in olive oil with pepper and tomatoes.

trigo (Sp) Wheat.

trigo negro (Sp) Buckwheat.

tripa (Pg) Tripe.

tripe (US) Stomach lining of veal or beef; needs long cooking. Sheep or pig tripe is also used for food.

tripes à la mode de Caen (Fr) A tripe casserole as prepared in the style of Caen, in northern France; with calf's foot, garlic, leeks, herbs, spices, Calvados, and cider.

triple-crème (Fr) A very rich French dessert cheese containing 75 percent butterfat.

triple sec (US) A strong, colorless orange-flavored liqueur.

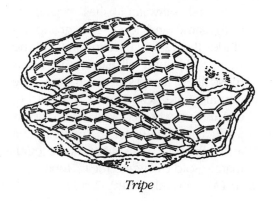

Tripe

trippa alla bolognese (It) Tripe fried in olive oil, bacon, onion, and garlic with egg yolks added.

trippa alla fiorentina (It) Casserole of tripe; served with beans and cheese.

trippa al sugo (It) Tripe with meat sauce.

triticale flour (US) A high-protein, low-gluten flour produced as a hybrid of three different grains: durum wheat, hard red wheat, and rye. Because it is low in gluten, a high-gluten flour must be added for baking purposes.

Trockenbeerenauslese (Gr) An excellent German wine made from individually picked grapes that are allowed to remain on the vines until nearly dry and rich in sugar.

tronçons de homard (Fr) Lobster chunks.

trota (It) Trout.

trota salmonata (It) Salmon trout.

trotter (GB) The foot of a livestock animal.

trout (US) Any salmonlike fish with a delicate white to pinkish sweet-flavored flesh. Flavors vary from nearly bland for freshwater species to salmonlike taste and texture for steelheads and other saltwater varieties. The steelhead is a freshwater rainbow trout that migrates from western mountain streams to the Pacific Ocean for feeding.

trouvillaise (Fr) A shrimp sauce garnish that also contains mussels and mushrooms.

trucha (Sp) Trout.

trufa (Pg) Truffle.

truffe (Fr) Truffle.

Trüffel (Gr) Truffle.

truffle (US) Any of a variety of fleshy underground fungi. They range in color from white through beige and brown to black and in size from a fingernail to an apple. They have a raw flavor similar to garlic that becomes delicate when cooked for use as a garnish.

truite (Fr) Trout.

truite au bleu de meunière (Fr) Trout in oil and butter.

truite saumonée (Fr) Salmon trout.

trunzo (It) Collards.

truskawki (Po) Strawberries.

truss (US) To skewer and tie a fowl or a cut of beef into a compact shape before cooking.

truta (Pg) Trout.

Truthahn (Gr) Turkey.

Truthahn mit Reis gratiniert (Gr) Baked turkey and rice with melted cheese and bread crumbs.

tryptophan (US) An essential amino acid and a parent chemical to niacin, a B-complex vitamin. It occurs in meat, milk, eggs, and some leafy vegetables and is necessary for normal growth and nitrogen balance.

tsai (Gk) Tea.

tsài tāng (Ch) Vegetable soup.

tsán-dòu (Ch) Lima beans.

tsău-méi (Ch) Strawberries.

tsetov (Tr) With olive oil.

tsetov gangar (Tr) Artichokes in olive oil.

tsetov leetsk (Tr) Stuffed vegetables.

tsetov tzavari yeghintz (Tr) Bulghur pilaf.

tsgnaganch (Tr) Mussels.

tsgnaganchi leetsk (Tr) Stuffed mussels.

tsgnaganchi meechoog (Tr) Pilaf with mussels.

tsoog (Tr) Fish.

tsoogi aghtsan (Tr) Fish salad.

tsù (Ch) Vinegar.

tsukemono (Jp) Pickled vegetables.

tsukimi udon (Jp) Noodles with raw egg.

tsukudani (Jp) Fish, shellfish, and seaweed simmered with sweetened soy sauce; preserved foods.

tsumamimono (Jp) Literally, "thirst provokers"; appetizers on skewers.

tswèi-pí jī (Ch) Deep-fried chicken, wrapped in paper.

tsyplyata tabaka (Rs) Boned, pressed chicken; fried and served with sour cream.

tubettini (It) Small tubular macaroni.

tufaa (Af–Swahili) Apple.

tuffaaha (Ar) Apple.

tuile (Fr) A thin crisp cookie in the shape of a tile.

tükör tojás (Hu) Fried eggs.

tulband (Du) Raisin cake.

tulipe (Fr) A ruffled pastry shell shaped to hold a dessert filling.

tulsee (Ia) Basil.

tum (Ar) Garlic.

tuna (US) Any of several kinds of mackerel-related saltwater fishes prized as both game and food. The group includes the 12-foot bluefin tuna and the small, 10-pound albacore, the kinds most likely to appear on a table. The raw albacore flesh is very soft but becomes firm when cooked. Albacore has a much milder flavor than other tuna and is the only species that can be legitimately sold as "white meat" tuna.

tuna (Mx) Prickly pear.

tuňák (Cz) Tuna.

tunge (Da) Tongue.

tunge (Nw) Tongue.

tungeflyndre (Nw) Sole.

tungule (Af–Swahili) Tomatoes.

tunjevina (SC) Tuna.

Tunke (Gr) Gravy or sauce.

tunnied veal (GB) See **vitello tonnato.**

tunny (GB) Tuna.

tuoremebu (Fi) Fresh fruit juice.

tuorlo d'uova (It) Egg yolk.

tur (Ia) Pigeon peas.

turbinado sugar (US) A partially refined light brown sugar produced by washing raw sugar in a turbina (centrifuge) to remove the molasses.

turbot (US) A European flatfish, family Bothidae; valued for its firm, white flesh; usually poached. Although similar in shape to sole or flounder, sometimes offered as "type of turbot," most turbots are much larger and have both eyes on the left side of the head. However, most gourmets prefer a small "chicken turbot." Also called *Bannock fluke,* **piggvar.**

turbot poché hollandaise (Fr) Poached turbot served with a sauce of egg yolks and butter.

tur dal (Ia) Pigeon peas; usually served with chilis.

turkey (US) A large North American fowl related to the pheasant and highly prized as a food. Originally a wild bird, the turkey has been domesticated and bred like other poultry to produce large males (Toms) and hens with plump tender flesh.

Turkish Delight (US) A Middle Eastern pink, white, or green confection coated with icing. Flavored with rose water, vanilla or peppermint, the sweet may also contain nuts. Also called **lokum.**

türlü (Tr) A casserole of mixed vegetables, such as green string beans, potatoes, eggplant, and onions, with lamb or veal stewed in olive oil.

turmeric (US) A brown-skinned root of a plant, *Curcuma domestica*, native to India; the slightly bitter, yellow flesh is used in curries, lentil dishes, and ground to a powder for spice mixtures or as a substitute for saffron.

turn (US) To make sour.

turnedo (It) Fillet of beef.

turnip (US) A white cruciferous vegetable (*Brassica rapa*) with a round fleshy root. It is boiled, mashed, used in stews, and, when young, eaten raw. The tops are boiled as greens.

Turnip

301

turnip greens (US) See **turnip.**

turnip-root celery (US) See celeriac.

turnip-rooted cabbage (US) Kohlrabi.

turnover (US) A pastry round folded over a fruit or savory filling.

túrós (Hu) Noodles.

túrós gombóc (Hu) Cottage cheese dumplings.

túróscsusza (Hu) Noodles with cottage cheese curds, sour cream, and bacon cracklings; served as a dessert.

turska (Fi) Cod.

turşu (Tr) Mixed pickles.

turtle (US) Any of about three hundred species of reptiles covered by a horny protective shell (carapace) that live in or near water. The favorite species used for food are the green turtle, a brown creature named for its green fat utilized in green turtle soup, and the diamondback terrapin, highly prized both for its flesh and its contribution to Maryland terrapin soup.

tutmaj (Tr) Yogurt noodle soup.

tutoo (Tr) Sour.

tutoo aboor (Tr) Sour soup.

tutoom (Tr) Squash.

tutoomi bahadzo (Tr) Pumpkin preserve.

tutoomi leetsk (Tr) Stuffed squash.

tutti-frutti (It) Literally, "all fruits"; any ice cream, cake, or other sweet food containing a mixture of chopped fruits and nuts.

tutvash (Tr) Pickled, pickles.

tuz (Tr) Salt.

tvaroh (Cz) Farmer or pot cheese.

tvorog (Rs) Cottage or pot cheese.

tvrda jaja (SC) Hard-boiled eggs.

twaalfuurtje (Du) Cold luncheon.

twelfth-night cake (GB) A traditional rich spice cake with candied fruits and almond paste filling. It may be topped with a coin used to choose a "king" or "queen" of the festival marking the twelfth day after Christmas.

tyán chéng chá (Ch) A beverage made with oranges, sugar, and rice flour boiled in water.

tyán-gwā (Ch) Melon.

tyán swān gú lău ròu (Ch) Pork braised with bamboo shoots, green peppers; served with sweet-and-sour sauce.

tyán swān yú (Ch) Sweet-and-sour fish; served in a vinegar and sour sauce.

Tybo (Da) A loaf-style cheese somewhat like samsø but milder.

tykmælk (Da) A clabbered milk dessert.

tyrolienne (Fr) A garnish of tomatoes and fried onion rings.

tyrosine (US) A naturally occurring amino acid essential for formation of the nerve tissue chemical epinephrine, melanin skin pigment, and the thyroid hormone thyroxine.

tyttebær (Da) Lingonberry.

tyttebær (Nw) Red whortleberries.

tzavar (Tr) Cracked wheat.

tzavari aghtsan (Tr) A salad of cracked wheat, onions, potatoes, tomato paste, olive oil, and spices.

tzavari yeghintz (Tr) Cracked wheat pilaf.

tzimmes (Jw) A dish made with a variety of combinations of meats, vegetables, or fruits cooked over low heat, such as beef brisket and sweet potatoes or prunes and farfel.

tzoren (Tr) Whole wheat.

U

überbacken (Gr) Oven browned.

uborka (Hu) Cucumbers.

uborkamártás (Hu) Cucumber sauce.

uborkasaláta (Hu) Cucumber salad with garlic and sugar.

uccèlletti (It) Strips of veal, rolled and stuffed.

uccèlletti scappati (It) Rolled veal birds, sausages, or other meat chunks grilled and served with toast.

uccèlli (It) Birds, fowl.

udang (In) Shrimp, prepared in many ways.

udang asam manis (In) Sweet-and-sour shrimp.

udang goreng (In) Shrimp in batter, deep-fried.

udang karang (In) Crayfish or lobster.

udang kerie (In) Curried shrimp.

udang pindang ketjap (In) Shrimp in soy sauce.

udo (Jp) A bushy plant, *Aralia cordata*, cultivated in Japan; valued for its aromatic, crunchy root and tender young stalks; used as a vegetable or in salads.

udon (Jp) Broad noodles of wheat or buckwheat flour.

udonsuki (Jp) Broad wheat noodles in broth.

udruk (Ia) Green ginger.

ugli fruit (Cb) See **tangelo.**

ugnsbakat (Sw) Baked.

ugnspannkaka (Sw) A thick, oven-baked pancake.

ugnsstekt (Sw) Roasted.

úhoř (Cz) Eel.

uien (Du) Onions.

uitsmijter (Du) Literally, "thrower-outer"; a snack of an open sandwich topped with a slice of ham or beef, fried eggs, tomato, lettuce, and pickles.

uji (Af–Swahili) Hot cereal or porridge.

ukad (Ia) Red-brown, unpolished rice used to make a batter for dosas.

ukha (Rs) A clear soup of freshwater fish such as whitefish or perch; wine and a bouquet garni may be added.

uku (Pl) Gray snapper.

ukwaju (Af–Swahili) Tamarind.

ulje (SC) Oil. Also called **zejtin.**

ulu-ulu (Pl) Red snapper.

umani (Jp) Vegetables with chicken cut in strips; simmered in seasoned broth.

um ar-rubiyam (Ar) Literally, "mother of the shrimp"; a type of lobster harvested in the Arabian Gulf.

umchur (Ia) Raw sun-dried mango with a sour taste; used in chutney.

umeboshi (Jp) Pickled sour plums.

ume maki (Jp) Pickled plum.

umeshu (Jp) Plum wine.

umewan (Jp) A clear soup containing small rolled omelets, vegetables, shrimp, and fish.

umido (It) Stewed or boiled meats.

umido di coniglio (It) Rabbit stew.

umintas (Sp) A Bolivian dish of baked corn.

umm ali (Ar) A pastry and milk pudding with raisins.

unagi (Jp) Eel.

unagi domburi (Jp) Broiled eels served on rice.

unagi maki (Jp) Cooked eel.

unbleached flour (US) Wheat flour that has not been treated with chemicals to produce whiteness.

unday (Ia) Eggs.

unday brinjal (Ia) Spicy scrambled eggs mixed with cooked, mashed eggplant.

unelmapannukakku (Fi) Baked whipping cream pancakes.

uni (Jp) Edible, raw sea urchin.

univalve (US) A single-shelled edible mollusk, such as abalone, conch, snail, and whelk.

unleavened (US) Describes bread or other baked products that contain no rising agent such as yeast or baking powder. Examples include tortillas, matzos, and chapaties.

unpolished rice (US) See **brown rice.**

unsaturated fat (US) A fatty substance that contains unsaturated fatty acids. Most liquid vegetable oils are unsaturated fats.

unsaturated fatty acid (US) See **fatty acids.**

uova (It) Egg.

uova affogate (It) Poached egg.

uova affogate con acciughe (It) Poached egg with anchovies.

uova al prosciutto (It) Ham and eggs.

uova bollite (It) Boiled eggs.

uova fritte (It) Fried eggs.

uova morene (It) "Black eggs"; a dessert of crepelike omelets flavored with chocolate and almonds and layered with a custard filling.

uova piccante (It) Deviled eggs.

uova sode con tonno (It) Hard-boiled eggs stuffed with tuna.

uova strapazzate (It) Scrambled eggs.

upside-down cake (US) A cake made by lining a pan with butter, brown sugar, nuts, and fruit; batter is poured over this layer. When baked, the cake is inverted to place the fruit mixture on top.

urad (Ia) Lentils.

urap (In) A salad of bamboo shoots, cabbage, carrots, green beans, and bean sprouts with a grated coconut dressing.

urme (SC) Dates.

ürühús (Hu) Mutton.

ushio wan (Jp) A fish broth made with the head of a red snapper.

ushki (Rs) Small dumplings filled with meat or mushrooms; boiled, sautéed, or deep-fried.

ústřice (Cz) Oysters.

ustritsy s ikroi (Rs) Oysters with caviar.

usukuchi shoyu (Jp) Light, delicate-flavored soy sauce.

uszka (Po) A soup garnish; small pieces of dough stuffed with mushrooms.

uthappam (In) Doughy, slightly sour pancakes.

utrunj (Ar) A variety of large lemon used to make a Middle Eastern confection. Strips of inner rind are marinated in the lemon's juice with sugar.

uuden vuoden malja (Fi) A New Year's Eve nonalcoholic punch of currant juice and lemon soda.

uunijuustoa (Fi) Baked cream cheese.

uuni riisipuuro (Fi) Baked rice pudding.

uunissa paistettu (Fi) Baked.

uunissa paistettu perunakakkuja (Fi)
Baked potato cakes.

uva (Pg, Sp) Grape.

uva (It) Grape, or grapes in a bunch.

uva passa (It) Raisin.

uva spina (It) Gooseberry.

uyoga (Af–Swahili) Mushrooms.

uzená šunka (Cz) Smoked ham.

uzený jazyk (Cz) Smoked tongue.

üzüm (Tr) Grapes.

uzura (Jp) Quail.

uzura no tamago (Jp) Quail eggs.

vaca (Pg) Beef. Also called **bife.**

vaca cozida (Pg) Boiled beef.

vaca estufada (Pg) Pot roast cooked with bacon, onions, tomatoes, garlic, and soy sauce.

vaca guisada (Pg) Beef stew.

vacherin (Fr) A dessert of meringue or almond paste formed in layers or a shell filled with whipped cream or ice cream; also, any of several different cheeses of France and Switzerland.

Vacherin Mont d'Or (Fr–Swiss) A cow's milk cheese; beige rind, pale, soft interior; rich, creamy taste with an aroma of pine from being wrapped in spruce or balsam.

vad (Hu) Game.

vadas (Ia) Fried balls of ground lentils or chick-pea flour, spices and herbs; served with chutney or yogurt.

vadelmia (Fi) Raspberries.

våfflor (Sw) Waffles.

vafler (Nw) Waffles.

vaflya (Rs) Waffles.

vahva juusto (Fi) Strong-flavored cheese.

vainilla (Sp) Vanilla.

vaj (Hu) Butter.

vajas pogácsa (Hu) Sweet butter biscuits.

vajbab (Hu) Wax or yellow beans.

vajgaluska (Hu) Dumplings made with eggs, butter, and flour.

vaktel (Sw) Quail.

val (Ia) See **hyacinth bean.**

Valencay (Fr) A goat's milk cheese; pyra-mid-shaped; ash-coated; chalky-white interior; tangy, strong taste.

valenciano (Mx) A sweet green chili pepper sometimes used when a milder hot pepper dish is desired.

Valencia orange (US) A sweet, juicy orange with a spherical shape and thin skin.

Valencienne, à la (Fr) 1. Describes certain dishes of northern France such as rabbit with prunes and raisins. 2. In the style of Spanish (Valencia) cooking, such as a rice dish garnished with smoked ham and peppers.

valine (US) One of the essential amino acids required for normal growth in children and nitrogen balance in adults. Food sources include wheat gluten, wheat germ, brewer's yeast, and whole eggs, in addition to meat, poultry, fish, and dairy products.

valkosipuli (Fi) Garlic.

valkosipulisilakka (Fi) Pickled herring and thin slices of carrots in a garlic flavored brine.

valkoviiniä (Fi) White wine.

valnødkage (Da) Walnut cake.

valnødromkager (Da) Walnut rum cookies.

valnötter (Sw) Walnuts.

valnøtter (Nw) Walnuts.

Valois, sauce (Fr) Béarnaise sauce with added meat glaze or jelly.

valpolicella (It) A dry, red wine produced in northern Italy.

vanaspati (Ia) A vegetable shortening used as a butter substitute.

vand (Da) Water.

vaniglia (It) Vanilla.

vanilia fagylalt (Hu) Vanilla ice cream.

vaniljajäätelö (Fi) Vanilla ice cream.

vanilje (Nw) Vanilla.

vaniljepudding (Nw) Custard.

vaniljglass (Sw) Vanilla ice cream.

vaniljsås (Sw) 1. Cold vanilla sauce; served with cake or other desserts. 2. A custard.

vanilla (US) An extract from the bean of a light green orchid, *Vanilla planifolia*, native to Mexico; the raw bean is tasteless; flavor develops by drying and fermenting; vanilla essence is brown and fragrant; Cortes tasted it in the court of Montezuma and took it back to Spain.

vanilla extract (US) A flavoring obtained from chopped, cured vanilla beans processed with a solvent in a similar way that coffee beans are percolated.

vanilla sugar (US) 1. Finely ground, cured vanilla bean mixed with sugar,

Vanilla

used in producing sweet chocolate. 2. Sugar flavored by storing with a vanilla bean in a sealed jar.

vanille (Fr) Vanilla.

Vanilleeis (Gr) Vanilla ice cream.

vanilleijs (Du) Vanilla ice cream.

vanillin (US) Synthetic vanilla made from an aromatic substance (eugenol) in clove oil.

vann (Nw) Water.

vannbakkelse (Nw) Cream puffs.

vannmelon (Nw) Watermelon.

vanocka (Cz) A Christmas pastry in the shape of a braid.

vapeur, à la (Fr) Cooked in steam.

varak (Ia) Delicate, tissue-thin silver or gold leaf used to decorate food.

vařené (Cz) Boiled.

vařené brambory (Cz) Boiled potatoes.

vařené hovězi maso (Cz) Boiled beef.

vařené vejce (Cz) Boiled eggs.

vareniki (Rs) Noodle dumplings filled with cheese or fruit; similar to Chinese dim sum or Italian ravioli.

varerdrikke (Nw) Beverages.

varié (Fr) Assorted.

variety meats (US) See **offal.**

varkenskarbonaden (Du) Fried pork chops.

varkenskotelet (Du) Pork chops.

varkensvlees (Du) Pork.

varm choklad (Sw) Hot chocolate.

varme pølser (Nw) Cooked frankfurters; hot dogs.

varm krabbsmörgås (Sw) Canapés of hot crabmeat on toast.

vartaassa (Fi) Cooked on a skewer.

vasikanleike (Fi) Veal cutlet.

vasikanliha (Fi) Veal.

vasilopeta (Gk) A traditional New Year's

307

cake flavored with almonds, sesame seeds, and a spice derived from the black cherry kernel (mahlepi).

västkustsallad (Sw) Literally, "west coast salad"; shellfish salad made with lobster, prawns, mussels, peas, mushrooms, tomato, and asparagus; dressed with oil and vinegar or lemon juice, and dill.

vatapá (Pg) An Afro-Brazilian, highly spiced dish of shrimp with coconut milk and palm oil.

vath ka salun (Ia) Duck curry.

vatkattu marjapuuro (Fi) Whipped cranberry pudding.

vatrushki (Rs) Pastry shells filled with curd cheese.

vatten (Sw) Water.

vattenglass (Sw) Sherbet.

vaxbönor (Sw) Waxbeans.

veado (Pg) Venison.

veal (US) Meat from a calf.

veal Cordon Bleu (US) A French-Swiss dish with ham and Emmentaler cheese layered between slices of veal; coated in egg and bread crumbs, then fried; garnished with lemon and parsley; served with fried potatoes.

veal flory (Sc) A meat pie with veal, bacon, forcemeat balls, and mushrooms. The name is said to be derived from the influence of the Medici family of Florence, Italy.

veal Orloff (US) A dish of center cut veal chops prepared with two sauces, a soubise onion sauce and a béchamel sauce; reportedly created in the nineteenth century for a Prince Orloff in France.

veal parmigiana (US) Italian-style, baked or fried veal chops coated with bread crumbs and Parmesan cheese; served with tomato sauce.

veau (Fr) Veal.

veau thonné (Fr) See **vitello tonnato.**

vegetable extract (US) A dark brown concentrated extract made from vegetables; may have yeast added; used for flavoring soups and casseroles or as a beverage with hot water.

vegetable marrow (GB) The fruit of a trailing vine, *Cucurbita pepo*; green, smooth skin; tender, juicy flesh; used in savory dishes, jam, or chutney.

vegetable oyster (US) See **salsify.**

vegetable pear (US) See **chayote.**

vegetarian (US) One with a diet that is primarily of plant origin. A *vegan* eats only food from plant sources. An *ovo-lactovegetarian* does not eat meat, but uses milk, milk products, and eggs. A *lactovegetarian* refrains from eating meat and eggs.

vegetarian duck (US) See **mock duck.**

vegyes saláta (Hu) Mixed salad.

vejce (Cz) Eggs.

vejce na měkko (Cz) Soft-boiled eggs.

vejce na tvrdo (Cz) Hard-boiled eggs.

vellutata (It) Soup thickened with egg yolk.

velouté, sauce (Fr) A basic white sauce of butter, flour, and a stock usually from veal, chicken, or fish, sometimes vegetables; lemon juice or cream may be added.

velouté de légumes (Fr) Thick vegetable soup.

velouté de volaille (Fr) Cream of chicken soup.

velstekt (Nw) Well done (meat).

velveting (US) A Chinese technique of marinating fish in egg white, corn starch, and rice wine before cooking in a thin layer of oil in a wok. The fish is finished crisp on the outside and tender inside.

venado (Sp) Venison.

venaison (Fr) Venison.

vengi bath (Ia) Eggplant with rice.

venison (US) The term technically refers to the edible flesh of a variety of animals with hooves and antlers, such as deer, elk, moose, and reindeer, but is commonly associated with the meat of deer.

vénitienne, sauce (Fr) Allemande sauce with added vinegar, spinach puree, tarragon, and chervil.

venkel (Du) Fennel.

vepřová pečeně (Cz) Roast pork with caraway seeds; served with dumplings and sauerkraut.

vepřové maso (Cz) Pork.

verbena (US) An herb with a flavor and scent of lemon; used as a substitute for lemongrass and in sweet dishes or fruit salads.

verde (It, Mx) Green.

verdura (It) Green vegetables.

verduras (Pg) Green leafy vegetables.

verdure cotte (It) Cooked vegetables.

verdurette, sauce (Fr) A mixture of chives, egg yolks, chervil, and tarragon with oil, vinegar, salt, and pepper.

véres hurka (Hu) Blood sausage.

verikoka (Gk) Apricots.

veriohukaiset (Fi) Blood pancakes; a fried batter made with rye and barley flour, beer, calf or sheep's blood, and beaten egg; served with cranberry jelly.

veripalttu (Fi) Black pudding made with a batter as for blood pancakes; baked.

verjuice (US) The sour juice of unripe fruits, usually grapes; sometimes used in prepared mustards and other sauces.

verlorene Eier (Gr) Poached eggs.

vermicelli (It) Very thin spaghetti.

Véronique (Fr) A term for any savory dish garnished with grapes; often poultry or white fish.

verschieden (Gr) Various or mixed, such as a choice of items on a menu.

verte, sauce (Fr) Green mayonnaise, colored with spinach, watercress, tarragon, or other green herbs.

vert-pré, au (Fr) Garnished with watercress and potatoes cut in sticks; garnished with a mixture of asparagus tips, peas, and green beans in butter; also, fish or chicken coated with green sauce.

very-low-sodium (US) A term meaning that a food product contains less than 35 milligrams of sodium per serving and per 100 grams of the food in question; proposed by the U.S. Food and Drug Administration for food labels.

verza (It) Savoy cabbage.

verzata di riso (It) Cabbage and rice soup.

vešalica (SC) Grilled smoked veal or pork.

vese gombával (Hu) Kidney with mushrooms.

vesék (Hu) Kidneys.

vese velö tojással (Hu) Scrambled eggs, kidney, calf's brains, and onions seasoned with paprika.

vetchina (Rs) Ham.

vettä (Fi) Water.

viande (Fr) Meat.

viande froides (Fr) Sliced cold meats.

viazi (Af–Swahili) Potatoes.

viazi vya kuchemsha (Af–Swahili) Boiled potatoes.

viazi vya kukaanga (Af–Swahili) Fried potatoes.

viazi vya kuvuruga (Af–Swahili) Mashed potatoes.

viazi vitamu (Af–Swahili) Sweet potatoes.

viceroy's dessert (Mx) A traditional Mexican dessert, similar to English trifle; sponge cake or ladyfingers sprinkled with sherry and arranged in layers with fruit preserves, custard and egg white; topped with chocolate and almonds.

vichy (Fr) A dish of sweetened carrots cooked in Vichy water; often served with veal cutlets.

vichyssoise (US) A cold soup of leeks, potatoes, and fresh cream created by a New York City, Ritz-Carlton Hotel chef Louis Diat in 1910. Any cold soup with potatoes and another vegetable in chicken broth may be called vichyssoise.

vichyssoise à la Russe (Fr) Leek and potato soup with beets and sour cream.

Vichy water (US) A French mineral water, from the town of Vichy.

Victoria, à la (Fr) In the style of Victoria; with a garnish of lettuce, tomatoes, macaroni, and potatoes; sometimes artichokes.

Victoria sandwich (GB) A layered sponge cake named for Queen Victo-ria; filled with whipping cream or preserved fruits.

Vidalia onions (US) Officially F-1 hybrid yellow granex onions; golden skin; fat, round, juicy, mild and sweet; first harvested in 1931 by a Vidalia, Georgia, farmer.

vídeňský řizek (Cz) Wiener schnitzel.

Viennoise, à la (Fr) In the style of Vienna; usually meaning roast meat with a garnish composed of noodles, spinach, and potatoes or referring to a breaded veal cutlet.

Vierfrüchtkuchen (Gr) Fruitcake or tart with four different fruits.

viikunoita (Fi) Figs.

viili (Fi) Yogurtlike curdled sour milk.

viinimarjoja (Fi) Currants.

viinirypäleitä (Fi) Grapes.

vijgen (Du) Figs.

vild hönsfågel (Du) Grouse.

Villalón (Sp) A ewe's milk cream cheese; white; mild, fresh taste.

villeroi, sauce (Fr) Velouté sauce with the essences of truffles and ham.

vin (Sw) Wine.

vin, au (Fr) Prepared with wine.

vinäger (Sw) Vinegar.

vinagre (Sp) Vinegar.

vinagre (Pg) Vinegar.

vinaigre (Fr) Vinegar.

vinaigré (Fr) Seasoned with vinegar.

vinaigrette (Fr) A mixture of oil and vinegar, seasoned with salt and pepper; herbs may be added; often served with asparagus, cauliflower, poached fish, or as a green salad dressing.

vinaigrette huile de noix (Fr) Walnut oil vinaigrette.

vinbär (Sw) Currants.

vin blanc (Fr) White wine.

Vincent, sauce (Fr) Green herbs pureed and added to mayonnaise with hard-boiled egg yolks.

vindaloo (Ia) A curry made with tamarind juice, lemon juice, or white vinegar and a spice paste of cayenne pepper, cumin, ginger, turmeric, cinnamon, black pepper, salt, and oil; used as a marinade for fatty meats such as pork, duck, or goose; served with rice.

vindruer (Da) Grapes.

vindruva (Du) Grape.

vindruvor (Sw) grapes.

vinegar (US) Literally, "sour wine"; a liquid containing acetic acid, produced by fermentation of cider, malt, or wine; used for pickling, as a condiment, and in sauces or salad dressings.

vine leaves (US) Grapevine leaves, fresh, salted or canned, used for stuffing; often an ingredient in Greek and Middle Eastern dishes.

vinete cu carne (SC) Baked eggplants stuffed with ground meat, garlic, and onions; topped with tomatoes.

vinho branco (Pg) White wine.

vinho do Porto (Pg) Port wine.

vinho tinto (Pg) Red wine.

vin hvit (Nw) White wine.

vino (Cz) Wine.

vino bianco (It) White wine.

vino da tavola (It) Table wine.

vino rosso (It) Red wine.

vino secco (It) Dry wine.

vin rød (Nw) Red wine.

vin rouge (Fr) Red wine.

vinsuppe (Nw) Wine soup.

vintage (US) In wines, the year of a grape harvest for a particular wine.

violet (US) Any of various herbs, genus *Viola*; the blue to purple flower may be preserved in sugar and used as a cake decoration; leaves and buds, with a peppery taste, used in salads.

Virginia ham (US) Originated in Virginia, it is produced from pigs fed on peanuts and chestnuts; salted and smoked over hickory and apple wood fires.

virgin olive oil (US) A light flavored, slightly acid oil made by pressing without any other treatment. See also **olive oil.**

Viroflay, à la (Fr) In the style of Viroflay near Paris; roast meat served with a gravy and a garnish of spinach croquettes, artichokes, and potatoes.

vis (Du) Fish.

visciola (It) Sour cherry.

višisoaz (SC) Vichyssoise.

viskoekjes (Du) Fish cakes.

višně (Cz, Tr) A sour cherry.

vişne suyu (Tr) Juice of sour cherries.

vispgrädde (Sw) Whipped cream.

vitamin (US) Any of a group of substances that are coenzymes needed to make enzymes work. They were first called "vitamines" in 1911 by Polish biochemist Casimir Funk under the belief all contain nitrogen (amine) and are essential to life (vita). The name was changed to vitamin in 1920 by British biochemist J. C. Drummond, who started the letter system, such as vitamin A and vitamin B.

vitamin A (US) A fat-soluble vitamin essential for vision and growth; retinol is a form of vitamin A and requirements are expressed in retinol equivalents (RE). The recommended daily allowance (RDA) is 800 RE for adult females and 1000 RE for adult males. Good dietary sources include liver, orange or yellow vegetables and fruits, and dark green, leafy vegetables.

vitamin B complex (US) A term used to identify six water-soluble B vitamins, including B_1 (thiamine), B_2 (riboflavin), B_3 (niacin), B_5 (pantothenic acid), B_6 (pyridoxine), B_{12} (cyanocobalamin), as well as biotin and folic acid. In general, all members of this group are found in the same principal food sources, such as liver and the bran of cereal grains.

vitamin B_1 (US) A water-soluble vitamin essential for the metabolism of carbohydrates; the recommended daily allowance (RDA) ranges from 1.0 to 1.5 milligrams for adults. Good dietary sources include pork, wheat germ, whole-grain cereals, brown rice, and most vegetables. Also called **thiamine.**

vitamin B_2 (US) A water-soluble vitamin essential for cell growth and tissue maintenance; the recommended daily allowance (RDA) ranges from 1.2 to 1.6 milligrams for adults. Good dietary sources include liver, brewer's yeast, milk, cheese, eggs, and leafy, green vegetables. Also called **riboflavin.**

vitamin B_3 (US) A water-soluble vitamin essential for tissue respiration, oxidation of glucose, and prevention of pellagra; the recommended daily dietary allowance (RDA) ranges from 13 to 19 milligrams for adults. Good dietary sources include liver, lean meat, fish, poultry, and whole-grain products. Also called **niacin.**

vitamin B_5 (US) A water-soluble vitamin essential for the production of energy from sugars and fats; a recommended daily allowance (RDA) has not been established but 4–7 milligrams per day is considered safe and adequate for normal adults. Good dietary sources include liver and other organ meats, legumes, and brewer's yeast. Also called **pantothenic acid.**

vitamin B_6 (US) A water-soluble vitamin essential for normal metabolism and specific enzyme systems; the recommended daily allowance (RDA) is about 2 milligrams for adults. Good dietary sources include liver, chicken, fish, and whole-grain cereals. Also called **pyridoxine.**

vitamin B_{12} (US) A water-soluble vitamin essential in fat and carbohydrate metabolism, nucleic acid formation, and termed the antipernicious anemia factor; the recommended daily allowance (RDA) is 3 micrograms for adults. Good dietary sources include liver, lean meats, eggs, and dairy products. Also called **cyanocobalamin.**

vitamin C (US) A water-soluble vitamin essential in the formation of collagen, a supportive tissue in skin, tendons, cartilage, bone, and connective tissues; and necessary for the prevention of scurvy; the recommended daily allowance (RDA) is 60 milligrams for adults. Good dietary sources include citrus fruits, strawberries, tomatoes, and potatoes. Also called **ascorbic acid.**

vitamin D (US) A fat-soluble vitamin essential in the proper formation of the skeleton and necessary in the efficient utilization of calcium and phosphate; the recommended daily allowance (RDA) is 5 micrograms for adults. Exposure to sunlight results in the synthesis of vitamin D in the skin, but for a dietary supply the best sources include fortified milk, eggs, dairy products, and oily fish such as sardines, salmon, tuna, and herring.

vitamin E (US) A fat-soluble vitamin essential as a defense against oxidation of unsaturated fatty acids, which leads to cell damage and neurologic symptoms; the recommended daily allowance (RDA) expressed in international units (IU) is 12 IU for adult females and 15 IU for adult males. Good dietary sources include vegetable oils, wheat germ, nuts, and green, leafy vegetables.

vitamini (Rs) Vitamins.

vitamin K (US) A fat-soluble vitamin essential for normal blood clotting; a recommended daily allowance (RDA) has not been established but some authorities suggest that 1 microgram per kilogram of body weight should be sufficient to maintain clotting time in adults; good dietary sources include green vegetables such as spinach and cabbage, root vegetables, fruits, seeds, yogurt, and alfalfa.

Vitaminmangel (Gr) Vitamin deficiency.

vitaminy (Cz) Vitamins.

vitela (Pg) Veal.

vitello (It) Veal.

vitello alla Milanese (It) Breaded veal cutlets.

vitello tonnato (It) A popular dish of cold roast veal with tuna and wine sauce. Also called **tunnied veal, veau thonné.**

vitkålsoppa med kroppkakor (Sw) Cabbage soup with pork and potato dumplings.

vitling (Sw) Whiting.

vitlök (Sw) Garlic.

vitsås (Sw) White sauce.

vitt bröd (Sw) White bread.

vitt vin (Sw) White wine.

vitunguu (Af–Swahili) Onions.

viz (Hu) Water.

vla (Du) Custard.

vlašské ořechy (Cz) Walnuts.

vlees (Du) Meats.

vleespannekoekjes (Du) Meat pancakes.

vlees voor de boterham (Du) Sliced cold meats for sandwiches.

vleet (Du) Skate.

voće (SC) Fruit.

voćni sok (SC) Fruit juice.

voda (Cz) Water.

vodka (Rs) A colorless, odorless, alcoholic drink made from fermented grain or potatoes.

vodu sa ledom (SC) Water with ice.

vohveli (Fi) Waffle.

voi (Fi) Butter.

voileipä (Fi) Open-face sandwich.

voileipäpöytä (Fi) An assortment of cold foods; cold or open table.

voimakkaasti maustettua (Fi) Spicy.

volaille (Fr) Poultry.

volaille au vinaigre (Fr) Sautéed

chicken simmered in white wine, vinegar, and tomato puree.

vol-au-vent (Fr) Literally, "windward flight"; a puff pastry shell filled with a variety of mixtures bound together with a brown or white sauce.

vol-au-vent de ris de veau (Fr) Pastry shells filled with a mixture of calf's sweetbreads, mushrooms, truffles, and olives in a sauce.

volos (Gr) A variety of Greek olive.

vongole (It) Small clams.

vongole alla marinara (It) Clams with chopped parsley and garlic.

vongole ripiene al forno (It) Baked stuffed clams.

voorgerechten (Du) Appetizers; hors d'oeuvres.

vörösbort (Hu) Red wine.

Vorspeisen (Gr) Appetizers; hors d'oeuvres.

vörtbröd (Sw) Maltbread.

vørterkake (Nw) Spice bread.

vruća čokolada (SC) Hot chocolate.

vrucht (Du) Fruit.

vruchtensap (Du) Fruit juice.

vruchtentaart (Du) Fruit tart.

vutiro (Gk) Butter.

Wachenheimer (Gr) One of several varieties of white wine, originating near Wachenheim in the Rhineland.

Wachsbohnen (Gr) Wax or yellow beans.

Wachteln (Gr) Quail.

wadas (Ia) A fried lentil paste.

wadjid (In) Rice cookie.

wafels (Du) Waffles.

wafer (US) a thin, crisp biscuit, cracker, or cookie; also a thin disk of candy.

Waffeln (Gr) Waffles.

waffle (US) A crisp, egg batter cake baked in a greased waffle iron with an impressed design, usually squares; served with syrup, honey, and butter or fruit preserves.

wagashi (Jp) Sweet cakes.

waha dori teriyaki (Jp) Young chicken teriyaki.

Wähen (Gr–Swiss) Huge open-faced tarts filled with fruit, vegetables, or cheese. One is large enough for a group.

wahoo (US) A mackerel; dark-fleshed and fatty with an intense flavor; often served in bean dishes.

wain (Ml) Wine.

wajik (In) Sweet sticky rice cake.

wakame (Jp) A form of edible seaweed, *Undaria pinnatifida*, sold both dried and fresh; mild flavor; used in miso soups, with cellophane and soba noodles, and is sometimes fried to eat as chips.

wakasagi (Jp) Smelt; small silvery fish served on skewers.

wakasagi no furai (Jp) fried smelt.

wakegi (Jp) Young green onions.

Waldegerling (Gr) Tan and white field mushrooms.

Waldmeister (Gr) Woodruff.

Waldmeisterbraten (Gr) Braised beef.

Waldorf salad (US) A fruit salad of diced apples, celery, walnuts, and mayonnaise. First served at the Waldorf-Astoria in New York City; walnuts were not part of the original salad.

Waldschnepfe (Gr) Woodcock.

Walewska, à la (Fr) A style of fish preparation named after Countess Maria Walewska, the Polish mistress of Napoleon I. A poached fish, usually sole, is garnished with sliced lobster and truffles and served with Mornay sauce.

wali (Af–Swahili) Cooked rice.

Waller gebacken (Gr) Fried freshwater fish.

walleye (US) A freshwater fish, largest of the perch family, with prominent eyes; lean, white, flaky flesh; because of its size and shape, often called wall-eyed pike.

walnoot (Du) Walnut.

Walnuss (Gr) Walnut.

walnut (US) An edible nut from a tree, genus *Juglans*, a native of southeastern Europe. Most commonly eaten in the United States is the English walnut, so named because of its introduction from England. Eaten fresh, used in salads, soups, sauces, meat dishes, pickled, and as an oil. See also **black walnut.**

walnut oil (US) An oil made from walnuts with a delicate flavor; used in salad dressings.

wampi (Th) A small yellow fruit with a flavor resembling a gooseberry; used in jam.

wān dòu (Ch) Peas.

wanilia (Po) Vanilla.

warabi (Jp) Edible fern sprout.

warak al gar (Ar) Bay leaf.

warak inib (Ar) Grape leaf.

warak inib mihshee (Ar) Stuffed grape leaf rolls.

warm, to (US) To heat slowly to below the boiling point.

Warmbier (Gr) Hot beer soup.

Warme Wurstspeisen (Gr) Cooked sausages.

wasabi (Jp) A thick root of an Asian herb, *Eutrema wasabi*; grated like horseradish and sold in powdered form, then mixed with water; green color; a strong, potent taste; used in sushi and sashimi. Also called **Japanese horseradish.**

wash (US) See **egg wash.**

wassail (GB) A hot punch made of ale or beer, flavored with apples, spices, lemon, toast, and sugar, usually served at the Christmas holidays.

Wasser (Gr) Water.

Wassermelone (Gr) Watermelon.

Wasserteig (Gr) Water crust; a rich dough made with eggs, flour, butter, and water used for pasties or tarts.

water (US) Odorless, tasteless, colorless liquid (H_2O) essential to life.

water biscuit (US) Biscuit or cracker made with water instead of milk.

water chestnut (US) An edible walnut-size bulb with crisp, white flesh of an Asian water plant, *Trapa bispinosa*; not a true chestnut; used in stir-fried dishes, salads, soups, with meat, seafood, poultry, and the pulverized bulb makes a flour. Also called **má-tí.**

waterchocolade (Du) Hot chocolate made with water.

watercress (US) An aquatic herb, *Nasturtium officinale*; best known and most commonly available cress with dark green leaves and pungent, tangy flavor; used in salads, soups, and as a garnish.

watercress sauce (US) A sauce of pureed watercress, egg yolk, lemon juice, olive oil, salt, and pepper.

water ice (US) See **ices.**

watermelon (US) The edible fruit of a vine in the cucumber family; the many varieties have fruit of differing shapes, sizes, and colors. Most common are large, round or oblong fruit with sweet, juicy pink-red or yellow flesh which is eaten

Watercress

316

raw; the hard, green rind is sometimes pickled; the black seeds are roasted and salted as a snack.

waterzootje (Bl) A traditional Flemish dish made of freshwater fish poached in butter and seasoned stock.

waterzootje de poulet (Bl) Chicken soup.

wątróbka (Po) Liver.

wau (Ch) Snail.

wax bean (US) A variety of snap or string bean with yellow pods.

weakfish (US) An Atlantic and Gulf coast food fish of the croaker group; mild flavor, fine texture; often prepared like trout. Also called **sea trout.**

Weckklösse (Gr) Bread dumplings.

wedding cake (US) A cake served at a wedding celebration; often a white frosted sponge cake with several tiers and garnished with figurines of a bride and groom. The first piece is customarily cut by the bride and groom together.

wĕi (Ch) Tuna.

weichgekochte Eier (Gr) Soft-boiled eggs.

wèi-jing (Ch) Monosodium glutamate.

Wein (Gr) Wine.

Weinbergschnecken (Gr) An appetizer of snails.

Weinbrand (Gr) Brandy.

Weinkaltschale (Gr) Cold wine soup.

Weinkäse (Gr) A term used to mean a mild, creamy cheese good with a light wine.

Weinkraut (Gr) Sauerkraut cooked in white wine.

Weinsuppe (Gr) Wine soup made with eggs and cream.

Weintraube (Gr) Bunch of grapes.

Weissbrot (Gr) White bread.

Weisse Bohnen (Gr) White haricot beans; butterbeans.

Weisse Bratwürste (Gr) White sausages made with lean pork and veal, white bread, and white pepper. Also called **Weisswürste.**

Weisse Rüben (Gr) Turnips.

Weisse Sosse (Gr) White sauce.

Weissfisch (Gr) Whiting.

Weisskäse (Gr) Cream cheese; cottage cheese.

Weisskohl (Gr) White cabbage.

Weisslacker (Gr) A cow's milk cheese, semisoft, white interior; mild to pungent taste.

Weissrüben (Gr) Turnips.

Weisswein (Gr) White wine.

Weisswürste (Gr) See **Weisse Bratwürste.**

Weizen (Gr) Wheat; corn.

Welsh border tart (GB) A tart with dark and light raisins; topped with meringue.

Welsh rabbit (GB) Melted cheese, usually mixed with milk, ale or beer, and mustard; served over toast. Incorrectly known as Welsh rarebit.

Wensleydale cheese (GB) A cow's milk cheese; two kinds: white or blue-veined interior; mild, tangy taste.

Werderkäse (Gr) A rennet cheese.

west coast halibut royal (Ca) Baked halibut steaks marinated in lemon juice and paprika; topped with onions and peppers; a British Columbia specialty.

western (US) An omelet with ham, onions, and green pepper served on bread.

Westfälischer frischer Obstkuchen (Gr)

Westphalian fruitcake made with fresh sweet cherries.

Westfälischer Schinken (Gr) Westphalian ham; a German specialty; a boneless ham salted and brined, smoked with juniper berries; served in thin slices, often wrapped around melon pieces.

whale (US) Any of a family of mammals, order *Cetacea*; with a fishy, oily flavor, the flesh may be braised or stewed.

wheat (US) A grasslike grain of the genus *Triticum*; cultivated worldwide; important as a cereal food and in bread making; most important type is durum or hard wheat, yielding semolina. Major forms are: *bran*, outer covering of the kernel; *bulgar*, ground whole kernel; and *cracked wheat*, crushed whole kernel.

wheat flour (US) Flour milled from wheat.

wheat germ (US) The embryo or kernel of wheat; rich in nutrients; used as a supplement to breakfast cereals, added to salads, and as a coating for fried or baked fish and poultry.

whelk (GB) A large sea snail, *Buccinum undatum*, with a muscular foot and white flesh; eaten poached, baked, or grilled. Also called *waved whelk*.

whey (US) The serum or watery liquid that separates from the curds of soured or cultured milk.

whip (US) A frothy dessert made by adding whipped cream or egg whites to a gelatin base.

whip, to (US) To introduce air bubbles by beating ingredients briskly with an appropriate tool; usually done to increase the volume of cream or egg whites.

whipped cream (US) Cow's milk cream expanded by the incorporation of air through beating.

whipped topping (US) Ready-to-use sweet topping for desserts, similar to whipped cream; also used as an ingredient in desserts.

whipping cream (US) Cow's milk cream thick enough to whip; with butterfat between 32 percent (light cream) and 40 percent (heavy cream).

whisk, to (US) To combine mixtures or make frothy by beating; usually applies to egg whites.

whitebait (US) Any of a variety of small fish such as the young or "fry" of herring and sprat; also, smelt; usually coated with flour and deep-fried.

white basil (Ia) A potherb used in India in the making of curry.

white bean (US) A term used for certain light-colored beans including great northern beans, pea beans, and navy beans.

white butter sauce (US) See **beurre blanc.**

white chocolate (US) A product made of cocoa butter, milk solids, and sugar; used in confectionery; not a true chocolate as it contains no cocoa; although the flavor is similar.

whitefish (US) A freshwater fish, family Coregonus, with several species that migrate to and from the sea; weight 1 to 5 pounds; white, tender flesh.

white flour (US) Flour from which the wheat germ and bran have been removed.

white milk sauce (US) See **béchamel, sauce.**

white pepper (US) See **pepper, white.**

white pudding (GB) Large sausages made with ground pork, oatmeal, various seasonings and parsley; there may also be a mixture of meat combined with pork fat and bread crumbs.

white sauce (US) A term used for many sauces because of their color; usually made with white flour and milk, or with clear, white chicken or veal stock.

white vinegar (US) A colorless vinegar with a mild acid taste; used in salad dressings, mayonnaise, for pickling and other dishes where a pale color is desired.

white walnut (US) See **butternut.**

white wine sauce (US) White sauce with the addition of white wine; used on fish, chicken, and egg dishes.

whiting (US) Any of a variety of marine fish with white, lean flesh. On the European side of the Atlantic it is a member of the hake family. On North American shores it is usually a kingfish. Used baked, fried, grilled, poached, or steamed.

whole grain (US) The entire grain, including the bran or outer layer, such as that of corn, wheat, barley, rice, millet, bulgar, oats, and triticale; provides dietary fiber, complex carbohydrates, B vitamins, vitamin E, iron, zinc, and other minerals.

wholemeal flour (GB) whole wheat flour.

whole wheat flour (US) A coarse flour that includes the whole grain; with a high bran content; more nutrition and flavor than white flour.

whortleberry (GB) A variety of blueberry.

widjen (In) Sesame seed.

wiener (US) Frankfurter.

Wiener Backhendl (Gr) Deep-fried and baked chicken.

wienerbröd (Sw) Literally, "Vienna bread"; Danish pastry.

wienerbrød (Da, Nw) Danish pastry.

Wiener Krapfen (Gr) Doughnuts filled with apricot or raspberry jam and topped with icing.

wienerleipä (Fi) Danish pastry.

Wiener Rostbraten (Gr) Cube steak with onions.

Wiener Schlagobers (Gr–Austria) Viennese rich whipped cream with vanilla sugar.

Wiener Schnitzel (Gr) Veal cutlets pounded thin, breaded, and sautéed; a specialty of Austria.

Wienerwurst (Gr) Sausages of cured chopped or ground pork, beef, and veal; the original "hot dog."

wieprzowina (Po) Pork.

wijn (Du) Wine.

wild (Du) Game.

Wild (Gr) Game; venison.

Wildbretpastete (Gr) Venison pasty or pie.

wilde appel (Du) Crab apple.

wilde eend met sinaasappel (Du) Wild duck with orange.

Wildente (Gr) Wild duck.

wildfowl (US) A game bird, particularly aquatic.

Wildgeflügel (Gr) Game birds.

wild rice (US) An aquatic North American grass, *Zizania aquatica*, with long, slender, hard brown seeds; nutty flavor and chewy texture; usually combined in cooking with white or brown rice. Also called **Indian rice.**

Wildschweinbraten (Gr) Roast wild boar.

wild strawberry (GB) A native strawberry of Europe, *Fragaria vesca*, with small highly flavored fruit.

Windbeutel (Gr) Zephyrs; puff pastry filled with apricot, raspberry, or strawberry puree.

wine (US) A drink produced from the fermented juice of grapes; classified in four major divisions: appetizer wines, table wines, dessert wines and sparkling wines; and may be white, rosé or red and range from dry to sweet. Wine may also be made from the fermented juice of fruit other than the grape, such as the elderberry, or from a plant, such as the dandelion.

wineberry (US) A small, red, acid-tasting fruit, genus *Rubus*, related to the raspberry; native to Japan and China. Also refers to other fruits such as red currant and wine grapes.

wine vinegar (US) A vinegar made from both white and red wines; used in salad dressings, sauces, and cooked dishes.

winkle (GB) An edible sea snail, *Littorina littorea*; boiled in the shell, the flesh is removed and eaten with seasoning or vinegar, or in a prepared dish. Also called **periwinkle, bigaro, bigorneau.**

wino biale (Po) White wine.

wino czerwone (Po) Red wine.

winogrona (Po) Grapes.

wintergreen (US) An evergreen herb of the heath family with deep green, aromatic leaves yielding oil of wintergreen used in flavoring.

Winterkohl (Gr) Winter cabbage; kale.

winter melon (US) See **melon.**

winter pear (US) Any of various pears that ripen late in the fall such as Anjou and Bosc pears.

winter savory (US) A European herb of the mint family; leaves used fresh or dried as a flavoring.

Wirsingkohl (Gr) Savoy cabbage.

wiśnie (Po) Cherries.

witlof (Du) Belgian endive; chicory; used braised, au gratin, and in salads.

witte bonen (Du) White beans.

wittebrood (Du) White bread.

witte kool (Du) Cabbage.

witte wijn (Du) White wine.

wok (US) A large, bowl-shaped pan used for stir-frying foods in Chinese cooking.

Wolfsbarsch (Gr) Bass.

Wintergreen

wonton (US) Chinese appetizers made with egg-noodle wrappers rolled around a variety of fillings such as minced meat, fish, vegetables, and seasonings.

wonton wrappers (US) Egg-noodle wrappers smaller than egg roll wrappers.

wood ear (US) See **cloud ear.**

woodcock (GB) A fat, squat, pigeon-sized game bird, *Scolopax rusticola*, common in Europe; usually roasted and served on toast. Also called **bécasse.**

woodruff (US) An herb, *Asperula odoratum*, with a fragrant aroma; used in May wine and in wine punch.

Worcester sauce (GB) A sauce made with vinegar, anchovy essence, walnut ketchup, soy sauce, and shallots.

Worcestershire sauce (GB) A vinegar, molasses, and anchovy-based commercial condiment used on meats and to season other dishes; originated in Worcestershire, England.

wormseed (US) See **epazote.**

worst (Du) Sausage.

wortel (In) Carrot.

worteltjes (Du) Carrots.

wrasse (US) A marine fish found along the European coasts of the Atlantic.

wú-hwā-gwo (Ch) Figs.

wū lúng chà (Ch) Oolong tea.

Wurst (Gr) Sausage.

Wurstbrot (Gr) Sausage sandwich.

Würstchen (Gr) Small, link sausages.

Würze (Gr) Seasoning; spice.

Wurzeln (Gr) Carrots.

wŭ-syāng jī (Ch) Barbecued chicken in cinnamon, cloves, anise seed, and ginger.

wŭ-syāng-lyàu (Ch) Five-spice powder; a blend of star anise, cinnamon, clove, fennel, and red pepper.

wŭ-syāng pái-gŭ (Ch) Spareribs marinated with soy sauce, wine, cloves, anise seed, and mustard.

wuz (Ar) Roast goose.

xacutti (Pg) A dish from Portuguese India; lamb or chicken marinated in coconut milk and stewed with Indian spices.

xalota (Pg) Green onions; scallions.

xamfina (Sp) A Catalan side dish of sautéed eggplant and bell peppers.

xanthide (US) A yellow coloring matter that occurs in fruits and vegetables.

xapoipa (Sp) A kind of pancake.

xarel-lo (Sp) A variety of grapes, native to Spain, used in the manufacture of Cava wines.

xarope (Pg) Syrup.

Xavier (Fr) A cream soup made with chicken stock thickened with rice flour; garnished with diced chicken; said to have been created by Louis Stanislas Xavier, Count of Provence, who became King Louis XVIII.

xérès, au (Fr) With a sauce flavored with sherry; the term refers to the town of Jerez in Spain where the wine originated.

xia (Ch) See **syǎu-syār.**

xiangjiao (Ch) See **syāng-jyāu.**

xiangyóu (Ch) See **syāng-yóu.**

ximénia (Fr) A tropical shrub, widespread in Africa, with edible, sour fruit. In Florida, United States, one of the species, *Ximenia americana*, is known as the wild lime.

xìngrén dòufù (Ch) See **sying-rén dòu-fú.**

xingzi (Ch) See **sying-dz.**

xinxin de galinha (Pg) A Brazilian dish of chicken and shrimp simmered in dende oil; sometimes served with a peanut and coconut sauce.

xoconoxtles (Mx) Alligator pears.

xylitol (US) A carbohydrate sweetener that occurs naturally in a number of fruits and vegetables and is a normal constituent of human metabolism. Produced commercially, it has the same sweetness as sucrose.

yabloki (Rs) Apples.

yabloki sup (Rs) Cold apple soup with berry jam and white wine.

yā-dz (Ch) Duck.

yā-dz dàn-jywan (Ch) Rolled omelets stuffed with minced duck and steamed.

yagodni sup (Rs) Berry soup with cream, egg yolks, and sugar.

yahni (Tr) Stew.

yai la kukaanga (Af–Swahili) Fried egg.

yaita (Jp) Baked; grilled.

yaitsa (Rs) Eggs.

yā jyàng (Ch) Plum sauce for duck.

yakhni (Ia) Meat or poultry stock.

yakidofu (Jp) Broiled soybean curd.

yaki hamaguri (Jp) Broiled clams.

yaki ika (Jp) Grilled squid.

yakimono (Jp) Broiled, grilled, and pan-fried foods; meats are usually put first in a marinade of soy sauce, mirin, grated ginger, and sugar.

yakisoba (Jp) Noodles broiled with vegetables in miso.

yakitori (Jp) Small cubes of boneless chicken and sometimes chicken livers grilled on skewers; basted with a sauce of mirin, sugar, and soy sauce.

yakizakana (Jp) Grilled fish.

yakumi (Jp) Garnish; chopped flavorings.

yalanci (Tr) Vine leaves.

yalas çorbasi (Tr) A soup of beef broth and yogurt with onions, parsley, and mint or garlic.

yam (Th) Literally, "mix with the hands"; tossed salads.

yams (US) The tubers of tropical or subtropical plants, species *Dioscorea*; size, shape, and color varies with species but commonly have a thick brown skin and starchy yellow, white, or red flesh; bland flavor; some are harmful when raw; used boiled, mashed, roasted, or fried; term often erroneously applied to sweet potato.

yán (Ch) Salt.

yáng-bái-tsài (Ch) Cabbage.

yáng-ròu (Ch) Mutton.

yáng-tsài-hwār (Ch) Cauliflower.

yáng-tsūng (Ch) Onions.

yān-mài (Ch) Oats.

yansoon (Ar) Anise.

yān wō (Ch) See **bird's nest.**

yaourt (Fr) Yogurt.

yaout (Rs) Yogurt.

yaprek dolmasi (Tr) Grape leaves stuffed with rice, raisins, onions, pine nuts, herbs, and seasonings, baked; served cold.

yard-long bean (US) A legume, *Vigna sesquipedalis*, grown in the Caribbean and the Far East; related to the cowpea or black-eyed pea; very long, thin, green pods; delicate flavor; used as a fresh vegetable and dried pulse. Also called **asparagus bean.**

yarrow (US) An herb, *Achillea millefollium*, with deep green, lacy leaves; pungent odor and taste; used in salads or for tea.

yasai (Jp) Vegetables.

yasai sūpu (Jp) Vegetable soup.

yassa (Af) A lemon-based marinade for

meat, chicken, or fish that usually includes onions, hot peppers, and seasonings.

yassa au poulet (Af) A West African dish
of marinated chicken first fried, then
simmered in its marinade.

yataklete kilkil (Af) An Ethiopian casserole of potatoes, carrots, beans, and
onions with garlic, ginger, and hot
chilis.

yāu-dòu (Ch) Kidney beans.

yāu-dz (Ch) Kidneys.

yāu-gwo (Ch) Cashew nuts.

yautia (Sp) A vegetable tuber of a plant,
Xanthosoma sagittifolium, related to
taro; white to pink flesh; used in
dishes of West Africa, South America,
and the West Indies.

yawarakai rōru pan (Jp) Soft bread
rolls.

yeasts (US) Tiny cells of fungi that multi-
ply and make enzymes that, when
combined with liquid and carbohydrate foods, induce fermentation and
release carbon dioxide; important in
making raised bread, beer, and wine.
Baker's yeast is sold fresh in compressed cakes, and dried as active
granules. See also **brewer's yeast.**

yé-dz (Ch) Coconut.

yeghintz (Tr) Pilaf.

yēji (Ch) Pheasant.

yellowtail snapper (US) A delicate,
white-fleshed fish with a mild flavor;
often fried or broiled; abundant on
the south Atlantic coast of the United
States.

yema (Sp) Yolk, egg yolk.

yemiser selatta (Af) An Ethiopian lentil

salad with hot green chilis, shallots,
oil, and vinegar.

yemitas de mi bisabuela (Mx) A cooked
mixture of egg yolks and syrup
formed into balls; then dipped in
syrup and cinnamon.

yengeç (Tr) Crab.

yepvadz (Tr) Baked or cooked.

yerakot (Jw–Israel) Vegetables.

yerba maté (Sp) See **maté.**

yeşil salata (Tr) Green salad.

yě-wèi (Ch) Game.

yiaourti (GK) Yogurt.

yì-bèi (Ch) Mussels.

yīng-táu (Ch) Cherries.

yin-lyàu (Ch) Beverages.

yiouvetsi (Gk) Lamb braised with tomatoes, onions, and pasta; topped with
grated cheese.

yodo (Sp) Iodine.

yōgashi (Jp) French-style pastry.

yoghourt (Sw) Yogurt.

yoghurt (Da, Du, It) Yogurt.

yogur (Sp) Yogurt.

yogurt (US) A sheep's, goat's, or cow's
milk treated with bacteria, *Lactobacil-
lus bulgaricus*, turning it thick,
smooth, and slightly acidic; a high-
protein food with varying percentages
of fat. Yogurt is a common and favorite
food, used in many ways.

yoğurt (Tr) Yogurt.

yoğurtlu (Tr) A grilled round of flat
bread topped with yogurt, spicy meatballs, pieces of lamb, and tomatoes.

yoğurtlu paça (Tr) A stew of calf's feet
with yogurt.

yoğurt salçasi (Tr) Yogurt sauce flavored with garlic.

yoğurt tatlisi (Tr) Yogurt cake in syrup; served with cream.

yōkan (Jp) A sweet red bean (azuki) jellied confection; served cold in small squares.

yōniku (Jp) Mutton.

Yorkshire curd tart (GB) An open tart filled with a custardlike mixture of curd cheese, sometimes cottage cheese, eggs, currants, nutmeg, and grated lemon peel.

Yorkshire pudding (GB) A traditional accompaniment to roast beef; a batter of flour, eggs, and milk added to the drippings in the roasting pan and baked.

yosenabe (Jp) A stew of vegetables with meat or fish.

yóu (Ch) Oil.

yòu-dz (Ch) Pumelo; shaddock.

youghurt (Nw) Yogurt.

yóu-mài-yàn (Ch) Oatmeal.

youngberry (US) A large, dark red berry; a hybrid of the blackberry and dewberry; named for a U.S. horticulturist, B. M. Young.

you-tsài (Ch) Leeks.

yóu-yú (Ch) Cuttlefish, squid.

yú (Ch) Fish.

yuba (Jp) Bean curd skin; tissue-thin sheets skimmed from simmered soy milk; deep-fried and salted when dried. Fresh yuba (nama yuba) may be eaten with soy sauce.

yuca (US) See **cassava.**

yucatico (Mx) Baked red snapper with olives, red peppers, coriander, and fruit juice.

yú-chr (Ch) Shark's fin.

yudeta (Jp) Boiled.

yude tamago (Jp) Hard-boiled egg.

yufka (Tr) Unleavened bread.

yukka (Tr) See **phyllo.**

yukkai jang kuk (Kr) A spicy stew with beef, scallions, and chilis.

Yule log (GB) A rolled cake coated with chocolate buttercream ridged to resemble a log's bark; a traditional Christmas dessert.

yù-mi (Ch) Corn.

yù-mi-myàr (Ch) Corn meal.

yumurta başlama (Tr) Poached eggs.

yumurta lop (Tr) Hard-boiled eggs.

yumurta rafadan (Tr) Soft-boiled eggs.

yún er (Ch) See **cloud ear.**

yusafandi (Ar) Tangerines.

yuzu (Jp) A member of the citrus family similar to a lemon or lime; used for flavoring and as a garnish.

ywán-shwēi (Ch) Coriander; Chinese parsley.

zabady (Ar–Egypt) Yogurt.

zabaglione (It) A foamy custard made with egg yolks, sugar, and Marsala wine; served warm or cold. Also called **sabayon.**

zabibu (Af–Swahili) Grape.

zacht gekookte eieren (Du) Soft-boiled eggs.

začini (SC) Spices.

zadělavané žaludky (Cz) Stewed goose gizzards.

zaděnky (Cz) Clams.

zafferano (It) Saffron.

zahter (Ar) Thyme.

zahuštěná (Cz) Thickened, as in gravy.

zajac (Po) Baked rabbit.

zajíc (Cz) Hare.

zajíc na smetaně (Cz) Hare served in cream sauce.

zakhari (Gk) Sugar.

zakoussotchnyï (Rs) A pasteurized cow's milk cheese, similar to Camembert.

zakuski (Rs) An appetizer plate; may include blinis, caviar, anchovies, eggplant, and other tidbits. Legend has it that the tradition of an assortment of savories served before a meal, accompanied by vodka, was introduced by Rurik, Viking Prince of Kiev, in the ninth century.

zalivnoye iz rybi (Rs) Fish in aspic.

zalm (Du) Salmon.

zamikand (Ia) A type of yam with white to pink flesh, native to India.

zampe di maiale (It) Pig's feet.

zampone (It) Spiced pork sausage, usually garlic seasoned, stuffed into the skin of a pig's forefoot and boiled; served with lentils or a piquant sauce.

zampone al cedro (It) A zampone made with white wine and candied citron peel.

zanahorias (Sp) Carrots.

Zander (Gr) A large freshwater fish, pike perch, *Stizostedion lucioperca*, usually served in wine sauce.

Zander mit Mandeln (Gr) Pike perch cooked with almonds.

zanjabiyl (Ar) Ginger.

zapiekanka (Po) A baked dish of pork strips, sliced potatoes, onions, and mushrooms with sour cream.

zapote (Sp) See **sapodilla.**

zarda (Ia) Rice pudding flavored with saffron, cardamom, raisins, pistachios, almonds, and cashews.

zarigani (Jp) Crayfish.

zarusoba (Jp) Buckwheat noodles, dried seaweed, and wasabi; served with a soy and sweet sake sauce.

zarzamora (Sp) Blackberry.

zarzuela (Sp) Literally, "operetta"; a stew of fish, shellfish, tomatoes, onions, and peppers flavored with garlic and white wine.

zarzuela de mariscos (Sp) A Catalan shellfish stew.

zatar (Ar) An herb, *Thymbra spicata*, of the mint family with a flavor like hearty thyme; native to the Middle East and important in Arabic and North African cooking; used in many dishes including a bread dip.

zatziki (Gk) An appetizer made from

grated cucumber, yogurt, garlic, olive oil, vinegar, mint, and seasonings.

zavináč (Cz) Rolls of marinated herring stuffed with onions.

zavyvanets (Rs) Sweet dough filled with fruits and nuts.

zayetz zharini v suharyakh (Rs) Fried hare coated in bread crumbs.

zayt (Ar) Oil.

zayteem (Jw–Israel) Olives.

zbeeb (Ar) Raisins.

z cytryna (Po) With lemon.

zdoba (Rs) Sweet buns.

zedoary (US) A spice related to ginger and turmeric; used in Indonesian cooking. Also called **kentjoer.**

zeera (Ia) Cumin.

zeevis (Du) Seafish.

zejtin (SC) Oil. Also called **ulje.**

zelena salata (SC) Salad of greens; lettuce.

zelená paprika (Cz) Green peppers.

zelen fasul (Bu) A mix of cooked carrots, green beans, onions, peppers, and tomatoes.

zeleninová polévka (Cz) Vegetable soup.

zèleva chorba (Bu) Cabbage soup.

zeli (Cz) Cabbage.

zeljanica (SC) Spinach pastry.

zeller (Hu) Celery.

zellerkrémleves (Hu) Celery soup.

zellersaláta (Hu) Celery root salad.

zemičke (SC) Rolls.

žemle (Cz) Roll.

zenmai (Jp) Fern shoots.

zensai (Jp) Sweet or savory appetizers served hot or cold before a meal.

zenzero (It) Ginger.

zephyr (US) Literally, "gentle breeze"; any light, frothy, sweet or savory dish such as a soufflé, a mousse, a meat pudding, an ice cream dessert, or a small pastry.

zeppole (It) Sweet dough fritters; a kind of doughnut filled with sweetened ricotta cheese.

žervé (Cz) A type of cream cheese.

ze śmietanka (Po) With cream.

zest (US) The outermost layer of citrus-fruit rind, containing the aromatic oils, grated or cut and separated from the white pith; used for flavoring and garnishing.

zesto (Gk) Warm, hot.

zeytin (Tr) Olives.

zeytinyăği (Tr) Olive oil.

zeytinyăği sebzeter (Tr) A dish of vegetables, garlic, and seasonings simmered in olive oil; topped with chopped parsley; served cold.

zeytinyăği pirasa (Tr) Onions, leeks, and rice braised with olive oil.

zhá (Ch) Fried; deep-fried.

zhá dà xia (Ch) Fried shrimp.

zhá gèzi (Ch) Fried pigeon.

zhāng chá yā (Ch) Fried duck in spices.

zharennyi porosenok (Rs) Roast suckling pig.

zharini orgutzi (Rs) Fried cucumbers and onions.

zhá yú tíaor (Ch) Fried fish slices.

zhēng (Ch) Steamed.

zhou fàn (Ch) See **congee.**

zhug (Jw) An Israeli spice mix of garlic, hot peppers, caraway seeds, cardamom, and coriander; used in soups and sauces.

zibärtle (Gr) A wild, cherry-size plum found in the Baden region of Germany.

zibda (Ar) Butter.

Ziegen (Gr) Goat's milk cheese.

zielone oliwki (Po) Green olives.

ziemniaki (Po) Potatoes.

ziemniaki pure (Po) Mashed potatoes.

ziemniaki smazone (Po) Fried potatoes with paprika.

Zigeuner Art (Gr) Gypsy style; usually food cooked over an open fire.

Zigeunerspiess (Gr) An Austrian grilled kebab of meat cubes, peppers, and onions.

zik de venado (Mx) Cooked venison, shredded and served cold with chopped coriander, onions, serrano chilis, and Seville oranges.

ziminu (Fr) A Corsican fish stew similar to bouillabaisse.

Zimt (Gr) Cinnamon.

zinc (US) An essential trace element; the recommended dietary allowance (RDA) per day for adult males is 15 milligrams; for adult women, 12 milligrams; the best sources are meat, liver, eggs, and seafood, especially oysters; whole-grain products contain zinc in less available form.

Zinfandel (US) A California wine with a light-bodied, fruity, dry flavor when new.

zingara (Fr) Literally, "gypsy"; a sauce or garnish containing paprika, tomato, ham, tongue, mushrooms, and sometimes truffles; served with poultry or meat.

Zink (Gr) Zinc.

ziti (It) Long lengths of macaroni, which can be broken into shorter pieces; often served with meat or mushroom sauce.

ziti mezze (It) A thinner kind of ziti.

ziti tagliati (It) The cut or cooking length form of ziti.

žitne pahuljice (SC) Cereal.

žitný chléb (Cz) Rye bread.

zitoni (It) Pasta double the thickness of ziti.

Zitrone (Gr) Lemon.

Zitronenschale (Gr) Zest of lemon or other citrus fruits.

zmrzlina (Cz) Ice cream.

zoet (Du) Sweet.

zöldbab (Hu) Green beans.

zöldbableves (Hu) Green bean soup with vinegar, paprika, and sour cream.

zöldbabsaláta (Hu) Green bean salad.

zöldpaprika (Hu) Green pepper.

zöldségleves (Hu) Vegetable soup.

zöldségsaláta (Hu) Cold mixed vegetable salad.

zoni (Jp) Japanese New Year soup; a clear soup with vegetables cut in shapes according to tradition; served with rice cakes.

zosui (Jp) A rice porridge and miso soup served in many variations with added meats, fish, vegetables, grains, and seasonings. In the home, it is a way of using leftovers.

zout (Du) Salt.

zraziki w sosie (Po) Fried veal steaks served in a caper sauce.

zrazy (Po) Fried beef, lamb, or veal cutlets simmered in an onion and mushroom sauce.

zrazy baranie (Po) Thin slices of lamb cooked in tomato puree with red wine and soy sauce.

zsemlegombóc (Hu) Dumplings of bread, flour, egg, milk, and parsley.